# Peytonsville, TENNESSEE

## TWO HUNDRED YEARS

Paul M. Pratt Sr

This book would not have been possible without the
contributions of, Rick Warwick, Williamson County Historian.
His knowledge of the county is a gift to us all.

Peytonsville Press
Major Contributor: Rick Warwick
Cover design: Debbie Smartt
Book layout and design: Debbie Smartt
Front cover image: 1878 Beers Map of Williamson County
ISBN: 978-0-578-92905-7

# TABLE OF CONTENTS

Miss Katie Lou Gatlin spent her entire life educating and helping her students in many ways. She came to Peytonsville in 1940, with a plan for a very rural community with no pre-judgments of anyone because she was always looking for the best of everyone.

As I look back and remember those days, many events cross my mind. We always felt secure which created trust between us and Miss Katie and created a solid foundation for her teaching plan.

I remember practicing marching for the Rodeo Parade on Gosey Hill Road. It was a gravel road with a steep hill. As her other students have written, her posture was perfect and she expected your posture to be the same, so if we did not do well on the first practice which was a long way up and back; instead of going back in the school, yes we marched up and back again. Miss Katie had many ways to administer discipline. One was called "writing off". She would have you write the same sentence 500 times with no recess until you finished so I became really good holding two pencils and writing two sentences at once. One day while writing off, Miss Katie decided the wood floors needed to be cleaned and some type of oil spread which was very slick, so we worked hard to finish before recess was over. She had on a beautiful blue dress which she often wore. Well, Miss Katie picked up the mop, threw her shoulders back and with high heels on and perfect posture, took one step and landed on her rear end. The beautiful blue dress ruined. No one dared to laugh. Recess lasted longer than usual, but we still had to write off.

Miss Katie taught grades one through four in the same classroom. She was so organized that you had paperwork to finish while she taught one of the other grades, so we were busy all the time. This method taught us to be accountable and ready when our class time arrived. If you followed the system, you learned more than the average student and she would give you glowing credit.

Several of my classmates have written wonderful articles about Miss Katie Lou, which shows the love and respect her students had for her.

In September 2019, I decided to write the history of the community I grew up in, which was settled in the early 1800's. The first week was exciting until the reality set in that I had no experience writing a book and didn't know where to start. After a lot of thought, I realized this venture was like my career. This was going to be a lot of hard work and a challenge, but if you love what you are accomplishing, you will be successful.

I started by finding the first 10 residents of the community and working up a profile on each one, which was very time consuming. Again I remembered my career, hard work and many hours, so this became a mission because I wanted our community to be recognized as part of our great county, Williamson County, Tennessee, USA.

After about three or four months reality set in again and then a fortunate meeting happened by being in the right place at the right time. I was visiting the Williamson County Archives and noticed this man digging into the files and I asked the lady at the desk, "who is that man?" She said, "Rick Warwick, the County Historian, surely you know him!" So, I eased around and introduce myself and asked him a question. He stopped what he was doing and proceeded to answer my question. I had a name of a road called Harpeth Lick, which I felt it should be in south Williamson County, but could not find it. He looked at me without hesitation and said, "that road is now Peytonsville Road."

Since the community that I was trying to write a book on was Peytonsville, I began to become more confident. So for the next three or four months, I stopped by the Williamson County Historian's office and asked questions. He always welcomed me with a big smile. I could carry old pictures and he would say, "yes, that is so and so, born about 1880, in the 13th District." I became so comfortable around him, that one day I got the courage to say that I needed help. Before I knew it, I was receiving so much valuable information.

I originally intended to dedicate the book to one teacher. Now the book will be dedicated to two teachers, Miss Katie Lou Gatlin, Peytonsville School, 1940-1961 and Rick Warwick, Teacher and Williamson County Historian.

KATIE LOU GATLIN

RICK WARWICK

# INTRODUCTION BY RICK WARWICK

As Williamson County historian, I am so please to announce that the old 13th Civil District, embracing the communities of Peytonsville, Little Texas, Arno, Rudderville and Westwood, will finally have a written history. Under the leadership of Paul Pratt, Sr., Debbie Smartt and myself, the 13th has joined the ranks of Nolensville, Burwood, Flat Creek, College Grove, Brentwood, Thompson Station, Leiper's Fork, Triune and the First District with a published written history. Since serving as co-chair with Judy Hayes during the Tennessee and Williamson County Bicentennials era (1996-1999), it has been my goal to see that every community has a written history, a history that preserves the rich past of the community with stories of its people, places and notable events in words and period photographs. We have done our best to accomplish that goal.

Looking back about two years ago, I remember Paul Pratt coming to the Williamson County Archives while I was reading microfilm and asking if I knew where the Old Harpeth Lick Road was located. Since I had researched roads leading into Franklin, I told him it was on the same roadbed as Lewisburg Pike, starting at the corner of Fifth Avenue and South Margin, going south until reaching the Old Peytonsville Road, then running through the village of Peytonsville on to Arno, Owen Hill Road and reaching Harpeth Lick on Grove Creek. I could tell by the expression on Paul's face, it was the answer he wanted to hear.

From this brief encounter, Paul invited me to help him work on the history of the 13th District. Though I was not well-versed in the area, I did have a personal interest in the community since my wife, Martha Elaine Ladd, has deep roots in Peytonsville, being a descendant of the Smithson, Harrison, Ladd, Burnett, Sledge, Knott, and Knight families. She is kin, by birth and marriage, to a majority of the early families of the area, all from Lunenburg County, Virginia. With this said, I began a seven-month feast of devouring all the records in the Williamson County Archives. With what facts I could compile, I have written a brief history on schools, churches, and businesses. I have also compiled information on local cemeteries, roadways, tax records, census records, notable homes, and biographies of individuals of the 13th District.

Five interesting facts I discovered during my research:

1. The 13th District was created in 1836 with the Harpeth River its northern border, McCrory Creek on the east, the Duck River Ridge on the south, and the 10th District on the west.

2. In 1890, Arno Road, from Millview to Rudderville, was part of the Chrisman Mill Turnpike and from Rudderville to Harpeth Lick was known as the Duck River Ridge Turnpike.

3. The 13th District was diminished with the creation of the 23rd Civil District in 1887, losing the Rudderville area, and, later, it lost the Arno area to the 21st.

4. There have been three post offices in the area: Peytonsville P.O. (1836-1904); Arno P.O. (1890-1908); Rudderville P.O. (1888-1904).

5. Two notable historical figures from the 13th District were Col. James W. Starnes of the 4th Tennessee Cavalry CSA and Tom Little, 1957 Pulitzer Prize winner, a *Nashville Tennessean* cartoonist known as "Southpaw from Snatch".

Acknowledgements to Debbie Chunn, Ricky Smithson, Sara Vaden Davis, Howard Smithson, Ronny Mangrum, Elaine Warwick, Hilda Reynolds, Louise Gillespie Lynch and the Williamson County Archives for sharing their photographs. Special thanks to Mike Vaden, Jimmy Vaden, Nancy York, Nelson Dodd and Bill Hurt for sharing their memories of Miss Katie Lou Gatlin.

The Origins of the Peytonsville Community: How did Peytonsville get its name? This question has been a mystery for many years. Many have suggested it was named for a family of Peytons. Problem is, there were never any Peytons living in the 13th District. Some have thought it was named for Bailey Payton of Sumner County. Again, not likely. Paul Pratt Sr. has discovered the most plausible theory from his research on the early families who migrated here from the southwestern part of Virginia, today known as Lunenburg, Halifax and Pittsylvania. We can assume they chose Peytonsville for their post office in 1836, in honor of their home across the mountains.

Lunenburg County was formed in 1746, from the western two-thirds of Brunswick County. Halifax County was formed in 1752, from the western two-thirds of the original Lunenburg County. The first county seat of Halifax County was Peytonsville, which is now in Pittsylvania County, formed in 1766. From a 1911 Rand McNally map, we find that Peytonsville, in modern times, had become Peytonsburg. *The Therapeutic Gazette* of January 16, 1900, reported that Dr. Rowley White, who lived near Peytonsville, in Pittsylvania County, VA., had introduced a remedy for snake and spider bites, which he had acquired the recipe from Indians. So, we can assume the name changed between 1900 and 1911.

And there you have it; thanks to Paul Pratt, Sr.

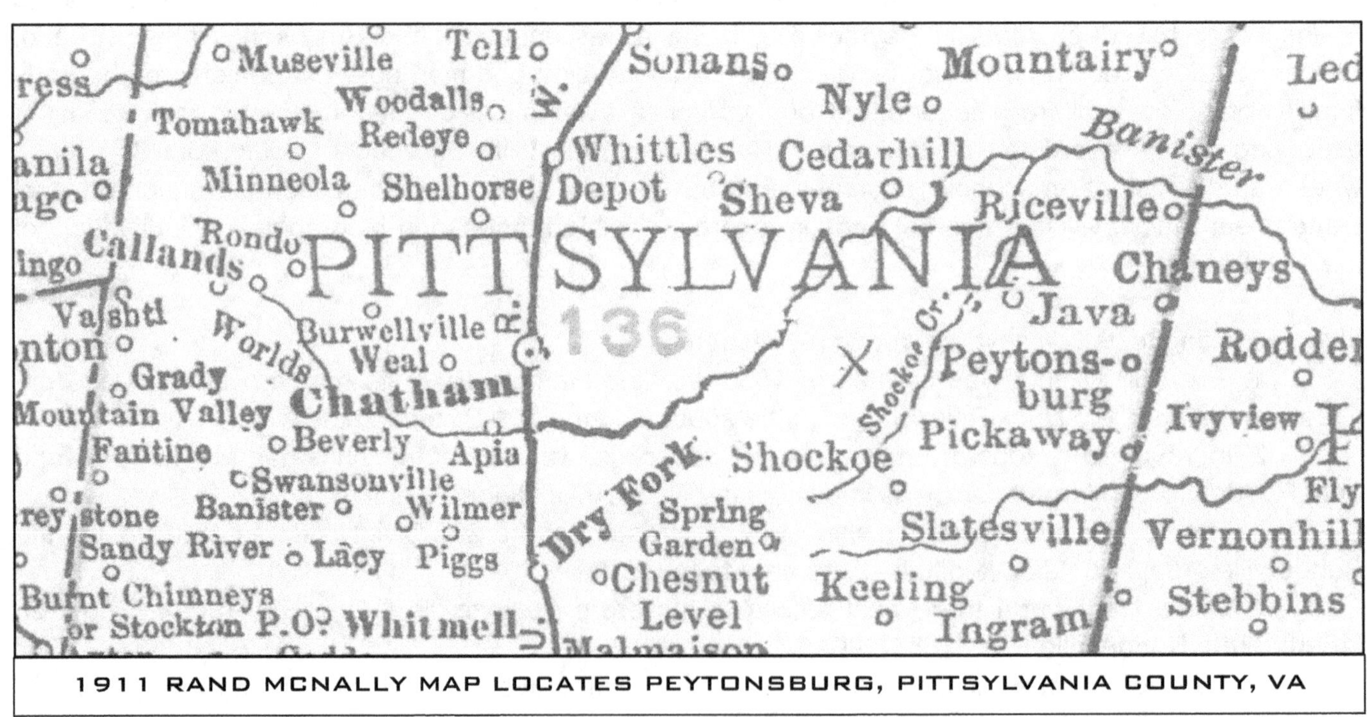


**1911 RAND MCNALLY MAP LOCATES PEYTONSBURG, PITTSYLVANIA COUNTY, VA**

# A DESCRIPTION OF THE 13TH DISTRICT AND ITS CREATION IN 1836

Williamson County was carved from Davidson County by an act of the Tennessee General Assembly on October 26, 1799. The county was then divided into military districts and musters and elections were held near the home of the captain of the company. In 1807, James Boyd was captain of the militia in the Peytonsville area. By 1836, the county was divided into civil districts and the Peytonsville, Rudderville and Arno communities were within the 13th District. In 1897, Rudderville and Arno were placed in the 23rd District.

## Williamson County Divided into Civil Districts
*The Western Weekly Review*
**February 12, 1836**
In pursuance of the act of the General Assembly of the state of Tennessee, entitled "An act to provide for the laying off the several size, within which Justices of the Peace and Constables shall be elected, and other purposes…"

"No. XIII. Bounded as follows: Beginning at the mouth of Neely's branch; thence south, with the east boundary liner of the tenth district, to the southeast corner of the same, including Hezekiah Smithson, Sr.; thence eastwardly, with the Duck River Ridge, to McCall's Gap; thence north with McCrory's Creek, to Big Harpeth; thence down the same to the beginning."

The store house of Andrew Campbell, at Snatch, was selected as a suitable place for holding elections.

Using the 1878 Beers map of Williamson County, the best available, it is obvious the 13th District has changed overtime. We can tell that by the tax rolls. The tax rolls indicate that I.W.P. West, J. Smithson, Hughes Bros., T. Priest, J. Andrews, J. Long were once in the 13th. Property owners may have petitioned the county court to move the boundaries for convenience or political reasons. According to the 1836 directions, the northern boundary of the 13th extended to the Harpeth River starting at Neeley's Branch, today Toon's Creek, which on the 1878 map was near Dr. H.R. Williams home. Following the boundary line with the 10th District to Hezekiah Smithson, Sr. land, who must have lived near W. Williams and P.S. Childress, then the line heads in a straight line south to the 12th District. The boundary line between the 12th and the 13th Districts runs in a southerly direction along the Duck River Ridge and makes a northeasterly turn near Cool Springs Road at what was once called McCall's Gap. Today, this would be the intersection with Bethesda-Arno Road. Since Arno wasn't named until 1890, it is not on the 1878 map. However, it is located at the intersection of the road coming from Peytonsville and the dotted line going to College Grove at McCrory Creek. The boundary line between the 13th and 21st Districts follows McCrory Creek until it empties into the Harpeth, just northeast of Rudderville on McDaniel Road.

Another interesting fact, Arno Road did not exist in 1878. The Chrisman Mill Turnpike (organized in 1881) began at the Franklin Third Avenue Bridge, then out what is known today as Murfreesboro Road or Highway 96 East to Chrisman's Mill at Millview. Before Chrisman Mill Turnpike was extended to Allisona in the late 1880s, to get to Rudderville from Millview, one would go Gosey Hill Road to Crowder Lane-Meeks Road. If you draw a line between Z. West to A. Hatcher, then south to C.W. Pennington, you will get some idea of where Arno Road is today.

Notice the cluster of families centered in the Peytonsville village. Also, notice that the road to Trinity was only a dotted line, as is the road going to Harpeth. In the village, one will notice the old familiar names that one would associate with Peytonsville i.e., N.L. Harrison, W. Nevils, M.C. Gosey, N.N. Smithson, T.L. Harrison, the Methodist Church, Dr. A. Reid, J. Lamb and J.B. Wilson. On the road to Franklin, one will find W.T. Smithson, M.L. Helm, W. Vaden, H. Clay,

E.S.B. Gosey, A. Pratt, W. Williams, G. McConnico, J.H. Merritt, and A. Boyd. Going north on Gosey Hill Road is J. Gosey, W.W. Reed, J.A. Johnson, G. Johnson and the Beech Cliff Academy. On Crowder Road, one would find the Thomas Methodist Church, Johnson School, E.M. Johnson and Westwood School. On Meeks Road, we find the wealthy Mrs. Mary C. Starnes, widow of Col. J.W. Starnes, and the largest landowner in the 13th, Thomas Burnett. T. Parrish, G. Crunk's cotton gin, H.L. Edmonds, and A. Hatcher. South to the Harpeth River, we find A.R. Pinkston, L.H. Holt, J.D. Patton, S.L. Crunk and J. Couch.

Going south towards Bethesda, we find Dr. W. West, the school and church at Cool Springs, J. Holland, T. Stegall, G. Low, W. Petway and W.H. Dodson. The traditional families who settled in Little Texas i.e., the Lillards, McGees, Bennetts, Garners, and Veaches are not identified yet, though L. Beard and S. Harris and N. Bennett are to the west. The numerous Tomlins will appear soon. Along Hurricane Creek we find, J. Gee, J. Buchanan, B. Sledge, J. Tanner, E.S.B. Gosey and Mrs. E.C. Smithson.

Clustered around the Crowder-Meek-Trinity Road area is the community of Westwood. A community made up largely of descendants of freedmen who settled on the cedar glades where land was cheap and the best they could afford. These families often took the name of their former owners, which can easily be identified, since the tax rolls were separated by race. The 1960 tax roll listed the following families: Beal, Crowder, Gentry, Hayes, Kinnard, Luster, Reynolds, Smithson, and Starnes.

The streams that drain the 13th District flow north to the Harpeth River. McCrory Creek, the largest stream, begins at the base of the Duck River Ridge at the Cool Springs and flows through Arno on to the Harpeth River providing narrow, fertile bottoms along the way. Hurricane Creek, the second largest stream, begins southwest of the village and flows northward to the Harpeth. On modern maps, Hurricane Creek has become Starnes Creek, named after the district's largest landowner Col. James W. Starnes. Toon Creek, the smallest and shortest

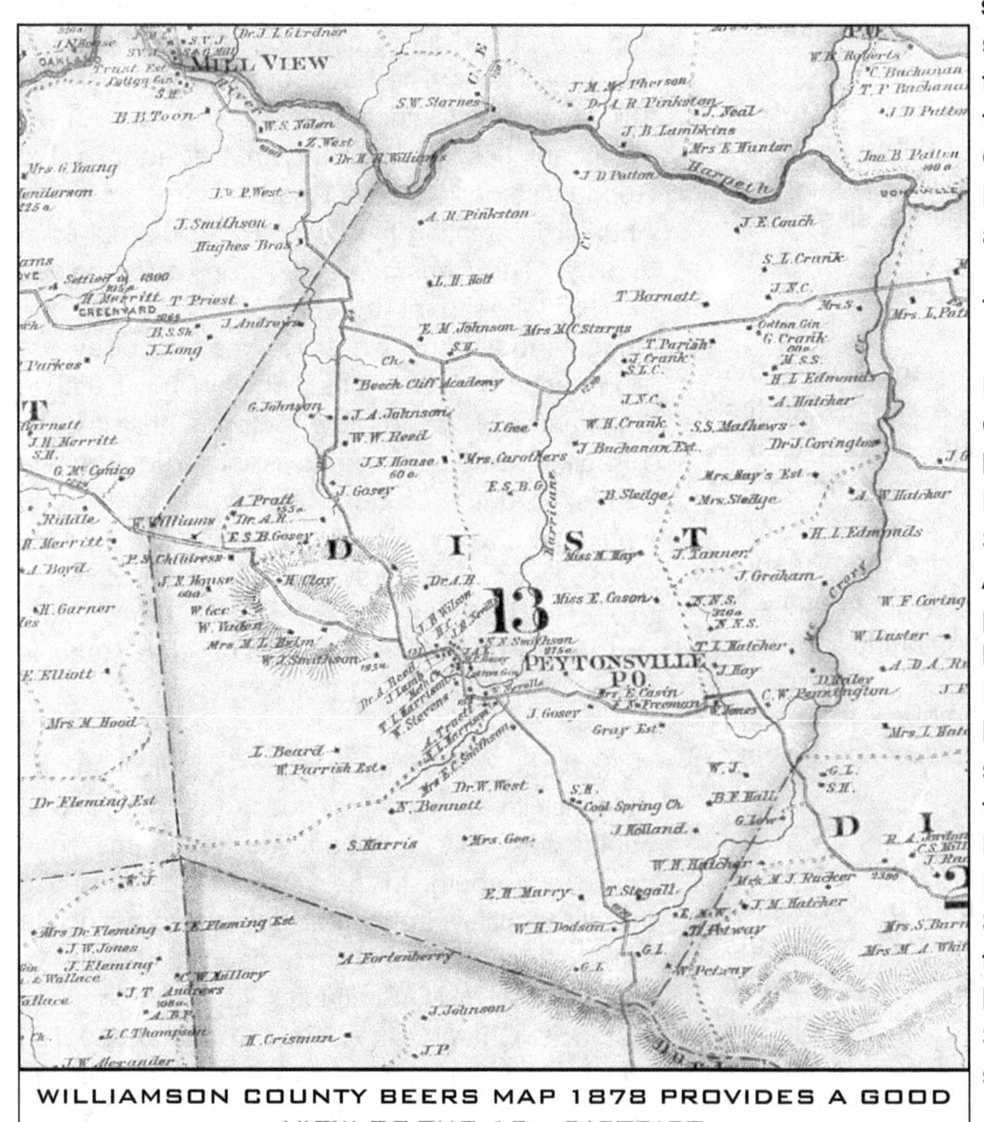



WILLIAMSON COUNTY BEERS MAP 1878 PROVIDES A GOOD VIEW OF THE 13TH DISTRICT

waterway, begins from springs on the north side of Gosey Hill and flows northward to Harpeth River east of Millview. In 1836, this stream was called Neely's Branch, after an early family to the area.

The numerous red cedar trees found throughout the 13th District foretell the viewer that limestone is close to the surface. The soils are shallow and easily depleted. The first farmers found patches of tobacco could be grown as a cash-crop soon after their arrival. Dairy and small grains could be grown with some success. Sawmills appeared with the coming of steam-power and soon depleted the virgins stands of oak, hickory, chestnut, and of course, cedar. Today, full-time farmers are rare. Landowners have discovered growing houses are more profitable than tobacco, corn or cattle.

The next map provides a good overview of the village of Peytonsville. Glenn's Store and R.W. Glenn's home may be seen at the intersection of Peytonsville Road and the road to Trinity. Between Glenn's Store and the Tomlin's Store, located at the intersection of Gosey Hill Road, was the old Smithson-McGee-Mangrum brick house, Richard Poteete and the Peytonsville Church of Christ which moved in 1951. G. W. Bruce lived between the store and the school. G.W. King lived across the road from the school. Gary Bruce (Webster) lived at the intersection of Gosey Hill and Peytonsville Road, across from the store. Peytonsville Methodist Church is across the road from the Tomlin-Bruce Store.

Mrs. Lela Warren Spears lived west of the Methodist church. The homes east of the Methodist church were occupied by the Harrisons, Tomlins and Maxwells.

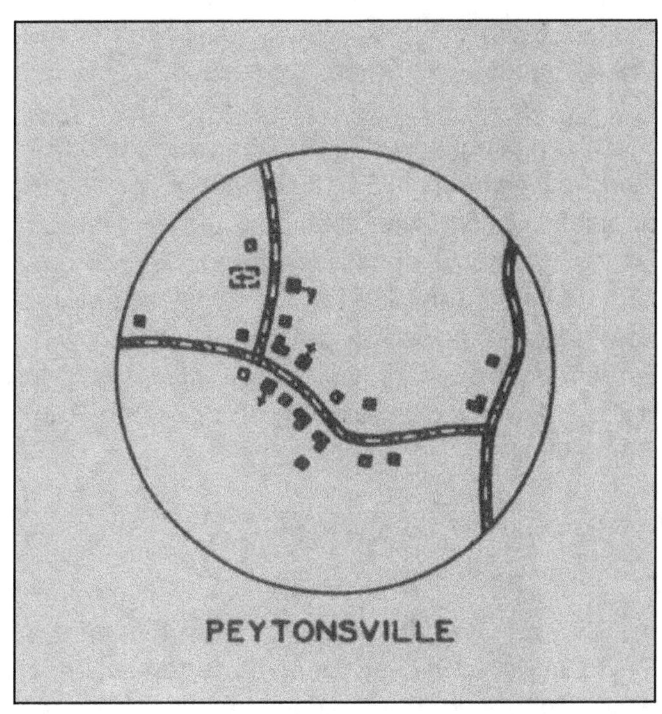



## RUDDERVILLE

In the northeast section of the 13th District is the settlement of Rudderville. Originally, a large portion of the community was owned by Richard Rudder and his son-in-law Dr. James W. Starnes. It is divided by Arno Road and is situated between the neighborhoods of Millview and Arno. Other roadways that bisect the community are Trinity-Peytonsville Road, McDaniel Road, Lampkin Bridge Road, Meeks Road, Nathan Smith Road and Eudaily-Covington Road. At one time, Rudderville had two grocery stores-Smithson's Store and White's Store & Feed Mill. Like other communities, it also had a blacksmith shop, operated by J.W. Culberson and gas-powered grist mill, owned by S.A. and Van Smithson. Today, one will notice the old Smithson store, under new management, is still operating, with the Milcrofton Utility District office next door. Milcrofton provides water to a large section of southeastern Williamson County. The name was created by the communities it serves, Millview-Clovercroft-Arrington. The major educational institutions, Page High School and Page Middle School dominate the opposite sides of Arno Road. Sadly, the ghost-like structures of

White's Store & Feed Mill still inhabit the corner of Arno and Meek's Road intersection.

Yes, surprisingly, Rudderville had a post office. First, on January 25, 1888, W.T. Ridley was appointed postmaster, but only until November 30, 1888, when it was discontinued. On February 17, 1894, John P. Tanner was appointed postmaster, followed by William J. Jordan, who served until January 14, 1904, when the post office was moved to Franklin and became Rural Route One.

## ARNO

In 1893 E.K. Smithson moved from his store in Peytonsville to the store at the intersection of Arno Road and the road connecting Harpeth-Peytonsville and College Grove. Arno had a post office from 1890 to 1908 with only two postmasters during that period, Robert Low (1890-1894) and E.K. Smithson (1894-1908). One would assume that Robert Low operated a store in the community before E.K. Smithson came. It is reported that the community got the name Arno from the River Arno in Italy. Since there were no Italians in the community, it is believed, a postal officer in Washington D.C. selected the name in honor of his homeland.

E.K. Smithson operated the store until 1925, turning it over to Eugene 'Red" Jordan and Earl Culberson, who ran it until 1946. The store has known many owners over the years: Bob White, Jimmy Robinson, John Paul Skinner, Frank Howell, and Fred Hughes. Milton Ryan was the final owner before this piece of Williamson County history burned October 1982.

E.K. Smithson served on the Williamson County Quarterly Court for nearly 50 years. He started when Arno was in the 13th District and continued when it was moved to the 23rd District, only missing one term between the gerrymandering.

ELIJAH KNOTT SMITHSON
(1860-1941)

During the July 1887 term of the Williamson County Quarterly Court, the justices voted to create a new civil district, called the 23rd, carved out of the 13th, 14th, 18th, 19th and 20th districts, with Arrington as the voting place. This placed the citizens of Rudderville in the 23rd District. Also, on the 1959 map, you will notice that the Arno community was placed in the 21st District, leaving the 13th a must smaller district. One could speculate that this gerrymandering of district lines could have been political. Apparently, someone wanted to serve as a magistrate on the county court and knew they could not compete against a Meek, Smithson, Lillard or Vaden successfully. Historically, the magistrates from the 13th District came from these four families.

## HISTORIC ROADS AND BYWAYS IN THE 13TH DISTRICT

In 1784, North Carolina appointed a group of commissioners to survey Middle Tennessee to establish the boundaries for the issuing of land grants to reward the officers and soldiers of the Continental Line, who fought the British. It appears there were two land grants that covered what would be the 13th District: James Moore's 12,000-acres and James Thackston's 4,362-acres. The surveyors found a well-travelled trail used by buffalo and Native Americans running north and south through the center of what would become Williamson County and the 13th District. They named this trail the Big South Road or the Buffalo Road. In 1805, Jones Glover purchased from Samuel Jackson of Washington County, Tennessee 250 acres of James Thackston's land grant that began east of the Commissioner's Road. This would place the boundary right in the heart of Peytonsville at Hurricane Creek. The accompanying map shows that the Big South Road is part of the Peytonsville-Trinity Road today. After passing through the village, it continues south on Cool Springs Road to the Duck River Ridge. On the 1878 Beers map, this road is located by a dash-line to Meek Road then disappears, only to appear across the Harpeth River at Starnes's Mill and on to Wilson Pike.

The second historic trail of the 13th District that passes through the village of Peytonsville was originally called Harpeth Lick Road. It started in Franklin at the corner of West Margin (5th Avenue South) and South Margin.  Going out to what is today Lewisburg Pike, to the Old Peytonsville Road at Berry Farm, crossed over I-65, to Peytonsville Road through the village, on to Arno, then south to Owen Hill Road. In time, one will reach the headwaters of the Harpeth River on Grove Creek, known historically, as Harpeth Lick. The Harpeth Lick Cumberland Presbyterian Church on Arno Road is the only landmark that bears the name of the once prominent destination.

The Williamson County Road Book 1816-1826, found in the county archives, provides some interesting details as to those families living along the Harpeth Lick Road.

**April 1816:** Ordered that Richard Hay be appointed to oversee the clearing out and keeping in repair the Harpeth Lick Road from the Five Mile Creek above Franklin to Glover's Gap and that Patrick Gibson, Richard Hay, William Williams, John Sledge, Jones Glover, John Williamson, Joseph Tanner, Richard Tanner, J. Roberts, Fredrick Taylor, H. Sledge work thereon under his directions.

**April 1816:** Ordered that David Pinkston be appointed to oversee the clearing out and keeping in repair the road leading from Franklin to Harpeth Lick beginning at Hurricane Creek running to the George Kinnard horse mill and that all those hands live in the bounds beginning and running so as to include William Young, Kracy Andrews' hands, Ephraim Bugg, Francis Young, Jacob Whithead, Wilie McCall, Mrs. Elizabeth Locke's hands, John Secrest, John Baker, Joseph Tanner, Richard Tanner, Edward Burton, Loami Stevens, Henry Walker, Matthew Pope, Pamplin Shelburne, Samuel Shelburne's hands and George Kinnard's hands.

**January 1817:** Ordered that Thomas Merritt be appointed to oversee the clearing out and keeping in repair that part of the Harpeth Lick Road beginning at Five Mile Creek to work to James Boyd's and that Barnett, Merritt, Mayfield & Boyd's hands and Oldham's hands work thereon under his directions.

**January 1817:** Ordered that Angus McPhail oversee the clearing out and keeping in repair the public road (Harpeth Lick) from the southeast corner of Franklin to McGavock's Spring Branch and that the hands of John Donelson's plantation, Moses Moore and others living on the plantation of McGavock, with the hands living where Nicholas Perkins formerly lived, together with the hands of said Angus McPhail work thereon under his directions.

**January 1817:** Ordered that Horatio Pettus oversee the clearing out and keeping in repair that part of the public road (Harpeth Lick) leading from James Boyd's to Hurricane Creek thence running so as to include Horatio Pettus, thence southeast with the knobs so as to include Patrick Gibson, thence down Hurricane Creek to

Thomas B. Walthall, thence to James Williams, thence to include John Harden, then to the beginning to work thereon under his direction.

**April 1817:** Ordered that Joseph Tanner oversee the clearing out and keeping in repair the Harpeth Lick Road from the fork nine miles from Franklin to Glover's Gap and that Patrick Gibson, Richard Hay, William Williams, John Sledge, Jones Glover, John Williams, Joseph Tanner, D. Tanner, Joseph Roberts, Fred Taylor, L.H. Sledge work thereon under his directions.

The 1878 Beers map of the 13th District provides a visual sighting of the dash-line that would become Peytonsville-Trinity Road and a straight line to Starnes Mill that would cross the future Arno Road and connect further north with Wilson Pike. Also, the route of Harpeth Lick Road from Peytonsville-Arno-Owen Hill Road and on to the headwaters of the Harpeth River are more defined. It should be noticed on this map that Arno Road is not there. The Chrisman Mill

Turnpike was chartered in 1882 but not built to Millview until 1890. This turnpike started in Franklin at the 3rd Avenue bridge across the Harpeth River, continued east to what is today Murfreesboro Road, turned south on what is the beginning of Arno Road today, then to Chrisman's Mill at Millview. In October 1891, the Chrisman Turnpike was extended further south through what is today Rudderville, then called Mrs. Starnes's plantation.

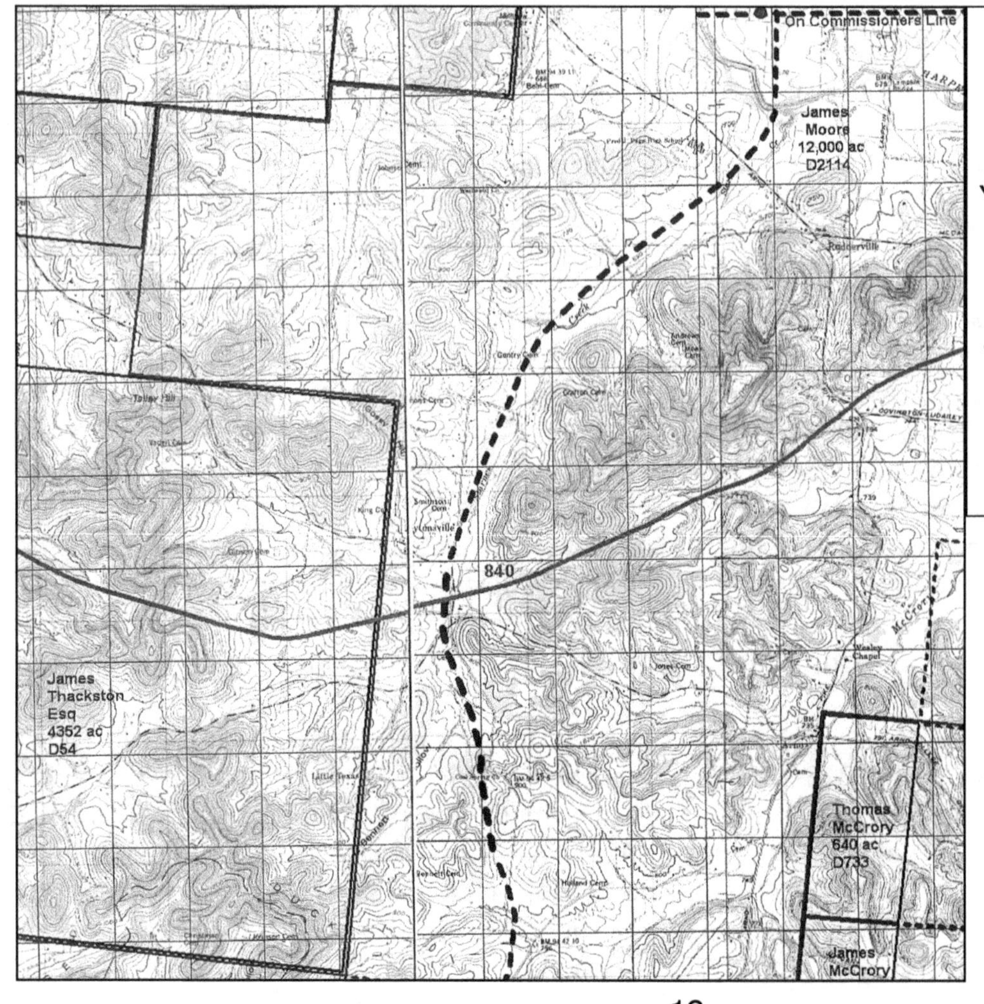


COMMISSIONERS' TRACE RUNS ALONG HURRICANE CREEK AND TRINITY ROAD THROUGH THE VILLIAGE, THEN SOUTH TO COOL SPRINGS ROAD. HARPETH LICK ROAD FOLLOWS PEYTONSVILLE ROAD TO ARNO, THEN SOUTH TO OWEN HILL ROAD, THEN THE HEADWATERS OF THE HARPETH RIVER.

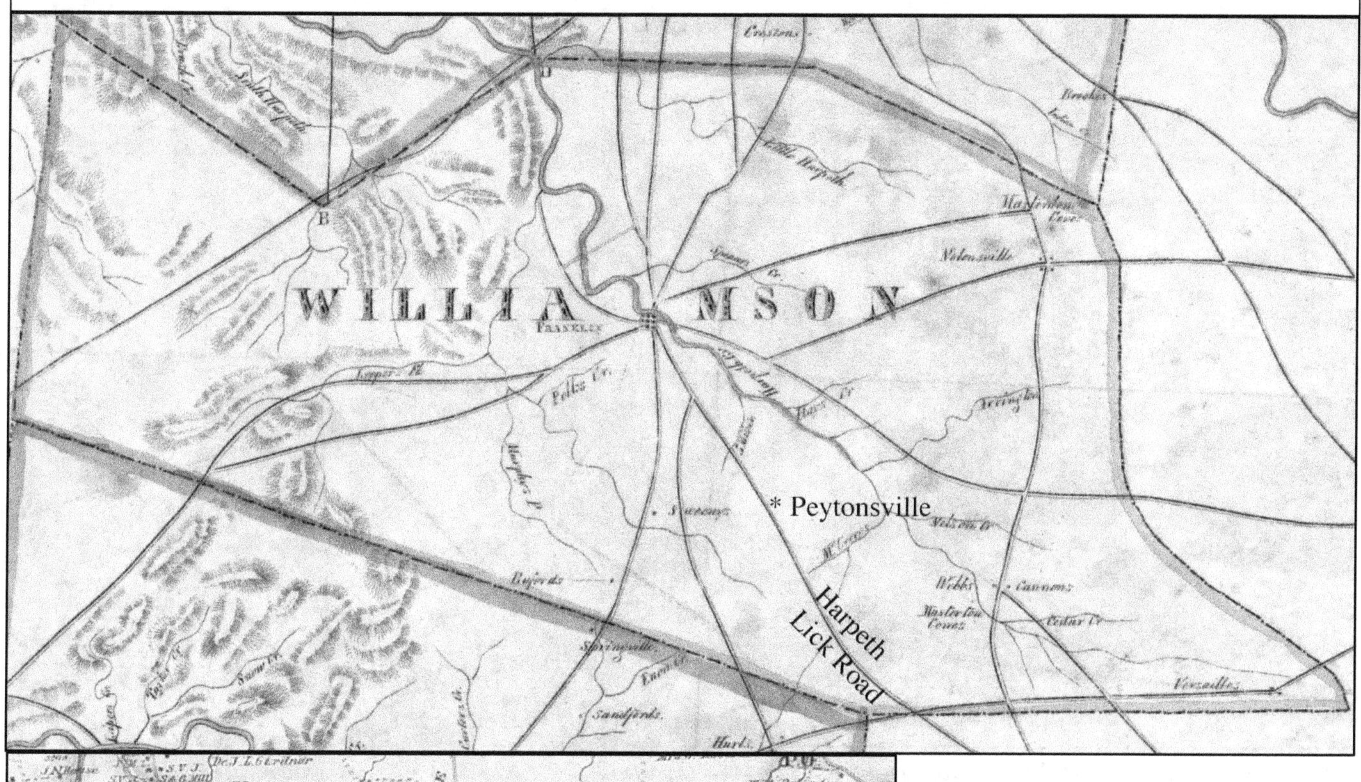


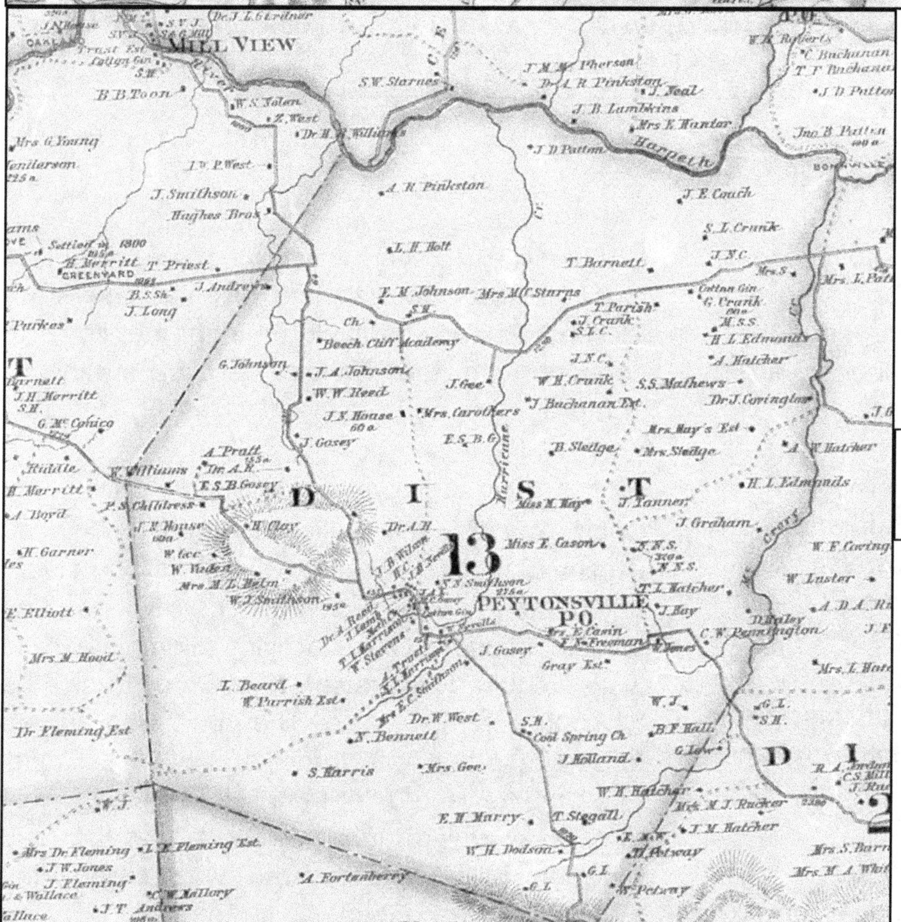


THE ORIGINAL 13TH DISTRICT OF 1836 AS SEEN ON THE 1878 BEERS MAP.

A plat of the J.H Parks's estate in 1917, today, owned by Sarah Louise Bratton Lillard, shows a tollgate located south of the Harpeth River, across the road from the late John Glenn's place.

Charles W. Hatcher mentions in his book, *Farm Strong*, that a tollgate stood at the corner of Arno Road and Nathan Smith Road, which would have been the second tollgate for the Chrisman-Arno Turnpike. The first being near Epworth Church. Hatcher also provides a view of the Duck River Ridge Turnpike, a.k.a Chrisman-Arno Turnpike, in front to the A.W. Hatcher place, today the Hatcher family compound, with Hatcher Dairy near the road.

In August 1890, the Duck River Ridge Turnpike was formed to run from Hubert T. Parrish's (Rudderville) to J.O. Petway's place (Arno), a four-mile distance with one tollgate. The Arno-Allisona Road was built through the cove to connect with the College Grove-Farmington Turnpike.

At the July term of the Williamson Quarterly Court of 1924, the justices agreed to buy the Chrisman Mill Turnpike, paying the stockholders $9,600 for the pike, rock crusher, gravel bar, and tollgate houses. Citizens living along the road were required to raise $2,400 to finish the $12,000 purchase price. The court also agreed to purchase the Arno turnpike at $300 per mile. The probate records of the estate of I.W.P. West of 1895 provides further evidence that the road between Millview and Arno was called "the turnpike between Chrisman to Arno."

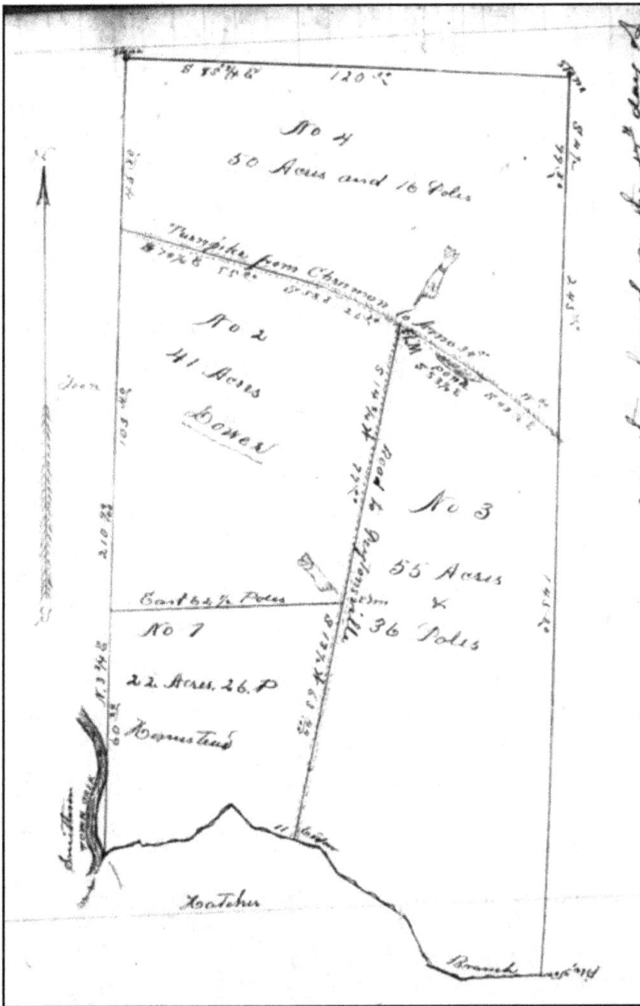

THE I.W.P. WEST PLACE WAS LOCATED AT THE CORNER OF ARNO ROAD AND GOSEY HILL ROAD. KNOWN AS THE LATE BOBBY T. LADD FARM. THE SOUTH CORNER OF THE FARM IS BORDERED BY TOONE CREEK AND WHAT WOULD BE KNOWN AS THE BILLY NOLAND PLACE.

## VOTERS IN THE 13TH DISTRICT IN 1835

The late Bud Smithson had in his possession an account book from a Smithson business in Peytonsville covering the years 1835 through 1855. On one page was a voters list of men from the 13th District, referred then as Snatchet. Unfortunately, only last names are used to identify the voters. However, those names provide us an idea of who was living in the 13th District in 1835.

| | |
|---|---|
| 1. H.P. Smithson | 11. Parish |
| 2. Tho. Helm | 12. Crews |
| 3. W. Vaden | 13. Sears |
| 4. J. Vaden | 14. Harris |
| 5. Carson | 15. Mosely |
| 6. Sappington | 16. G. Kinnard |
| 7. J. Mangum | 17. M. Kinnard |
| 8. W. Mangum | 18. J. Powel |
| 9. H. Smithson | 19. L. Powel |
| 10. M. Smithson | 20. Madaris |
| 21. R. Hay | 68. T. Hughes |
| 22. J. Hay | 69. Ja. Hughes |
| 23. Jorden | 70. Middleton |
| 24. M. Wilson | 71. Kennedy |
| 25. J. Wilson | 72. D. Sledge |
| 26. H. Walker | 73. R. Sledge |
| 27. W. Walker | 74. Z. Sledge |
| 28. Gray | 75. J. Crunk |
| 29. R. Tanner | 76. R. Crunk |
| 30. T. Tanner | 77. J. Andrews |
| 31. J. Walton | 78. W. Andrews |
| 32. Wm. Walton | 79. M. Andrews |
| 33. W. Walton | 80. J. Andrews |
| 34. T. Walton | 81. E. Hardeman |
| 35. Gee | 82. Ja. Hardeman |
| 36. Skinner | 83. Dotson |
| 37. Pennington | 84. Baily |
| 38. J. Jones | 85. Starnes |
| 39. H. Jones | 86. Kirkpatrick |
| 40. Tignor | 87. Vaughn |
| 41. I. Allen | 88. J. West |
| 42. J. Allen | 89. P. West |
| 43. Nichols | 90. Redmon |
| 44. R. Jones | 91. Farmer |
| 45. Clark Jones | 92. Gray |
| 46. H.C. Smithson | 93. J. Secrest |
| 47. J. Smithson | 94. T. Secrest |
| 48. Rucker | 95. N. Smithson |
| 49. Early | 96. S. Smithson |
| 50. J. Patton | 97. C. Smithson |
| 51. S. Patton | 98. N. Smithson |
| 52. Utley | 99. H. Moss |
| 53. Ja. William | 100. N. Smithson |
| 54. Jon. E. Williams | 101. Davis |
| 55. W. Williams | 102. Gordon |
| 56. Tho. Williams | 103. P. Gibson |
| 57. Ja. McGuire | 104. Wm. Gibson |

58. Tho. McGuire
59. Johnson
60. Sample
61. Rudder
62. Hays
63. Osburn
64. J. Layne
65. R. Layne
66. Wm. Layne
67. J. Hughes
115. Peoples
116. G. Brooks
117. J. Brooks
118. Olmon
119. Poindexter

105. Cook
106. Andrews
107. Bond
108. D. Sr. Pinkston
109. D. Jr. Pinkston
110. Roberts
111. Shelburn
112. Cheatham
113. Merritt
114. Stewart
120. Harrison
121. Scruggs
122. Sage
123. Elliot
124. Hudgins

When the boundaries for the 13th District were drawn in 1836, it was reported in the *Western Weekly Review* of February 12, 1836 this interesting sentence, "And have designated, in like manner, the store house of Andrew Campbell, at Snatch, as a suitable place for holding elections, & c." Since there has been a long tradition in the 13th District that elections were held in the store at the intersection of Franklin-Peytonsville Road and Peytonsville-Trinity Road, it is likely, Andrew Campbell's store was in this location.

The accompanying photograph of 1910 illustrates the interest local voters had in exercising their right to vote. In this case, good weather allowed an open-air ballot box with election officials overseeing the event beside Smithson's Store. Of course, this was a "men's only" event until 1920 when women obtained the privilege cast their ballot. Until 1948, voters were required to pay a $2 poll tax for the privilege of casting a vote. This discouraged a lot of poor black and white voters from voting. In days past, courthouse politicians were known to pay the poll tax for a promise to vote the straight party ticket.

Election Day 1910 in Peytonsville

There was a long tradition of candidates or their proxies offering half-pints of whiskey for a vote. Let us hope, those illegal practices are in our past.

## PEYTONSVILLE POSTMASTERS

U.S. Post Offices have been numerous in Williamson County, seventy-three to be exact, Franklin being the first in 1801. As a general rule, these rural post offices were located in the country stores usually located at a crossroads. Postmasters were most likely the owners of the local store and politically in favor with the present president. At the beginning of the 20th century and the advent of the Rural Free Delivery system, the number of post offices declined throughout the county.

Oral history tells us that Peytonsville was first known as Snatchit, also Snatch. This humorous, catty handle for the village was derived, we are told, as a result of a ten-dollar debt. The creditor collected his due bill by snatching a ten-dollar bill from the hand of the unsuspecting debtor, hence the name Snatchit. From the following list of Peytonsville postmasters, it would appear the village took the name Peytonsville in 1836.

| Postmasters: | Effective Date |
| --- | --- |
| Orlando Davis | 11 Mar, 1836 |
| George Andrews | 13 Nov, 1837 |
| John G. Boyd | 30 Mar, 1843 |
| John Andrews | 12 Jan, 1844 |
| John B. Critchlow | 24 Feb, 1849 |
| Thomas J. Gray | 7 Feb, 1854 |
| Moses G. Gosey | 18 Sep, 1856 |
| Patrick G. Smithson | 29 Sep, 1860 |
| Discontinued | 22 Sep, 1866 |
| John M. Nevils | 20 Feb, 1867 |
| John H. Criswell | 19 Apr, 1867 |
| John W. Smithson | 17 Jun, 1868 |
| Alexander Stephens | 25 Jan, 1870 |
| A.B. Fleming | 4 Sep, 1872 |
| John M. Nevils | 2 Oct, 1872 |
| Tandy Smithson | 12 Aug, 1880 |
| Elijah K. Smithson | 14 Aug, 1884 |
| Turnel L.G. Harrison | 23 Jun, 1892 |
| James F. West | 17 Oct, 1893 |
| Thomas W. Smithson | 31 Jan, 1894 |
| Henry L. Thomas | 14 Jan, 1897 |
| Discontinued | 15 Feb, 1904 |

## REVOLUTIONARY SOLDIERS AND THEIR FAMILIES IN THE 13TH DISTRICT

After reviewing the early families of the 13th District, it is obvious that many of them came from Lunenburg County, Virginia. Many of these families were brought here by their patriot father in the first decade of the 19th century. Others were children of patriots whose fathers died before they could accompany their neighbors on the migration West. The following list are those patriots who left Lunenburg County, Virginia and settled in Williamson County. The date of their coming was determined by tax rolls, land purchases, or family records.

1. John Crafton (    -1816) left Lunenburg County, Virginia in 1808 and bought land on Hayes Creek.
2. Daniel Crenshaw (1757-1831) left Lunenburg County, Virginia in 1813 to live with his son Cornelius Crenshaw in the center of Peytonsville.
3. Alexander Lester, (1754-1834) left Lunenburg County, Virginia in 1806.
4. Drury Murrell (    -1842) left Lunenburg County, Virginia in 1805.
5. Jeffrey Murrell (    -1823) left Lunenburg county, Virginia in 1805.
6. Robert Parrish (1756-1836) left Lunenburg County, Virginia in 1826.
7. Henry Sledge (dates unknown) left Lunenburg County, Virginia in 1815.

One of the most numerous families in the 13th District were the Smithsons, descendants of John S. Smithson (1739-1782) and Drusilla Ann Walker Smithson (1748-1811) of Lunenburg County, Virginia. John S. Smithson served in the 6th Virginia Regiment in the Continental Line but died before he could resettle to Williamson County. His son, Clement S. Smithson was the first Smithson to come into the 13th District. In 1814 Clement purchased 125 acres on McCrory Creek from Samuel Shelburne for $556.75. Unfortunately, Clement died in 1814, soon after arriving, leaving his wife, Nancy Pettus, and his children: Susan Smithson Pennington, Sally Smithson Roberts, Martha Smithson Gilliam, Sylvanus W. Smithson, Drucilla Smithson,

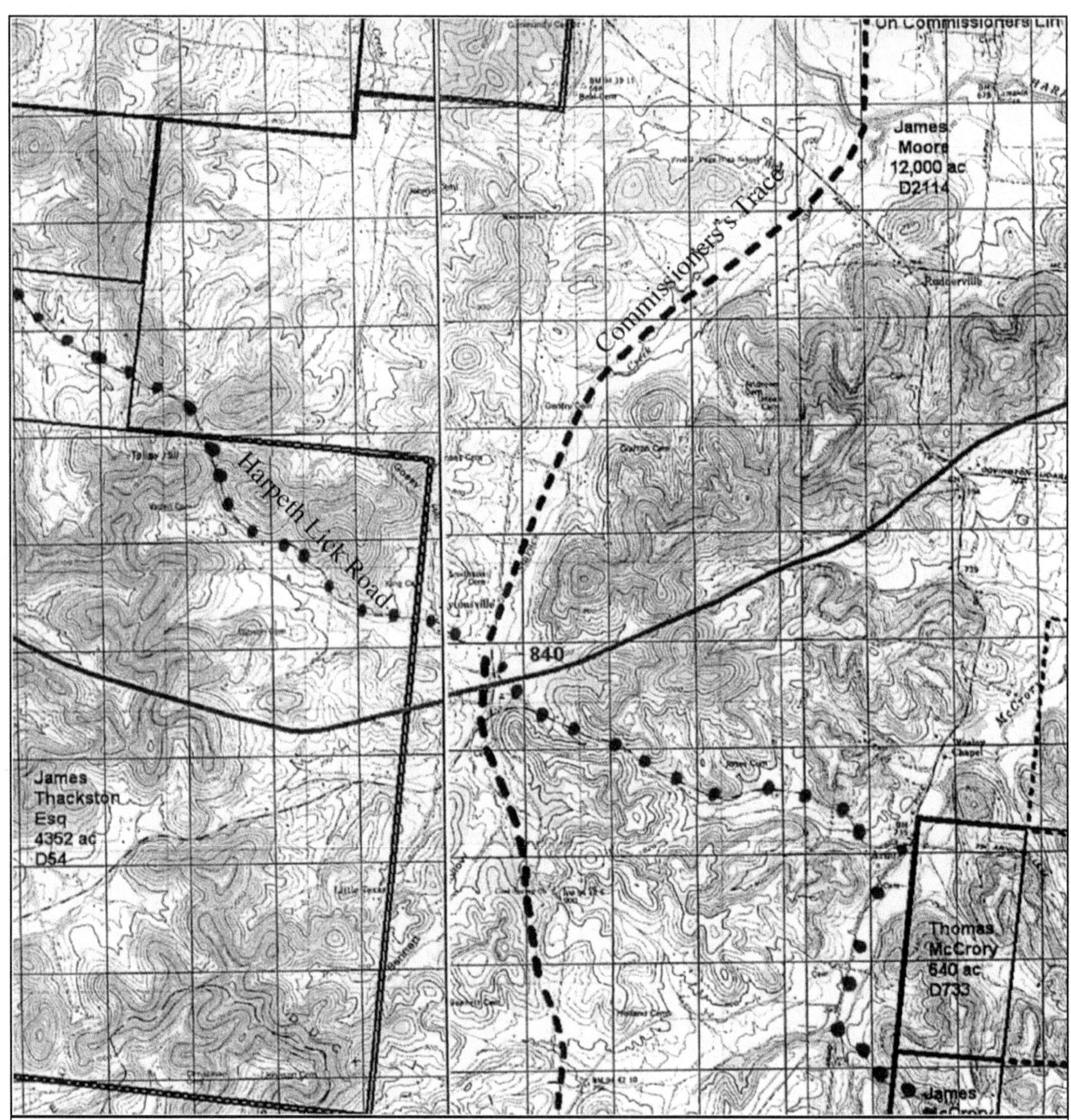


MAP COURTESY OF THOROUGHFARE FOR FREEDOM VOLUME II BY JACK MASTERS AND BILL PURYEAR 2011

Charles Smithson, Clement Smithson, Jr., Horatio Smithson, John P. Smithson and William Smithson.

The following patriots settled in Williamson County, outside the 13th District, from Lunenburg County, Virginia. John Cook, Henry Cook, Andrew Goff, William Jordan, Miles Priest and Moses Priest.

The following are Revolutionary patriots who settled in the 13th District but were not from Lunenburg County, Virginia:

1. Lodwick B. Beech (1758-1841) left Charlotte County, Virginia in 1821 to live with daughter Sarah and son-in-law Josiah Nevils.
2. John Gee (1742-1839) was paying taxes in Williamson County in 1806.
3. William Kennedy (1755-1853) left Lincoln County, N.C. in 1818 to live on McCrory Creek, where Hatcher Dairy is today.
4. James Merritt (1747-1837) left Edgecomb
5. County, N.C. in 1805 to live on Long Lane.
6. John Secrest (1858-1847) left Mecklenburg, County, N.C. in 1816 to live in the heart of Peytonsville.
7. Henry Sledge (dates unknown) left Virginia (possibly from Luneburg County) in 1815 to settle on Hurricane Creek.

Contrary to what many believe, families living in the 13th District did not receive a North Carolina Land Grant. The two large land grants of James Moore (12,000 acres) and James Thackston (4,352 acres) covered the whole 13th District and then some. Those early settlers coming to the 13th District either bought their land from Moore or Thackston or their agents.

## A 13TH DISTRICT REVOLUTIONARY VETERAN

**William Kennedy (1755-1853), Revolutionary Veteran**

***Our Valiant Men***
**Louise Gillespie Lynch**
William Kennedy was born April 13, 1755, in Culpepper County, Virginia. He was living there when he was drafted into Capt. Lewis Yancey's Company during the Revolutionary War. They marched to a ford on the Rappahannock River toward Fredricksburg. Before arriving there, orders were received that they were not needed. They marched back home and were discharged. This tour was for 2 months.

He again entered service in 1781 in Capt. Robert Pollard's Company and Col. James Slaughter's Regiment. Charles Barnes was an orderly Sergeant in this company. They marched from Culpepper Courthouse through Fredricksburg, crossing James River at Sandy Point. They met the British forces there and were pursued to Petersburg, where they engaged in battle. This was the first battle that William Kennedy was in. After sustaining the enemy's fire for an hour or two, the army retreated to Richmond where they joined LaFayette and marched down the north side of James River 8 or 9 miles below Richmond, under the command of LaFayette, where the Americans were encamped.

Kennedy, with a guard of about 120 men, under Joseph James of Fauquier County, Virginia, was sent to Chesterfield. While on the engagement Kennedy and about 60 other men were taken prisoners and sent to Norfolk. He remained there four months and ten days. He was taken prisoner in May of 1781 and liberated in the latter part of September. He described his sufferings in the horrible prison-house as, 'perfectly intolerable". Their only food for the greater part of the time being bad, "horse-beef," with water but once a day and sometimes not that. The hot weather, close confinements and bad food soon caused the death of most of the prisoners, only 7 surviving to be exchanged. William Kennedy was in such a weak condition, that he fell by the roadside on his way home and was discovered and relieved by some passing soldiers.

He moved to Lincoln County, North Carolina, in 1786 and to Williamson County, Tennessee, in 1818. In 1826, he deeded 50 acres of land to Rachel Kennedy. He was paying taxes on 72 acres of land on McCrory's Creek.

In May 1852, there was an article written about him in the South-Western Monthly stating that even though he was over 90 years of age, he still made his yearly walk to Nashville, a distance of more than 25 miles, to receive his yearly pension.

William Kennedy died in 1853 intestate. The remainder of his land was sold to Daniel Sledge and Octavias Hatcher. He is said to have been buried on his land in the Arno community.
His children were:
1. Celia, who married Daniel Sledge
2. Mary Ann, who married John Sledge
3. Sarah, who married Birdnear Beard
4. Elizabeth, who married _______ Corzine
5. Rachel, never married
6. Nancy, who married ______ Perkins.

**Rachel Kennedy Estate 1872**
***Miscellaneous Records Volume 7***
***Louise Gillespie Lynch***

Rachel Kennedy Estate Advertisement-Mary Ann Sledge et al vs. Sally Beard et al
Sale January 20, 1872-50 acres land belonging to the estate of Rachel Kennedy, deceased, in the 13th District, bounded by the lands of John Tanner, heirs of Alphonzo Andrews, deceased, A.W. Hatcher, Daniel Sledge, N.N. Smithson. Said tract of land has a neat little dwelling, a fine spring and good orchard.

Deposition of William Johnson- March 1880-I was acquainted with William Corzine, a legatee of the estate of Rachel Kennedy. I do not know if he is now dead. I have not heard from him in about 20 years. He was a citizen of Kentucky when I last saw him, and he was visiting his relatives in Williamson County. His heirs would be Mrs. A.M. Crunk, the heirs of Elizabeth Corzine, Easter Corzine, who never married and Rachel Atkinson, who is dead and left children.

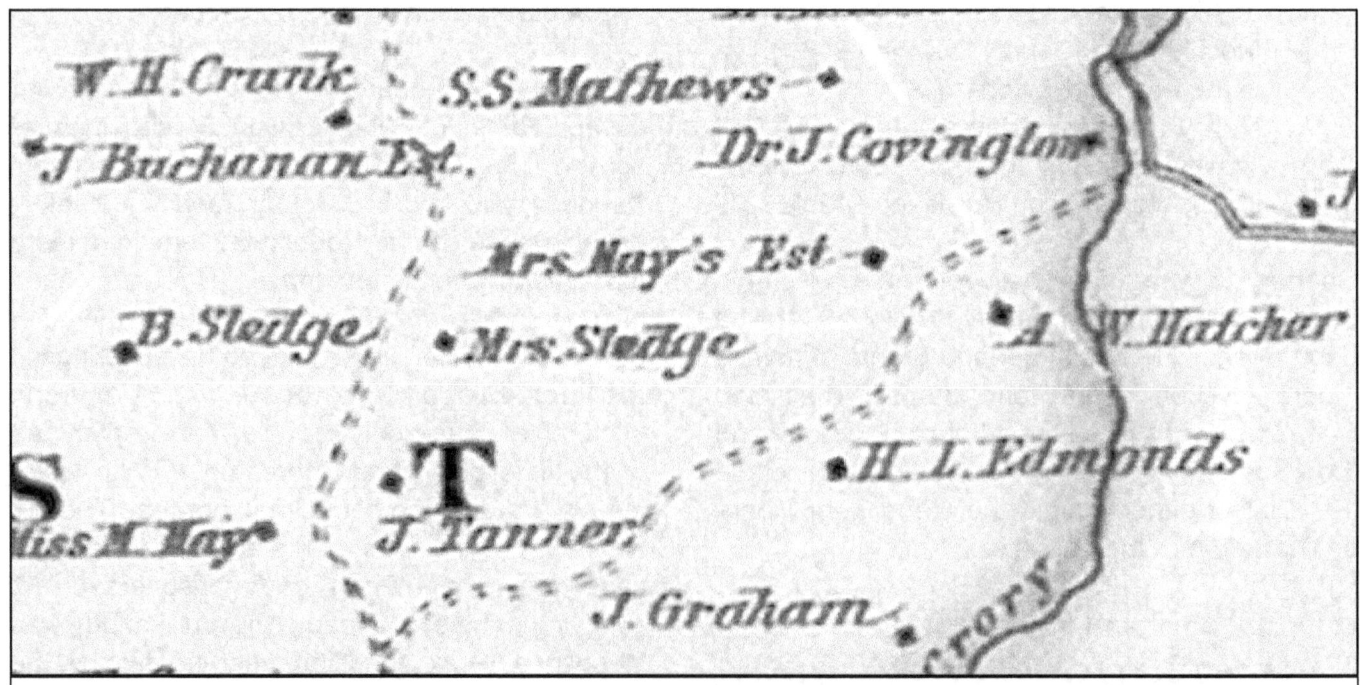


THE 1878 BEERS MAP OF THE LAND BETWEEN RUDDERVILLE AND ARNO MAY LOCATE THE ORIGINAL FARM OF WILLIAM KENNEDY AND RACHEL KING ON THE MCCRORY'S CREEK WATERSHED. THE J. BUCHANAN ESTATE WOULD BE THE ALPHONZO ANDREWS FARM.

Rachel Kennedy departed this life December 1870 intestate. She left heirs, sister Mary Ann Sledge, wife of John Sedge, Celia Sledge, wife of Daniel Sledge, her sister, her deceased sister Elizabeth Corzine's heirs, Sena Crunk, wife of Joseph Crunk, Rachel Atkinson, wife of Stephen Atkinson, William Corzine, who has not been heard from for many years and may be dead. The land was sold to A.W. Hatcher for $10.50 per acre.

## CHURCHES IN THE 13TH DISTRICT

On July 7, 1839, Robert Gray sold to Richard Hay and Theophilus Gentry, deacons of the United Baptist Church at Cool Springs, a one-acre and two poles lot adjoining the lands of Richard Hay and Michael Kinnard for ten dollars. On December 5, 1895, N.N. Smithson, "for the love and affection I have for the congregation and membership of Cool Springs Church," gave a lot of land in the form of a triangle adjoining Thomas W. Pate and __ Neely and the present church, by estimation of one acre. The deacons accepting the additional lot were William Jones, S.K. Adair and Joe Harris. The **Cool Springs Primitive Baptists** are in fellowship with the Cumberland Association of Primitive Baptists.

On November 29, 1849, Nathaniel L. Harrison sold for $25 a one-acre and forty poles lot, adjoining the old meeting house lot, to Hugh Thompson, John Andrews, James A. Neely, George Long, Richard W. Hays, John B. Crichlow, William Neely, William Andrews, and John S. Parks trustees in trust of the **Thomas Chapel Methodist Episcopal Church, South**. The mention of the old meeting house indicates that an earlier congregation was already established. The 1849 building was of log and in 1853 this was replaced with a larger frame structure. In 1857 an additional one-half acre of was given by Jesse Johnson to provide hitching space. Also, in 1857 a large brick church was constructed. Quarterly Conference minutes of the 1880s and 1890s state that Thomas Church was 40 X 50 feet and would seat 300 persons. In 1891 its value was priced at $1,500. In 1909, Thomas Church and North Chapel merged to

Cool Springs Primitive Baptist Church est. 1818, built in 1856, Elder Milton Lillard, in center.

become Epworth Methodist Church on Arno Road in the Millview community.

On January 1, 1857 William Parrish, "for the love I have for Christ," conveyed to M.G. Gosey, John C. Helm, John Andrews, Rufus Ledbetter, and Alexander Reid trustees of the **Peytonsville Methodist Church South** a lot of between one-fourth and one-half acre.

Cool Springs Primitive Baptist Church 2nd Sunday June 1894 Foot-washing & Communion

THOMAS METHODIST CHURCH
1857-1909

PEYTONSVILLE METHODIST CHURCH
EST. 1857

PEYTONSVILLE METHODIST CHURCH,
2020

This church structure stands today across from the intersection of Peytonsville Road and Gosey Hill Road, though no longer a Methodist congregation. It disbanded in the 1980s due to declining membership. Today, the building is occupied by a non-denomination congregation lead by Pastor Herschel Osborne.

On January 20, 1874, Mary Rudder Starnes, widow of Col. J.W. Starnes, leased for fifteen years a one acre and a half lot for a school and church for the Black citizens of the 13th District known as Westwood. Located at the corner of Meeks Road and Peytonsville-Trinity Road, **Westwood Missionary Baptist Church** and Westwood School shared the same building until 1922. In that year, R.H. Thompson and wife sold to trustees-Joe West, George Davis, Oscar Hardeman, Neely Beale and Lunn Gibson a lot next to the school for seventy-five dollars for the erection of a new church. The Westwood congregation joined the Cumberland Association Primitive Baptists in 1999.

EPWORTH UNITED METHODIST CHURCH
EST. 1909

WESTWOOD MISSIONARY BAPTIST CHURCH EST. 1874 ON PEYTONSVILLE-TRINITY ROAD.

## CHARTER MEMBERS OF THE PEYTONSVILLE CHURCH OF CHRIST

William L. Johnson

A.J. Craig

Jacob Halfacre

Nathaniel B. Vaden

William Knott Gee

D.J. Halfacre

J.B.Gibson

H.L. Edmonds

E.A. Harrison

S.J. Vaden

S.E. Helm

S.A. Edmonds

B.A. Johnson

N.T. Warren

A.L. Pratt

Exudes Halfacre

We, the undersigned, on December 26, 1948, assembled at the Peytonsville Church of Christ, Williamson County, Tennessee, in the presence of the congregation at worship service, have witnessed the open election of trustees, named below, to work with the congregation at this place, to carry on the financial dealings, and have authority concerning the construction of a new building to be erected in the year 1949.

The same will hold the deeds for both the old and new building, disposing of the old property for the betterment of the new at the time they deem best for the congregation.

Trustees:
Bro. Roy G. Meek
Bro. Billy Boyd

23

Bro. Leonard Henry
Bro. John Pratt
Bro. Edward K. Ware
Witness: Preacher of day-Wm. T. Brown
       Sec'y-Treas.-Edward K. Ware

PEYTONSVILLE CHURCH OF CHRIST WAS COMPLETED IN 1951 CONSISTING OF 198 INDIVIDUAL SEATS AND A FULL BASEMENT FOR CLASSROOMS. MRS. LELIA WILLIAMS GIFTED THE PROPERTY FOR THE NEW CHURCH.

**Peytonsville Baptist Church**, located on the Harpeth-Peytonsville Road, was organized in August 1959, under the sponsorship of First Baptist Church of Old Hickory. The small congregation met in a tent, then moved to a country store with dirt floors. The first pastor of the mission was Bro. Don Burnett, followed by Bro. F.T. Carroll. In 1962, the congregation built a small building, with an auditorium and five Sunday school classrooms, on Peytonsville-Trinity Road. Rev. Clinton Wright, a retired employee of the Baptist Sunday School Board, was called to serve this church in 1965. In 1997, when 840 planned to take their church, the congregation, under Rev. Gerry Price, was able to purchase 11-acres nearby on Peytonsville-Harpeth Road, and build a new, larger building.

THE PEYTONSVILLE BAPTIST CHURCH, BUILT IN 1962, ON PEYTONSVILLE-TRINITY ROAD, WAS REPLACED IN 1997 WITH A NEW, LARGER CHURCH.

PEYTONSVILLE BAPTIST CHURCH, LOCATED ON PEYTONSVILLE-HARPETH ROAD, HAS COME A LONG WAY FROM A TENT, COUNTRY STORE AND FIVE SUNDAY SCHOOL CLASSROOMS.

**St. Ignatius Orthodox Church**, located at 4671 Peytonsville Road, was founded in 1987. It began as a home Bible study group known as Grace Fellowship in Rev. Gordon Walker's living room. Walker a former Campus Crusade of Christ staff member, led the group in their religious studies. Along with six other staff members and their "house churches," Walker helped form the Evangelical Orthodox Church, that eventually joined the historic Antiochian Orthodox Church.

The church's name has changed from Grace Fellowship to Holy Trinity to St. Ignatius. The gold dome and cross on the roof and the detailed iconography on the inside may seem far from the

members' religious upbringings. But for these former Baptists, Presbyterians, Lutherans, and Roman Catholics—to name a few—this church is a return to the original religious practices that were taught some 2,000 years ago.

St. Ignatius Orthodox Church is sometimes referred to as the blueberry church. Its bucolic setting is known to locals as the Walter Vaden farm. The accompanying photograph was taken from the Sledge-Smithson-Vaden Cemetery and shows the picturesque church in the background.

**Wesley Chapel United Methodist Church** was started in 1834 by the "Four Billies," William Hatcher, William Rucker, William Burns, and William Lanier. Land for the building was donated by William Rucker on Owen Hill Road and the first church was built of homemade bricks. It was built near a spring so the congregation could have good drinking water. In 1835 the church was dedicated and used until 1907 when the building was torn down to make way for a new structure. This chapel was made of wood and built on Arno Road. Brick from the

original building was sold and the original lumber put in the second building. Wesley Chapel became part of the College Grove circuit, along with the church at College Grove and the one at Triune. The current church was completed in 1962, on the same site, and built of brick.

Mary Hatcher. A large fellowship hall and educational annex were added in 1987. Today, the congregation makes use of two buildings, the 1910 church and the 2009 building one mile further down Arno Road.

**Epworth United Methodist Church** was formed by the union of two earlier churches, Thomas Church (1855) on Crowder Road and North's Chapel (1866) on North Chapel Road. Land for the church was given by Jesse A. and Mittie Toon Pierce. The chancel rail from the old Thomas Church and the pulpit from North's Chapel were incorporated in the new building. The Good Shepherd window was dedicated to Beverly B. and Sara Nolen Toon, and W.M. Toon. The Toon's home, Riverside, still stands across Arno Road. In 1952, Sunday school rooms were added. The next year Epworth became a charge, and a parsonage was built on land donated by

## SCHOOLS IN THE 13TH DISTRICT AND THE 23RD DISTRICT

Unfortunately, there has never been a thorough history of education written for Williamson County. One of the best sources we have to locate schools in the 13th District may be the 1878 Beers map. On this map, one will find Beech Cliffe Academy on Gosey Hill Road near the intersection of Crowder Road. No deed in the county archives can provide any further information. However, Dolly Stanfield mentioned in her interview with *The Review-Appeal* columnist Jane Owen in 1942 that she attended Johnson School under Miss Lizzie Knott before her family moved to Rudderville and there she attended Accident School. She also mentioned that she attended Thomas Methodist Church on Crowder Road, which may lead one to think that Beech Cliffe Academy later became Johnson School. The 1878 map also identifies a school next to Cool Springs Primitive Baptist Church, which would make school number two. In 1879, a list of county teachers by districts attributes C.E. Johnson, Mrs. M.J. Moore and S.A. Jefferson as teaching in the 13th District.

The village of Peytonsville doesn't seem to have a public school until 1896 when School Directors B.M. Meeks, G.M. Smithson, and Robert Gray received a deed of two and one-half acres from George W. and Nancy King for a school near the Peytonsville Church of Christ. Enoch R. Chest may have been the first teacher in this building since he lived near-by and gave a right-away and use of his well in 1898. The original wooden school was replaced in 1950 with a concrete-block- structure that had two classrooms, a cafeteria and indoor restrooms.

Talented, dedicated teachers are the makings of a successful school and Peytonsville has surely had those. It is difficult to compile a complete list of teachers after Enoch R. Chest but Miss Alice Vaden has been mentioned as one in the early 1900s. The following list is the best that can be provided at this time: 1912-Miss Maude

Logan;1920-Miss Mary Hatcher; 1924-E.C. McCormick & Miss Martha Alexander; 1926-E.C. McCormick & Miss Fannie Griffin; 1927-Miss Fannie Griffin; 1928-Walter J. Parks & Miss Fannie Griffin; 1929-W.J. Parks & Miss Nelle Smithson; 1930-1937-W.J. Parks & Norine Hussey; 1938-1939 W.J. Parks & Miss Mary Smithson; 1939-40 W.J. Parks, Brownie Anderson; 1940-1941-W.J. Parks, Katie Lou Gatlin, Vivennie Watson; 1942-1949-W.J Parks & Katie Lou Gatlin; 1950-1952-T.J. Jones & Katie Lou Gatlin; 1952-1954-Katie Lou Gatlin & Mr. Guy Ferrell; 1955-1962- Katie Lou Gatlin & Elizabeth Houser. In September of 1961, Peytonsville School closed, and Miss Gatlin and Miss Houser were transferred to Bethesda School.

1ST ROW: HATTIE SIMMONS, MARY ALICE SIMMONS, ODELL SIMMONS, ANN DERRYBERRY, REBECCA HUGHES, SARA SIMMONS, FRANCES PRATT, DOROTHY MOSLEY, FRANCES TOMLIN. 2ND ROW: ROBBIE ELLA BENNETT, LOU ELLEN TOMLIN, VIRGINIA TOMLIN, ALLENE DERRYBERRY, ALMA BENNETT 3RD ROW: T.K. BENNETT, RICHARD POTEET, LLOYD WARREN, MR. WALTER PARKS, GRADY POTEET, JAMES BEARD, DOUGLAS HARPER, ALBERT WATSON, JOSEPH DEASON, MALCOM HARPER, HOWARD TOMLIN, JAMES MCGEE, THOMAS PRATT

1ST ROW: VIRGINIA TOMLIN, LOU ELLEN TOMLIN, EVIE DODD, REBECCA HUGHES, DOROTHY RADER, MARY ALICE SIMMONS, RUBY DODD, SARA WALTON, BETTY MAY IVORY 2ND ROW: JAMES MCGEE, JOSEPH DEASON, FRED BUCHANAN, CRUNK MATHIS, MILTON TOMLIN, HOWARD TOMLIN, T.K. BENNETT, LLOYD WARREN, RICHARD POTEET 3RD. ROW: JEWELL BENNETT, ROBBIE ELLA BENNETT, JOSEPHINE JAY, MR. WALTER PARKS, FRANCES SIMMONS, GRACE BUCHANAN, HERBERT BENNETT, ALBERT WATSON, ALVA LEE TOMLIN

DAN VEACH, J.B. ROBINSON, TOMMY CRAWFORD, JANE MCGEE, UNKNOWN, JERRY SKINNER, ANN VEACH, MARGARET ANN WILLIAMS

PEYTONSVILLE SCHOOL BOYS: MIKE VADEN, UNKNOWN, JIMMY WARF, NELSON DODD, UNKNOWN, TONY PRATT, RONNIE MAUPIN, JIMMY VADEN AND RANDY YORK

The 1878 Beers map also identifies a school on Peytonsville-Trinity Road. In 1874, Mary C. Starnes, widow of Confederate Col. James W. Starnes, leased one acre and a half for fifteen years at one dollar for a school and church for the Black families in the 13th District. School Directors E.S. Gosey, W.F. Johnson and J.M. Nevils were to oversee Westwood School. The early teachers of this school are lost to history, but the county school records related the following: 1935-36-Hannah L. Dotson; 1936-1939-John T. Gentry; 1940-1961-Mrs. Jimmy Gentry; 1962-1964-Mrs. Jimmy Gentry & Helen Thomas; 1964-1966-Mrs. Jimmy Gentry & Eva Myers Lee. In the spring of 1966, Westwood School closed, and Mrs. Gentry and Mrs. Lee were transferred to the new Evergreen School, near Thompson Station.

WESTWOOD SCHOOL, LOCATED ON THE PEYTONSVILLE-TRINITY ROAD, WAS BUILT IN 1926. MRS. JIMMY GENTRY TAUGHT HERE FROM 1940 UNTIL THE SCHOOL CLOSED IN 1966.

WESTWOOD SCHOOL STUDENTS IN 1936

INSIDE WESTWOOD SCHOOL IN 1949, MRS. JIMMY GENTRY, TEACHER, STANDS BEHIND HER HUSBAND, MR. JOHN T. GENTRY, WHO TAUGHT AT WESTWOOD FOR MAY YEARS EARLIER. A RECEPTION IS PREPARED FOR THE STUDENTS AND COMMUNITY VISITORS.

For the students in the southeastern part of the 13th District (in 1897 it became the 23rd) attended Arno School, located on Arno Road near the crossroads. The land for a school was donated by William P. Lester in 1883. Some of the teachers included: Mr. and Mrs. J.H. Pylant, A.R. Parks, Tom Pettus, Miss Stella Parks, Sally Hudson, Miss Nimmie Cullum, T.R. Beasley, Miss Ellen Smithson, Miss Virginia Graves, Mildred Beasley Arnold, Josephine Miller, Miss Mary Walton, Hatcher Graham, Eugene McMahon, and Elmira Petway. Arno School, grades 1-8, closed in 1947.

The school registers of Miss Josephine Miller (4-8) and Mrs. J.H. Pylant (1-3) for 1935-36 will provide a look at the students who attended Arno School and their large numbers for two teachers:

**1st** James Beard, Sampson Beard, Bill Jordan, Leon Lillard, Ralph Moses, Homer Robinson, Billy Ryan, C.P. Ryan, Milton Ryan, Robert Sanford, James Sledge, Lowett Hood, Jr. Edwards, Leslie Hartley, Eunice Smythia, Esther Buford, Lucy Pearl Buford, Lucy Hartley, Bettie Johnson, Rachel Logan, Alma McCoy, Elizabeth McCoy, Hazel Poteete.

**2nd** Leslie Buford, Houston Harper, Murrey Poteete, Bobby Sledge, Elizabeth Beard, Robert Stem.

**3rd** Gipson Johnson, Walter Lillard, Delma McCoy, Elmer McCoy, Henry Poteete, Wesley Robinson, William Ryan.

**4th** grade: Alvin Buford, Walter Johnson, R.G. Lillard, Norma Maxwell, Elgan Moses, Lightall Poteete, James Stanford, Edward West, Alma Stem, Willie Blythe Poteete, Martha Sledge, Christine Smithson, Louise Morton, Rose Bell Harrell.

**5th** W.J. Buford, Milton Lillard, Roy Harpeth, John Sanford, Ada Davis, Imogene Harper, Ethel McCoy, Hazel Williams.

**6th** Chester Poteete, Raymond Smythia, Mary Jordan, Mildred McDaniel, Lillie Vaughan.

**7th** Jimmie Johnson, Thomas Ware, Ralph Smithson, Catherine Crunk, Ethel Morton, Margaret Stem.

**8th** Willie Davis, Martha Jordan, Frances Ryan

The students in the northeastern part of the 13th District (later the 23rd) attended Accident School, later called Sunnyside, a 1-8 grade facility. Accident was located on Arno Road between McDaniel Road and Eudailey-Covington Road. Teachers at Accident included: Alice Pollard, Kate Waddey and Willie Reams. Accident closed in 1921 and the students were moved to a new school at Rudderville. Also, on Arno Road, Rudderville School was located east of the Smithson-Akin Store on the present-day Page High School campus. Rudderville School opened in 1921, as a two-teacher school for grades 1-8, with Miss Mary White and Miss Allie Wilson as the teachers. In 1924, Mrs. A.K. Walters and Miss Winfrey were the teachers, followed by Mrs. A.M. Pollard and Miss Sue Lamb. Other teachers were who taught here: Cleo Grigsby, Mary Hatcher Sims, Mrs. Velma Windrow, Josephine Miller, Mrs. Eleanor Noland.

ACCIDENT SCHOOL ON ARNO ROAD BEFORE 1923

ACCIDENT SCHOOL 1906; 1. BOB T. EDMONDS, GENE GRAVES, ANICE SIMMONS, GEORGIA CRUNK, JODIE SLEDGE, MIKE SIMMONS, JIMMY KINNARD 2. ELMER GRAVES, NANCY HARPER, LULA SIMMONS, LENA STANFIELD, EVELYN SLEDGE, 3. EMOGENE TOMLIN, ROB GRAVES, ROBERT SIMMONS, WILL GRAVES, MARGARET KINNARD, PAULINE KINNARD, 4. MINNIE STANFIELD, MISS BESSIE PARKS

The school registers for Miss Mary Sims Hatcher (1-4) and Miss Cleo Grigsby (5-8) for Rudderville School (1935-36) will provide the enrollment of the students:

1st grade: Howard Hamm, Charles Mosley, Raymond Williams, Billie Ruth Edmunds, Annie Walker Ivery, Sarah Wade Ivery, Martha Ryan, Frances Waters, Willie Davis, Ethel Ladd.

2nd grade: Clyde Mosley, Stanley Tallant, Thomas Roy Ivery, Virginia Meek.

3rd grade: Carl McGee, Leon McGee, C.W. Ryan, Clifton Taylor, John Will Ivery, Willodene Churchwell, Rubye Mosley, Edith Jeanette, Ovie Tallant.

4th grade: Glenn Noland, Howard Stanfield, Lena Mai Ivery, Lillian Gentry.

5th grade: Robert Edmunds, Jesse Johnson, Norman Noland, Robert Taylor, Bonnell Tallent

6th grade: Eugene Harper, Roy Ryan, Tilman Waters, Pearl Hartley, Tilman Waters.

7th grade: Lonnie Harper, Nannie Hamm, Mary Ryan, Hazel Stanfield, Kitty Waddey, Irene Waters.

8th grade: John Hamm, Jr., Raymond Parrish, Donald Taylor, Edward Taylor, Thomas Ladd, Marianna Meek.

Rudderville School closed in 1950 with Miss Joyce Glenn as the teacher.

Mrs. Hayden Stephens, the Nellie Culberson pictured, supplied this photograph of the Rudderville Elementary School students, taken in 1932. They are, left to right, front row: Richard Frank Waddey, Donald Taylor, Robert Taylor, Buford Stevens, Dallas Ryan, Dickie Covington, Emma Jean Harper, Norman Noland, Emma Gray Coop, Doris Culberson; second row: Thomas Ladd, James Noland, unknown, John Ham, Jr.; Kitty Margaret Waddey, Mary Ryan, Marianna Meeks, Lonnie Harper, Roy Harper, Eugene Harper, unknown, Joe Deason; third row: George Ryan, J. B. Smithson, Earl Ryan, Perry Gee Johnson, Thomas Ham, Thomas Stevens, unknown, Elmer Ryan, Douglas Harper, Raymond Parrish, James Culberson, John Knox Coop, Edward Taylor; fourth row: Irene Waters, Nellie Culberson, unknown, Sara Ladd, Mrs. Alice Pollard, teacher, Johnnie Mai Waters, Carolyn Stevens, Miss Cleo Grigsby, teacher; Rebecca Noland, Elizabeth Smithson, Lillie Mai Deason, Dorothy Covington, Virginia Parrish.

**RUDDERVILLE SCHOOL 1932 WITH MRS. ALICE POLLARD AND MISS CLEO GRIGSBY**

This picture was given to me of a winning girls team of Rudderville School in 1934. (This was in the location of Fred J. Page School.) The members are left to right Mary Ryan Johnson, Kitty Margaret Waddey Johnson, Hazel Stanfield McGee, Nannie Mai Ham Shannon, Mary Amy Lillard Greer (deceased) Marianna Meek, Irene Waters Clark and Dorothy Covington, (deceased). The managers were Edward Taylor (deceased) and Richard Frank Waddey. Miss Cleo Grigsby was coach and teacher. (I didn't know this.)

# MISS KATIE LOU GATLIN, MASTER EDUCATOR AND BELOVED TEACHER

Public school teachers in Williamson County are a long-suffering lot, who dedicated their lives to the profession of teaching their students the basics of reading, writing, arithmetic, spelling, science, history, geography, music and art. While they were at it, they instilled the importance of honesty, sharing, cleanliness, good citizenship, and, if they were really good, a love of beauty. They labored under harsh conditions, such as over-crowded classes, classrooms heated by a smoky pot-belly stove burning wood or coal, if they were lucky, no running water and outside toilets. On the poorly equipped playground, they taught sportsmanship, rules of the game, and protected the smaller students from the bullies. All this for $55 a month, no insurance or sick days.

Miss Katie Lou Gatlin, born February 28, 1904 to John and Letitia Gatlin of the Grassland community, labored under all the above and excelled with a cheerful heart. Her exemplary teaching career spanned 41 years in Williamson County. The following is an outline of her teaching assignments, many were one-teacher schools in the far-reaches of the county.

1924-27- She taught at Ballow School in McClanahan Hollow, off Murray Lane.
1927-29- She taught at Cherokee School (1-8) in the 1st District near Fernvale.
1929-31- She taught at Forest Hill School on Carter's Creek Pike near Overbey's Store.
1932-34- She taught at Ash Hill School off Lewisburg Pike.

1934-35- She taught at Shoals Branch School on Lick Creek.
1935-36- She taught at Post Oak School on Pinewood Road.
1936-1938- She taught at Parman School on Spencer Creek Road, near Hillsboro Road.
1938-1939- She taught at Pleasant Hill School on Clovercroft Road.
1940-1961- She taught at Peytonsville School on Gosey Hill Road, a two-teacher school.
1961-1965- Bethesda School (1-12)

An amazing fact about Miss Katie Lou is that she never owned a car. She always rented a room from some family near the school. She walked to school in sunshine, rain, sleet and snow. Out of her meager salary, she paid her room and board. How she managed to obtain transportation to the rural schools and attend the monthly teacher's meeting to collect her check in Franklin is unimaginable. When she started teaching in 1924, white teachers were paid $55 a month and black teachers were paid $40 a month. When she retired in 1965, her salary was more in the range of $500 a month.

While teaching at Peytonsville and Bethesda, she boarded with Mrs. Lela Warren Spears, who lived next to the Peytonsville Methodist Church, a short walking distance from the school. When Peytonsville School closed in 1961, she rode the school bus along with the students to Bethesda. In 1980, she moved to West End Home for Ladies at 2811 West End in Nashville to spend her remaining days in retirement. On December 15, 2001, Miss Gatlin passed to the big classroom in sky. Her former students held a graveside memorial for their beloved teacher at Mt. Hope Cemetery, beside her parents. A resounding chorus replied, "Well done! Miss Katie Lou. You have earned your rest."

The Williamson County Archives has on microfilm many old school registers, which recorded attendance of the students, the names of the parents and their occupation, and some facts about the teachers. In 1935, while teaching at Post Oak School, Miss Katie Lou reported that she paid $15 a month board, taught grades 5,6,7 & 8th for a total of 47 students. She listed her places of education as Grassland Elementary School, Franklin High School, State Teachers College at Murfreesboro and Peabody College. She obtained her Bachelor of Science degree in 1954 from M.T.S.C.

The number of degrees a teacher collects doesn't measure their ability to instill the basics. Miss Katie Lou taught most of her career without a college degree. Yet, her lessons were more powerful than any Ph.D. could provide. Her ability to mold a student into problem solving and thinking before acting is still remembered by her students today. Discipline was not a problem for Miss Katie Lou. One of her former students remembered that her word was law, yet she was firm, loving but just.

## MISS KATIE LOU GATLIN REMEMBERED BY HER STUDENTS

**Jimmy Vaden Remembers:**

I am an old man who is a graduate of Vanderbilt University, the University of Tennessee College of Dentistry and the Orthodontic Residency Program at the University of Tennessee. During my lifetime, I have probably had between seven- and nine-hundred teachers. I cannot remember most of them. About ten of them steered my life and my career. These people were role models and their interests in me allowed me to succeed in whatever endeavor I chose. I seemed to have someone at every fork in the road who steered me down the right fork of life.

She instilled a sense of responsibility, determination and integrity to all the kids with whom she interacted. She expected us to do our best. She realized that some were more gifted than others, so she gave the more gifted ones more to do and tried to find things that the less gifted could do well so that they would feel very good about themselves. Every kid in her classrooms loved her, respected her and would stand on their heads and spit up quarters for her. Discipline was not a problem. I can remember the time when someone strayed and she would send them outside to get a switch and have everybody watch the exercise of her switching the bare legs of the "rascal" with a green switch. Nobody wanted to get switched after they saw this demonstration of discipline! Those who got switched always knew they had it coming! We started every school day with the pledge to the flag. There were four grades in one room. When each grade recited their lessons, the other grade was either reading a book or learning from the grade ahead of them that was reciting. It is interesting to remember that if you were in the first grade, you learned your multiplication tables quickly because the third grade had to recite them over and over. You listened and you learned.

Perhaps the thing I remember and love the most about Ms. Katie was all the reading she did for us. We were introduced to the classics. I can remember her reading the *Silver Chalice*, *Ben Hur*, James Fenimore Cooper's *Last of the Mohicans*, and I think my favorite was *Lady of the Lake* by Sir Walter Scott. She encouraged us to read by getting books from the library and doling them out to us on a weekly basis. If you were in the fourth grade, you read books while the other students were doing their lessons. Once she started teaching fifth, sixth, seventh and eighth grade, it was the same. You did a lot of reading. She also had us memorize many poems. I can still quote Rudyard Kipling's *If* and the last nine lines of William Cullen Bryant's *Thanatopsis*. All this is due to Katie Lou Gatlin. One more thing I should mention is that at our recess periods she was the umpire for the baseball games and the announcer for all the "Red Rover" games.

All in all, Katie Lou Gatlin was a remarkable lady who was much more than a teacher. She was a role model for us all and a surrogate mother for many of the kids who had poor family situations.

I am sure that she bought clothes for some of these children and continually brought treats to all of us. She did this out of the goodness of her heart. She was a remarkable woman. All of us who were lucky enough to have had her as a teacher gained an exponential amount of love and learning each and every day. Katie Lou Gatlin started us out on our life journey.

**Mike Vaden Remembers:**

Miss Katie Lou not only was able to teach 4 different grades in the same room, but students with such diverse backgrounds...from the disparately poor (with no shoes and worn clothes) to the average (no one was rich)... and all different levels of ability in each class. She took the time to help everyone.

She dealt with students having to be off for tobacco planting and cutting. Several students would come in with black-stained hands during walnut harvesting time and a few students would come in smelly after they had worked with trap lines. Many would come in smelling of wood-burning smoke during the winter and others smelling of cow milking that morning.

At recess, Miss Katie Lou was there not only supervising, but was an umpire and referee for baseball and basketball games. During the afternoons, there was always a milk break (government funded) where students could buy milk for 1-2 cents. Here again, Miss Katie Lou would pay for milk for those who could not afford it.

Most importantly, in addition to teaching the basics to the four different grades, Miss Katie Lou brought literature to her students. She read novels in class....*The Thread That Runs So True* by Jesse Stewart, *The Last of the Mohicans* by James F. Cooper, even parts of *Macbeth*, along with classic poetry. Her students were totally enthralled and loved listening to these adventures as she read with such expression.

Imagine young rural elementary students being exposed to such advanced high school literature! She was an amazing teacher!

Mike Vaden remembers more, with humor:
she inspired us, made us want to achieve and showed us we could. She inspired young minds. the world in those days was pretty small. some kids had no tv. Peytonsville was moonshine, tobacco and small farms with milk cows and hogs. families got clothes and new shoes when the tobacco crop was sold in December. we knew nothing of the world. Miss Katie opened horizons and gave us some hope. my brother, Jim, still recites poems she opened his eyes to. my brother, Paul, named his daughter Katie because of his admiration for Miss Katie Lou.

I often reflect on those days and how rural we were and how much this world has changed. young folks today cannot comprehend life and hard work in those days. and we didn't know it was hard or that we had nothing-because no one else did either. it was the norm. but she gave us a window to the world and taught us so much more than the 3 r's. and–yes–Miss Katie taught me how to capitalize. I'm just a lazy typist!

**Nancy York Remembers:**

Miss Katie was brilliant, talented, gifted and used her talents and gifts to the fullest. When she came to Peytonsville the existing schoolhouse was set to be torn down. I do not remember that schoolhouse except for a photo she took of our oldest brother and two friends at the front steps, the whole building is not in the picture. In 1950 the county had built and opened a new school at Peytonsville and also Flat Creek. Our new school had two classrooms, two teachers, a kitchen and cafeteria and two restrooms - indoors. In February 1951, there was a deep snow, the old timers called it a "blizzard". Miss Katie had a small camera, and that camera was used for the rest of her life capturing all of her student's lives at Peytonsville. The first picture she captured was the new schoolhouse in that deep snow and that was her Christmas card to all the families that year. Of course, everything was in black and white.

In one classroom was first through third grade. In the other was fourth through eighth. Each class had three to four students only. After the pledge to the flag, she would announce "students it's time to take up books", and she spent the allotted time with each class and subjects. When she finished with one, they were to pick up their next subject and study while she spent the allotted time with the other classes and subjects and so on. And of course, we were supposed to be quiet and study. She taught English, History, Science, Geography, Spelling, History was a favorite. Art and Music were not required subjects for her to teach but she introduced us to these. Remember I said she was gifted and talented. One day she began a painting and we all asked her what it was, she said " let me finish and I will tell you about it " I can't remember how long it took to finish but she announced " students, I have finished the painting ". She held it up to us and told us it was her homeplace, where she was born. She had made something so plain, beautiful. It was a wood structure, maybe three rooms, a small loft, the front porch steps were at the side and not in the middle. In the yard she painted in wildflowers, all around the house, chickens, a few outbuildings and a creek flowing in front. Now Music. It was, I'm sure for her, a blessing that it was not required. Miss Katie could not carry a tune, but Miss Katie appreciated music - all kinds. She had a record player and she brought it to school.

After sending the first page Randy York informed me that it was not a record player. It was a Victrola. She brought this, along with records so that we would have music, regardless whether it was a subject to be taught. One day she announced that she wanted us to know names of composers: John Phillip Sousa, she announced, and I can hear those farm boys at Peytonsville: "who was that Miss Katie; what did you say Miss

Katie; Miss Katie, you will have to write that one down on the board ". Then she told us he composed our marches, and when we heard Hail to the Chief, we would know the composer. Of course, we had radios at home and had heard The Star Spangled Banner, our National Anthem, she wanted us to know it was Francis Scott Key that composed the words while viewing the battle in Baltimore Harbor. She even let us move our desks to the center of the room and said we were to march around the room while the marches played on that victrola.

History was her favorite, but Tennessee History was at the top as well. Yes, we had a textbook of Tennessee History and we had to draw the state and put the counties in. No one, that I remember, was perfect, but we did it.

She planned field trips for us and, yes, she was forever the teacher with field trips.The Hermitage; The State Capitol; War Memorial Building; The Parthenon; Belle Meade Mansion.

How she did it, I don't know, but she arranged for us to have our sack lunch picnic on the front grounds of Belle Meade. And, of course Centennial Park. Tommy Glenn was always booked to take us on all our trips. He was our bus driver as well. There were other field trips to other schools in the county and she was not going to let her students be left out of anything. An art exhibit, Spelling Bee, where ribbons would be given. One year it was music. Again, Miss Katie would not let her students be left out; but what would she do? She formed a girls' chorus; she did not sing or direct; on the other hand, the girls did not either. We knew our Sunday School songs and church hymns but did not read music, we listened to the radio. So, she brought a record to school thinking we could learn by ear: it was Marty Robbins, A White Sport Coat with a Pink Carnation. She wanted us to be dressed alike and went to the fabric store to make sure there was one whole bolt of navy blue and one white bolt of material to make skirts and blouses for each one. Miss Katie was a seamstress, (another of her talents/gifts) with a sewing machine and she helped our mothers with the sewing.

Miss Katie's penmanship was perfect and beautiful. it's called calligraphy today. Another of her gifts/talents. Books, oh she loved reading, it broadens your mind she would tell us.  On some Saturdays Miss Lela would drive her to town to the material center, not sure of the location, but that is where she would get books and supplies for us.  She would, but not every day, take time in afternoon before dismissing us for the school bus, to read to us.  Imagine, especially the boys, so engrossed as she read *Mutiny on the Bounty* and Jesse Stuart's *The Thread That Runs So True*.  We did not go to sleep. At my high school graduation rehearsal, we were told that our guest speaker would be Jesse Stuart, the author. I called Miss Katie to tell her and I sensed in her voice how pleased she was that I remembered her reading this to us.

She had one sister that lived in Nashville.  A nephew, Jackie, loved his Aunt Kate and would occasionally surprise her with a visit to the school.  Some summers she did visit with her sister. On one occasion they were walking Church Street in downtown Nashville.  Back then there were three movie theaters on Church Street and passing by one, probably the Tennessee, she noticed what was showing and stopped.  Her sister, stunned, "why Katie Lou Gatlin surely you are not going in to see that". Yes, sister, she said, I want to see what my girls are talking about.  It was *Love Me Tender* with Elvis Presley.  When school opened at the end of that summer, she told us about it. We were stunned also but, gosh, she was thinking of us on summer break. We asked her what she thought of the move -" I enjoyed it", she said.

In May 1958, I was in eighth grade with two other girls ending our time at Peytonsville School. She took us to Gatlinburg by Greyhound bus of course since she did not drive. I am not sure who took us to Nashville to the bus station, could

have been my daddy, I can't remember.  We stayed at Marshall's Creek Rest Court. It was very nice with a front porch with chairs.  We did not travel back then so this was a treat and entirely new to us. After unpacking and getting settled, she said, " girls I have hired a taxi and a driver/guide for tomorrow to take us over the Smoky Mountains and into Cherokee with stops on the way." Well, when she said taxi the picture of a taxi in downtown Franklin popped in my head.  It was dispatched from the cab stand, about where Baskin Robbins is, and it was always dusty, scratched and dented and the driver's left arm was always hanging down outside the door, bent at the elbow with a cigarette.   Next morning, she was already outside and called into the motel for us " girls, our taxi is here". We are three 13-year-old girls, we get to the top step, lo and behold, there is a 1955 Ford convertible, top down, and standing beside it is the best-looking young man we had ever seen.  He was a gentleman. He held the door for all four of us, opened the trunk and handed each one of us a blanket. He said we would need it before we got to the top of the mountain.

On our trip to Gatlinburg Miss Katie was still the forever teacher as we traveled over the mountain and into Cherokee where we met the chief and braves. He too was a gentleman, talked to us and posed for pictures with us.  That night she took us to an outdoor drama, Unto These Hills, the story of the Oconaluftee Indian Tribe.  I don't know if she paid for all of this or not.

Miss Katie planned our meals. We ate healthy and nutritiously.   Robert Orr and Company delivered the food and J. W. Little's Dairy delivered the milk.   We all had duties from stacking the shelves with the food, refrigerating the milk, cleaning, etc.  Aunt Nannie B Smithson was our cook.   She and Mr. John and their children, Mary and Clarence, lived on the Peytonsville-Trinity Road and she walked to school every day.   She had a path on the Mr Mike Simmons property that took her to the woods and that path came out at the school at the boys' baseball field.  She wore white every day.  Aunt Nannie B. was the best - she never burned anything, never over cooked or under cooked, her cornbread, in that special pan, was perfect and I'm pretty sure each child received the same size square.  Yes, we were children, and some things were not pleasing to eat but Miss Katie wanted us to at least taste.  Every day when we returned our tray of dishes, we told her - " I enjoyed my dinner Aunt Nannie B. " And she always thanked us. Let me explain back then, down in the country, the noon meal was dinner, not lunch. Some days before she left to go home, she would tap on the classroom door and leave us a treat - like peanut butter balls. We all loved Aunt Nannie B. deeply and she loved us.

Did we fuss, argue, scuffle, fight, yes.  The punishment would fit the crime.  I still have an indentation in my second finger for having to write off sometimes 200 times and the sentences would always start with those three words "I should not".

Women have come a long way since the 50's but I believe we could refer to Miss Katie with the modern slogan "I AM WOMAN, HEAR ME ROAR, and it would fit her to a tee. She never backed away from anything when it came to defending and providing for her students.

How blessed we all are when we can have these memories to share.

**Bill Hurt Remembers:**

Peytonsville was my home and where I grew up. That beautiful rural countryside was home also to my first learning and Peytonsville School was housed in two rooms. Grades 1-4 in one room and grades 5-8 in the other. This was connected by a small cafeteria and dining room that we all used. It also was where plays, and holiday performances took place.

Miss Katie Lou Gatlin was both teacher and principal. She had been a teacher there for decades before me.  She taught my mother. No guy wants to constantly be compared to his mother's high achievement. I didn't know it at first, but she was to become my mentor and my inspiration to be a teacher and eventually a principal as well.

Times were much simpler then. But innovation was the order of Miss Katie's day every day. She taught a multi-age classroom before it was an innovative approach. Everything she taught was about life. Very little was just memorizing. In that classroom we were encouraged to listen to and respond on each other's class. She loved history and geography. She told us we all needed a visual picture of the world in our heads because she knew that one day we may travel across the globe. When we finished our work, she had selected cities for us to find on the old globe in the corner of the classroom. I remember trying for days to find the city of Vladivostok in Russia.

Miss Katie was always interested in you and your whole life. She was fair but firm. She was the most patient person to me. I know I was so insecure and asked constantly "Is this right? Is this ok?" She never criticized but always encouraged. We had many projects to complete back then, shoebox dioramas, leaf collections, and nutrition notebooks.

Nutrition was very important to her. She was always asking us if we brushed our teeth and she sometimes would check you herself. We back then had to clean our plates. You must eat everything. That wasn't a good thing, but the idea was to eat nutritious foods that you might not get at home.

Our cafeteria had an excellent cook. She was a sweet African American lady called Aunt Nannie Bea. She kept Miss Katie informed if you didn't clean your plate.  One of my most traumatic moments involved this clean plate policy. I had seen others that couldn't get a specific food down and threw up get another plate. My nemesis was broccoli! Steamed broccoli! To this day it gags me. I knew that the next day we were having it on the menu. I took a small plastic bag to school and scraped that broccoli into it and stuffed it into my pocket. By afternoon it had begun to ooze out into my pants. I told Miss Katie I had to go to the bathroom. She looked down at that wet spot and excused me. Oh my, I never did that again.

Another part of the curriculum that Miss Katie emphasized was art. She wanted us to appreciate that it was everywhere in our lives and we needed to acknowledge that all the time.

At the holidays we would make our own Christmas ornaments to go on the cedar trees most of us had. These ornaments were very unique. She provided the paint and glitter and we brought to the classroom, dried okra pods from the garden, sweet gum balls from the trees, and long bean pods. All these were given new life. Red, green and a rainbow of creative ornaments emerged. We were so proud and claimed their beauty to our parents when we put them on our Christmas tree. She was an artist in her own right. She lived in the little village across the street from Bruce's Country store. She had an apartment with a widower, Mrs. Lela Spears. Now, Mrs. Lela was the antithesis of Miss Katie. She owned and ran a farm with many cows and chickens. You would see her riding an old Farmall tractor any day.

But Miss Katie was ever the "lady". She carried herself with a regal presence. Her posture was perfect, and I never saw her wear anything but a bright colored flowing dress. She had her cats that were her passion when not at school. So many cats! They were everywhere. She never turned away a stray.

In her spare time, she painted. I would say her style was much like that of Grandma Moses. It was very primitive and colorful. The subjects were always scenes in nature.

She gave me one of her paintings framed back in 1971. I have cherished it to this day. It is supposedly Mount Olympia in Washington state.

Eventually the school closed, and she moved to Bethesda School to teach Art and Social Studies. I again had the fortune of being a student in those seventh-grade classes.

She instilled in me a love of learning. School was a happy place especially to those of us who were poor living in rural Williamson County. She took us to places in our imagination that we would never have gone. She made everyone feel special and I knew I wanted to be a teacher like Miss Katie.

I regret I never visited her again before her death. But she will always live in my heart because she placed the "seeds" of learning in me!

**Nelson Dodd Remembers:**

I was asked by a lifelong friend, Paul Pratt, to write a story about Miss Katie Lou Gatlin. Miss Katie was a teacher at Peytonsville Grammar School for many years. I say grammar school, because that's what they were called back in the day. There was no mention of elementary schools. Miss Katie (a maiden) was a very strict teacher, who loved her extended family (her students). I had her in grades 1 though 5. The year I was to move to the 6th grade, I was ecstatic, because I was not going to have Miss Katie as a teacher anymore. Well, as luck would have it, Miss Katie took the principals position. She made the decision to teach grades 6 through 8. I was getting my Karma, and did not know it at the time. Miss Katie was as strict in the lunchroom as she was in the classroom. You were required to clean your plate or stay until you did. One day, we had boiled okra. Now anybody who knows me at all, knows I don't even want to be at the table where boiled okra is. Well, I have gotten over that, but still will not let okra touch my lips, boiled, fried, or any other way.

Aunt Nannie Bee Smithson was our cook. She knew each student as well as Miss Katie did. She put as small amount of okra on my plate as she could, without Miss Katie sending me back for more. God bless Aunt Nannie Bee. She was the sweetest lady, and one of the very best cooks ever. When we finished our meal that day, I covered my okra with my dessert bowl. Aunt Nannie Bee saw it and just smiled. I was so relived that she did not tell on me. Well, as you can imagine, Miss Katie spotted the bowl, and turned it over to find my okra. She asked who left okra on their plate, and nobody answered, because nobody knew, except Jimmy Warf, and he wasn't about to tell on his best friend. So Miss Katie went down the line, asking everyone whose it was. When she got to me and asked me, I thought for a millisecond about telling a lie, but my Mother's face appeared in my mind, and I knew to tell the truth. I told her it was mine and I was not going to eat the okra, she told me I would sit in the lunchroom until I ate it. Well, about 3 P.M., Miss Katie made her third or fourth trip to see how much okra I had eaten. I think by now everyone knows the answer, but for those who don't, the answer is not one single bite, nada, none, not gonna. The bus ran, and I was still in the lunchroom. She told me to get my books, and go catch the bus at Bruces store. Instead I just cut through the thicket to Mr and Mrs Simmons place, and scooted right on home. Mother asked me why I walked home alone, and I related the days events to her. That was the only time in my eight years as a student of Miss Katie's that my mother sent a note to school. She told Miss Katie to not try to make me eat anything I did not like, as I was not forced to eat things I did not like at home. Needless to say, the rest of my years at Peytonsville Grammar School, I was never served okra, except in a very small amount. I know now that Miss Katie knew I was not eating it, and could see the dessert bowl turned over the okra. She never mentioned it again and neither did I. By the way, they closed Peytonsville Grammar School in 1961. Guess who my History teacher was in my Senior year. Yep, you're right, the one and only Miss Katie Lou Gatlin. I studied under her tutelage for 8 years, in grammar school, and my Senior year at Bethesda High School. It did not take me very long to understand and know that I was a very blessed youngster to have Miss Katie for a teacher. She was beyond a doubt, the best teacher I ever had, THE VERY BEST.

Thank you to Miss Katie who is now holding classes in Heaven, Thank you Paul for asking me to write this true story. It has brought back so many memories, and has been an honor for me to do this.

Thanks and Love to all,
Nelson Dodd

## ENROLLMENT AT PEYTONSVILLE SCHOOL, TAKEN FROM MISS KATIE LOU GATLIN'S STUDENT REGISTERS

**1947-48-Miss Katie Lou Gatlin's classes: (Yes, count them 54 students in 4 grades)**
1st grade Boys: Neil Beard, Harry Bennett, Elijah Garner, James Moses Bruce, Glendon Wayne King, Henry C. Roberson, Willie Roberson, Bennie T. Smithson, James W. Ivey, Wendel Lee Howell, Douglas A. Pratt, William E. Guthrie, Girls: Maggie Estelle Beard, Nancy L. Crawford, Marion Dodd, Nancy L. McGee, Margaret Ann Redman, Zelma L. Ivey.
2nd grade Boys: Dan German Beard, Sammie Lee Crawford, Girls: Nancy E. Beard, Janice E. Beech, Elizabeth Glass, Bessie Jo Ivey, Joyce Rawls, Lillie J. Tomlin, Alta Pearl Veach
3rd grade Boys: Dan Bennett, Johnny F. Bennett, Gary Bruce, Earl Dodd, Bob Garner, Alton Garner, James Hinson, William Jackson, Jimmie Maxwell, John P. McGee, Pete Tomlin, Larry Beech, Filmore Bruce, Girls: Yvonne Bruce, Betty lee Garner, Belvin Jackson, Betty Jean Poteete, Betty J. Ivey
4th grade Boys: Thomas Bennett, Joe Mangrum, Wilson Vaden, William Warf, Girls: Catherine Bruce, Roger Glenn, Fanny Jean McGee, Jean Tomlin, Bobby June Howell

**1950-51-Miss Katie Lou Gatlin's classes:**
1st grade Boys: Joseph Beard, Henry Roberson, Roy Roberson, Lloyd C. Ivey, Girls: Patsy Skinner, Nancy York, Georgia McGee
2nd grade Boys: James King, Milton Hinson, Paul Pratt, James Robertson, Ralph Ivey, Girls: Linda Dodd, Billie Tomlin, Janet King
3rd grade Boys: John Beard, Carl Jackson, Gary York, Dan Ivey, Girls: Estell Beard, Margie Warf
4th grade Boys: Glendon King, Joe Roberson, Girls: Marion Dodd, Ethel Roberson, Evelyn Roberson, Nancy McGee, Rebecca Ivey

**1951-52-Miss Katie Lou Gatlin's classes:**
1st grade Boys: Nelson Dodd, Thomas King, Buford Roberson, James Vaden, Albert Johnson, Girls: Betty Goodman, Carol Maxwell, Barbara Roberson
2nd grade Boys: Roy Roberson, Henry Roberson Girl: Nancy York
3rd grade Boys: Donald Glenn, Milton Hinson, James King, Paul Pratt, James Roberson, Girls: Linda Dodd, Janet King, Eva Simmons, Billie Tomlin
4th grade Boys: Carl Jackson, Gary York, Douglas Harper, Welvon Ivey, Girls: Nellie Bruce, Margie Warf, Marie Harper

**1953-52-Miss Katie Lou Gatlin's classes:**
1st grade Boy: Howard Harper, Girls: Brenda Bruce, Shirley Mai Hosford, Shirley Ann Tate, Carol Sue Tate
2nd grade Boys: Nelson Dodd, Albert Johnson, Thomas King, Buford Roberson, James Warf, Jerry Wayne Tate, Girls: Lejune Givens, Betty Goodman, Carol Maxwell, Barbara Roberson
3rd grade Boys: Henry Roberson, Roy Roberson Girls: Nancy York
4th grade Boys: Guy Ferrell, Milton Hinson, Donald Glenn, James King, Paul Pratt, James Roberson, Bobby Plunkett, Girls: Nellie Bruce, Linda Dodd, Marie Harper, Janet King, Carolyn Simmons, Billie Tomlin

**1954-55-Miss Katie Lou Gatlin's classes:**

1st grade Boys: Harry Bruce, Michael Bruce, Tom Crawford, Tony Pratt, Blythe Roberson, jerry Skinner, Paul Vaden, Dan Veach, Joseph York, Girls: Jane McGee, Ann Veach, Margaret Williamson
2nd grade Boys: Helton Bruce, Ronnie Bruce, David Tomlin, Randy York, Girl: Bertha Holt
3rd grade Boys: Michael Vaden, Robert Bennett Girls: Brenda Bruce, Sue McGee, Barbara Roberson
4th grade Boys: Nelson Dodd, Albert Johnson, James Vaden, James Warf

**1955-56-Miss Katie Lou Gatlin's classes:**
5th grade Boys: Nelson Dodd, James Vaden, James Warf, Girls: Minnie Harpeth, Betty Goodman, Carol Maxwell
6th grade Boys: Jesse Crawford, Henry Roberson, Roy Roberson, Girls: Patsy Skinner, Nancy York
7th grade Boys: Donald Glenn, Milton Hinson, Paul Pratt, Girls: Nellie Bruce, Linda Dodd, Georgia McGee, Carolyn Simmons, Billie Tomlin
8th grade Boy: Gary York, Girls: Linda Maupin, Margie Warf

**1956-57-Miss Katie Lou Gatlin classes:**
5th grade Boy: Mike Vaden, Girls: Brenda Bruce, Mary Crawford, Barbara Roberson
6th grade Boys: Jesse Crawford, Nelson Dodd, Jimmy Vaden, James Warf, Girls: Betty Goodman, Carol Maxwell
7th grade Girls: Patsy Skinner, Nancy York
8th grade Boys: Don Glenn, Paul Pratt, Girls: Carol Simmons, Billie Tomlin

**1959-60-Miss Katie Lou Gatlin's class:**
5th grade Boys: Harry Bruce, Helton Bruce, Ronnie Bruce, Thomas Crawford, William Hurt, William Crawford, Danny Brigman, Girl: Josephine Tomlin
6th grade Boys: Tony Pratt, Joe York, Girls: Brenda Rader, Margaret Williams
7th grade Boys: Ronnie Maupin, David Tomlin, Randy York, Girls, Mary Crawford

**1960-61-Miss Katie Lou Gatlin's classes-Her last classes at Peytonsville**

5th grade Boys: Richard Bruce, Tandy Bruce, Horace Coleman, Donald Watkins, Girls: Nancy Anderson, Helon Pratt

6th grade Boys: Helton Bruce, Ronald Bruce, Harry Bruce, William Crawford, Thomas Crawford, Claude Coleman, William Hurt, Don Veach, Girls: Patrice Burge, Josephine Tomlin

7th grade Boys: Ton Pratt, Joe York, Girls: Bobbie Jean Burge, Brenda Rader, Margaret William, Ann Veach

8th grade Boys: Ronnie Maupin, David Tomlin, Randy York, Girls: Mary Crawford, Carolyn Coleman, Barbara Jean Morris

PEYTONSVILLE SCHOOL, TEACHER MISS KATIE LOU GATLIN, 1ST ROW: JERRY SKINNER, PAUL VADEN, UNIDENTIFIED, MICHAEL BRUCE, UNIDENTIFIED, 2ND ROW: JANE MCGEE, TONY PRATT, J.B. ROBINSON, UNIDENTIFIED, MARGARET ANN WILLIAMS, UNIDENTIFIED, ANN VEACH

MISS KATIE'S DRAMA CLUB, JIMMY VADEN, JANE MCGEE, MARY WARF, GARY YORK, ALBERT JOHNSON

MISS KATIE'S LAST 8TH GRADE CLASS AT PEYTONSVILLE SCHOOL, MAY 1961. CAROLYN COLEMAN, BARBARA JEAN MORRIS, MARY CRAWFORD, DAVID TOMLIN, RANDY YORK, RONNIE MAUPIN

43

GARY YORK, HARRY BENNETT, CARL JACKSON

MISS GATLIN'S STUDENTS ON THE LAST DAY OF SCHOOL IN THE OLD SCHOOL IN 1950

PEYTONSVILLE SCHOOL'S BALL FIELD AND OUTSIDE BASKETBALL GOAL

MISS KATIE'S BOYS: HELTON BRUCE, RONNIE MAUPIN, UNKNOWN, UNKNOWN, BLYTHE ROBERSON, DAVID TOMLIN, RANDY YORK

MISS KATIE'S BOYS IN 1950, HARRY BENNETT, CARL JACKSON, GARY YORK

MISS KATIE'S GIRLS

MISS KATIE'S BOYS

# THE HISTORY OF PEYTONSVILLE HOME DEMONSTRATION CLUB

**By: Addie Louise (Meek) Pratt**

The Peytonsville Home Demonstration Club was first suggested and discussed by two ladies of the community one morning as they were going to the school building to plant flowers on the school grounds and later in the spring of 1930 the Peytonsville Home Demonstration was organized by Miss Virginia Carson, H.D. County Agent.

At which time, Mrs. Dee Stanfield was elected president, Mrs. O.C. Boyd, vice president, Mrs. Pink Johnson, secretary. They had no need for a treasurer at that time but, not for long, as the club begin to grow, they soon had to have a treasurer.

The Club began with the following members: Mrs. Reece Tomlin, Mrs. Nell Warren, Mrs. Sam McGee, Miss Nell Meek, Mrs. Wave Glenn, Mrs. Ewell Ladd, Miss Polly Stanfield, Mrs. John McGee, Mrs. Blythe Johnson, Mrs. Ella Smithson, Mrs. Albert Tomlin, Mrs. Bennie

Tomlin, Mrs. Pink Johnson, Mrs. Thomas Smithson, Mrs. Douglas York, Mrs. Dave Tomlin, Mrs. John Pratt, Mrs. Roy Mosley, Mrs. Sam Mosley, Mrs. Mary Ann Deason, Mrs. Mary Deason, Miss Sadye Johnson and Mrs. George Campbell.

The first year the Club met in a vacant room of the school building. They learned to can pineapple, other fruits and vegetables. All enjoyed learning handicrafts i.e., making fire screens, painting jars and jugs, weaving baskets, making flowers, braiding and crocheting rugs, framing pictures, etc. Every member had to have something to carry home that was made at the club that day.

Our second president was Mrs. O.C. Boyd with Mrs. Pink Johnson, secretary, and Miss Nell Meek was elected treasurer. The second year was somewhat like the first year except the members liked it so well they carried baskets of food and spent the day and, later in the year, they decided to meet in the homes, which I think everyone enjoys on through the years.

The third president was Mrs. Pink Johnson, and, on through the years with Miss Carson, the following have served as president: Mrs. Heton Pate, Mrs. Thomas Smithson, Mrs. Douglas York, Mrs. John Pratt, Mrs. Roy Meek and Mrs. James Boyd.

Down through the years the Club has tried to help many worthy causes such as Red Cross, Cripple Children, Library Fund, Cancer Fund and others. We were always ready to help when someone lost a home. We gave donations to the library and a book in honor one of our soldiers. We painted road signs for the different roads of the community. We donated dishes to the Club Room in the basement of the courthouse. We have entered many things in the county and state fairs, such as rugs, artwork, baskets, canned fruit and other items in which we received prizes and ribbons.

Through the years the Club has had the pleasure of adding many new members, both young and old. In 1942 Miss Virginia Carson was married to Mr. Robert Jefferson, a farmer in the 10th district. We were all hurt over losing her but was glad for her to have a home in the county.

In a short time, Miss Jeanne Gilmore took Miss Carson's place and the Club rolled on two and a half years and Miss Gilmore was married to Mr. John Webb, then Miss Sara Wood came to us in 1944, but she only stayed a year, and she too married. In 1946, Miss Lois Crowley came to us and brought new life to the Peytonsville Club. With history repeating itself, Mrs. O.C. Boyd was elected president, Mrs. Ben Smithson, secretary, Mrs. George Bruce, vice president, and Mrs. James Boyd, treasurer.

In 1948, the Peytonsville Club had the honor of first prize on their exhibit at the Williamson County fair, over the other thirty clubs of the county. Following Mrs. Boyd, we have had the following presidents: Mrs. Bill Gatlin, Mrs. Leonard Henry, Mrs. King Henry, Mrs. Gene Smithson and Mrs. Wesley York.

We all enjoy working with Miss Crowley, who has been with us for eleven years.

All history has a sad part and during the many years the Club has been together, they have lost some of their members. At this time, I will bring to our memory the ones who have gone to rest: Mrs. Dee Stanfield, Mrs. George Campbell, Mrs. Mell Warren, Mrs. Lou Gee, Mrs. Ana Stanfield, Mrs. Claude York, Mrs. Fannie Thompson, Mrs. Ella Smithson, Mrs. Wave Glenn, Mrs. Ewell Ladd, Mrs. John McGee, Mrs. Dave Tomlin, Mrs. Roy Mosley, Mrs. Mary Ann Deason, and Mrs. O.C. Boyd.

And in memory of these, we must keep the Club rolling on. We now have the following members: Mrs. Wesley York, Mrs. Dennis Skinner, Mrs. A.T. Pate, Mrs. Leonard Henry, Mrs. Thomas Smithson, Mrs. Gene Smithson, Mrs. W.A.

Jordan, Mrs. Walter Jordan, Mrs. John Pratt, Jr., Mrs. Wave Williams, Mrs. William Moss, Mrs. Sam Johnson, Mrs. John Pratt, Sr., and Mrs. Ben Smithson.

LADIES OF THE PEYTONSVILLE HOME DEMONSTRATION CLUB: 1. UNKNOWN, 2. SAMMIE LOU JOHNSON, 3. GLADYS BEARD BRUCE, 4. BLANCHE MOSS, 5. ELIZABETH PATE MCGEE, 6. SADIE PRATT YORK, 7. EVELYN VADEN, 8. WILLIE MAE BUCHANAN, 9. UNKNOWN, 10. DIXIE MEEK PATE, 11. UNKNOWN 12. EMMA HENRY, 13. ALICE HUME JORDAN, 14. LOUISE MEEK PRATT, 15. JOSEPHINE JAY WALTON, 16. ELAINE MOSS, 17. FRANCES PRATT HENRY, 18. ALLENE HENRY, 19. SARAH HENRY, 20. CATHERINE MAXWELL PRATT, 21. UNKNOWN, 22. NELLIE YORK, 23. JANE MCGEE, 24. MARGARET WILLIAMS, 25. BIRDIE MAI SKINNER WILLIAMS

MISS VIRGINIA CARSON

MISS LOIS CROWLEY

47

# LOCAL CEMETERIES

The information on these cemeteries was obtained from *Directory of Williamson County, Tennessee Burials Volumes 1, 2 and 3*, published in 1973, 1975, and 1991 by the Williamson County Historical Society.

## Anderson-Maupin Cemetery

Location: 11th or 13th District on the Harpeth-Peytonsville Road.

| | |
|---|---|
| Anderson, J.W. | B. Aug 27, 1854 |
| | D. Apr 9, 1930 |
| ,John W. | B. 1939 |
| | D. 1965 |
| ,Luther Thomas | B. Mar 10, 1910 |
| | D. Jan 15, 1977 |
| Harper, Bessie L. | B. Jun 22, 1916 |
| | D. |
| ,Daniel R. | B. 1956 |
| | D. 1957 |
| ,Fred Bly | B. 1938 |
| | D. 1938 |
| Poteete, Adora Maupin | B. Feb 29, 1908 |
| | D. Oct 10, 1980 |

## Andrews-Hatcher-Pollard Cemetery

Location: 13th District on Meeks Road

| | |
|---|---|
| Allen, Mrs. Jane C. | B. Nov 29, 1815 |
| | D. Aug 3, 1856 |
| Andrews, Alphonso | B. Nov 9, 1818 |
| | D. Jan 25, 1863 |
| ,James (70-years) | B. 1780 |
| | D. Jun 12, 1850 |
| ,Jane | B. May 5, 1785 |
| | D. Sep 11, 1811 |
| ,Lutie | B. Apr 1, 1858 |
| | D. Jun 7, 1858 |
| ,Mary P. | B. Apr 14, 1812 |
| | D. Jul 25, 1844 |
| ,Samuel | B. Feb 28, 1827 |
| | D. Mar 27, 1860 |
| ,Thomas | B. Aug 8, 1824 |
| | D. Jan 20, 1851 |
| ,William | B. Sep 14, 1807 |
| | D. Feb 28, 1860 |

| | |
|---|---|
| Andrews, William M. | B. Feb 25, 1861 |
| | D. Jan, 1881 |
| Hatcher, George W. | B. May 1, 1858 |
| | D. Oct 11, 1865 |
| ,Mary J. | B. Jan 20, 1832 |
| | D. Aug 3, 1870 |
| ,Mortimer | B. Mar 31, 1875 |
| | D. Sep 24, 1875 |
| ,Mamie | B. Nov 27, 1862 |
| | D. Nov 17, 1865 |
| Matthews, Sallie Andrews | B. May 15, 1820 |
| | D. Mar 21, 1879 |
| Pollard, Robert L. | B. Oct 13, 1838 |
| | D. Oct 19, 1863 |
| Pollard, W.R.A. | B. Nov 18, 1861 |
| | D. July 13, 1862 |

## Barnett Cemetery (destroyed)

Location: 10th District on Peytonsville Road near the Old Barnett School site.

| | |
|---|---|
| Barnett, Arixney | B. Jul 22, 1819 |
| | D. Dec 6, 1856 |
| ,James P. | B. Jan 18, 1783 |
| | D. Jan 10, 1827 |
| ,Josephus | B. Apr 11, 1811 |
| | D. Apr 8, 1878 |
| ,Margaret Gibson | B. Apr 3, 1789 |
| | D. Jan 25, 1873 |
| ,Mary | B. Mar 13, 1742 |
| | D. Mar 17, 1827 |
| ,Mohulda Ann Short | B. Mar 22, 1819 |
| | D. Dec 22, 1887 |

## Beal Cemetery (Black)

Location: 13th District, Peytonsville-Trinity Road

| | |
|---|---|
| Beal, Cornelia | B. |
| | D. 1928 |
| ,Elizabeth | B. 1871 |
| | D. May 26, 1961 |
| ,Hattie | B. |
| | D. |
| ,Henry | B. |
| | D. |
| ,Janie | B. |
| | D. |
| ,John | B. 1883 |
| | D. Sep 29, 1958 |

| Beal, Lena | B. 1893 |
| | D. Feb 27, 1953 |
| ,Minnie | B. |
| | D. |
| ,Susie | B. 1873 |
| | D. Nov 4, 1938 |
| ,Tilton | B. 1881 |
| | D. Aug 8, 1853 |
| Gentry, Hattie Pearl | B. 1905 |
| | D. Mar 31, 1960 |
| Starnes, Dee | B. 1874 |
| | D. Jan 2, 1959 |

## Beard Cemetery

Location: 13th District at the end of Buchanan Road on a hill to the southwest.

| Beard, Mary Lucinda Young | B. |
| | D. Dec 12, 1932 |
| ,George Fred | B. Dec 15, 1900 |
| | D. Dec 1, 1935 |
| ,Louis Jackson | B. |
| | D. |
| ,Jack | B. Dec 17, 1859 |
| | D. Jan 24, 1943 |
| Shedd, Ester M. | B. May 2, 1913 |
| | D. Dec 10, 1943 |

## Beech-Simmons Cemetery

Location: 13th District, Peytonsville-Trinity Road, Mrs. Hattie Bruce Farm.

| Beech, Debra Jean | B. |
| | D. Feb 27, 1956 |
| Beech, Michel | B. 1869 |
| | D. 1944 |
| Bruce, Garrett W. | B. 1925 |
| | D. 1963 |
| ,James Moses | B. Jan 29, 1892 |
| | D. May 10, 1963 |
| ,Roy G. | B. 1918 |
| | D. 1966 |
| Robinson, Audie | B. 1910 |
| | D. May 18, 1968 |
| ,Willie Reams | B. 1901 |
| | D. |
| Simmons, Alice | B. Dec 15, 1900 |
| | D. |

| Simmons, Frances | B. 1916 |
| | D. 1970 |
| ,Henry W. | B. 1885 |
| | D. |
| ,Lena B. | B. 1895 |
| | D. 1958 |
| ,Margaret | B. Aug 27, 1857 |
| | D. Oct 6, 1933 |
| ,Mike | B. Dec 21, 1899 |
| | D. Mar 22, 1968 |
| ,Obe W. | B. Nov 17, 1852 |
| | D. Apr 30, 1939 |
| Sledge, Emma B. | B. 1893 |
| | D. |
| Spain, L. | B. |
| | D. |
| ,M. | B.. |
| | D. |
| ,Dorothy L.S. | B. |
| | D. |
| ,Mary A.S. | B. |
| | D. |
| ,Sara A.S. | B. |
| | D. |

## Bennett Cemetery

Location: 13th District, owned by the Bennett family and located at the end of Bennett Hollow Road, beyond Peytonsville. Many graves marked with one fieldstone or faded funeral markers.

| Bennett, Alexander | B. Dec 25, 1843 |
| | D. Nov 30, 1906 |
| ,Allen | B. 1900 |
| | D. 1914 |
| ,Ennie | B. 1898 |
| | D. 1914 |
| ,Felix M. | B. Jul 31, 1912 |
| | D. Feb 10, 1962 |
| ,Hattie D. | B. |
| | D. Apr 18, 1855 |
| ,James T. | B. Dec 10, 1905 |
| | D. Aug 22, 1909 |
| ,James Thomas | B. 1870 |
| | D. 1914 |
| ,Joe A. | B. July 2, 1906 |
| | D. Oct, 1958 |

| Bennett, Lincoln | B. 1903 |
| | D. 1933 |
| Bennett, Menurvie J. Tucker | B. Mar, 1844 |
| | D. Oct 14, 1890 |
| ,Milton | B. 1915 |
| | D. 1957 |
| ,Modie Frances | B. Mar 8, 1884 |
| | D. Jan 7, 1947 |
| ,Neola Culberson | B. 1873 |
| | D. 1951 |
| ,Phil | B. Jan 10, 1878 |
| | D. Oct, 1968? |
| ,Richard B. | B. 1911 |
| | D. 1961 |
| ,Sadie Low | B. Apr 20, 1936 |
| | D. Aug 12, 1936 |
| ,Sam Jr. | B. Mar 22, 1927 |
| | D. Jun 1, 1927 |
| Chapman, Catherine | B. Feb 17 |
| | D. |
| Garner, son of Andrew | B. Dec 5, 1939 |
| | D. Mar 26, 1944 |
| ,Ernie I. | B. Sep 19, 1897 |
| | D. May 24, 1918 |
| ,Lee | B. |
| | D. |
| ,Mollie | B. Oct 20, 1866 |
| | D. Sep 24, 1897 |
| ,Mrs. Susie | B. |
| | D. Apr 10, 1968 |
| ,Wavie | B. May 14, 1903 |
| | D. Nov 28, 1906 |
| Hilliker, Bernard J. | B. Aug 27, 1938 |
| | D. Feb 16, 1962 |
| ,Lillie J. | B. Aug 24, 1938 |
| | D. Oct, 1968 |
| ,Baby Boy | B. Feb 14, 1962 |
| | D. |
| Johnson, Noney D.R. | B. Aug 31, 1902 |
| | D. |
| ,Robert E. | B. Dec 24, 1892 |
| | D. Apr 2, 1948 |
| Poteete, Bertha | B. Mar 24, 1894 |
| | D. Oct, 1968 |
| ,Daisey Odell | B. |
| | D. |

| Poteete, Dan | B. Jan 5, 1905 |
| | D. Aug 20, 1931 |
| Poteete, Harvey | B. |
| | D. Sep 13 |
| ,Henry L. | B. May 26, 1905 |
| | D. Feb 3, 1910 |
| ,James Edward | B. |
| | D. |
| ,Lena Pearl | B. |
| | D. |
| ,Ruby | B. |
| | D. |
| ,Ruth | B. |
| | D. |
| ,Sallie J. Bennett | B. Sep 6, 1871 |
| | D. Apr 27, 1946 |
| ,Will Brice | B. Jun 8, 1863 |
| | D. Apr 17, 1927 |
| ,Willie West | B. Aug 23, 1891 |
| | D. Sep 29, 1955 |
| Rodgers, Billie Jane | B. |
| | D. Dec, 1933 |
| Tomlin, Dick | B. |
| | D. |
| ,Jim H. | B. Jan 30, 1876 |
| | D. Sep 24, 1938 |
| Veach, Addie | B. 1896 |
| | D. |
| ,Carmack | B. Jun 25, 1908 |
| | D. Apr 22, 1962 |
| ,Israel | B. 1890 |
| | D. 1953 |
| ,Jack | B. 1899 |
| | D. 1942 |
| ,Jack W. | B. 1898 |
| | D. 1963 |
| ,Jess | B. Dec 23, 1870 |
| | D. Dec 18, 1939 |
| ,Laura | B. Aug 7, 1872 |
| | D. Sep 2, 1928 |
| ,Linda Sue | B. Jan 29, 1945 |
| | D. Jul 28, 1945 |
| ,Logan | B. |
| | D. |
| ,Mollie | B. 1904 |
| | D. |

| Veach, Nellie | B. 1913 |
| | D. Oct, 1968 |
| Veach, Susie L. | B. 1917 |
| | D. |
| ,Thomas Oscar | B. |
| | D. Jun 2, 1954 |
| ,Tommie | B. |
| | D. Jun 10, 1964 |
| ,Virginia Oden | B. |
| | D. Nov 11, 1941 |
| ,Wesley | B. 1913 |
| | D. |
| ,William L. | B. Jan 4, 1919 |
| | D. Jun 11, 1936 |

## Burnett Cemetery

Location: 13th District, now 23rd, on the farm of Norman Noland on Arno Road. The cemetery is on the side of a hill about .2 miles from Lampkin Bridge Road and .3 miles from both Arno and McDaniel Road.

| Burnett, Eliza J. | B. Dec, 1828 |
| | D. Feb 4, 1887 |
| Burnett, Rev. Thomas | B. Oct 6, 1820 |
| | D. Sep 20, 1881 |

## Cook-Ford Cemetery

Location: 13th District on Peytonsville Road, on Kenneth Groves Farm.

| Cook, Lucinda | B. Aug 16, 1816 |
| | D. Sep 24, 1865 |
| Ford, Henry | B. Jun 20, 1830 |
| | D. Mar 29, 1920 |
| ,Irene Hood | B. Jan 5, 1899 |
| | D. Jun 24, 1919 |
| ,Sarah E.J. | B. Jan 8, 1834 |
| | D. Jan 8, 1907 |
| Hood, John Edward | B. Aug 12, 1887 |
| | D. Sep 20, 1905 |
| Walton, P.J. | B. Sep 11, 1851 |
| | D. May 24, 1923 |
| ,Rebecca | B. Apr 29, 1858 |
| | D. |

## Cool Springs Cemetery

Location: 13th District, follow Lewisburg Pike to Harpeth-Peytonsville Road, turn left, go to Cool Springs Road near Peytonsville. Turn right and the cemetery is next to Cool Springs Primitive Baptist Church.

| Adair, Annie E. | B. 1865 |
| | D. 1921 |
| ,Cora White | B. 1879 |
| | D. 1921 |
| ,Henry L. | B. 1883 |
| | D. 1949 |
| ,John R. | B. 1859 |
| | D. 1940 |
| ,Margaret | B. 1889 |
| | D. 1930 |
| ,Mary | B. 1834 |
| | D. 1912 |
| ,Robert | B. 1868 |
| | D. 1949 |
| ,William L. | B. 1858 |
| | D. 1942 |
| Bagsby, Mrs. W.T. | B. |
| | D. 1958 |
| Beard, Addie | B. 1932 |
| | D. 1933 |
| ,Alice | B. 1880 |
| | D. 1904 |
| ,Charlie | B. 1872 |
| | D. 1945 |
| ,Charles W. | B. 1933 |
| | D. 1933 |
| ,Clifton D. | B. 1898 |
| | D. 1963 |
| ,George M. | B. 1867 |
| | D. |
| ,James L. | B. 1895 |
| | D. 1953 |
| ,Larry | B. |
| | D. 1961 |
| ,Michael D. | B. 1961 |
| | D. 1963 |
| ,Myrtle | B. 1907 |
| | D. 1934 |
| ,Nancy C. | B. 1869 |
| | D. 1949 |
| ,Richard D. | B. 1902 |
| | D. 1962 |
| Beard, Sara Rebecca | B. 1882 |
| | D. 1951 |

| Beard, Walter B. | B. 1882 | Golden, John W. | B. 1878 |
| | D. 1961 | | D. 1958 |
| Bennett, Robert A. | B. | Graham, Addie | B. 1923 |
| | D. 1965 | | D. 1923 |
| Crafton, Emmie R. | B. | ,Evie S. | B. |
| | D. 1956 | | D. 1964 |
| ,G.W. | B. 1874 | Green, G.W. | B. 1882 |
| | D. 1951 | | D. 1942 |
| ,Jerry | B. 1947 | Haley, Ellen C. | B. 1875 |
| | D. 1954 | | D. 1932 |
| ,Leslie P. | B. 1891 | ,R. Emmett | B. 1869 |
| | D. 1937 | | D. 1938 |
| ,Rosie T. | B. 1888 | Harper, Salle E. | B. 1898 |
| | D. 1941 | | D. 1953 |
| ,Tom P. | B. 1873 | ,William H. | B. 1923 |
| | D. | | D. 1964 |
| ,Walter | B. | Hartley, Charles H. | B. |
| | D. 1960 | | D. 1961 |
| Culberson, Benj. | B. 1854 | ,Ewin | B. 1894 |
| | D. 1934 | | D. 1963 |
| ,Emma E. | B. 1886 | ,Mary | B. |
| | D. 1956 | | D. |
| ,Harden S. | B. 1869 | Hinson, Albert | B. |
| | D. 1934 | | D. 1917 |
| ,Lucy Ann | B. 1848 | ,Ella | B. 1878 |
| | D. 1920 | | D. 1917 |
| ,Mary P. | B. 1873 | House, Burneter | B. 1872 |
| | D. 1922 | | D. 1907 |
| ,Norman A. | B. 1923 | ,Eliza | B. 1843 |
| | D. 1923 | | D. 1901 |
| ,Wallace A. | B. 1883 | Hughes, John T. | B. 1887 |
| | D. 1958 | | D. 1954 |
| ,Walter T. | B. 1877 | ,Lottie | B. 1862 |
| | D. 1927 | | D. 1916 |
| Davis, Anna | B. 1872 | ,Marion | B. 1918 |
| | D. 1907 | | D. 1931 |
| ,Nancy | B. 1841 | Ivery, John Will | B. 1920 |
| | D. 1925 | | D. 1951 |
| ,T.A. | B. 1840 | ,Tony Allen | B. 1943 |
| | D. 1919 | | D. 1950 |
| ,W.E. | B. 1870 | Ivey, infant daughter | B. |
| | D. 1945 | | D. 1950 |
| Dillard, Allie C. | B. | Jackson, John P. | B. 1874 |
| | D. 1853 | | D. 1953 |
| Dobson, Sue Ella Denton | B. 1833 | Jackson, Luticia | B. 1880 |
| | D. 1915 | | D. 1938 |

|  |  |
|---|---|
| Jackson, William H. | B. 1932 / D. 1952 |
| Johnson, Fannie C. | B. 1908 / D. 1959 |
| Jones, Betty J. | B. / D. 1961 |
| ,Wiley | B. 1869 / D. 1957 |
| King, Alva | B. 1912 / D. 1951 |
| ,Elizabeth O. | B. 1887 / D. 1939 |
| ,Fealon | B. 1918 / D. 1949 |
| ,Samuel | B. 1881 / D. 1949 |
| Kiger, John T. | B. 1896 / D. 1949 |
| Lavender, Lizzie | B. 1867 / D. 1939 |
| Lester, J.H. | B. 1847 / D. 1929 |
| ,Martha J. | B. 1851 / D. 1909 |
| Lillard, Alice | B. 1883 / D. 1958 |
| ,Daisy | B. 1910 / D. 1951 |
| ,Davis | B. 1903 / D. 1938 |
| ,Ethel G. | B. 1902 / D. 1958 |
| ,Greer Davis | B. 1879 / D. 1926 |
| ,James A. | B. / D. 1967 |
| ,Lemuel | B. 1880 / D. 1933 |
| ,Oliver C. | B. 1924 / D. 1926 |
| ,Ollie C. | B. 1873 / D. 1953 |
| ,R. Graham | B. 1913 / D. 1953 |
| Lillard, Richard M. | B. 1878 / D. 1940 |
| Lillard, Woodard M. | B. 1878 / D. 1937 |
| Mathis, Allen M. | B. 1912 / D. |
| ,Charlie M. | B. 1890 / D. 1943 |
| ,Francis | B. 1849 / D. 1909 |
| ,Jerry B. | B. 1847 / D. 1926 |
| ,Mary A. | B. 1892 / D. 1912 |
| ,Mattie | B. 1881 / D. 1958 |
| ,Sam T. | B. 1875 / D. 1939 |
| McGee, John L. | B. 1880 / D. 1946 |
| ,John P. | B. 1938 / D. 1962 |
| ,Willie Eunice | B. 1885 / D. 1939 |
| Meek, Britton | B. 1835 / D. 1919 |
| ,Caroline J. | B. 1838 / D. 1920 |
| ,Lena S. | B. 1873 / D. 1913 |
| ,Thomas R. | B. 1870 / D. 1957 |
| Mosley, Amy P. | B. 1865 / D. 1925 |
| ,Elsie Russman | B. 1887 / D. 1925 |
| ,Henry O. | B. 1888 / D. 1951 |
| ,L.H. | B. 1864 / D. 1936 |
| ,Willie | B. 1907 / D. 1933 |
| Pate, Mary E. | B. 1877 / D. 1914 |
| ,Mattie | B. 1900 / D. 1907 |
| Pate, Sophia | B. 1863 / D. 1950 |

Pate, Thomas H.     B. 1867
                          D. 1941

,Thomas W.     B. 1828
                          D. 1897

,William     B. 1858
                          D. 1935

,William Lundy     B. 1936
                          D. 1936

,W.L.     B. 1811
                          D. 1895

Russell, Charles C.     B. 1894
                          D. 1966

,Janie     B. 1929
                          D. 1931

,John L.     B. 1861
                          D. 1947

,Nancy     B. 1862
                          D. 1946

Sears, Dee     B. 1876
                          D. 1956

Smith, J.H.     B. 1880
                          D. 1908

,W.M.     B. 1858
                          D. 1940

Smithson, Lizzie C.     B. 1830
                          D. 1900

Stevens, O.A.     B. 1895
                          D. 1916

Tanner, Jodie M.     B. 1864
                          D. 1925

Taylor, Henryetta     B. 1873
                          D. 1928

,James E.     B. 1920
                          D. 1940

,William Mc     B. 1868
                          D. 1940

Thomas, Lundy     B. 1892
                          D. 1911

Thomason, Emma L. Taylor     B. 1899
                          D. 1959

Tomlin, Ben A.     B. 1877
                          D. 1957

,David M.     B. 1848
                          D. 1933

Tomlin, Martha E.     B. 1855
                          D. 1907

Tomlin, Myrtle     B. 1906
                          D. 1918

,Richard A.     B. 1887
                          D. 1931

Turnage, Mildred     B. 1932
                          D. 1934

Vaughn,     B. 1886
                          D. 1951

,James E.     B. 1924
                          D. 1946

,Margaret L.     B. 1927
                          D. 1928

White, Caroline E.     B. 1843
                          D. 1922

,Elder F.M.     B. 1839
                          D. 1924

,Luther     B. 1905
                          D. 1956

Wiley, W.R.     B. 1884
                          D. 1906

**Crafton-Beech-Heithcock Cemetery**
Location: 13th District on the George Jack Crafton farm, at the end of Meeks Road.

Beech, William     B. 1869
                          D. 1929

Crafton, G.W.     B. Dec 1, 1847
                          D. Nov 1, 1923

,Maggie     B. Jul 26, 1876
                          D. Jul 12, 1972

,Susan E. Young     B. Jun 21, 1850
                          D. Apr 21, 1916

,W. Henry     B. Dec 28, 1874
                          D. May 10, 1962

Heithcock, Linnie Crafton     B. 1873
                          D.

,Sidney B.     B. 1879
                          D. 1950

**Crenshaw-Parrish-Shelburn Cemetery**
Location: 13th District, originally in cedar thicket to the left of David H. Jones place near Peytonsville. It was moved to Williamson Memorial Gardens in 1997 due to Interstate 840.

Crenshaw, Daniel     B.
                          D. Sep 20, 1831

Crenshaw, Mary     B. Oct 25, 1794

|  | D. Apr 14, 1875 |
| ,Mattie L. | B. Sep 9, 1837 |
|  | D. Jul 20, 1862 |
| ,Nancy J. | B. Oct 9, 1772 |
|  | D. Dec 11, 1859 |
| ,Nathie | B. Jun 2 |
|  | D. Jan 18, 1859 |
| Parish, James A. | B. Mar 26, 1856 |
|  | D. Jul 19, 1856 |
| Shelburn, Mary Crenshaw | B. Oct 25, 1794 |
|  | D. Apr 14, 1875 |
| Shelburn, Pettus | B. Jul 21, 1787 |
|  | D. Jun 11, 1864 |

## George Crunk Cemetery

Location: 14th District on the old Jack Crunk place on Caruthers Road at Millview.

| Crunk, George N. | B. Dec 14, 1842 |
|  | D. Mar 25, 1913 |
| Crunk, Seth Lewis | B. Jun 6, 1886 |
|  | D. Jun 6, 1886 |
| Bush, Pairlee V. | B. Jun 30, 1854 |
|  | D. Mar 15, 1889 |
| House, E.J. | B. May 11, 1877 |
|  | D. Jul 31, 1911 |
| House, John N. | B. Dec 9, 1810 |
|  | D. Nov 16, 1888 |
| House, Mary Jane | B. Jan 7, 1824 |
|  | D. Jul 12, 1856 |
| Jamison, Eddie Marshall | B. 1875 |
|  | D. 1952 |
| Jamison, Pattie May | B. Jan 7, 1881 |
|  | D. |
| Long, James N. | B. 1859 |
|  | D. 1913 |
| Long, Nancy J. | B. 1872 |
|  | D. 1951 |
| Stanfield, Thomas | B. Jan 1, 1828 |
|  | D. Oct 20, 1888 |
| Talley, Robbie Inez | B. Sep 22, 1883 |
|  | D. Aug 23, 1886 |
| Wagner, Irene May | B. Aug 19, 1872 |
|  | D. Mary 18, 1892 |

## Flack Cemetery

Location: 13th District on the John Boyd farm on Long Lane.

| Flack, Jane | B. Feb 2, 1799 |
|  | D. Mar 16, 1842 |
| Flack, James | B. |
|  | D. |
| Potter, James | B. Dec 1, 1836 |
|  | D. Aug, 1839 |

## Gee Cemetery

Location: 13th District on the Peytonsville-Trinity Road on the Shelby Stanfield farm.

| Gee, James Lucas | B. Jul 13, 1829 |
|  | D. May 8, 1896 |
| ,Louise | B. Jun 9, 1910 |
|  | D. Jun 9, 1910 |
| ,Owen Lucas | B. Dec 7, 1921 |
|  | D. Oct 6, 1926 |
| ,Sallie Ann Johnston | B. Sep 11, 1843 |
|  | D. Dec 26, 1915 |

## Gentry Cemetery (Black)

Location: 13th District on the Peytonsville-Trinity Road.

| Ewing, M.B. | B. |
|  | D. Sep 22, 1921 |
| Gentry, Annie L. | B. 1901 |
|  | D. 1933 |
| ,John T. | B. Nov 15, 1868 |
|  | D. May 2, 1958 |
| ,Josephine T. | B. Oct 16, 1877 |
|  | D. Sep 20, 1928 |
| ,Roxanne | B. |
|  | D. Jan 17, 1961 |
| Johnson, Jim | B. 1892 |
|  | D. 1958 |
| McAdams, Walter | B. |
|  | D. |
| Patton, Felix Edward | B. 1900 |
|  | D. 1946 |
| Woods, Martha | B. 1885 |
|  | D. 1958 |
| Woods, Solomon | B. 1882 |
|  | D. 1964 |

**Gilliam-Smithson Cemetery**
Location: 13th District, now 21st, on Arno Road across from Wesley Chapel Methodist Church, behind the home of Mrs. Leonard Harmon.

| | |
|---|---|
| Gilliam, Martha Smithson | B. Nov 11, 1800 |
| | D. Jun 3, 1846 |
| Smithson, Mrs. Sarah | B. Apr 25, 1825 |
| | D. Jul 3, 1847 |

**Gibson Cemetery**
Location: 13th District on Peytonsville Road on the W.L. Williams farm.

| | |
|---|---|
| Collins, John A. | B. JUn 22, 1811 |
| | D. Jun 25, 1813 |
| Gibson, James | B. Jan 27, 1772 |
| | D. Jan 25, 1831 |
| ,Mary | B. May 16, 1750 |
| | D. Feb 25, 1818 |
| ,Patrick | B. 1740 |
| | D. 1817 |
| ,Rachel | B. Jan 14, 1774 |
| | D. Dec 9, 1838 |
| ,Sarah A. | B. Jan 13, 1775 |
| | D. Sep 5, 1846 |

**Gosey Cemetery**
Location: 13th District on Gosey Hill Road on the Billy and Barbara Noland farm.

| | |
|---|---|
| Compton, Catharine M.E. | B. |
| | D. May 5, 1853 |
| Compton, Catharine R. | B. Dec 4, 1823 |
| | D. Mar 7, 1853 |
| Dobson, Mary Tomie | B. Oct 25, 1874 |
| | D. Jul 16, 1882 |
| ,Sarah Gosey | B. Sep 18, 1848 |
| | D. May 19, 1878 |
| ,William Henry | B. Aug 8, 1947 |
| | D. Jan 18, 1929 |
| Gosey, E.S.B. | B. Sep 8, 1820 |
| | D. Feb 20, 1887 |
| ,James | B. Feb 11, 1772 |
| | D. Oct 3, 1854 |
| ,James G. | B. Apr 23, 1847 |
| | D. Apr 25, 1856 |
| Gosey, M.G. | B. |
| | D. Jan 21, 1903 |

**Gosey, Mary A.**

| | |
|---|---|
| Gosey, Mary A. | B. Aug 12, 1823 |
| | D. Aug 26, 1896 |
| ,Mary T. | B. Dec 2, 1849 |
| | D. Feb 2, 1869 |
| ,Mattie Lieu | B. Oct 16, 1853 |
| | D. Apr 9, 1856 |
| ,Rebecker Bowers | B. 1785 |
| | D. 1859 |
| Nevils, Christina | B. Mar 14, 1844 |
| | D. Jul 25, 1858 |
| Smith, Nema Smithson | B. Nov 29, 1874 |
| | D. Jul 1, 1906 |
| Smithson, J.P. | B. Sep 9, 1840 |
| | D. Feb 12, 1902 |
| ,M.E. | B. Jan 23, 1870 |
| | D. Feb 29, 1870 |
| ,P.G. | B. Oct 7, 1867 |
| | D. Feb 11, 1868 |

**N.L. Harrison Cemetery**
Location: 13th District on Crowder Road.

| | |
|---|---|
| Harrison, Christina Knight | B. Oct 15, 1811 |
| | D. Sep 4, 1862 |
| ,Nathaniel Lundy | B. Dec 2, 1808 |
| | D. Nov 21, 1885 |
| Pate, Arabella T. | B. Mar 18, 1861 |
| | D. Dec 3, 1861 |
| ,Sarah Harrison | B. Jan 15, 1833 |
| | D. Jul 18, 1867 |

**Harrison-Burge-Stevens Cemetery**
Location: 13th District, now 23rd, on the Jack Stanfield property on Lampkin Bridge Road.

| | |
|---|---|
| Burge, George R. | B. 1880 |
| | D. 1975 |
| Burge, Lucy C. | B. 1894 |
| | D. 1926 |
| Burge, Mary E. | B. 1854 |
| | D. 1934 |
| Burge, Wilburn | B. 1843 |
| | D. 1913 |
| Stevens, Fannie | B. Aug 29, 1872 |
| | D. Aug 15, 1954 |
| Stevens, Kirk | B. May 25, 1870 |
| | D. Jan 3, 1943 |
| Harrison, William P. | B. Apr 2, 1785 |
| | D. Feb 20, 1842 |

Harrison, C.      B. Jan 15, 1815
     D. 1825

Foster, James (no dates)

## Hall-Holland Cemetery

Location: 13th District on the C.R. Wood farm on Bethesda-Arno Road.

| | |
|---|---|
| Hall, Jemima Ann | B. 1811 |
| | D. 1895 |
| ,John G. | B. Jan 21, 1808 |
| | D. May 6, 1872 |
| Holland, J.J. | B. Jan 18, 1843 |
| | D. Jul 12, 1933 |
| ,Nannie E. | B. Mar 4, 1844 |
| | D. Sep 27, 1897 |
| ,Sarah Jemima | B. Sep 12, 1873 |
| | D. Oct 27, 1874 |
| Stanfield, Dee | B. 1871 |
| | D. 1953 |
| ,Dolly | B. 1877 |
| | D. 1946 |
| ,Elsie Mae | B. Jun 16, 1888 |
| | D. |
| ,J.D. | B. Dec 28, 1884 |
| | D. Jan 16, 1894 |
| ,John Leonard | B. Oct 1, 1898 |
| | D. Sep 26, 1930 |
| ,J.S. | B. Jul 14, 1870 |
| | D. May 1, 1871 |

## B.F. Hall Cemetery

Location: 13th District, now 21st, on Arno Road, farm of Mrs. George Holt, on east side of the road.

| | |
|---|---|
| Hall, Benjamin Franklin | B. Nov 10, 1841 |
| | D. Sep 3, 1899 |
| Hall, Bettie | B. Jan 13, 1879 |
| | D. Jul 18, 1916 |
| Hall, Ernest W. | B. Jul 28, 1871 |
| | D. Jul 18, 1916 |
| Hall, James F. | B. Jan 23, 1862 |
| | D. May 10, 1913 |
| Hall, Zachariah G. | B. July 18, 1869 |
| | D. Jun 30, 1905 |
| Holland, Mitchel B. | B. Jan 16, 1849 |
| | D. Mar 3, 1892 |

## Heithcock Cemetery

Location: 13th District, Trinity Road near its junction with Arno Road, on the farm now owned by Jim Crowell.

| | |
|---|---|
| Beech, J.W. | B. Aug 20, 1868 |
| | D. Oct 26, 1943 |
| Heithcock, Mary E. | B. Nov 2, 1839 |
| | D. Oct 18, 1913 |
| Page, Oscar R. | B. Jul 6, 1891 |
| | D. May 14, 1922 |

## Jones-Gillespie Cemetery

Location: 13th District on Peytonsville-Arno Road.

| | |
|---|---|
| Jones,__________ | B. |
| | D. Dec 12, 1858 |
| ,Anna | B |
| | D. |
| ,Anne | B. |
| | D. |
| ,Elizabeth | B. |
| | D. 1824 |
| ,James | B. |
| | D. 1820 |
| ,Judith | B. 1784 |
| | D. Mar 18, 1857 |
| ,Martha J. | B. 1826 |
| | D. |
| ,Sarah A. | B. |
| | D. |
| ,Thomas H. | B. |
| | D. 1840 |
| ,William | B. Sep 20, 1822 |
| | D. Sep 2, 1898 |
| Gillespie, Isaac Jasper | B. Mar 6, 1833 |
| | D. Nov 10, 1906 |

## Jordan-Helm-Taylor Cemetery

Location: 13th District on Cool Springs Road, behind the residence of Mrs. Willie Joe Buford.

| | |
|---|---|
| Helm, Elizabeth W. | B. Jan 27, 1827 |
| | D. Dec 1, 1853 |
| ,G. Burnton Jordan | B. Jan 27, 1827 |
| | D. Dec 1, 1853 |
| Helm, James G. | B. Nov 8, 1852 |
| | D. Sep 15, 1853 |

| Jordan, James H. | B. Feb 14, 1812 |
| | D. Oct 20, 1812 |
| ,Mary M. Petway | B. Aug 4, 1805 |
| | D. Aug 18, 1873 |
| ,Nancy J. | B. Mar 15, 1833 |
| | D. Feb 17, 1855 |
| ,Rebecca Burton | B. Jun 4, 1806 |
| | D. Feb 12, 1839 |
| Taylor, Richard W. | B. Jul 11, 1817 |
| | D. Jun 10, 1851 |

## King Cemetery

Location: 13th District on Gosey Hill Road, near the intersection with Peytonsville Road.

| Glenn, Ada | B. 1868 |
| | D. 1966 |
| ,F.A. | B. 1870 |
| | D. 1966 |
| King, George M. | B. Jul 30, 1857 |
| | D. |
| ,George W. | B. Aug 3, 1828 |
| | D. Feb 7, 1914 |
| ,J. Watt | B. Oct 21, 1874 |
| | D. Nov 21, 1940 |
| ,Lillie | B. Oct 5, 1890 |
| | D. Dec 22, 1946 |
| ,Nancy E. | B. Jun 6, 1837 |
| | D. Jun 8, 1911 |
| ,Tennie S. | B. Jul 20, 1860 |
| | D. Jan 27, 1842 |
| Reed, Sarah Anna | B. Aug 4, 1903 |
| | D. Feb 22, 1920 |

## George Kinnard Cemetery

Location: 13th District, now 21st, one mile south of Arno Road on and in front of the Adair farm. Two illegible monuments and 11 field stone markers.

| Crump, John Osburn | B. Apr 16, 1816 |
| | D. Sep 10, 1849 |
| Dodson, Adeline B. | B. Dec 6, 1805 |
| | D. Nov 4, 1853 |
| Kinnard, Catherine Cannon | B. |
| | D. Oct, 1849 |
| Kinnard, Gabriel | B. Sep 10, 1837 |
| | D. Apr 25, 1850 |
| Kinnard, George, Jr. | B. Nov 13, 1808 |
| | D. Jul 28, 1820 |

| Kinnard, George, Sr. | B. Sep 23, 1768 |
| | D. Oct 7, 1845 |
| Kinnard, James William | B. |
| | D. |
| Kinnard, Michael | B. |
| | D. Nov, 1847 |
| Kinnard, Rufus | B. Sep 10, 1829 |
| | D. Dec 20, 1859 |
| McConnico, Garner | B. Jul 20, 1771 |
| | D. Sep 16, 1883 |
| Parrish, Susan C. | B. Jan 22, 1836 |
| | D. Dec 20, 1859 |
| Tanner, Mrs. Nancy | B. |
| | D. Sep 11, 1810 |

## Kirkpatrick Cemetery

Location: 13th District on the Ben Givens farm, near the intersection of Gosey Hill Road with Arno Road.

| Hill, Sarah | B. Feb 5, 1839 |
| | D. Feb 22, 1856 |
| Kirkpatrick, H.A. | B. Apr 29, 1828 |
| | D. Jul 2, 1851 |
| ,J.O. | B. Apr 28, 1824 |
| | D. Jun 8, 1847 |
| ,Mary M. | B. Feb 9, 1792 |
| | D. Dec 24, 1863 |
| ,Henry | B. Jul 3, 1790 |
| | D. Sep 14, 1845 |
| ,Elizabeth | B. Sep 15, 1822 |
| | D. Oct 24, 1942 |
| ,Lucinda M. | B. Sep 18, 1819 |
| | D. Aug 9, 1842 |
| ,Samuel | B. Mar 2, 1833 |
| | D. Mar 2, 1833 |

## W.P. Ladd Cemetery

Location: 13th District on the south side of the Harpeth-Peytonsville Road on the Jesse Crawford farm.

| Ladd, Bessie A. | B. Sep 15, 1892 |
| | D. Dec 3, 1918 |
| Ladd, Leonard L. | B. Sep 4, 1883 |
| | D. Jul 8, 1949 |
| ,Martha Burnette | B. Sep 2, 1847 |
| | D. Jul 30, 1930 |
| ,Robert N. | B. Dec 24, 1879 |

D. Sep 12, 1953

,William P.     B. Feb 12, 1847

D. Jan 20, 1915

## Luster Cemetery (Black)
Location: 13th District, now 23rd, on Arno Road on the right before Interstate 840 exit.

Luster, Grant B.     B. Nov 27, 1895
D. Apr 26, 1981

Luster, James Lee     B. May 10, 1922
D. Aug 23, 1985

Luster, William Thomas     B. Dec 2, 1929
PFC CE USAR Korea     D. Feb 23, 1969

Luster, Alex, uncle of Grant Luster

Luster, Grant, Sr., grandfather of Grant Luster

## McConnico Cemetery
Location: 10th District on Peytonsville Road on the Lawrence Hussey farm.

McConnico, Catharine K.     B. Jan 23, 1811
D. Nov 27, 1860

## Charles Meek Cemetery
Location: 23rd District on Meek Road.

Meek, Charles     B. Sep 1, 1857
D. Nov 28, 1917

Meek, Mary Ann     B. Nov 21, 1859
D. Jan 16, 1891

## Merritt Cemetery
Location: 10th District on the W.A. Jordan farm on Peytonsville Road.

Dorris, Lutie Merritt     B.
D.

Merritt, Addiee     B. Apr 12, 1842
D. Sep 14, 1876

,Henry J.     B. Dec 23, 1803
D. Jan 22, 1873

,James Henry     B. 1837
D. 1922

Merritt, Rebecca     B.
D.

,Rebecca Newsom     B. 1808
D. Mar 16, 1863

,Thomas     B. Feb 18, 1770
D. Jul 6, 1857

Newsom, B.L.     B. Feb 27, 1829

D. Jan 24, 1849

## Mallory-Johnson Cemetery
Location: 13th District on Gosey Hill Road, on the former C. Douglas York farm.

Johnson, Blyth     B. Apr 8, 1883
D. Dec 20, 1896

,Elin     B. Dec 10, 1888
D. May 9, 1894

,Fannie O.     B. 1892
D. Broken stone

,Gregory     B. Oct 26, 1809
D. Mar 24, 1887

,J. Pinkney     B. 1894
D. 1934

,Maggie Lee     B. 1898
D.

,P. Jane     B. May 18, 1837
D. Oct 7, 1905

Mallory, Addie V.     B. Apr 27, 1835
D. Mar 11, 1901

,William A.     B. Oct 13, 1814
D. Jan 29, 1865

McMahon, Betty Lou     B. Jun 17, 1875
D. Mar 27, 1922

,F.E.     B. Jul 9, 1867
D.

Parks, W.V.     B. Oct 3, 1837
D. Jul 14, 1896

## Parks Cemetery
Location: 10th District on the Earl Campbell farm on Long Lane.

Parks, Andrew Baker     B. Mar 20, 1793
D. Sep 19, 1870

,Elizabeth Barnett     B. Mar 22, 1815
D. Feb 18, 1901

,Josephus Barnett     B. Apr 30, 1850
D. Feb 12, 1906

Parks, Margaret Rachel     B. Jul 15, 1848
D.

,Mary E.     B. Aug 18, 1831
D. Oct 25, 1854

,Rhoda Neely     B.
1st wife of Andrew     D.

,Sophronia A.     B. Oct 7, 1846
D. Mar 12, 1920

,Addie O. Sweeney B. Mar 21, 1858
D. Jun 24, 1887

## Pennington Cemetery
Location: in the yard of Mrs. Maggie Beech on Arno Road, near the intersection of Peytonsville-College Grove and Arno Road.

| | | |
|---|---|---|
| Pennington, C.R. | B. 1877 | |
| | D. 1952 | |
| ,Charles Robert | B. | |
| | D. Aug 18, 1952 | |
| ,Ella Tomlin | B. 1872 | |
| | D. 1955 | |
| ,William Albert | B. Dec 17, 1906 | |
| | D. Feb 15, 1907 | |
| Shepherd, James Timothy | B. | |
| | D. Mar 31, 1965 | |
| Sledge, Alma Pennington | B. 1905 | |
| | D. 1931 | |

## Peytonsville Methodist Church Cemetery
Location: 13th District at the intersection of Peytonsville Road and Gosey Hill Road.

| | |
|---|---|
| Farabee | B. May 1, 1841 |
| | D. Aug 10, 1857 |
| Harrison, Ellen Martin | B. Feb 13, 1842 |
| | D. Apr 2, 1899 |
| ,Turnel Lundy Green | B. Jun 5, 1838 |
| | D. May 23, 1918 |
| Harrison, Goldie | B. Aug 19, 1877 |
| | D. Dec 9, 1900 |
| Martin, Jane Alston | B. Jan 24, 1825 |
| | D. Nov 5, 1906 |
| More, Mary | B. |
| | D. 1825 |
| Reid, John T. M.D. | B. Dec 25, 1825 |
| | D. May 4, 1858 |
| Wilson, Catherine | B. Oct 1, 1796 |
| | D. Oct 16, 1871 |
| Wilson, Isaac | B. Dec 10, 1874 |
| | D. Jan 24, 1877 |

## Pinkston-Low-Nevils Cemetery
Location: 13th District, now 21st, on the west side of Arno Road, one mile south of Arno College Grove Road intersection and just past the Owen Hill Road intersection, both on the east side of Arno Road. The cemetery is near the road and to the left of the drive going to the house of the late Herbert Crunk.

| | |
|---|---|
| Low, Gabriel | B. Mar 8, 1808 |
| | D. Feb 13, 1882 |
| Low, Vinnia Pinkston | B. Jun 13, 1820 |
| | D. May 13, 1893 |
| Nevils, Ella G. | B. 1851 |
| | D. 1932 |
| Nevils, J.W. | B. 1834 |
| | D. 1893 |
| Nevils, Joe W. | B. Oct 31, 1876 |
| | D. Dec 23, 1876 |
| Nevils, Jonnie Lee | B. Feb 16, 1872 |
| | D. Dec 23, 1876 |
| Nolen, Augie Nevils | B. Apr 23, 1874 |
| | D. Oct 21, 1954 |
| Nolen, Charley Powell | B. Apr 13, 1874 |
| | D. Oct 21, 1954 |
| Pinkston, J.D. | B. Aug 22, 1850 |
| | D. Sep 28, 1906 |
| Pinkston, Mrs. S.F. | B. Feb 20, 1849 |
| | D. Mar 10, 1919 |
| Pinkston, Mary | B. |
| | D. Nov 11, 1889 |
| Pinkston, William | B. Aug 16, 1807 |
| | D. Feb 28, 1837 |
| Yarbrough, Richard S. | B. Aug 29, 1837 |
| | D. Mar 23, 1855 |

## Pollard Cemetery
Location: 23rd District on the F.M. Bass farm on McDaniel Road.

| | |
|---|---|
| Cotton, J. Howard | B. May 14, 1896 |
| | D. Jul 5, 1966 |
| Pollard, Malachi W. | B. 1822 |
| | D. 1881 |
| Pollard, Mary Kate | B. 1835 |
| | D. 1911 |
| Pollard, Sallie Madorah | B. 1853 |
| | D. 1904 |

## Poteete Cemetery
Location: 11th District on the north side of Harpeth-Peytonsville Road. Though the 11th District, many buried here lived in the 13th District.

| | |
|---|---|
| Amick, Abraham Lincoln | B. Sep 2, 1904 |
| | D. Oct 20, 1904 |

|  |  |  |
|---|---|---|
| ,Capt. F.H. | B. 1843 | D. 1907 |
| ,Laura Poteete | B. 1869 | D. 1928 |
| Anderson, Elizabeth | B. | D. Aug 19, 1905 |
| ,Johnnie Buchanan | B. Dec 31, 1883 | D. Sep 4, 1906 |
| Barnes, William Thomas | B. | D. Apr 27, 1968 |
| Bennett, Emma M. | B. Jan 19, 1892 | D. |
| ,Joe | B. Feb 9, 1893 | D. Jan 22, 1958 |
| ,John | B. Dec 19, 1922 | D. Jan 22, 1960 |
| ,Oscar | B. 1914 | D. 1943 |
| ,William | B. Apr 23, 1838 | D. Jan 14, 1902 |
| Buchanan, Annie Grace | B. Jul 7, 1895 | D. Jul 22, 1896 |
| ,Charles Asa | B. Dec 18, 1885 | D. Apr 21, 1939 |
| ,Maudie H. | B. 1891 | D. 1967 |
| Buchanan, Willie Mai | B. 1899 | D. |
| Burns, Nathaniel | B. 1880 | D. 1931 |
| Cole, Frank | B. Jul 5, 1903 | D. May 8, 1959 |
| ,Myrtle | B. Mar 12, 1902 | D. |
| Crawford, Alta L. | B. Mar 5, 1892 | D. Jan 13, 1967 |
| Crawford, Sam P. | B. Feb 3, 1895 | D. Jan 10, 1964 |
| Dalton, Ollie May Reynolds | B. Aug 30, 1876 | D. Sep 29, 1948 |
| Deason, Charles Dan | B. Feb 15, 1935 | D. Sep 2, 1966 |
| ,James Thomas | B. Feb 11, 1900 | D. Apr 28, 1921 |
| ,Tena Poteete | B. Nov 22, 1880 | D. Dec 9, 1958 |
| ,Walter Lee | B. Mar 4, 1874 | D. Jul 6, 1950 |
| Hassell, Helen | B. 1926 | D. |
| ,John Merritt | B. Jul 11, 1893 | D. Jul 20, 1952 |
| ,Milton | B. 1915 | D. 1957 |
| Hood, Mrs. Forrest | B. Jun 15, 1883 | D. Jun 10, 1964 |
| ,Green M. | B. Mar 9, 1903 | D. Feb 7, 1904 |
| ,James Walter | B. Dec 1, 1915 | D. Jul 8, 1917 |
| ,Paul M. | B. 1916 | D. 1932 |
| ,Senie Angeline | B. Jun 13, 1883 | D. Nov 23, 1902 |
| ,Thomas L. | B. 1875 | D. 1945 |
| Jackson, Ada Tomlin | B. Dec 23, 1884 | D. Aug 15, 1954 |
| ,Annie M. | B. 1894 | D. |
| ,Charles | B. Dec 13, 1842 | D. Dec 13, 1923 |
| Jackson, Charles T. | B. 1872 | D. 1946 |
| ,Elizabeth | B. Jul 20, 1845 | D. Nov 23, 1922 |
| ,Henry | B. Sep 18, 1878 | D. Oct 8, 1916 |
| ,Inez | B. Jun 4, 1916 | D. Jan 23, 1917 |
| ,Jesse | B. Sep 27, 1876 | D. Jul 20, 1906 |
| Jackson, John E. | B. 1887 | D. 1939 |
| ,Josephine H. | B. May 20, 1907 | D. May 7, 1927 |
| ,Josephine Poteete | B. Jun 9, 1885 | D. Nov 19, 1926 |
| ,Lillie M. | B. Jan 18, 1914 | D. Dec 25, 1914 |
| ,Mary | B. 1930 | D. 1961 |
| ,Mildred Irene | B. Nov 14, 1904 | D. Mar 10, 1944 |

| ,Owen | B. |
| | D. 1927 |
| Jones, Jim M. | B. 1895 |
| | D. 1965 |
| ,Lucille H. | B. 1902 |
| | D. Oct 13, 1962 |
| King, Beverly J. | B. |
| | D. Oct 3, 1962 |
| ,J.W. "Doc" | B. 1918 |
| | D. 1964 |
| ,James W. | B. Feb 9, 1918 |
| | D. Oct 30, 1964 |
| ,Jerry P. | B. 1955 |
| | D. Aug 3, 1955 |
| Marlin, Horace L. | B. Dec 30, 1928 |
| | D. May 18, 1955 |
| McCall, Edward Taft | B. Dec 23, 1911 |
| | D. Nov 14, 1949 |
| McGee, Allen Reece | B. 1879 |
| | D. 1952 |
| ,James A. | B. Mar 26, 1866 |
| | D. Oct 3, 1952 |
| ,James L. | B. Jun 14, 1888 |
| | D. Oct 3, 1918 |
| McGee, Janie Ingram | B. 1887 |
| | D. 1959 |
| ,John F. | B. Aug 22, 1857 |
| | D. Dec 30, 1944 |
| ,John R. | B. Jul 11, 1828 |
| | D. Aug 3, 1899 |
| ,Mary Alice | B. May 5, 1861 |
| | D. Aug 4, 1941 |
| ,Mary E. | B. Jun 7, 1859 |
| | D. Jan 28, 1941 |
| McGee, Mildred L. | B. Mar 17, 1915 |
| | D. Nov 3, 1920 |
| ,Sam F. Jr. | B. 1917 |
| | D. 1927 |
| Poteete, Baby | B. |
| | D. Nov 17, 1927 |
| ,Clarence | B. 1907 |
| | D. 1958 |
| ,Effie R. | B. Jul 20, 1884 |
| | D. Jan 25, 1933 |
| ,Ethel | B. 1918 |
| | D. |
| ,Fannie | B. 1880 |

| | D. |
| ,Filmore | B. Jun 1, 1889 |
| | D. Mar 19, 1909 |
| ,H. Baker | B. 1869 |
| | D. 1960 |
| ,H. Munroe | B. 1873 |
| | D. |
| ,Hannah Pearl | B. Mar 22, 1945 |
| | D. Feb 6, 1948 |
| ,Harvey M. Jr. | B. 1926 |
| | D. 1948 |
| ,Harvey M. Sr. | B. Aug 10, 1849 |
| | D. Jun 13, 1936 |
| ,Harvey Munroe III | B. 1908 |
| | D. 1952 |
| ,Iva | B. Mar 14, 1904 |
| | D. Mar 15, 1904 |
| ,J.B. | B. Mar 16, 1878 |
| | D. May 2, 1921 |
| ,J.R. Sr. | B. Nov 25, 1846 |
| | D. Nov 21, 1898 |
| ,Jack | B. 1875 |
| | D. 1950 |
| Poteete, James | B. 1908 |
| | D. 1958 |
| ,James M. | B. May 29, 1812 |
| | D. Feb 10, 1896 |
| ,James Pat | B. Aug 10, 1878 |
| | D. Oct 29, 1918 |
| ,James R. Sr. | B. Mar 29, 1875 |
| | D. Jun 16, 1846 |
| ,John Henry | B. Jun 11, 1880 |
| | D. Jan 26, 1921 |
| Poteete, John W. | B. 1885 |
| | D. 1910 |
| ,Lillie Irene | B. Feb 16, 1898 |
| | D. Jul 14, 1899 |
| ,Mandy Lee | B. Apr 14, 1897 |
| | D. Oct 21, 1897 |
| ,Manirvie | B. 1810 |
| | D. Sep 14, 1892 |
| ,Mary Ann | B. Jun 2, 1929 |
| | D. Jul 4, 1959 |
| ,Mary Ella | B. Jan 25, 1876 |
| | D. Sep 18, 1966 |
| ,Paul | B. 1911 |
| | D. 1961 |

| | |
|---|---|
| ,Sennie E. | B. Jul 23, 1855 |
| | D. Jan 13, 1939 |
| ,William Clyde | B. Jul 8, 1909 |
| | D. Nov 20, 1911 |
| ,William Harvey | B. Apr 7, 1901 |
| | D. Apr 16, 1901 |
| Tomlin, Bobby Calvin | B. 1937 |
| | D. 1959 |
| ,Buddy | B. 1887 |
| | D. 1957 |
| ,Charles Reece | B. Jul 12, 1880 |
| | D. Feb 12, 1964 |
| ,Dessie Reynolds | B. Dec 1, 1882 |
| | D. Sep 25, 1961 |
| ,Eugene Ellis | B. Sep 11, 1904 |
| | D. Mar 17, 1906 |
| ,Jerry | B. Sep 13, 1882 |
| | D. |
| ,Joe | B. 1877 |
| | D. 1963 |
| ,Lillie M. | B. 1891 |
| | D. 1918 |
| Tomlin, Lula | B. Sep 12, 1880 |
| | D. Sep 2, 1909 |
| ,Nathan | B. 1851 |
| | D. 1928 |
| ,Susan B. | B. 1861 |
| | D. Jan, 1962 |
| ,Viola H. | B. 1899 |
| | D. 1965 |
| ,William T. | B. Oct 26, 1915 |
| | D. Aug 7, 1917 |
| Tomlin, Willie Mai | B. Sep 7, 1892 |
| | D. |
| Weaver, Herman | B. 1892 |
| | D. 1965 |
| ,Pearlee | B. 1892 |
| | D. |
| Watkins, Lucretia Tomlin | B. 1880 |
| | D. 1924 |
| ,W.H. (Billy), Sr. | B. 1877 |
| | D. 1954 |

## Pratt Cemetery

Location: 13th District on Peytonsville Road on the farm of James O. Boyd and Mrs. Elmer Groves.

| | |
|---|---|
| Pratt, Elizabeth P. Akin | B. Oct 1, 1837 |
| | D. Nov 17, 1899 |
| ,George W. | B. Jul 6, 1829 |
| | D. Mar 8, 1903 |
| ,Sammie Lou | B. 1904 |
| | D. |
| ,Samuel Houston | B. Mar 15, 1868 |
| | D. Oct, 1904 |
| ,Will | B. Feb 29, 1900 |
| | D. 1916 |
| Amis, Nancy Boyd | B. 1810 |
| | D. Jan 26, 1830 |

## Ratcliffe Cemetery (Black)

Location: 13th District on Gosey Hill Road on the former C. Douglas York farm.

| | |
|---|---|
| Burns, Mrs. Winnie | B. |
| | D. Dec 17, 1964 |
| Caruthers, John L. | B. May 8, 1915 |
| | D. Dec 25, 1964 |
| Ratcliffe, Rev. Willie L. | B. |
| | D. Mar 24, 1966 |
| Reynolds, Ruben B. | B. |
| | D. Mar 22, 1965 |

## Rudder-Starnes-Boyd Cemetery

Location: 13th District, now 20th, on the property of Mrs. Elizabeth Boyd Lamb on McDaniel Road. The cemetery is on a hill to the left of her home.

| | |
|---|---|
| Boyd, Effie Mai | B. 1888 |
| | D. 1914 |
| Boyd, J. Thaddeus | B. 1837 |
| | D. 1907 |
| Boyd, Jimmie M. | B. 1891 |
| | D. 1906 |
| Boyd, Sarah Brown | B. 1844 |
| | D. 1901 |
| Haley, Martha E. | B. Jun 7, 1846 |
| | D. Jul 31, 1861 |
| Harper, Sadie Pearl | B. 1890 |
| | D. 1900 |
| Hayes, Richard W. | B. July 29, 1809 |
| | D. May 8, 1883 |
| Hayes, Robert | B. Jul 29, 1774 |
| | D. Mar 24, 1860 |

| Hayes, Thomas | B. Dec 10, 1841 |
| Co. A. 4th TN Cavalry | D. Feb 2, 1862 |
| Neal, Emily F. | B. May 3, 1818 |
|  | D. |
| Neal, James J. | B. Jun 7, 1814 |
|  | D. Sep 10, 1849 |
| Rudder, infant | B. |
|  | D. |
| Rudder, John B. | B. Jul 4, 1824 |
|  | D. Jun 27, 1844 |
| Rudder, Mary | B. Mar 9, 1764 |
|  | D. Jun 24, 1826 |
| Rudder, Noah B. | B. Jun 20,, 1820 |
|  | D. Jul, 1841 |
| Rudder, Richard | B. Jul 4, 1788 |
|  | D. Nov 4, 1852 |
| Starnes, Mary C. Rudder | B. 1830 |
|  | D. 1904 |
| Starnes, oldest daughter | B. Apr 7, 1850 |
|  | D. May 9, 1859 |
| Starnes, Cora D. | B. Arp 7, 1850 |
|  | D. May 9, 1859 |
| Starnes, Henry M. | B. Nov 12, 1851 |
|  | D. Jan 19, 1859 |
| Starnes, Col. James W. | B. Jul 9, 1817 |
|  | D. Jun 30, 1863 |
| Starnes, James W. Jr. | B. Jul 10, 1853 |
|  | D. Feb 16, 1894 |
| Starnes, Marian | B. Dec 12, 1860 |
|  | D. Aug 7, 1895 |
| Starnes, William R. | B. Aug 10, 1863 |
|  | D. 1881 |
| Vaughn, D.L. | B. Feb 10, 1833 |
|  | D. 1881 |

## Secrest Cemetery

Location: 13th District on Peytonsville-Trinity Road on the Mrs. Hattie Bruce farm.

| Rea, Tabitha | B. Apr 4, 1795 |
| | D. Jul 8, 1854 |
| Secrest, Elias | B. Aug 9, 1807 |
| | D. Jun, 1829 |
| Secrest, Isaac | B. Jul 16, 1792 |
| | D. Jul 18, 1864 |
| Secrest, John | B. May 16, 1805 |
| | D. Sep 29, 1825 |
| Secrest, John | B. Apr 23, 1758 |

D. Nov 30, 1847

## Smithson Cemetery

Location: 13th District on the Peytonsville-Trinity Road near the village of Peytonsville.

| Hicks, L.S. | B. Jan 11, 1857 |
| | D. Oct 28, 1857 |
| Gee, Elizabeth | B. Jan 29, 1827 |
| ,Louisa G. | B. Nov 11, 1830 |
| | D. Aug 30, 1831 |
| Gibson, John | B. Nov 21, 1840 |
| | D. Aug 8, 1866 |
| Gosey, Charles T. | B. Nov 11, 1840 |
| | D. Nov 17, 1876 |
| ,Pamelia W. | B. Jun 17, 1824 |
| | D. Feb 20, 1873 |
| Kinnard, Addie | B. Jan 23, 1833 |
| | D. Aug 2, 1885 |
| Smithson, Ada | B. May 23, 1867 |
| | D. Jul 31, 1884 |
| ,Alice | B. Jun 8, 1861 |
| | D. Dec 18, 1923 |
| Smithson, Ann | B. May 3, 1804 |
| | D. May 17, 1888 |
| ,Bettie | B. Aug 31, 1879 |
| | D. Nov 14, 1880 |
| ,Effie | B. Aug 31, 1881 |
| | D. Jul 22, 1884 |
| ,J. | B. May, 1844 |
| | D. Oct 5, 1877 |
| ,J.P. | B. Dec 29, 1855 |
| | D. Apr 18, 1889 |
| Smithson, Jesse | B. Nov 18, 1877 |
| | D. Jan 8, 1878 |
| ,Maggie N. | B. Feb 7, 1884 |
| | D. Aug 13, 1884 |
| ,Margaret K. | B. Mar 8, 1833 |
| | D. |
| ,Mrs. Mary | B. Oct 12, 1777 |
| | D. May 16, 1850 |
| ,Nathaniel B. | B. May 16, 1773 |
| | D. Aug 8, 1859 |
| ,Nathaniel N. | B. Apr 20, 1826 |
| | D. Apr 10, 1896 |
| ,Tandy S. | B. Jan 17, 1801 |
| | D. May 26, 1873 |
| ,Tandy S. | B. Nov 9, 1857 |

| | D. Jul 12, 1884 |
| Todd, Elizabeth G. | B. Feb 24, 1827 |
| | D. Jul 27, 1850 |

## Stanfield Cemetery

Location: 13th District, now 23rd, on the Jack Stanfield property on Lampkin Bridge Road, between the bridge and McDaniel Road.

| | |
|---|---|
| Stanfield, Thomas Edward | B. 1832 |
| | D. 1903 |
| Stanfield, Louella | B. 1845 |
| | D. 1918 |

## Starnes-Pinkston Cemetery

Location: 13th District on Trinity Road, near the Arno Road intersection on the Jim Crowell farm.

| | |
|---|---|
| Pinkston, Alexander Rufus | B. May 25, 1826 |
| | D. Oct 22, 1904 |
| Pinkston, Camelia Starnes | B. |
| | D. |
| Starnes, Ebenzer | B. |
| | D. Apr 10, 1863 |
| Starnes, Nancy | B. |
| | D. |
| Starnes, Rachel | B. |
| | D. |
| Starnes, Samuel Scott | B. |
| | D. Nov 20, 1841 |

## Steagall Cemetery

Location: 13th District on the Lloyd Warren farm, on the east side of Bethesda-Arno Road. The cemetery is east and a little south of where Cool Springs Road comes into Bethesda-Arno Road.

| | |
|---|---|
| Carson, R.A. | B. Apr 2, 1858 |
| | D. Mar 12, 1893 |
| Edmunds, James T. | B. Aug 18, 1787 |
| | D. Feb 18, 1859 |
| Harper, Mary Peny Lillard | B. Apr 24, 1847 |
| | D. Sep 24, 1917 |
| Lillard, Ira Grace | B. Mar 25, 1911 |
| | D. Jan 17, 1914 |
| Steagall, Elizar A. | B. Oct 22, 1821 |
| | D. Jun 6, 1872 |
| Steagall, Julia K. | B. Sep 15, 1833 |
| | D. Aug 17, 1881 |
| Steagall, Mary S. | B. Nov 23, 1838 |

| | D. Jun 18, 1862 |
| Steagall, Nancy | B. Aug 30, 1801 |
| | D. Aug 9, 1856 |
| Steagall, Samuel | B. May 22, 1798 |
| | D. Oct 22, 1873 |
| Tracy, Silas W. | B. Aug 7, 1847 |
| | D. Jan 3, 1915 |

## Elige Tomlin Cemetery

Location: 13th District on the David White farm, off Peytonsville-Harpeth Road. The cemetery is on a hill within view of the Bennett Cemetery.

| | |
|---|---|
| Tomlin, Elige | B. Mar, 1856 |
| | D. 1932 |
| ,Mary E. Bennett | B. 1846 |
| | D. 188_ |
| ,Lizzie Hay | B. 1863 |
| | D. 1949 |
| ,George | B. |
| | D. |
| ,Henry | B. Nov, 1884 |
| | D. |
| Tomlin, Martha Season | B. |
| | D. |
| ,John Wesley | B. Mar 13, 1889 |
| | D. |
| Pugh, Sennie Tomlin | B. 1876 |
| | D. |

## John Tomlin Cemetery

Location: 13th District on the Charles Meek farm. It is a quarter mile due west of the Beard Cemetery on Buchanan Road. Many graves have no markers.

| | |
|---|---|
| Tomlin, Bettie Tucker | B. Aug 10, 1853 |
| | D. Mar 10, 1912 |
| ,John Abner | B. 1854 |
| | D. |
| ,Charles William | B. Dec, 1878 |
| | D. |
| ,Agnes Beard | B. |

## Vaden Cemetery

Location: 13th District on Peytonsville Road, on the former farm of Walter Vaden, today St. Ignatius Orthodox Church.

| | |
|---|---|
| Pennington, Jennie | B. May 15, 1875 |

|                      | D. Jan 26, 1927      |
|----------------------|----------------------|
| ,Joe                 | B. 1900              |
|                      | D. 1952              |
| ,John                | B. 1870              |
|                      | D. 1952              |
| Sledge, Nathaniel    | B. May, 1838         |
|                      | D. 1869              |
| Smithson, Charles W. | B. 1895              |
|                      | D. Dec 10, 1968      |
| Vaden, Albert C.     | B. Jan 10, 1893      |
|                      | D. Oct 29, 1895      |
| ,Charles Wilson      | B. 1869              |
|                      | D. 1935              |
| ,N.B.                | B. Feb 22, 1845      |
|                      | D. 1942              |
| ,Nora Alice Sledge   | B. 1873              |
|                      | D. 1942              |
| ,Tennie              | B. Feb 1, 1849       |
|                      | D. May 10, 1895      |

## West Cemetery

Location: 13th District on Gosey Hill Road, near Arno Road.

|                  |                 |
|------------------|-----------------|
| Crowder, Beauty T. | B. Feb 8, 1887 |
|                  | D. May 12, 1927 |
| West, Mary D.    | B. Nov 20, 1818 |
|                  | D. Oct 8, 1877  |
| ,W.P.            | B. 1812         |
|                  | D. May 14, 1895 |

## Westwood Cemetery (Black)

Location: 13th District at the intersection of Crowder Road and Peytonsville-Trinity Road, across the road from Westwood Baptist Church. No markers found.

|                      |           |
|----------------------|-----------|
| Caruthers, Theoplis  | B. 1932   |
|                      | D. 1934   |
| Hughes, Eula         | B.        |
|                      | D. 1928   |
| Hughes, William Brice | B.       |
|                      | D. 1930   |
| Ratcliffe, Bulla     | B.        |
|                      | D. 1927   |

**The following photographs were taken by C. A. Wood from his beautiful book entitled *Images of 190 Cemeteries in Williamson County, Tennessee* (2020) and offered here with a generous heart.**

THE HALL-HOLLAND CEMETERY ON BETHESDA-ARNO ROAD

THE COOL SPRINGS PRIMITIVE BAPTIST CHURCH CEMETERY ON COOL
SPRINGS ROAD

THE SMITHSON-GEE-KINNARD CEMETERY ON PEYTONSVILLE-TRINITY ROAD

THE POTEETE CEMETERY ON HARPETH-PEYTONSVILLE ROAD

RIGHT: THE ALEXANDER BENNETT CEMETERY, AT THE END OF BENNETT HOLLOW ROAD

LEFT: THE BEECH-SIMMONS CEMETERY ON PEYTONSVILLE-TRINITY ROAD

RIGHT: THE JOHN T. GENTRY CEMETERY ON PEYTONSVILLE-TRINITY ROAD

LEFT: THE PEYTONSVILLE METHODIST CHURCH CEMETERY

RIGHT: THE GEORGE WASHINGTON KING CEMETERY ON GOSEY HILL ROAD

LEFT: THE JAMES GOSEY CEMETERY ON GOSEY HILL ROAD, BEHIND THE NEW SCHOOL

RIGHT: THE GARNER MCCONNICO JORDAN CEMETERY ON COOL SPRINGS ROAD, NEXT TO THE BUFORD HOME, TAKEN BY RICK WARWICK SOON AFTER IT WAS CLEANED

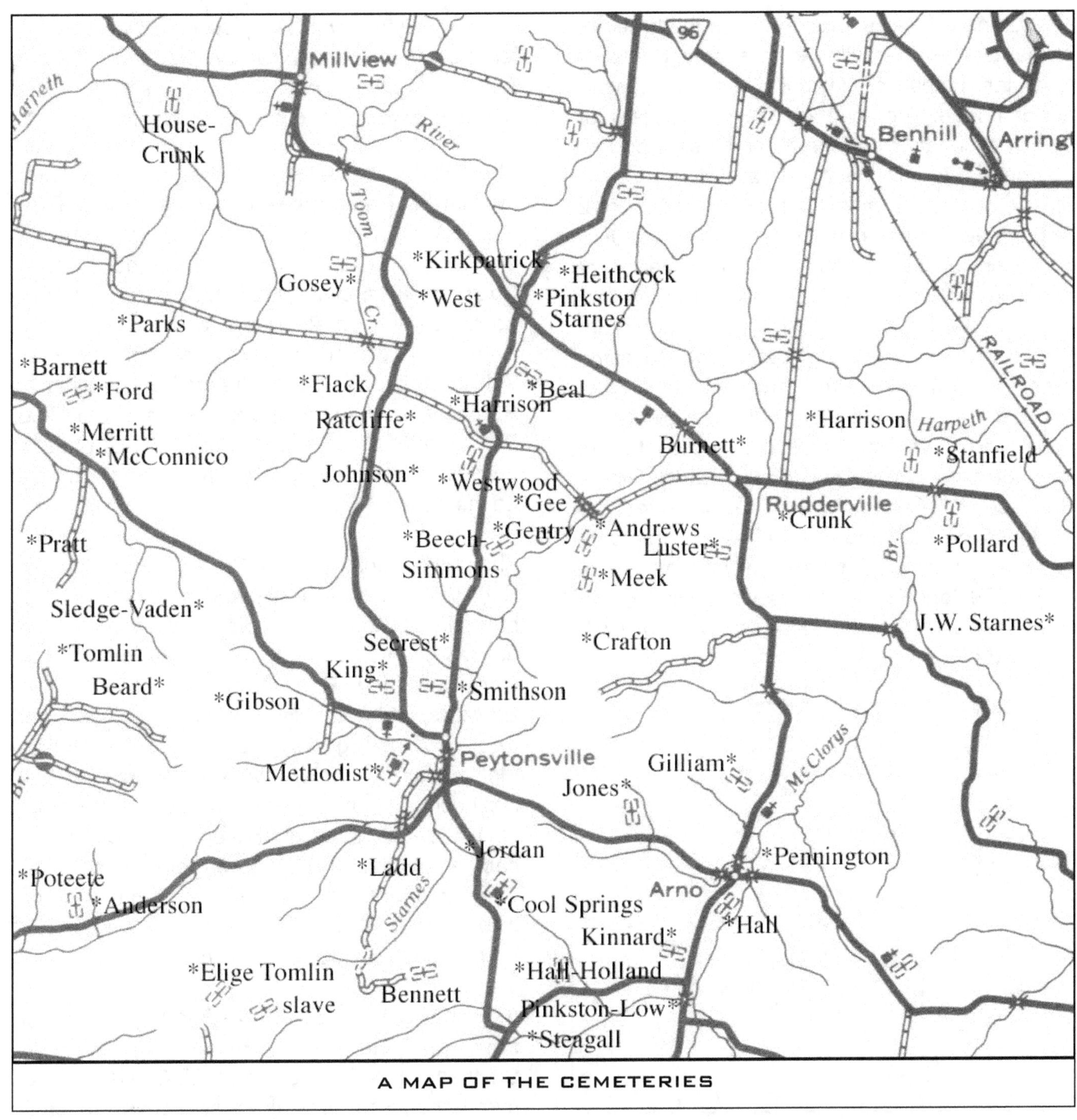


## BUSINESSES AND VARIOUS OCCUPATIONS IN THE 13TH

Every community seems to have had at least one country store at its crossroads. Often times, the community's post office was located in that store. In times past, each community had at least one, and sometimes two blacksmith shops. When flocks of sheep were kept by local farmers, there may have been a building used to card the wool, grade it, put it in bales and then send it to market. According to the U.S. Census, as early as 1850, Peytonsville had all these. The 1878 Beers map shows a cotton gin owned by M.G. Gosey in the village. Also, George Crunk had a cotton gin in the Rudderville community.

The late Bud Smithson had in his possession an account book dating back to 1835, which detailed the business of wool-carding, tobacco

71

sales, whiskey sales, groceries and the breeding of mares at Peytonsville. Interestingly, Snatchett is written instead of Peytonsville at the heading of each page. The June 27, 1835 entry [as seen below] accounts for Richard Tanner's 34 pounds of wool made into white rolls at a cost of $3.40 and 19 pounds of mixed-color wool at $2.371/2. Apparently, the book originally belonged to John Smithson, Jr. (1775-1838), who recorded large quantities of tobacco purchased by his son Sylvanus W. Smithson, Bud's great-grandfather. On October 8, 1835, Smithson made a list of mares covered by his stud horse, "Davy Crockett", in the spring of 1835. The owners of the mares were listed and, if a successful colt was born, the stud fee was $5.00. Patrick Gibson Smithson, Sylvanus's son, took over the business on November 7, 1844, so the book indicates. Interestingly, at the bottom of the page, "Peytonsville 1836", is written instead of Snatchett. This was the year Peytonsville received a post office.

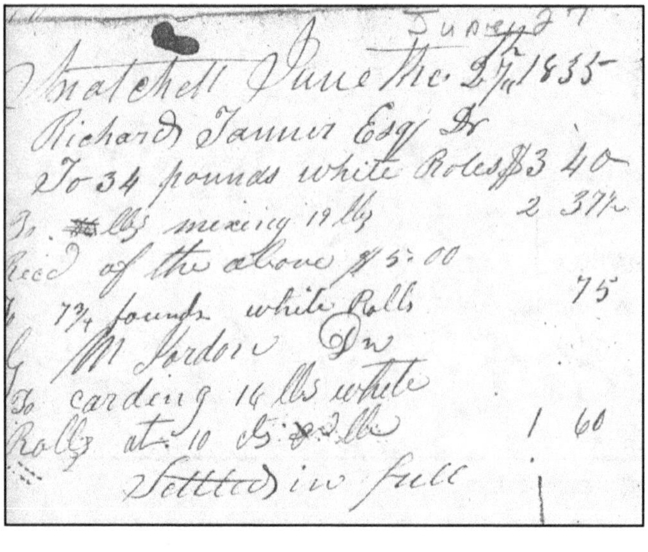
Snatchett June the 27th 1835
Richard Tanner Esq Dr
To 34 pounds white Roles $3 40
To lbs mixing 19 lbs 2 37½
Recd of the above $5:00
7¾ pounds white Rolls 75
M Jordon Dr
To carding 16 lbs white
Rolls at 10 cts pr lb 1 60
Settled in full

**The *Western Weekly Review* on December 18, 1835, carried this announcement:**

*New Tanning Establishment-the undersigned having lately commenced the tanning business at Peytonsville, (formerly known as Snatchet) on the road from Franklin to Harpeth Lick in Williamson County would respectfully inform the public that they are prepared to carry on the business in all its various branches. They will purchase hides at the highest customary prices of the country and will pay in either cash or leather. They will also tan on the shares at one half for the other. They respectfully solicit a share of public patronage. Gibson and Cook.*

The 1850 census listed Moses G. Gosey and William C. Parks as woolcarders; Jacob Rich, Robert Rich and John W. Osborne as blacksmiths; John B. Crichlow as a merchant; C. Smithson as a clerk in Crichlow's store and as postmaster; Conrad Hicks as a tailor; John Andrews and John McGuire as cabinetmakers; William Andrews, Henry Steagell and William P. Robinson as wagonmakers; Dr. Alexander Reid, Dr. James M. Critz and Dr. James W. Starnes as physicians and George W. Layne and Demarcus Layne as teachers.

The 1860 census listed Dr. A.R. Pinkston, Dr. E.J. Pinkston, and Dr. Alexander Reid as physicians; Moses G. Gosey and Thomas Helm as merchants; J.M. Nevils as a clerk; C.M. Comstock and R.J. Odle as teachers; S.T. Edwards, John L. Hall, William Robinson and and J.V. Bugg as tobacconists; William McGinness as sadler; William Poynor and L.G. Heithcock as shoemakers; James Robinson and H.W. Steagall as wagonmakers; John Batey as a cabinetmaker; J.R. Holt as a stonemason; M.W. Gray as a Methodist minister; and Andrew Cook, J.S. Parrish, J.A. Barnes, H.L. Edwards, R.L. Pollard and George White as carpenters.

Skipping to the 1900 census, we find Dr. Robert Low, physician; Rev. Felix Johnson; E.K. Smithson, H.L Thomas, and T.L.G. Harrison as merchants; Sam L. Graham as a clerk; Enoch R. Chest and Mary L. Shannon as teachers; Jackson Southern as mail-carrier; Boney Stanfield and Spy M. Stanfield as stone masons; George King, Dan Kinnard, James Graves and James W. Beard as blacksmiths; Charlie Waddy, William T. Hall and Reece Mills as carpenters; and Mack Roberts as tollgate-keeper.

The 1910 census listed Walter J. Parks as teacher; Brice Hughes and Perkins H. Crunk as traders; Henry T. Warren, Hyman Korman and

Aaron Frank as merchants, George Marion King and Thomas Stevens as blacksmiths; and Henry Tomlin as a salesman.

Interestingly, Hyman Korman and his father-in-law Aaron Frank were Jewish merchants who lived in the village of Peytonsville in 1910 and 1911 before folding their tent and moving back north. Their store seems to be east of the old Church of Christ building and west of Richard Poteete's home. Korman sold the house and store to Henry Tomlin for $500 in 1911.

T.L.G. Harrison (1838-1918) lived on the east side of the Methodist Church, where Marvin Tomlin later lived, and, according to the 1900 census, Harrison operated a store in the village. Most likely, the store was next to his home and near the Methodist church.

The corner of Peytonsville Road and Gosey Hill Road appears to have had a store in that location for over a hundred years. In recent memory, Percy and Hazel Simmons Bruce were the last to operate the store, after Marvin and Nell Tomlin served the community there for many years. The store building was owned by Mrs. Lela Maud Williams Warren Spears, who lived west of the Methodist Church. Mrs. Spears's first husband, J.A. Warren, acquired the store from his father, Henry T. Warren for $100 in 1920. H.T. Warren bought the store site from W.L. McCall for $255 in 1909. Whether W.L. McCall operated a store here is lost to history.

At the intersection of Peytonsville-Trinity Road and the Peytonsville-Franklin Road, R. W. and Odell Pate Glenn operated the Glenn Store after J.M. Warren. In 1945, the Glenn's purchased the store from Jesse Marshall and Elizabeth Warren, who had owned the store since 1928. J.M. Warren was an amazing merchant, who was blind, yet he operated the business without help. He also served in the Tennessee General Assembly from 1933-1937 and gave up the village store to manage the lunchroom in the Tennessee Capitol.

In 1928, J.M. Warren purchased the store from J.B. Mathis, Jr. In 1911, Mr. Mathis and his wife, Mollie, purchased one acre for $333.33 from Joe G. Vaden and his wife, Ophelia Smithson Vaden. Ophelia was the daughter of Nathaniel N. Smithson, who in 1898 paid $2,000 for 214 ½ acres from her brothers, John and E.K. Smithson, for the old Smithson homeplace, today, the home of Ronny Mangrum. A 1901 photograph shows a group of locals standing in front of the Smithson's Store. The store appears to be new and not the 1836 store John Smithson, Jr. or Patrick Gipson Smithson operated. Most likely, it was the store E.K. Smithson operated before he left Peytonsville and moved to Arno in 1893.

The old Glenn's store has been replaced with a new building in 1987, which services the local trade and travelers on 840. A short-order cook provides breakfast, lunch and supper for those on-the-go. Multiple gas pumps have replaced the single pump with a hand-crank used to pump the gas up to a bubble and released into the tank by gravity-flow.

BRUCE'S STORE, CORNER OF GOSEY HILL ROAD

BUD AND HAZEL BRUCE AWAIT

PERCY "BUD" BRUCE AND TRUCK

PERCY "BUD" BRUCE AND MULES

BRUCE'S STORE, READY TO SERVE

JACKIE, JIMMY, WAYNE BRUCE & JIMMY
MAXWELL AT BRUCE'S STORE

BEN TOMLIN AND ALLEN BRUCE SIT ON
THE STEPS OF BRUCE'S STORE

E.K. SMITHSON

MARY ELLEN AND TOMMY GLENN SHOW
A 1901 PHOTO OF THE STORE

MAY ELLEN (CLARK) AND TOMMY GLENN WITH LOCAL CUSTOMERS

HAZEL AND PERCY BRUCE AT GAS PUMPS

MOSES AND MARY BRUCE OPERATED A SMALL COUNTRY STORE ON THE PEYTONSVILLE-TRINITY ROAD, A COUPLE OF MILES EAST OF THE VILLAGE, IN THE MID-20TH CENTURY. ONLY A FEW FOUNDATION STONES MARK THE SPOT OF ITS LOCATION

PATSY SKINNER, CAROLYN SIMMONS, BILLY TOMLIN, JUDY BRUCE, RICKY POTEETE, WAYNE BRUCE, JACKIE BRUCE ON THE STEPS AT BRUCE'S STORE

LOCAL MEN IN FRONT OF SMITHSON'S STORE IN 1901

PEYTONSVILLE'S GLENN'S GROCERY IN 2021

Election Day, August 4, 1912 in Peytonsville: 1st row: Felix Bennett, Doc Gee, Bob Jackon & son, Buford, Patton Jackson & son, Dick, Ennis Bennett, Hugh Bennett, T. Wray, Ella McMahan, Andrew Warren, Will Scruggs, Haley Hall, Prentice Warren, unknown, Paul House, and unknown, (3 boys: Lincoln Bennett, unknown, Sam Bennett) 2nd row; Will Graves, Jason Harper, Phil Bennett, Israel Veech, Henry Warren, Ewen Hartley, Ed Warren, Ollie Lillard. Zeed Mathis, John Nevils, Billy Dotson, Henry Simmons, Willy Nevils, Eural Ladd, Richard Tomlin, Sam Burgress, unknown, Bill Ladd, Will Fay McCall, and Jocky Bill Poteete, back row John Waddey, Byrant Dodd, Lee Gardner, Earley Davis, John Crunk, Fieldon Glenn, Ira Waddey, Dick Waddey, Elijah Tomlin, Cal Mathis, Doctor Graham, Howard Nevils, Joe Harrison, Modey Harrison, Jhnny Tomlin, Henry Simmons, Greeny Hartley, Jent Jones

THIS PHOTOGRAPH CAME FROM STELLA SMITHSON LADD (MRS. W.P. LADD) WHOSE GRANDFATHER, T.L.G. HARRISON, OPERATED THE STORE ON THE LEFT AND OWNED THE BLACKSMITH SHOP ON THE RIGHT. IT IS BELIEVED THE MAN IN FRONT OF THE MULE IS GEORGE MARION KING, THE VILLAGE BLACKSMITH.

Since Rudderville and Arno were once part of the 13th District, it seems appropriate to include these neighbors to this. Rudderville may have had a store as early as 1888, since W.T. Ridley was the postmaster there, followed by John P. Tanner and William J. Jordan in 1894 to 1904. In 1906, James Newton Akin and his brother-in-law Sylvanus Andrew Smithson bought the general store and ran it for fifty-five years. Then it was operated by Van Smithson, followed by Howard Parks Smithson, Sr., who ran it or another twenty-three years. The blacksmith shop near the store was run by J.W. Culberson, who also ran the gas-powered gristmill. At the intersection of Arno and Meeks Road, we find another general store operated by Walter Smith and Louis Parrish, later operated by Robert and Jimmy White. The feed mill was added about 1960.

The Rudderville community had three resident physicians. Dr. Alexander R. Pinkston (1826-1904) lived on the Peytonsville-Trinity Road on what was later the Jim Crowell farm. He is buried with his wife Camelia Augusta Starnes on the farm, along with the Samuel Starnes family. Dr. John W. Hatcher (1855-1929), son of Spotwood H. and Mary Jane Andrews Hatcher, grew up on Gosey Hill Road and Long Lane. He graduated from Vanderbilt Medical School and served his community for many years. Dr. J.J. Covington (1845-1918), son of William F. and Margaret D. Covington, lived on the Eudailey-Covington Road, serving both Rudderville and College Grove. He graduated from Vanderbilt Medical School in 1897.

DR. A.R. PINKSTON

DR. JOHN W. HATCHER

DR. JAMES J. COVINGTON

BEULAH, SYLVANUS, HOWARD SMITHSON, J.N. AND MAMIE SMITHSON AKIN, MATTIE PARKS SMITHSON IN FRONT OF THE SMITHSON-AKIN STORE ON ARNO ROAD IN 1913

SMITHSON STORE AT RUDDERVILLE ON ARNO ROAD

SMITHSON'S DELIVERY TRUCK

LEFT: ROBERT AND JIMMY WHITE'S STORE AND FEED MILL AT ARNO ROAD AND MEEKS ROAD

RIGHT: E.K. SMITHSON'S STORE AND ARNO POST OFFICE, AT THE INTERSECTION OF ARNO ROAD AND HARPETH-PEYTONSVILLE-COLLEGE GROVE ROAD

Arno is located at the intersection of Arno Road and the road connecting Harpeth, Peytonsville and College Grove. Robert Low may have had a store there as early as 1890, when the community got a post office. E.K. Smithson left Peytonsville in 1893 and moved to Arno. His store remained the center of the community until it burned in 1982. Dr. Walter W. Graham (1868-1928) lived across the road from the store and served the neighborhood until his death.

At one time, Williamson County was a large producer of mules. The mating of a jack with a mare produces mules, which were in great demand before the advent of tractors. E.K. Smithson, besides being a merchant at Peytonsville and Arno, also produced mules. He is proudly showing off his prized jack "Brigham Young" in the following photograph provided by his grandson, Frank Woodruff Smithson.

E.K. SMITHSON WITH BRIGHAM YOUNG, HIS PRIZED JACK

## THE BATTLE OF SNATCH (PEYTONSVILLE)

**From Hale and Merritt Vo. III. Page 658)**

There was a company of guerrillas in Williamson County who rendered the women and non-combatant citizens of Southern sympathies much protection during a part of the war. In Ridley's "Battle and Sketches," the story an adventure he calls the Battle of Snatch is related. He explains that Snatch, now Peytonsville, was a hamlet in Williamson County. General Morgan's cavalry was stationed at Liberty, and General Forrest's at Columbia, when Bragg's army was at Tullahoma. The commands of these two generals guarded for a time the left and right outposts of the army of Tennessee. An order came to a lieutenant in Morgan's cavalry (George Ridley, now of Florence, Texas) from the general commanding to select ten picked men to go by way of Alexandria, Lebanon, and Goodlettsville, and as near to Edgefield (East Nashville) as practicable and send a messenger to Nashville to ascertain the location of the Federals, their force, and the approaches. It was but little trouble always to find some woman of southern blood who was not only willing but glad to do anything to promote the Southern cause. Accordingly, the scouts pursued their way across the Cumberland, near Payne's Ferry, and found a trusty young lady for the mission. They scattered in the vicinity until her return. In twelve hours, she came back with a complete diagram of the Federal works around Nashville, with the location of every regiment and battery, and the exact force. Lieutenant Ridley started back posthaste for Liberty, but to his astonishment, found out that General John T. Wilder, with a large force of Federal cavalry, had marched from Murfreesboro by way of Lebanon and was then on his way via Alexandria to meet Morgan at Liberty. He changed his course and started for Columbia to report to Forrest.

Reaching a two-story frame farmhouse in the vicinity of Snatch at nightfall, he sent an orderly sergeant to the house to seek a guide, making his approach through a lawn. A lady came to the door and said there was no one who could act as guide although the sergeant had seen a man on the premises. It was a time when the citizen could not readily distinguish a Federal from a Confederate by his dress, for when a Confederate captured a Federal, he invariably took his prisoner's overcoat. The Federals were killing many of those caught on suspicion, and it behooved the citizens to be wary. The sergeant assured her they were rebel scouts trying to reach Columbia, but she was skeptical, and was not moved when the lieutenant approached and made the same assurance. She slammed the door on the scouts, and hollered to her girls, occupying the second floor, the "ring the bell and blow the horn." The command was obeyed, while the scouts continued to parley for a guide.

For quite awhile the ringing and blowing continued, and at last Lieutenant Ridley heard the pattering gallop of horses. He suspected an attack, and he and his scouts made ready to receive it. Horses were mounted and navies drawn. They were charged by a company. A running fire ensued for miles. The forest was dense, however, and after two hours of excitement they evaded the pursuers. Near dawn they discovered another farmhouse across open fields. Cautiously they approached, and the speaker announcing that they were seeking a guide, a voice inside called with some excitement: "Marthy Ann, ring the bell." Again, the clatter of hoof-beats on the road, and again a running battle, in which the pursuers escaped.

In the forenoon, sometime Lieutenant Ridley met an acquaintance who had been to see a friend in the Confederate service. After having told the scouts they were on the road to Columbia, he explained the mystery of the horn-blowing and bell-ringing. It was a signal the southern sympathizers gave Cross's guerrillas on the appearance or suspected appearance of Federals in the neighborhood.

| Name | District | | | | |
|---|---|---|---|---|---|
| Andrews, John | 13 | 3 | $ 2,900 | 223 | $ 8,475 |
| Allen, John estate | 13 | | | | $ 100 |
| Andrews, Alphonzo | 13 | 3 | $ 3,400 | 238 | $ 7,185 |
| Andrews, Samuel | 13 | 2 | $ 2,200 | 207 | $ 5,305 |
| Allen, James estate | 13 | | | 65 | $ 780 |
| Allen, James W. | 13 | | | | $ 300 |
| Boyd, John O. | 13 | 2 | $ 1,900 | 80 | $ 3,100 |
| Boyd, J.W. estate | 13 | 2 | $ 1,900 | 154 | $ 5,680 |
| Boyd, J.F. | 13 | 1 | $ 1,200 | | $ 1,200 |
| Beard, Louis | 13 | | | | |
| Beech, R.W. | 13 | 1 | $ 300 | 115 | $ 1,475 |
| Buchanan, J | 13 | 3 | $ 2,800 | 150 | $10,050 |
| Buchanan, J.P. | 13 | | | | |
| Boyd & Long | 13 | | | | $ 150 |
| Buchanan, T.P. | 13 | | | 54 | $ 1,620 |
| Corzine, Elizabeth | 13 | | | | $ 331 |
| Crenshaw, C.A. | 13 | | | | $ 50 |
| Crowder, J.J. | 13 | 4 | $ 3,600 | 124 | $ 5,460 |
| Cordal, Elizabeth | 13 | | | 100 | $ 1,200 |
| Crunk, richard | 13 | 1 | $ 900 | 235 | $ 4,125 |
| Crafton, Dennis M. | 13 | | | 330 | $ 9,900 |
| Dobson, Eli | 13 | 7 | $ 6,000 | 329 | $12,911 |
| Dalton, M.H. | 13 | 10 | $ 9,600 | | $ 9,600 |
| Edwards, P.T. | 13 | | | | $ 300 |
| Edwards, S.T. | 13 | | | | |
| Gray, Robert | 13 | | | 245 | $ 4,900 |
| Gosey, E.S.B. | 13 | 6 | $ 6,300 | 231 | $11,120 |
| Gosey, M.N. | 13 | 2 | $ 1,700 | 89 | $ 2,735 |
| Gee, N.W. estate | 13 | | | 50 | $ 800 |
| Gibson, J.B. | 13 | 4 | $ 3,650 | | $ 9,913 |
| Gardner, J.L. | 13 | | | | |
| Gee, J.M. | 13 | | | | $ 624 |
| Gray, James | 13 | | | | |
| Gray, John | 13 | | | | |
| Gray, R.D. | 13 | | | | |
| Gibson, J.W. | 13 | 1 | $ 1,100 | | $ 1,100 |
| Gardner, P.C. | 13 | | | | |
| Harrison, S.K. | 13 | 1 | $ 700 | 220 | $ 4,000 |
| Helm, John C. | 13 | 1 | $ 900 | | $ 900 |
| Helm, Thomas | 13 | 5 | $ 4,100 | 256 | $ 7,940 |
| Heathcock, M.C. | 13 | | | | |
| Heathcock, L.S. | 13 | | | | |
| Hazelwood, M.E. | 13 | | | | $ 384 |
| Helm & Gray | 13 | | | | $ 100 |
| Hatcher, John estate | 13 | 7 | $ 5,200 | 353 | $10,848 |

| Name | | | | | |
|---|---|---|---|---|---|
| Harris, Samuel | 13 | | | 175 | $ 2,800 |
| Hatcher, A.W. | 13 | 2 | $ 2,200 | | $ 2,400 |
| Hall, J.G. | 13 | 3 | $ 2,600 | 390 | $10,400 |
| Hale, Thomas I. | 13 | | | | |
| Helm, F.M. | 13 | | | | |
| Heathcock, L.G. | 13 | | | | |
| Hatcher, T.L. | 13 | 1 | $ 1,000 | 135 | $ 3,155 |
| Hatcher, L.H. | 13 | 1 | $ 1,000 | 133 | $ 3,095 |
| Jordan, G.M. | 13 | 15 | $14,400 | 345 | $20,070 |
| Johnson, Gregory | 13 | | | 166 | $ 4,150 |
| Johnson, E.M. | 13 | | | | |
| Johnson, W.L. | 13 | | | 58 | $   870 |
| Jarrett, W.A. | 13 | | | | |
| Johnson, Jesse | 13 | | | | |
| Johnson, Wilson | 13 | | | 167 | $ 4,175 |
| Jones, William | 13 | 2 | $ 2,200 | 172 | $ 4,780 |
| Jones heirs | 13 | | | 133 | $ 1,995 |
| Jones, Judith estate | 13 | | | 55 | $   925 |
| Johnson, J.A. | 13 | | | 40 | $ 1,000 |
| Kennedy, Rachel | 13 | | | 50 | $ 1,000 |
| Kinnard, G.G. | 13 | 4 | $ 4,200 | 208 | $ 8,260 |
| Knight, Sarah | 13 | 4 | $ 3,500 | | $ 3,500 |
| Kinnard, N.C. | 13 | | | | $ 1,831 |
| Kinnard, A.E. | 13 | | | | $ 1,895 |
| Kinnard, F.V. | 13 | | | | $ 1,818 |
| Kinnard, N.c. | 13 | 9 | $ 8,400 | | $ 8,400 |
| Long, George | 13 | | | 41 | $ 1,625 |
| Lester, G.F. | 13 | | | 56 | $ 1,120 |
| Lamb, B.F. | 13 | | | | |
| Low, Gabriel | 13 | 9 | $ 9,300 | 274 | $14,615 |
| Maxwell, Elmira | 13 | | | 273 | $ 6,825 |
| Merritt, H.J. | 13 | | | | $   500 |
| McGinnis, William | 13 | | | | |
| McGuire, William | 13 | | | | |
| McGuire, S.B. | 13 | | | | |
| Nichol, Allen estate | 13 | 3 | $ 2,400 | 88 | $ 3,700 |
| Nichol, F.S. | 13 | | | | |
| Nevils, J.M. | 13 | | | | |
| Nevils, V.R. | 13 | | | | $   530 |
| Osborn, J.W. | 13 | | | | |
| Osburn, R.E.D. | 13 | | | 86 | $ 1,290 |
| Osburn, J.T. | 13 | | | | |
| Petway, W.J. | 13 | 8 | $ 7,600 | 249 | $17,744 |
| Pinkston, Francis | 13 | 2 | $ 1,900 | 123 | $ 4,400 |
| Pinkston, E.T. | 13 | | | | |
| Parks, W.C. | 13 | | | | |

| Name | | | | | |
|---|---|---|---|---|---|
| Pennington, W.P. | 13 | | | | |
| Pennington, C.S. | 13 | 1 | $ 1,000 | 260 | $ 6,200 |
| Pennington, C.N. | 13 | | | | $ 780 |
| Parrish, J.S. | 13 | | | | |
| Parks, B.F. | 13 | | | | |
| Parks, W.B. | 13 | | | 100 | $ 1,500 |
| Pinkston, A.R. | 13 | 6 | $ 5,200 | 308 | $11,745 |
| Pinkston, F.M. | 13 | 2 | $ 2,400 | | $ 2,550 |
| Patton, Lucy | 13 | | | 195 | $ 5,850 |
| Parrish, William | 13 | 15 | $15,000 | 586 | $28,115 |
| Reid, Alexander | 13 | 2 | $ 2,100 | 194 | $ 5,655 |
| Redmond, B.O. | 13 | 4 | $ 4,300 | 100 | $ 5,875 |
| Ray, C.S. | 13 | | | | |
| Redmond, Young | 13 | 31 | $30,000 | 482 | $45,460 |
| Rucks, J.J. | 13 | | | | |
| Smithson, C.W. | 13 | | | | $ 500 |
| Smithson, W.O. | 13 | | | | |
| Scruggs, J.H. | 13 | | | | |
| Smithson, C.G. | 13 | 1 | $ 900 | 74 | $ 2,720 |
| Smithson, W.J. | 13 | | | | $ 1,170 |
| Sledge, J.W. | 13 | | | | |
| Smithson, T.S. | 13 | 2 | $ 2,100 | 166 | $ 6,825 |
| Smithson, N.N. | 13 | 1 | $ 900 | 226 | $ 6,360 |
| Sledge, Robert | 13 | | | 83 | $ 664 |
| Sledge, Daniel | 13 | | | 22 | $ 330 |
| Smithson, P.G. | 13 | | | | $ 25 |
| Shelburn, Pettus | 13 | 10 | $ 9,700 | 340 | $19,800 |
| Shelburn, J.M. | 13 | 3 | $ 2,800 | | $ 4,040 |
| Steagall, H.W. | 13 | | | | |
| Steagall, Samuel | 13 | | | 70 | $ 1,436 |
| Stokes, J.E. | 13 | | | | |
| Smithson, S.W. | 13 | 4 | $ 2,900 | 372 | $ 9,080 |
| Starnes, S.S. | 13 | 5 | $ 5,200 | 211 | $ 8,465 |
| Starnes, E. | 13 | 5 | $ 400 | | $ 6,786 |
| Starnes, J.W. | 13 | 22 | $22,200 | 1,582 | $72,335 |
| Secrest, Isaac | 13 | 6 | $ 5,260 | 228 | $15,388 |
| Taylor, R. estate | 13 | | | | $ 400 |
| Taylor, S.J. | 13 | 1 | $ 1,000 | | $ 1,700 |
| Tulloss, P. | 13 | 1 | $ 900 | | $10,140 |
| Vaden, C.A. | 13 | | | | |
| Vaden, W.H. | 13 | | | 112 | $ 1,820 |
| West, I.W.P. | 13 | 4 | $ 3,400 | 157 | $ 8,310 |
| West, Sarah G. | 13 | 2 | $ 350 | 127 | $ 5,525 |
| Williams, William | 13 | | | | |
| Williams, F.W. | 13 | | | | |
| Williams, J. estate | 13 | 4 | $ 4,300 | 104 | $ 5,860 |

| Yarborough, W.J. | 13 | 2 | $ 2,100 | $ 2,900 |
| Young, M.A. | 13 | 1 | $ 1,000 | $ 1,000 |
| Young, John | 13 | | | |

## 1850 CENSUS FOR THE 13TH DISTRICT

# 543 (Overseer)

| William Walton | | 40 m Tenn. |
| Nancy | " | 35 f Tenn. |
| James | " | 12 m Tenn. |
| John | " | 10 m Tenn. |
| Thomas | " | 5 m Tenn. |
| Nancy | " | 3 f Tenn. |

# 544 (Farmer)

| Anthony Lavender | | 46 m Va. |
| Parabe | " | 35 f Tenn. |
| Poindexter J. Lavender | | 13 m Tenn. |
| Virginia R. | " | 11 f Tenn. |
| Emaline E. | " | 9 f Tenn. |
| Delila P. | " | 7 f Tenn. |
| Richard B. | " | 4 m Tenn. |
| Gustavus A. | " | 1 m Tenn. |

# 545 (Farmer)

| Thomas Anderson | | 57 m N.C. |
| Sarah A. | " | 43 f N.C. |
| Marinda | " | 30 f Tenn. |
| Robert | " (Farmer) | 23 m Tenn. |
| Mary | " | 16 f Tenn. |
| William | " | 14 m Tenn. |
| Nancy | " | 12 f Tenn. |
| Martha | " | 10 f Tenn. |
| Frances | " | 8 f Tenn. |
| Ophelia | " | 6 f Tenn. |
| Octavia | " | 4 f Tenn. |

# 546

| Susan Pettus | | 77 f Va. |
| Thomas | " (Teacher) | 23 m Ala. |

# 547 (Farmer)

| Thomas B. Spratt | | 24 m Tenn. |
| Sarah | " | 19 f Tenn. |

# 548

| Frederick Fisher | | 40 m Va. |
| Lucy | " | 28 f Tenn. |
| Robert | " | 13 m Tenn. |
| Henry C. | " | 6 m Tenn. |

# 549

| Nelson Lavender, Jr. | | 38 m Va. |
| Parmelia | " | 36 f Tenn. |
| Nancy N. | " | 17 f Tenn. |
| Tobitha A. Lavender | | 15 f Tenn. |
| Mary E. | " | 13 f Tenn. |
| Margaret | " | 11 f Tenn. |
| Alexander | " | 9 m Tenn. |
| Lafayette | " | 8 m Tenn. |

# 549

| Caledonia V. Lavender | | 3 f Tenn. |

# 550 (Farmer)

| Blythe Spratt | | 58 m N.C. |
| Martha | " | 27 f Tenn. |
| Rachael M. Spratt | | 21 f Tenn. |
| Mary E. | " | 18 f Tenn. |
| William H. | " | 15 m Tenn. |
| Zarilda A.C. | " | 12 f Tenn. |

Dwellings 125     Families 125

White males     328
White females   334
                662

Slaves, male    151
Slaves, female  199
                350

Deaths  10          Farms  81

Pages*  26

<u>District #13    September 23, 1850</u>

Page 279

# 551 (Farmer)

| William H. (?) Baden | | 44 m Ga. |
| Martha | " | 44 f Va. |
| Charles Baden (Farmer) | | 17 m Tenn. |
| Mary | " | 15 f Tenn. |
| Catherine Baden | | 12 f Tenn. |
| Martha | " | 9 f Tenn. |
| Nathaniel | " | 7 m Tenn. |
| William | " | 5 m Tenn. |

# 552 (Farmer)

| Thomas Holme | | 65 m Va. |
| Elizabeth Holme | | 50 f N.Y. |
| John C. Holme (Farmer) | | 24 m Tenn. |

# 553 (Farmer)

| James Holme | | 69 m Va. |
| Susanna | " | 70 f N.C. |
| Susan Cochran | | 14 f Tenn. |

# 554

| William Smithson | | 26 m Va. |
| Mary A. | " | 23 f Tenn. |

# 554
Jno. G. Smithson          2 m Tenn.
Sarah E.    "           6/12 f Tenn.

# 555 (Farmer)
Robert Carson            76 m Va.
Jane     "               53 f Va.
William  "               39 m Va.
James    "   (Farmer)    23 m Tenn.
Thomas   "               20 m Tenn.
Mary     "               18 f Tenn.
James Helme (Laborer)    15 m Tenn.

# 556
Parmelia M. Helme        40 f Tenn.
W.H. Helme (Laborer)     16 m Tenn.
J.P.    "                14 m Tenn.
David N. Helme           11 m Tenn.
Robert L.   "             9 m Tenn.
George B.   "             4 m Tenn.
P.O.        "             3 m Tenn.

# 557
Catharine Parrish        59 f Va.
William    "  (Farmer)   23 m Tenn.

# 558
Jno. S. Parrish          35 m N.C.
Mary      "              24 f Tenn.
Martha A.M. Parrish     9/12 f Tenn.

# 559 (Farmer)
Lundy L. Smithson        49 m Va.
Ann        "             46 f Va.

# 560
Parmelia Gibson          26 f Tenn.
Nathaniel Smithson       24 m Tenn.
Jno. B. Gibson            1 m Tenn.

# 561 (Farmer)
Sylvanus Smithson        35 m Va.
Mary J.     "            30 f Tenn.
Patrick     "            12 m Tenn.
James       "            10 m Tenn.
Benj.       "             8 m Tenn.
Sarah       "             5 f Tenn.
William     "             3 m Tenn.
John        "           4/12 m Tenn.
William Helme (Laborer)  16 m Tenn.

# 562 (Farmer)
M.W. Gee                 66 m Va.
Catharine Gee            60 f N.C.

# 562
Sally Gee                30 f Va.
Drury  "   (Farmer)      24 m Va.
George "                 21 m Va.
Elizabeth Gee            20 f Va.
J. Henry Marks           13 m Tenn.

# 563 (Farmer)
Samuel Harris            53 m Va.
Mary       "             59 f Va.
Eliza Walson             35 f Va.

# 564
Rebecca Harris           41 f Va.
Robert    "   (Farmer)   16 m Va.
James     "              14 m Va.
Sarah     "              12 f Va.
William   "              10 m Va.
Reuben    "               8 m Va.
John      "               6 m Va.
Susan     "               4 f Tenn.

# 565 (Farmer)
Bartholomew Crowder      65 m Va.
Elizabeth    "           41 f Va.
John C. Crowder (Farmer) 30 m Va.
Mary G. Hazlewood         9 f Tenn.

# 566 (Farmer)
C.W. Kinnard             28 m Tenn.
Martha V. Kinnard        22 f Tenn.
Adaline T.   "            4 f Tenn.

# 567
A.B. Kinnard             44 f Tenn.
M.M.    "  (Farmer)      19 m Tenn.
George G. Kinnard        16 m Tenn.
Susan C.      "          14 f Tenn.
Gabriella H.  "          12 f Tenn.
Newton C.     "          10 m Tenn.
Adaline E.    "           8 f Tenn.
Frances V.    "           6 f Tenn.

Page 280

# 568 (Farmer) (Overseer)
Holcomb P. Harvey        30 m Va.
Mary C.      "           30 f Va.
Rufus W.     "            6 m Va.
Mary E.      "            2 f Va.
Isham O.     "          2/12 m Va.

# 569 (Farmer)
Samuel Steigall          52 m Va.

# 569
Nancy Steigall                    49 f Va.
Eliza        "                    28 f Va.
Harry        "   (Wagon maker)    23 m Va.
Martha       "                    21 f Tenn.
Julia        "                    18 f Tenn.
Lucy         "                    16 f Tenn.
Mary         "                    13 f Tenn.
Thomas       "                    10 m Tenn.
William      "                     7 m Tenn.

# 570 (Farmer)
Samuel S. Allen                   35 m Tenn.
Jane C.        "                  33 f Tenn.
Sarah J.       "                  10 f Tenn.
William T.  "                      8 m Tenn.
Mary A.        "                   3 f Tenn.

# 571 (Farmer)
Robert Bigger                     30 m Tenn.
Elizabeth "                       35 f Tenn.
Mary         "                     8 f Tenn.
Cynthia A. Bigger                  6 f Tenn.
Clementine    "                    4 f Tenn.
William J.    "                    3 m Tenn.
Lucy          "                 6/12 f Tenn.

# 572 (Farmer)
Jno. R. Hatcher                   32 m Va.
Matilda F.  "                     27 f Va.
Mary C.       "                    5 f Tenn.
Wilson        "                    4 m Tenn.
Jno. M.       "                    2 m Tenn.
Lucy F.       "                 3/12 f Tenn.

# 573 (Farmer)
David Pinkston                    77 m N.C.
Frances    "                      53 f N.C.
George     "   (Farmer)           26 m Tenn.
Thomas     "                      25 m Tenn.
Ephraim T. Pinkston               23 m Tenn.
Turner         "                  21 m Tenn.
H.R. Pinkston (Physician)         22 m Tenn.
Adaline "                         17 f Tenn.

# 574 (Farmer)
John P. Smithson                  33 m Va.
Clarissa    "                     29 f Va.
Harriet E.T. Smithson              8 f Tenn.
O.P.             "                 6 m Tenn.
Thos. J.         "                 3 m Tenn.
Caroline V.      "                 1 f Tenn.

# 575 (Farmer)
C.L. Pennington                   60 m Va.
Susan       "                     59 f Va.
David       "   (Farmer)          24 m Tenn.
Martha      "                     21 f Tenn.
Charles     "   (Farmer)          19 m Tenn.
John        "                     11 m Tenn.

# 576 (Farmer)
William Pennington                29 m Tenn.
Jane         "                    23 f Tenn.

# 577 (Farmer)
Clemence Pennington               27 m Tenn.
Martha         "                  22 f Tenn.

# 578
Judith Jones                      60 f Va.
John B.  "   (Farmer)             36 m Ky.

# 579 (Farmer)
Robert Gray                       63 m Ky.
Martha   "                        50 f Va.
Joel A.  "   (Farmer)             22 m Tenn.
Sarah    "                        18 f Tenn.
Samuel   "                        20 m Tenn.
Frances  "                        15 f Tenn.
Robert   "                        12 m Tenn.
America  "                        11 f Tenn.

# 580 (Farmer)
James Gray                        32 m Tenn.
Mary A. "                         27 f Tenn.
Jno. W. "                         12 m Tenn.
David    "                        10 m Tenn.
Andrew   "                         8 m Tenn.
Nancy    "                         6 f Tenn.
Henry    "                         4 m Tenn.
Robert   "                         2 m Tenn.

# 581 (Farmer)
G.M. Jordan                       47 m Tenn.
Mary M. "                         45 f Tenn.
Elizabeth Jordan                  23 f Tenn.
William Petway (Farmer)           22 m Tenn.
Rebecca Jordan                    21 f Tenn.
Sarah J.  "                       20 f Tenn.
Nancy J.  "                       17 f Tenn.
John Petway (Student)             18 m Tenn.
Ann Eliza Jordan                  15 f Tenn.

Page 281


Susan Jordan                      13 f Tenn.

# 581
Garner Jordan     11 m Tenn.
Mary T.C. Jordan     1 f Tenn.

# 582 (Farmer)
Richard Hay     72 m Va.
Martha   "     64 f Va.

# 583
Polly Robertson     43 f Va.
Louisa   "     17 f Tenn.
Adaline   "     14 f Tenn.
Rebecca   "     11 f Tenn.
John   "  (Farmer)     17 m Tenn.

# 584 (Blacksmith)
Jacob Rich     32 m N.C.
Ann   "     35 f Va.
Catharine Rich     21 f Ala.
Elizabeth   "     19 f Ala.
Robert   "     17 m Tenn.
  (Blacksmith)
Sally C. Rich     15 f Tenn.
Granville   "     13 m Tenn.
Mary   "     8 f Tenn.
Jane   "     8 f Tenn.
Lucy Lane     18 f Tenn.
Benjamin Lane     14 m Tenn.
Eliza Rich     11 f Tenn.

# 584 (Farmer)
Pettus Shelburne     63 m Va.
Mary J.   "     56 f Va.
Nancy Crenshaw     78 f Va.
Martha   "     13 f Tenn.
America V. Crenshaw     11 f Tenn.
Henry J.   "     9 m Tenn.

# 585 (Farmer)
W.M. Kinney     96 m Va.
Rachel Kennedy     45 f N.C.
Eliaabeth Corsine     32 f Tenn.

# 586 (Merchant)
Henry S. Crichlow     40 m Tenn.
Martha A.   "     38 f Tenn.
Catharine   "     16 f Tenn.
Elizabeth   "     12 f Tenn.
John   "     8 m Tenn.
Nancy   "     1 f Tenn.

# 587 (None)
Richard Williamson     76 m Va.

# 588 (Merchant)
John B. Crichlow     30 m Tenn.
Martha J.   "     36 f Tenn.
Wm. B.   "     12 m Tenn.

# 589 (Clerk)
C. Smithson     37 m Tenn.

# 590 (Physician)
Alexander Reid     32 m Va.
Sarah   "     29 f Tenn.
Elizabeth Morpin     17 f Tenn.
Augustine Adridge     17 f Tenn.

# 591 (Taylor)
Conrad Hicks     42 m Prus.
Henry   "     4 m Tenn.
Mary E.   "     2 f Tenn.

# 592 (Woolcarder)
William C. Parkes     23 m Tenn.

# 593 (Woolcarder)
M.G. Gocey     35 m Tenn.
Mary   "     27 f Tenn.
Gentry   "     4 m Tenn.
Sarah   "     2 f Tenn.
Thomas   "     1 m Tenn.

# 594 (Farmer)
Nathl. B. Smithson     77 m Va.
William J.   "     33 m Tenn.
Polly   "     27 f Tenn.

# 595
Sarah W. Knight     76 f Va.
Coleman G. Smithson     31 m Tenn.
Celia   "     27 f Tenn.
James B.   "     5 m Tenn.
Mary A.   "     4 f Tenn.

# 596 (Farmer)
Issac Secrest     58 m N.C.

# 597
Tobitha Rhea     56 f N.C.
Jane Curd     30 f Ire.
Tobitha Curd     9 f Tenn.
Martha Rhea     22 f Tenn.
Malissa   "     20 f Tenn.
Susan   "     18 f Tenn.
Claiborne Rhea     17 m Tenn.
Mary   "     10 f Tenn.

# 597 (Farmer)
Stephen Smithson . . . . . . . . . . 53 m Va.
Sally      "     . . . . . . . . . . 54 f Va.
Elizabeth  "     . . . . . . . . . . 23 f Va.
Allen      "   (Farmer) . . . . . . 22 m Va.
Amanda     "     . . . . . . . . . . 20 f Va.
Martha     "     . . . . . . . . . . 16 f Va.
Jno.       "     . . . . . . . . . . 14 m Va.

# 598 (Farmer)
Daniel M. Walker . . . . . . . . . . 55 m Va.
Mary G.      "   . . . . . . . . . . 43 f Va.
Daniel M.    "   . . . . . . . . . .  3 m Tenn.
Lucy Westbrook . . . . . . . . . . . 25 f Va.

# 599 (Farmer)
William Cheatham . . . . . . . . . . 59 m Va.
     (Mulatto)

Page 282

Betsy Cheatham (Mulatto) . . . 30 f Va.
Sarah      "        "    . . . 13 f Tenn.
William E. Cheatham . . . . . . 11 m Tenn.
     (Mulatto)
Jas. C. Cheatham (Mulatto) . .  8 m Tenn.
Buley W.    "       "   . . . .  6 m Tenn.
John A.     "       "   . . . .  3 m Tenn.
Sally E. Evans (Mulatto) . . . 81 f Tenn.

# 600 (Farmer)
Thomas Chapman . . . . . . . . 43 m Tenn.
Catharine "  . . . . . . . . . 30 f Tenn.
Saml.     "  . . . . . . . . . 14 m Tenn.
Thomas J. "  . . . . . . . . . 12 m Tenn.
Tennessee "  . . . . . . . . .  9 f Tenn.
Caledonia "  . . . . . . . . .  4 f Tenn.
Meridith G. Chapman . . . . . .  1 m Tenn.

# 601 (Farmer)
Jesse Johnson . . . . . . . . . 46 m Va.
Dolly     "   . . . . . . . . . 38 f Va.
William L. Johnson . . . . . . 21 m Tenn.
     (Farmer)
John A. Johnson (Farmer) . . . 18 m Tenn.
Margaret     "   . . . . . . . 17 f Tenn.
Adeline V.   "   . . . . . . . 15 f Tenn.
Mary J.      "   . . . . . . . 13 f Tenn.
Martha P.    "   . . . . . . . 10 f Tenn.
Dolly S.     "   . . . . . . .  9 f Tenn.
L.L.         "   . . . . . . .  7 m Tenn.
Lucy         "   . . . . . . .  4 f Tenn.
Benj. M.     "   . . . . . . 6/12 m Tenn.

# 602 (Farmer)
John A. Merritt . . . . . . . . 44 m Tenn.
Ann        "    . . . . . . . . 40 f N.C.
Rebecca    "    . . . . . . . . 19 f Tenn.
Susan      "    . . . . . . . . 17 f Tenn.
Mary       "    . . . . . . . . 12 f Tenn.
Frances    "    . . . . . . . . 10 f Tenn.
Sarah      "    . . . . . . . .  8 f Tenn.

# 603 (Wagon Maker)
William Andrews . . . . . . . . 43 m Tenn.
William M.  "   . . . . . . . . 10 m Tenn.
John S.     "   . . . . . . . .  7 m Tenn.
Saml. M.    "  (Farmer) . . . . 23 m Tenn.

# 604
Bathenia Andrews . . . . . . . 45 f Va.
Alpheus V.  "  (Farmer) . . . . 29 m Tenn.
Thomas      "  (Farmer) . . . . 25 m Tenn.

# 605 (Cabinet Maker)
John Andrews . . . . . . . . . 36 m Tenn.
Manerva "    . . . . . . . . . 29 f Tenn.
Nancy R. Andrews . . . . . . .  9 f Tenn.
Mary E.     "   . . . . . . . .  5 f Tenn.
Lucy J.     "   . . . . . . . .  4 f Tenn.
John McGuin (McGuire?) . . . . 25 m Tenn.
     (Cabinet Maker)
Fidella Helme (Farmer) . . . . 23 m Tenn.
S.S. Mathews (Farmer) . . . . . 28 m Tenn.

# 606 (Farmer)
John Russell . . . . . . . . . 29 m Tenn.
Rosetta "    . . . . . . . . . 37 f Tenn.
Cynthia D. Russell . . . . . .  6 f Tenn.
V.C.T.       "   . . . . . . .  3 f Tenn.
Sarah C.     "   . . . . . 10/12 f Tenn.
Rhoda H.     "   . . . . . . . 26 f Tenn.

# 607 (Farmer)
Robert Sledge . . . . . . . . . 37 m Tenn.
Catharine "   . . . . . . . . . 39 f Tenn.
Mary L.   "   . . . . . . . . . 17 f Tenn.
John W.   "   . . . . . . . . . 14 m Tenn.
Nathl.    "   . . . . . . . . . 12 m Tenn.
Sarah E.  "   . . . . . . . . .  9 f Tenn.
Ann E.    "   . . . . . . . . .  5 f Tenn.

# 608 (Farmer)
James S. Gee . . . . . . . . . 35 m Va.
Martha J. "  . . . . . . . . . 37 f Va.
Mary A.   "  . . . . . . . . . 14 f Tenn.
Cornelia S. (?) Gee . . . . . 12 f Tenn.
James M.        "   . . . . . 10 m Tenn.

# 608
Martha J. Gee                         6 f Tenn.

# 609
William Jones                        28 m Tenn.
Ann E.P.    "                        22 f Tenn.
James       "                         6 m Tenn.
Martha      "                         4 f Tenn.
Ann E.      "                         2 f Tenn.

# 610 (Farmer)
James Allen                          64 m Va.
Mary      "                          57 f Va.
Aluezea ? Allen                      34 f Tenn.
Sarah J.    "                        24 f Tenn.
James W.    "                        19 m Tenn.

# 611
Eva (Era?) Nichol                    55 f S.C.
Allen T. Nichol (Farmer) 22 m Tenn.
Frederick S. Nichol                  15 m Tenn.
   (Farmer)
Mary J.S. Nichol                     12 f Tenn.

# 612
O.C. Hatcher                         33 m Tenn.
Caledonia Hatcher                    25 f Tenn.
Mary          "                       6 f Tenn.

Page 283

Oliver Hatcher                        4 m Tenn.
William   "                           2 m Tenn.

# 613 (Farmer)
Daniel Sledge                        45 m Tenn.
Celia      "                         45 f Tenn.

# 614 (Overseer)
Joseph Crunk                         32 m Tenn.
Scena?    "                          34 f Tenn.
Nicholas  "                           7 m Tenn.
John      "                           2 m Tenn.
Hardy     "                           1 m Tenn.

# 615 (Overseer)
John Allen                           37 m Tenn.
Lucind "                             34 f Tenn.
Mary   "                             13 f Tenn.
Martha "                             10 f Tenn.
Elizabeth Allen                       7 f Tenn.
Margaret    "                         5 f Tenn.

# 616
Peggy Walton                         45 f Tenn.
Jane Tignor                          22 f Tenn.
John   "                             12 m Tenn.

# 617
Matilda Smithson                     40 f Tenn.
Caroline    "                        14 f Tenn.
Susan       "                        10 f Tenn.

# 618 (Farmer)
John Patton                          61 m Ga.
George Maxwell (None)                24 m Tenn.

# 619
Elizabeth Corsine                    63 f N.C.

# 620
Naomi Wall                           37 f Tenn.
Cephus "                             10 m Tenn.
Jordan "                              7 m Tenn.
Alexander Wall                        7*m Tenn.

# 621 (Wagon Maker)
William P. Robinson                  43 m Ky.
Nancy        "                       32 f Tenn.
Caroline     "                       16 f Tenn.
Andrew       "                       12 m Tenn.
Frances      "                       10 f Tenn.
Ba'alam      "                        7 m Tenn.
Henry        "                        5 m Tenn.
Davis        "                        1 m Tenn.
James Stephenson                     10 m Tenn.
Andrew T.  "                          8 m Tenn.

# 622 (Farmer)
James McGuire                        64 m Va.
Rachel   "                           55 f Va.
Elizabeth McGuire                    38 f Tenn.
Jane       "                         30 f Tenn.
Rebecca    "                         28 f Tenn.
William    "                         18 m Tenn.
Saml.      "                         15 m Tenn.

# 623 (Farmer)
John Scruggs                         70 m Va.
Sarah   "                            58 f N.Y.

# 624 (Teacher)
Geo. W. Lane                         24 m Tenn.

# 625 (Farmer)
James Mangum                         27 m N.C.
Sarah E. "                           26 f N.C.

# 625
| Mary J. Mangum | 7 | f | Tenn. |
| W.H.           " | 5 | m | Tenn. |
| Nancy A.E. Mangum | 4 | f | Tenn. |
| Saml. J.       " | 2 | m | Tenn. |
| Jno. C.        " | 3/12 | m | Tenn. |

# 626 (Farmer)
| Thomas Wall | 23 | m | Tenn. |
| Mary     " | 37 | f | N.C. |

# 627 (Farmer)
| James Hughes | 30 | m | Tenn. |
| Martha     " | 26 | f | Tenn. |
| Elizabeth Hughes | 7 | f | Tenn. |
| William     " | 5 | m | Tenn. |
| Mary J.     " | 1 | f | Tenn. |

# 628 (Farmer)
| Richard Crunk | 36 | m | Tenn. |
| Nancy C.   " | 53 | f | Tenn. |
| Elizabeth S. Crunk | 13 | f | Tenn. |
| Mary S.     " | 11 | f | Tenn. |
| Seth L.*     " | 9 | m | Tenn. |
| George M.     " | 7 | m | Tenn. |
| John A.*E.     " | 5 | m | Tenn. |
| James N.     " | 3 | m | Tenn. |
| Richard T.     " | 2 | m | Tenn. |

# 629 (Farmer)
| Saml. Patton | 58 | m | Ga. |
| R.J.     " (Farmer) | 17 | m | Mo. |
| William Crunk | 5 | m | Tenn. |

# 630 (Physician)
| James M. Critz | 39 | m | Tenn. |
| Ann E.     " | 22 | f | Tenn. |
| Willie Ann " | 5 | f | Tenn. |
| Narcissa   " | 2 | f | Tenn. |

# 631 (Farmer)
| Richard Rudder | 62 | m | Va. |
| R.W. Hayes (Farmer) | 35 | m | Va. |

# 632 (Physician)
| James W. Stearns | 33 | m | N.C. |
| Mary C.     " | 24 | f | Tenn. |
| Cora       " | 3/12 | f | Tenn. |
| Elizabeth Haley | 4 | f | Tenn. |

Page 284

# 633 (Farmer)
| Jno. R.* Holt | 27 | m | Tenn. |

# 633
| Jane Holt | 24 | f | Va. |
| John J. Holt | 5 | m | Tenn. |
| Mary J.     " | 4 | f | Tenn. |
| William Zack Holt | 2 | m | Tenn. |

# 634 (Farmer)
| Josiah Nevils | 57 | m | Va. |
| Sarah     " | 49 | f | Va. |
| Martha     " | 20 | f | Tenn. |
| John M.   " (Farmer) | 18 | m | Tenn. |
| Watkins     " | 16 | m | Tenn. |
| Ann E.     " | 11 | f | Tenn. |
| Virginia " | 9 | f | Tenn. |
| Catharine J. Nevils | 6 | f | Tenn. |

# 635 (Farmer)
| Francis Tisdale | 24 | m | Tenn. |
| Emaline     " | 22 | f | Tenn. |
| Ellen       " | 2 | f | Tenn. |

# 636 (Overseer)
| Robert Lane | 32 | m | Tenn. |
| Susan A. Lane | 17 | f | Tenn. |
| Wm. J.       " | 3 | m | Tenn. |
| Albert       " | 2 | m | Tenn. |
| Parmelia F. Hogan | 16 | f | Tenn. |

# 637 (Farmer)
| W.R. Layne | 51 | m | Va. |
| Frances Layne | 26 | f | Tenn. |
| Damascus " (Teacher) | 23 | m | Tenn. |
| Washington Layne (Farmer) | 22 | m | Tenn. |
| John Layne (Student) | 21 | m | Tenn. |

# 638 (Farmer)
| William Warf | 40 | m | Va. |
| Sarah       " | 50 | f | N.C. |
| James R.   " (Farmer) | 17 | m | Va. |
| Roger A.   " | 15 | m | Va. |
| William T. Warf | 13 | m | Va. |
| Benj. S.     " | 11 | m | Tenn. |
| Edward P.     " | 8 | m | Tenn. |

# 639 (Farmer)
| Joseph Clark | 28 | m | Tenn. |
| James     " | 25 | m | Tenn. |

# 640 (Farmer)
| John Farmer | 60 | m | N.C. |
| Elizabeth Farmer | 21 | f | Tenn. |
| Benj. Farmer (Farmer) | 17 | m | Tenn. |
| Richard " | 5 | m | Tenn. |
| Susan   " | 3 | f | Tenn. |

| # 641 (Blacksmith) | | | # 648 (Laborer) | | |
|---|---|---|---|---|---|
| John W. Osborne | 67 m N.C. | | William Allen | 30 m Tenn. |
| Mary " | 54 f S.C. | | Sarah " | 27 f Tenn. |
| Jane " | 26 f Tenn. | | Turner " | 10 m Tenn. |
| David " (Farmer) | 27 m Tenn. | | John " | 8 m Tenn. |
| Eliza " | 24 f Tenn. | | | |
| Martha " | 22 f Tenn. | | Page 285 | |
| Rosanna " | 20 f Tenn. | | | |
| John T. " (Farmer) | 17 m Tenn. | | William Allen | 6 m Tenn. |
| Christina C. Osborne | 13 f Tenn. | | Sarah " | 4 f Tenn. |
| | | | Martha " | 2 f Tenn. |

# 642 (Farmer)

| N.L. Harrison | 41 m N.C. | | # 649 | |
| Christina Harrison | 39 f Va. | | Mary T. Crump | 34 f Tenn. |
| Saml. " | 19 m Tenn. | | Martha J. " | 12 f Tenn. |
| Arabella " | 15 f Tenn. | | George K. " | 8 m Tenn. |
| L.G. " | 12 m Tenn. | | John O.* " | 6 m Tenn. |
| W.H. " | 9 m Tenn. | | Ann M. " | 4 f Tenn. |
| Susan T. " | 7 f Tenn. | | Roena " | 2 f Tenn. |
| James G. " | 5 m Tenn. | | | |
| D. Jones " | 3 m Tenn. | | | |

Dwellings 99    Families 99

# 643 (Farmer)

| Thomas W. Pate | 22 m Tenn. | White males | 255 |
| Sarah A. " | 17 f Tenn. | White females | 251 |
| Henry Clay " | 1/12 m Tenn. | | 506 |
| | | Col. males | 4 |

# 644 (Farmer)

| | | Col. females | 3 | Deaths 13 |
| Gregory Johnson | 40 m Va. | | 7 |
| Rachel " | 38 f N.C. | | 513 | Farms 65 |
| Eli Johnson (Farmer) | 16 m Tenn. | Slave males | 271 |
| Elizabeth Johnson | 13 f Tenn. | Slave females | 323 | Pages* 26 |
| William " | 10 m Tenn. | | 594 |
| Jesse " | 7 m Tenn. | | |
| Martha J. " | 5 f Tenn. | | |
| James " | 2 m Tenn. | District #14    September 26, 1850 |

# 645 (Farmer)

| Isham Harvey | 60 m Va. | Page 286 |

# 646 (Farmer)

| | | # 649 (Farmer) | |
| J.W.P. West | 38 m Tenn. | John W. Gibson | 33 m Tenn. |
| Mary D. " | 32 f N.C. | Martha " | 35 f Va. |
| Margaret H. West | 12 f Tenn. | Martha J. " | 9 f Tenn. |
| Eliza L. " | 7 f Tenn. | John H. " | 8 m Tenn. |
| Mary E. " | 6 f Tenn. | Mary A. " | 6 f Tenn. |
| Isaac Q.* " | 2 m Tenn. | Sarah E. " | 5 f Tenn. |
| Hannah Price | 74 f N.C. | Susan " | 3 f Tenn. |
| | | Parmelia " | 2 f Tenn. |
| | | C. " | 3/12 f Tenn. |

# 647 (Farmer)

| | | # 650 (Farmer) | |
| Josiah Long | 27 m Tenn. | John J. Hudgins | 47 m Va. |
| Cromer " | 20 f Tenn. | Mary H. " | 35 f Va. |
| Mary E. " | 1 f Tenn. | | |

1920 WILLIAMSON COUNTY CENSUS

**END DISTRICT 12**

ENUMERATED BY
BOND, Leonard P.

**13 TH DISTRICT**

**#1-1 (Farmer)**

| | | |
|---|---|---|
| HARPER, Earnest | 30 | TN |
| Sally | 21 | TN |
| Fannie | 8 | TN |
| Robert | 4 | TN |
| Margaret | 8/12 | TN |

**#2-2 (Farmer)**

| | | |
|---|---|---|
| BENNETTE, Phillix | 33 | TN |
| Hattie | 33 | TN |
| Elexander | 13 | TN |
| Odell | 11 | TN |
| Phillix | 7 | TN |
| William | 4 | TN |

**#3-3 (Farmer)**

| | | |
|---|---|---|
| MCGEE, J. L. | 33 | TN |
| Willie | 34 | TN |
| Wade | 13 | TN |
| Clide | 10 | TN |
| Florence | 6 | TN |
| Herbert | 3 | TN |
| Herman | 3 | TN |

**#4-4 (Farmer)**

| | | |
|---|---|---|
| HARGROVE, Henry | 38 | TN |
| Maude | 35 | TN |
| Norene | 14 | TN |
| MCGEE, Willy | 56 | TN |

**#5-5 (Farmer)**

| | | |
|---|---|---|
| TOMLIN, Ben | 48 | TN |
| Anna | 31 | TN |
| Alma | 5 | TN |
| Claton | 2 | TN |

**#6-6 (Farmer)**

| | | | |
|---|---|---|---|
| VAUGHAN, Tom | 32 | | TN |
| Mamie | 32 | | TN |
| Mary | 11 | | TN |
| Irvine | 6 | | TN |
| Johnie | | 6/12 | TN |

**#7-7 (Blacksmith)**

| | | | |
|---|---|---|---|
| KING, G. M. | 62 | | TN |
| Tinnie | 59 | | TN |
| HUGHES, Tom | 32 | | TN |
| Earsle | 29 | | TN |
| M. T. | 1 | 11/12 | TN |
| Gladis | | 1/12 | TN |

**#8-8 (Farmer)**

| | | |
|---|---|---|
| KING, W. R. | 55 | TN |
| Willie | 33 | TN |

**#9-9 (Farmer)**

| | | |
|---|---|---|
| MEEK, T. R. | 63 | TN |
| Roy | 26 | TN |
| Dixie | 23 | TN |
| Louise | 17 | TN |
| Will | 9 | TN |

**#10-10 (Merchant)**

| | | |
|---|---|---|
| MATHIS, C. M. | 34 | TN |
| M.C. | 19 | TN |
| G. C. | 33 | TN |

**#11-11 (Farmer)**

| | | |
|---|---|---|
| WARREN, C. A. | 36 | TN |
| Lela | 23 | TN |

**#12-12 (Farmer)**

| | | |
|---|---|---|
| MATHIS, Sam | 45 | TN |
| Mattie | 39 | TN |
| Samie Lou | 16 | TN |
| Johnie May | 14 | TN |
| Susie Lee | 7 | TN |
| Charley A. | 5 | TN |
| Comer | 2 | TN |

#13-13 (Blacksmith)

| Name | Age | | State |
|---|---|---|---|
| MCNEAL, Tom | 33 | | TN |
| Magy | 52 | | TN |
| ANDERSON, Stand | 40 | | TN |
| Herman | 9 | | TN |
| POTEET, Frank | 28 | | TN |

#14-14 (Farmer)

| Name | Age | | State |
|---|---|---|---|
| WEST, Joe (B) | 59 | | TN |
| Mary J. (B) | 57 | | TN |
| John (B) | 29 | | TN |
| Annie (B) | 27 | | TN |
| Pearl (B) | 25 | | TN |
| Walter (B) | 22 | | TN |
| Charley (B) | 17 | | TN |

#15-15 (Farmer)

| Name | Age | | State |
|---|---|---|---|
| TALLY, Addie (MU) | 46 | | TN |
| George (MU) | 21 | | TN |
| Johnie (MU) | 17 | | TN |
| CROWDER, John (B) | 23 | | TN |
| Laula (MU) | 18 | | TN |

#16-16 (Farmer)

| Name | Age | | State |
|---|---|---|---|
| WARREN, H. T. | 33 | | TN |
| Mary | 31 | | TN |
| Lucile | 13 | | TN |
| Ramon | 10 | | TN |
| Rolf | 8 | | TN |
| Lorine | 5 | | TN |
| Priney | 1 | | TN |

#17-17 (Farmer)

| Name | Age | | State |
|---|---|---|---|
| WARREN, Herman | 24 | | TN |
| Parilee | 19 | | TN |
| VEACH, Bud | 55 | | TN |
| Ranie | 47 | | TN |
| Tom | 26 | | TN |
| Georgie Lee | 16 | | TN |
| Clint | 14 | | TN |
| R | 10 | | TN |
| Wade | 8 | | TN |

#18-18 (Farmer)

| Name | Age | | State |
|---|---|---|---|
| POTEET, Monrow | 46 | | TN |
| Fannie | 39 | | TN |
| Ethel | 26 | | TN |
| Fred | 21 | | TN |
| Bertha | 19 | | TN |
| Annie May | 15 | | TN |
| Pollene | 14 | | TN |
| Harris | 11 | | TN |
| Philmore | 9 | | TN |
| Mary | 6 | | TN |

#19-19 (Farmer)

| Name | Age | | State |
|---|---|---|---|
| DODSON, E.L. | 40 | | TN |
| Lee | 35 | | TN |
| Willie | 7 | | TN |
| Gertrue | 6 | | TN |
| Nora | 4 | | TN |
| W. H. | 72 | | TN |

#20-20 (Farmer)

| Name | Age | | State |
|---|---|---|---|
| VADEN, Charley | 50 | | TN |
| Nora | 49 | | TN |
| Annie | 24 | | TN |
| Ada | 21 | | TN |
| Lera | 16 | | TN |
| Walter | 7 | | TN |

#21-21 (Farmer)

| Name | Age | | State |
|---|---|---|---|
| VADEN, W. B. | 75 | | TN |

#22-22 (Farmer)

| Name | Age | | State |
|---|---|---|---|
| SMITHSON, T. W. | 54 | | TN |
| Ella | 33 | | TN |
| Thomas | 9 | | TN |

#23-23 (Farmer)

| Name | Age | | State |
|---|---|---|---|
| HARDIMAN, Oscar (MU) | 54 | | TN |
| Martha (B) | 36 | | TN |
| Girtrue (MU) | 12 | | TN |
| Baxter (MU) | 10 | | TN |
| Patterson (MU) | 8 | | TN |
| Mattie (MU) | 5 | | TN |
| J. C. (MU) | 3 | | TN |
| Oscar, Jr. (MU) | 11/12 | | TN |

| #24-24 (Farmer) | | | |
|---|---|---|---|
| HAYES, Obey (MU) | 50 | | TN |
| Kitty (MU) | 39 | | TN |
| John (MU) | 10 | | TN |
| Rayburn (MU) | 8 | | TN |

| #25-25 (Farmer) | | | |
|---|---|---|---|
| TOMLIN, John Lee | 19 | | TN |
| S. B. | 16 | | TN |
| Robert | 1 | 2/12 | TN |

| #26-26 (Farmer) | | | |
|---|---|---|---|
| KING, J. W. | 49 | | TN |
| Lillie | 30 | | TN |
| Nancie | 6 | | TN |
| Rubie | 5 | | TN |
| George | 4 | | TN |
| James | 1 | 10/12 | TN |
| Jessie | | 7/12 | TN |

| #27-27 (Farmer) | | | |
|---|---|---|---|
| TOMLIN, Davis | 35 | | TN |
| Bessie | 31 | | TN |
| Albert | 15 | | TN |
| Lavese | 8 | | TN |
| Marvin | 6 | | TN |
| Mildred | 3 | | TN |
| SKINNER, R. | 28 | | TN |

| #28-28 (Farmer) | | | |
|---|---|---|---|
| SKINNER, Noland | 25 | | TN |
| Gertrue | 23 | | T N |
| Corine | 3 | | TN |
| George | 2 | | TN |
| Clarence | | 3/12 | TN |

| #29-29 (Farmer) | | | |
|---|---|---|---|
| MCMAHAN, F. E. | 52 | | TN |
| Belle | 45 | | TN |
| JOHNSON, Pink | 26 | | TN |
| Maggie | 22 | | TN |

| #30-30 (Farmer) | | | |
|---|---|---|---|
| BEARD, L. C. | 63 | | TN |
| Cindy | 53 | | TN |
| Fred | 19 | | TN |
| Walter | 37 | | TN |
| Sallie | 37 | | TN |
| Willie | 13 | | TN |
| Myrtle | 12 | | TN |
| Addie | 7 | | TN |
| Claud | 6 | | TN |
| Era May | 3 | | TN |
| Allen | 2 | | TN |
| Gladice | 1 | 1/12 | TN |

| #31-31 (Farmer) | | | |
|---|---|---|---|
| HAY, H. B. | 73 | | TN |
| M. P. | 65 | | TN |

| #32-32 (Farmer) | | | |
|---|---|---|---|
| HAY, Walter | 36 | | TN |
| Izora | 33 | | TN |
| Sadie | 5 | | TN |

| #33-33 (Farmer) | | | |
|---|---|---|---|
| TOMLIN, Elijia | 66 | | TN |
| Nansie | 57 | | TN |
| Johnie | 30 | | TN |
| Cleo | 28 | | TN |
| Mildred | 8 | | TN |
| Paul | 6 | | TN |
| W. P. | 4 | | TN |

| #34-34 (Farmer) | | | |
|---|---|---|---|
| SIMMONS, Oscre | 36 | | TN |
| Irene | 26 | | TN |
| Howard | 4 | | TN |
| Margret | 3 | | TN |

| #35-35 (Farmer) | | | |
|---|---|---|---|
| TOMLIN, DeWirtley | 61 | | TN |
| Martha | 63 | | TN |
| POTEET, Eddin | 29 | | TN |
| Jack | 13 | | TN |
| Clarence | 12 | | TN |
| Elijia | 9 | | TN |

#36-36 (Farmer)

| Name | Age | | State |
|---|---|---|---|
| BENNETTE, Robert | 28 | | TN |
| Lula | 24 | | TN |
| Herbert | 4 | | TN |
| Alma | | 1/12 | TN |

#37 (Farmer)

| Name | Age | State |
|---|---|---|
| BENNETTE, Nola | 48 | TN |
| Lincon | 16 | TN |
| Grata | 11 | TN |
| Richard | 8 | TN |
| Zelma | 6 | TN |

#37-38 (Farmer)

| Name | Age | State |
|---|---|---|
| SCHRUGGS, Will | 58 | TN |
| Willie | 47 | TN |

#38-39 (Farmer)

| Name | Age | State |
|---|---|---|
| POTEET, Will | 57 | TN |
| S. J. | 49 | TN |
| Emory | 25 | TN |
| Nancie | 17 | TN |
| Dan | 14 | TN |
| Bettie | 12 | TN |
| Myrtle | 8 | TN |

#39-40 (Farmer)

| Name | Age | State |
|---|---|---|
| BENNETTE, Allin | 58 | TN |
| Lillar | 34 | TN |
| Harrison | 12 | TN |
| Mamie | 9 | TN |

#40-41 (Farmer)

| Name | Age | State |
|---|---|---|
| VEACH, Lee | 38 | TN |
| Reallie | 27 | TN |
| Darnell | 10 | TN |
| Nellie | 7 | TN |
| James | 5 | TN |
| Clifton | 3 | TN |
| Frank | 1 | TN |

#41-42 (Farmer)

| Name | Age | State |
|---|---|---|
| BENNETTE, N. L. | 33 | TN |
| Dollie | 33 | TN |
| JONES, Wyly | 55 | TN |
| Mary | 67 | TN |
| George | 28 | TN |

#42-43 (Farmer)

| Name | Age | State |
|---|---|---|
| VEACH, Isreal | 29 | TN |
| Addie Belle | 22 | TN |
| Odie T. | 7 | TN |
| Laura May | 4 | TN |
| BEARD, Etter | 36 | TN |
| Louise | 3 | TN |

#43-44 (Farmer)

| Name | Age | | State |
|---|---|---|---|
| ANDERSON, Laura | 52 | | TN |
| POTEET, Neal | 25 | | TN |
| AMICK, Henry | 14 | | TN |
| HALL, Elma | 23 | | TN |
| Lena May | 21 | | TN |
| Melvin | | 3/12 | TN |

#44-45 (Farmer)

| Name | Age | State |
|---|---|---|
| VEACH, Jessie | 51 | TN |
| Laura | 47 | TN |
| Jack | 21 | TN |
| Andy | 13 | TN |
| Carmac | 11 | TN |
| Kittie | 9 | TN |
| Madie | 8 | TN |
| Wesley | 6 | TN |
| Eligie | 4 | TN |

#44-45

| Name | Age | State |
|---|---|---|
| HARTLEY, Charles | 36 | TN |

#45-46 (Farmer)

| Name | Age | State |
|---|---|---|
| BURGE, John | 42 | TN |
| Bettie | 28 | TN |
| Gladice | 10 | TN |
| Sherman | 6 | TN |
| V. G. | 2 | TN |

#46-47 (Farmer)

| | | |
|---|---|---|
| BENNETT, Phil | 36 | TN |
| Madie | 32 | TN |
| Ida May | 14 | TN |
| Unice | 11 | TN |
| Howard | 9 | TN |
| Fannie | 7 | TN |
| Milton | 5 | TN |
| Ella | 4/12 | TN |

#47-48 (Farmer)

| | | |
|---|---|---|
| SMITHSON, J. W. | 34 | TN |
| Rubie | 32 | TN |

#48-49 (Farmer)

| | | |
|---|---|---|
| NEVILS, W. W. | 42 | TN |
| Ella G. | 68 | TN |
| CRUNK, Jim Will | 16 | TN |

#49-50 (Farmer)

| | | |
|---|---|---|
| TOMLIN, J. A. | 37 | TN |
| Minervia | 27 | TN |
| LADD, Henry | 7 | TN |
| J. P. | 4 | TN |

#50-51 (Farmer)

| | | |
|---|---|---|
| POTEET, Tomie | 31 | TN |
| Bessie | 21 | TN |

#51-52 (Farmer)

| | | |
|---|---|---|
| TOMLIN, John | 62 | TN |

#52-53 (Farmer)

| | | |
|---|---|---|
| BENNETTE, Jimie Dee | 26 | TN |
| Beatrice | 25 | TN |
| Alline | 1 6/12 | TN |

#53-54 (Farmer)

| | | |
|---|---|---|
| BENNETTE, Hugh | 21 | TN |
| Bessie | 18 | TN |
| Margret | 1 9/12 | TN |

#54-55 (Farmer)

| | | |
|---|---|---|
| BENNETTE, Sherman | 52 | TN |
| Nancie | 46 | TN |
| Sam | 18 | TN |

#55-56 (Farmer)

| | | |
|---|---|---|
| GARNER, Lee | 48 | TN |
| Susie | 41 | TN |
| Mary | 20 | TN |
| Burtie | 15 | TN |
| Eliger | 12 | TN |
| Patterson | 9 | TN |
| Andrew | 5 | TN |
| Susie Lee | 2 | TN |
| VEACH, Maggie | 18 | TN |
| William | 11/12 | TN |
| POTEET, Roy | 1 | TN |

#56-57 (Farmer)

| | | |
|---|---|---|
| LADD, Mattie | 71 | TN |
| R. N. | 41 | TN |
| L. L. | 30 | TN |
| Estell | 7 | TN |

#57-58 (Wash Woman)

| | | |
|---|---|---|
| BEARD, Edna | 56 | TN |
| Lissie | 17 | TN |
| Henry | 10 | TN |

#58-59 (Farmer)

| | | |
|---|---|---|
| MATHIS, J. H. | 46 | TN |
| Eunice | 39 | TN |
| Bertie May | 14 | TN |
| Rachel F. | 13 | TN |
| Bratin | 10 | TN |

#59-60 (Farmer)

| | | |
|---|---|---|
| HARPER, Robert | 43 | TN |
| Bettye | 34 | TN |
| Robert L. | 14 | TN |
| Bula | 8 | TN |
| Clifton | 3 | TN |
| Douglas | 10/12 | TN |

| Household | Name | Age | | State |
|---|---|---|---|---|
| #60-61 (Mason) | DODD, W. A. | 51 | | TN |
| | Bettie | 52 | | TN |
| | Briant | 23 | | TN |
| | John | 18 | | TN |
| | Florence | 14 | | TN |
| | Graham | 11 | | TN |
| #61-62 (Farmer) | TRACY, Mary | 58 | | TN |
| | Sallie | 23 | | TN |
| | DAVIS, Mincie | 72 | | GA |
| #62-63 (Farmer) | DAVIS, Early | 43 | | AL |
| | Lillie | 24 | | AL |
| | Mary | 8 | | TN |
| | Hortense | 7 | | TN |
| | Jona | 5 | | TN |
| | Nell | 3 | | TN |
| | Rachel | | 8/12 | TN |
| #63-64 (Farmer) | LILLARD, O. C. | 46 | | TN |
| | Greer | 40 | | TN |
| | Jimmie | 22 | | TN |
| | Mary | 19 | | TN |
| | Davis | 16 | | TN |
| | Johnie | 13 | | TN |
| | Rena | 9 | | TN |
| #64-65 (Farmer) | RAY, W. M. | 67 | | AL |
| | Bettie | 53 | | TN |
| #65-66 (Farmer) | MOSLEY, Ky | 58 | | TN |
| | Alice | 55 | | TN |
| | Lee | 24 | | TN |
| | Roy | 20 | | TN |
| | Walter | 24 | | TN |
| | Ethel | 27 | | SD |
| | Doris | 1 | 1/12 | MO |
| #66-67 (Farmer) | WHITE, Marion | 79 | | GA |
| | Caline | 71 | | TN |
| #67-68 (Farmer) | HICKS, John | 25 | | TN |
| | Lummie | 20 | | TN |
| | Robert | 4 | | TN |
| | Mary | 2 | | TN |
| | William | | 8/12 | TN |
| #68-69 (Farmer) | HARTLEY, Ewin | 25 | | TN |
| | Frances | 20 | | TN |
| #69-70 (Farmer) | WADDIE, R. P. | 45 | | TN |
| | Maggie | 45 | | TN |
| | Lee | 21 | | TN |
| | Ira | 13 | | TN |
| #70-71 (Farmer) | SMITHSON, Jerry (B) | 24 | | TN |
| | Ophelia (B) | 19 | | TN |
| | John Lee (B) | | 1/12 | TN |
| #71-72 (Farmer) | LILLARD, Jim | 39 | | TN |
| | Allice | 36 | | TN |
| | Ollie | 16 | | TN |
| | William | 12 | | TN |
| 72-73 (Farmer) | WOOD, Charley | 50 | | TN |
| | Lena | 60 | | TN |
| | Reedie | 17 | | TN |
| | Roy | 16 | | TN |
| | HALL, Nancie | 75 | | TN |
| | Mina | 44 | | TN |
| #73-74 (Farmer) | WADDY, John | 48 | | TN |

#74-75 (Farmer)

| Name | Age | Birthplace |
|---|---|---|
| LESTER, Joseph | 39 | TN |
| Bula | 24 | TN |
| Hattie | 5 | TN |
| Mattie | 2 | TN |
| John | 73 | TN |
| INGRAM, Sarah | 61 | TN |

#75-76 (Farmer)

| Name | Age | Birthplace |
|---|---|---|
| HICKS, Mason | 68 | TN |
| Cora | 48 | TN |
| Odeam | 15 | TN |
| Emit | 22 | TN |
| Ira | 3 | TN |
| James | 1 | TN |
| TOMLIN, Lige | 27 | TN |
| Myrtle | 25 | TN |
| Walter | 9 | TN |
| Earnest | 7 | TN |
| Westley | 3 | TN |

#76-77 (Farmer)

| Name | Age | Birthplace |
|---|---|---|
| GROVES, Johnie | 34 | TN |
| Annibelle | 25 | TN |
| William | 9 | TN |
| Comer | 7 | TN |
| Calvert | 3 | TN |

#77-78 (Farmer)

| Name | Age | Birthplace |
|---|---|---|
| GROVES, Henry | 60 | TN |
| Loulia | 58 | TN |
| Willie | 30 | TN |
| Elmo | 25 | TN |
| Gertrue | 21 | TN |
| Ethel | 17 | TN |

#78-79 (Farmer)

| Name | Age | Birthplace |
|---|---|---|
| LILLARD, R. M. | 41 | TN |
| Lucy | 37 | TN |
| Tommie | 14 | TN |
| Woodard | 12 | TN |
| Gabon | 6 | TN |
| John Dee | 1 | TN |

#79-80 (Farmer)

| Name | Age | Birthplace |
|---|---|---|
| LADD, Johnie | 33 | TN |
| Mansie | 20 | TN |
| Sarah | 10/12 | TN |

#80-81 (Farmer)

| Name | Age | Birthplace |
|---|---|---|
| BEECH, W. C. | 50 | TN |
| Michael M. | 50 | TN |
| Emma | 26 | TN |
| George | 11 | TN |
| Audie | 9 | TN |

#81-82 (Farmer)

| Name | Age | Birthplace |
|---|---|---|
| HAYES, John (MU) | 54 | TN |
| Janie (MU) | 47 | TN |
| Charley (MU) | 18 | TN |
| James (MU) | 9 | TN |
| Janie (MU) | 7 | TN |
| Will (MU) | 5 | TN |

#82-83 (Farmer)

| Name | Age | Birthplace |
|---|---|---|
| JOHNSON, Watt (MU) | 55 | TN |
| Sally (MU) | 45 | TN |
| Will (MU) | 17 | TN |
| Rubie (MU) | 18 | TN |
| Flora (MU) | 11 | TN |

#83-84 (Farmer)

| Name | Age | Birthplace |
|---|---|---|
| CLABORN, Will | 36 | TN |
| Birter | 33 | TN |
| Willie B. | 12 | TN |
| Rosie Lee | 9 | TN |
| Robert | 8 | TN |
| Elma | 4 | TN |
| Edga | 5/12 | TN |
| Harris | 32 | TN |
| Ida | 37 | TN |
| LANE, Nancie | 6 | TN |

#84-85 (Farmer)

| Name | Age | Birthplace |
|---|---|---|
| SMITHSON, Ore (MU) | 31 | TN |
| Dosie (MU) | 28 | TN |
| Mattie (MU) | 7 | TN |
| Osie Lee (MU) | 4 | TN |

#84-85 (Continued)

#84-85 (Continued)

| Name | Age | State |
|---|---|---|
| SMITHSON, Susie (MU) | 2 | TN |
| Bessie (MU) | 1 | TN |
| HOUSE, Mattie (MU) | 64 | TN |

#85-86 (Farmer)

| Name | Age | State |
|---|---|---|
| SMITHSON, John (MU) | 35 | TN |
| Emit (MU) | 17 | TN |
| John Robert (MU) | 5 | TN |

#86-87 (Farmer)

| Name | Age | State |
|---|---|---|
| SIMMONS, Henry | 34 | TN |
| Lena | 24 | TN |
| Frances | 3 | TN |

#87-88 (Farmer)

| Name | Age | State |
|---|---|---|
| CRAFTON, G. W. | 74 | TN |
| POTEET, Bukner | 47 | TN |

#88-89 (Farmer)

| Name | Age | State |
|---|---|---|
| CRAFTON, Henry | 47 | TN |
| Maggie | 41 | TN |
| George | 3 | TN |
| SLEDGE, Sallie | 49 | TN |

#89-90 (Farmer)

| Name | Age | State |
|---|---|---|
| JOHNSON, W. L. | 48 | TN |
| Minnie | 42 | TN |
| Samuel | 25 | TN |
| Sadie | 23 | TN |
| Blyte | 20 | TN |
| Corie | 9 | TN |
| William | 6 | TN |
| Murry | 1 | TN |

#90-91 (Farmer)

| Name | Age | State |
|---|---|---|
| SIMMONS, O. W. | 67 | TN |
| Annie | 58 | TN |
| Robert | 25 | TN |
| Anise | 21 | TN |
| Mike | 20 | TN |
| Abert | 13 | TN |
| SPANN, Louisa | 77 | TN |
| Munrow | 50 | TN |

#91-92 (Farmer)

| Name | Age | State |
|---|---|---|
| MYRICK, E. B. | 29 | MS |
| Stella | 23 | KY |

#92-93 (Farmer)

| Name | Age | State |
|---|---|---|
| GLEN, F. A. | 48 | TN |
| Ada | 50 | TN |
| Beatrice | 23 | TN |
| Rogger | 17 | TN |
| Wane | 15 | TN |
| Elammy | 11 | TN |
| John | 7 | TN |

#93-94 (Farmer)

| Name | Age | State |
|---|---|---|
| TOMLIN, Pritchard | 33 | TN |
| Willie | 33 | TN |
| Pauline | 11 | TN |
| Don | 9 | TN |
| Elma | 7 | TN |
| Auther | 5 | TN |
| J. W. | 3 | TN |
| Arline | 11/12 | TN |

#94-95 (Farmer)

| Name | Age | State |
|---|---|---|
| GEE, James | 39 | TN |
| Louise | 36 | TN |
| THOMPSON, James | 77 | TN |

#95-96 (Farmer)

| Name | Age | State |
|---|---|---|
| GENTRY, John (MU) | 51 | TN |
| Jocie (MU) | 42 | TN |
| Edd (MU) | 16 | TN |
| Mittie (MU) | 14 | TN |
| James (MU) | 11 | TN |
| Gertie (MU) | 5 | TN |
| Howard (MU) | 1/12 | TN |

#96-97 (Farmer)

| Name | Age | State |
|---|---|---|
| LADD, E. C. | 48 | TN |
| Ola Mai | 46 | TN |
| Jamie A. | 20 | TN |

#97-98 (Farmer)

| SKINNER, W. R. | 46 | | TN |
|---|---|---|---|
| A. B. | 33 | | TN |
| Ella | 17 | | TN |
| Vergie | 12 | | TN |
| Oscra | 9 | | TN |
| Eula Kate | 7 | | TN |
| James | 4 | | TN |
| Jessie O. | 1 | | TN |

#98-99 (Farmer)

| GIBSON, Henry (B) | 56 | | TN |
|---|---|---|---|
| Laura (B) | 54 | | TN |
| Willie (B) | 12 | | TN |
| WADDY, James (MU) | 24 | | TN |
| Maggie (MU) | 22 | | TN |
| Woodrow (MU) | 3 | | TN |
| Elisabeth(MU) | 2 | | TN |
| Fred (MU) | | 4/12 | TN |

#99-100 (Farmer)

| GIBSON, Gosey (MU) | 53 | | TN |
|---|---|---|---|
| Beatrice (MU) | 38 | | TN |
| Jimmie (MU) | 12 | | TN |
| Philice (MU) | 10 | | TN |
| Ryan (MU) | 6 | | TN |
| T. G. (MU) | 3 | | TN |
| YARBROUGH, Birtha (MU) | 11 | | TN |

#100-101 (Farmer)

| REYNOLDS, Henry (MU) | 33 | | TN |
|---|---|---|---|
| Matilda (MU) | 40 | | TN |
| Gladice (MU) | 8 | | TN |
| Annie Belle (MU) | 4 | | TN |
| Henry (MU) | 2 | | TN |
| Johnnie May (MU) | | 4/12 | TN |

#101-102 (Farmer)

| REYNOLDS, R. B. (MU) | 64 | | TN |
|---|---|---|---|
| Mary Jane (MU) | 48 | | TN |
| Mable (MU) | 19 | | TN |
| Rubin White (MU) | 16 | | TN |
| Winnie (MU) | 13 | | TN |
| Clarrice (MU) | 7 | | TN |

#102-103 (Farmer)

| CROWDER, Oula (MU) | 26 | | TN |
|---|---|---|---|
| Amelia (MU) | 25 | | TN |
| Louise (MU) | 2 | | TN |
| James (MU) | | 3/12 | TN |

#104 (Farmer)

| RATCLIFFE, Will (MU) | 29 | | TN |
|---|---|---|---|
| Amely (MU) | 28 | | TN |
| William (MU) | 8 | | TN |
| Mary (MU) | 6 | | TN |
| Rueben (MU) | 4 | | TN |
| Berdie (MU) | 2 | | TN |
| Beula (MU) | | 1/12 | TN |

#103-105 (Farmer)

| VADEN, A. J. | 45 | | TN |
|---|---|---|---|
| Sallie | 42 | | TN |
| Elise | 19 | | TN |
| Jennie | 17 | | TN |
| Leonard | 12 | | TN |

#104-106 (Farmer)

| BAUGH, O. C. | 40 | | TN |
|---|---|---|---|
| Mamie Lou | 35 | | TN |
| Ralf | 13 | | TN |
| Corbin | 11 | | TN |
| Jane | 9 | | TN |
| Lissebeth | 4 | | TN |

#105-107 (Farmer)

| HARPER, Milt | 55 | | TN |
|---|---|---|---|
| Ella | 53 | | TN |

#106-108 (Farmer)

| DAVIS, Tom | 33 | | TN |
|---|---|---|---|
| Dora | 33 | | TN |

#107-109 (Farmer)

| YORK, Claud | 50 | | TN |
|---|---|---|---|
| Josephine | 47 | | TN |
| Doulas *Douglas* | 21 | | TN |
| Bulah *Beulah* | 19 | | TN |

#107-109 (Continued)

#107-109 (Continued)

| Name | Age | | Birthplace |
|---|---|---|---|
| YORK, Beal | 18 | | TN |
| Pauline | 18 | | TN |
| Wesley | 10 | | TN |

#108-110 (Farmer)

| Name | Age | | Birthplace |
|---|---|---|---|
| HADLEY, Turner (MU) | 61 | | TN |
| Ella (MU) | 33 | | TN |
| PICKIT, John (MU) | 28 | | TN |

#109-111 (Farmer)

| Name | Age | | Birthplace |
|---|---|---|---|
| CAMPBELL, G. A. | 55 | | TN |
| Sallie | 45 | | TN |
| Marvin | 25 | | TN |
| Myrtle | 19 | | TN |
| Owen | 14 | | TN |
| Earl | 12 | | TN |
| Robert | 11 | | TN |
| Leonard | 10 | | TN |
| Clifton | 7 | | TN |
| James | 4 | | TN |
| Vera | 1 | 10/12 | TN |

#110-112 (Farmer)

| Name | Age | | Birthplace |
|---|---|---|---|
| MCEWIN, Poter (B) | 56 | | TN |
| Racheal (MU) | 51 | | TN |

#111-113 (Farmer)

| Name | Age | | Birthplace |
|---|---|---|---|
| BAGGERS, George (MU) | 46 | | TN |
| Sophy (MU) | 48 | | TN |
| Booker (MU) | 18 | | TN |
| Natt (MU) | 15 | | TN |
| KINNARD, John Henry (MU) | 12 | | TN |

#112-114 (Farmer)

| Name | Age | | Birthplace |
|---|---|---|---|
| JOHNSON, Perry | 31 | | TN |
| Olyie | 25 | | TN |
| Perry, Jr. | 2 | | TN |

#113-115 (Farmer)

| Name | Age | | Birthplace |
|---|---|---|---|
| CROWDER, Will (B) | 29 | | TN |
| ? (MU) | 25 | | TN |

#114-116 (Farmer)

| Name | Age | | Birthplace |
|---|---|---|---|
| WEST, G. W. | 61 | | TN |
| Lillian | 48 | | TN |

#116-118 (Farmer)

| Name | Age | | Birthplace |
|---|---|---|---|
| JOHNSON, Joe | 46 | | TN |
| Racheal | 41 | | TN |
| Alma | 17 | | TN |
| Parker | 8 | | TN |
| MORRIS, Roger | 26 | | TN |

#117-119 (Farmer)

| Name | Age | | Birthplace |
|---|---|---|---|
| DANIELS, Fred | 51 | | MI |
| Nellie | 41 | | IL |
| LANDON, Roy | 11 | | TN |

#118-120 (Farmer)

| Name | Age | | Birthplace |
|---|---|---|---|
| SMITHSON, Syl | 35 | | TN |
| Minnie | 30 | | TN |
| James | 1 | 1/12 | TN |

#119-121 (Farmer)

| Name | Age | | Birthplace |
|---|---|---|---|
| BRYAN, Henry | 50 | | TN |
| Nora | 41 | | TN |
| Orbey | 21 | | TN |
| Charley | 19 | | TN |
| Mary J. | 17 | | TN |
| Thomas | 14 | | TN |
| Albert | 10 | | TN |
| Walter | 7 | | TN |
| Willard | 3 | | TN |

#120-122 (Farmer)

| Name | Age | | Birthplace |
|---|---|---|---|
| TOMLIN, C. D. | 40 | | TN |
| Lena | 33 | | TN |
| Della | 16 | | TN |
| Mildred | 12 | | TN |
| Emma | 9 | | TN |
| Davis | 6 | | TN |
| Olna | 4 | | TN |
| Jim Frank | | 5/12 | TN |
| James | 23 | | TN |
| L. E. | 15 | | TN |

#121-123 (Farmer)

| Name | Age | | Birthplace |
|---|---|---|---|
| STAUBER, Dee (MU) | 50 | | TN |
| Minsie (MU) | 37 | | TN |
| Hattie Pearl (MU) | 17 | | TN |

#122-124 (Farmer)

| Name | Age | | Birthplace |
|---|---|---|---|
| BRIDGE, George | 23 | | TN |
| Jammie | 25 | | TN |
| Susie | 4 | | TN |
| Willie | 3 | | TN |
| James | 1 | 9/12 | TN |
| Mattie | 65 | | TN |
| HOUSE, Permelia | 29 | | TN |

#123-125 (Farmer)

| Name | Age | | Birthplace |
|---|---|---|---|
| LADD, Jessie | 28 | | TN |
| Addie | 19 | | TN |

#124-126 (Farmer)

| Name | Age | | Birthplace |
|---|---|---|---|
| TOMPSON, Terrie (MU) | 26 | | TN |
| Mary (B) | 23 | | TN |
| Graham (MU) | 5 | | TN |
| Roggers (MU) | 2 | | TN |
| Turner (MU) | 65 | | TN |

#125-127 (Farmer)

| Name | Age | | Birthplace |
|---|---|---|---|
| BEAL, John (MU) | 35 | | TN |
| Lena (MU) | 21 | | TN |
| Louise (MU) | 4 | | TN |

#126-128 (Farmer)

| Name | Age | | Birthplace |
|---|---|---|---|
| BEAL, Neal (MU) | 62 | | TN |

#127-129 (Farmer)

| Name | Age | | Birthplace |
|---|---|---|---|
| TOMPSON, ? | 43 | | TN |
| Fannie | 42 | | TN |
| Charlie B. | 11 | | TN |

#128-130 (Farmer)

| Name | Age | | Birthplace |
|---|---|---|---|
| HATCHER, Henry | 53 | | TN |
| Mary Jane | 84 | | TN |
| Minie | 45 | | TN |

#128-130 (Continued)

| Name | Age | | Birthplace |
|---|---|---|---|
| HATCHER, Mary | 41 | | TN |
| Minervia | 7 | | TN |
| Sarah | 5 | | TN |
| Annie Bunch | 2 | | TN |
| Harase | 12 | | TN |
| ALDRAGE, Gallin | 21 | | TN |
| NEELEY, Bettie | 74 | | TN |

3129-131 (Farmer)

| Name | Age | | Birthplace |
|---|---|---|---|
| PATTON, J. (B) | 61 | | TN |
| Genevia (MU) | 38 | | TN |
| GREEN, Merret (MU) | 14 | | TN |

#130-132 (Farmer)

| Name | Age | | Birthplace |
|---|---|---|---|
| MANGRUM, Willie | 25 | | TN |
| Nelly | 19 | | TN |
| Jenny | | 2/12 | TN |

#131-133 (Farmer)

| Name | Age | | Birthplace |
|---|---|---|---|
| CRAFTON, Jaron | 48 | | TN |
| Molly | 39 | | TN |
| Leonard | 15 | | TN |
| Walter | 8 | | TN |

#131-134 (Blacksmith)

| Name | Age | | Birthplace |
|---|---|---|---|
| STEVEN, Tom | 45 | | TN |
| Pearl | 25 | | TN |
| Caroline | 4 | | TN |
| Thomas | | 4/12 | TN |

#132-135 (Farmer)

| Name | Age | | Birthplace |
|---|---|---|---|
| LESTER, Grant (B) | 55 | | TN |
| Grant, Jr. (B) | 21 | | TN |
| WEBB, Lucian (MU) | 24 | | TN |
| Mattie (MU) | 20 | | TN |

#133-136 (Farmer)

| Name | Age | | Birthplace |
|---|---|---|---|
| JOHNSON, G. M. | 51 | | TN |
| Elisebeth | 51 | | TN |

#134-137 (Farmer)  
PARRISH, Charley 31 TN  
    Letcher M. 34 TN  
    Charles Herbert 15 TN  
    Katie May 13 TN  
    Ruthie 10 TN  
    Louis 8 TN  
    Virginia 3 TN  
    Ramon 7/12 TN  

#135-138 (Farmer)  
HARPER, Ikey 50 TN  
    Sallie 51 TN  

#136-139 (Farmer)  
WRAY, W. T. 52 TN  
    Fannie 53 TN  
    Janie 12 TN  
    Gradie 10 TN  
    Caudie 7 TN  
    Frances 2 TN  
PRATT, John 22 TN  
    Sadie 17 TN  
SKINNER, Till 21 TN  

**END DISTRICT 13**

ENUMERATED BY  
    WRAY, W. T.

#3-3 (Farmer)  
HAGERTY, Willie 44 TN  
    Pat 40 TN  
    Olie 50 TN  
VAUGHN, Ann 54 TN  

#4-4 (Farmer)  
GALAVIN, Eugene 44 TN  
WARREN, James M. 70 TN  

#5-5 (Farmer)  
OSBORNE, James P. 48 TN  
    Melissa 46 TN  
    Mary 17 TN  
    James 12 TN  
    Nannie Lou 8 TN  

#6-6 (Farmer)  
YOUNG, Tom J. 59 TN  
    Eliza 59 TN  
    James H. 30 TN  
    Ohelia 31 TN  

#7-7 (Farmer)  
WARREN, Harve 74 TN  
    Sarah 73 TN

## TAX BOOK, 1950, WILLIAMSON COUNTY, TENN.

| | NAME | DESCRIPTION OF PROPERTY | | | | No. Acres Land or Town Lots | Value Acres Land or Town Lots Dollars | Value Pers'l Property Less $1,000 Dollars | Total Real, Personal and all Other Property Dollars | Poll Tax Dollars | COUNTY TAXES $ Cts. | Total County Taxes $ Cts. |
|---|---|---|---|---|---|---|---|---|---|---|---|---|
| | | NORTH | SOUTH | EAST | WEST | | | | | | | |
| 1 | Beech, Beulah Mrs. | Crunk | Hatcher | Rd. | Rd. | 35 | 800 | | 800 | | | 24 00 |
| 2 | Bennett, Felix | Garner | Bennett | Boyd | Bennett | 25 | 300 | | 300 | | | 9 00 |
| 3 | Bennett, J.D. | Bennett | Bond | Bond | Bond | 150 | 2000 | | 2000 | | | 60 00 |
| 4 | Bennett, P. B. | " | Poteete | Veach | Garner | 43 | 500 | | | | | |
| 5 | " " | " | " | Hatcher | Boyd | 25 | 300 | | 800 | | | 24 00 |
| 6 | Bennett, Sam | Rd. | Ladd | Buford | Smithson | 8 | 400 | | 400 | | | 12 00 |
| 7 | Bennett, Tom Estate | McGee | Tomlin | Boyd | Bennett | 58 | 500 | | 500 | | | 15 00 |
| 8 | Bennett, Willie | Garner | Poteete | Bennett | Tomlin | 21 | 200 | | 200 | 2.00 | 6 00 | 8 00 |
| 9 | Boyd, James O. | Parks | Smithson | Rd. | West | 125 | 2500 | | 2500 | | | 75 00 |
| 10 | Boyd, Mrs. O. C. | Rd. | York | " | York | 228 | 5900 | | 5900 | | | 177 00 |
| 11 | Bruce, Allen J. L. | King | King | King | King | 34 | 600 | | 600 | | | 18 00 |
| 12 | Bruce, G. W. | " | " | McGee | School | 45 | 1200 | | 1200 | | | 36 00 |
| 13 | Bruce, Mose | Ladd | Nolen | Smithson | Rd. | 71 | 1200 | | 1200 | | | 36 00 |
| 14 | Buchanan, Mart | Rd. | Ladd | Deason | " | 36 | 700 | | | | | |
| 15 | " " | Smithson | Tomlin | King | McGee | 127 | 1200 | | 1900 | | | 57.00 |
| 16 | Buford, Alvin Lee | Ladd | Hall | Hall | Rd. | 115 | 3500 | | 3500 | 2.00 | 105 00 | 107 00 |
| 17 | Buford, L.W. | Buchanan | McGee | Hughes | Maupin | 75 | 1000 | | 1000 | | | 30 00 |
| 18 | Buford, Willie Joe | Rd. | " | Ladd | Nevils | 98 | 2700 | | 2700 | | | 81 00 |
| 19 | | | | | | | | | | | | |
| 20 | | | | | | | | | | | | |
| 21 | | | | | | | | | | | | |
| 22 | | | | | | | | | | | | |
| | | | | | | 1,319 | 25,500 | | 25,500 | 400 | | 769 00 |

## TAX BOOK, 1950, WILLIAMSON COUNTY, TENN.

| | NAME | DESCRIPTION OF PROPERTY | | | | No. Acres Land or Town Lots | Value Acres Land or Town Lots Dollars | Value Pers'l Property Less $1,000 Dollars | Total Real, Personal and all Other Property Dollars | Poll Tax Dollars | COUNTY TAXES $ Cts. | Total County Taxes $ Cts. |
|---|---|---|---|---|---|---|---|---|---|---|---|---|
| | | NORTH | SOUTH | EAST | WEST | | | | | | | |
| 1 | Campbell, Earl | Castleman | Thompson | Pinkston | Rd. | 44 | 600 | | 600 | 2.00 | 18 00 | 20 00 |
| 2 | Campbell, George | Vaden | Campbell | Vaden | " | 37 | 1400 | | 1400 | | | 42 00 |
| 3 | Campbell, Mrs. Sallie | York | Pratt | " | " | 25 | 700 | | 700 | | | 21 00 |
| 4 | Crafton, W. H. | Meek | Ware | Ware | Ware | 29 | 300 | | 300 | | | 9 00 |
| 5 | | | | | | | | | | | | |
| 6 | | | | | | | | | | | | |
| 7 | Dodd, W. B. | Smithson | Glenn | Crafton | Rd. | 78 | 1400 | | 1400 | | | 42 00 |
| 8 | Dodson, E.L. | West | Vaden | Johnson | " | 50 | 400 | | 400 | | | 12 00 |
| 9 | | | | | | | | | | | | |
| 10 | | | | | | | | | | | | |
| 11 | G Garner, Lee | Bennett | Bennett | Nevils | Tomlin | 125 | 1600 | | 1600 | | | 48 00 |
| 12 | Givens, B. E. | River | Rd. | River | Givens | 99 | 2500 | | 2500 | | | 75 00 |
| 13 | Glenn, F. A. estate | Dodd | McGee | Ogilvie | Smithson | 137 | 3400 | | 3400 | | | 102 00 |
| 14 | Glenn, R. W. | House and lot | | Peytonsville | | 1 | 1000 | | 1000 | 2.00 | 30 00 | 32 00 |
| 15 | | | | | | | | | | | | |
| 16 | | | | | | | | | | | | |
| 17 | Hatcher, Miss Mary | Wallace | Rd. | Givens | Boyd | 293 | 10000 | 1000 | 11000 | | | 330 00 |
| 18 | Heithcock, Mrs.Sid | Heithcock | Hatcher | Crafton | Gee | 29 | 300 | | 300 | | | 9 00 |
| 19 | Houser, Mrs. F. M. | Givens | Hatcher | Castleman | Hatcher | 42 | 1200 | | 1200 | | | 36 00 |
| 20 | | | | | | | | | | | | |
| 21 | | | | | | | | | | | | |
| 22 | | | | | | | | | | | | |
| | | | | | | 989 | 24,800 | 1,000 | 25,800 | 400 | | 778 00 |

# TAX BOOK, 1950, WILLIAMSON COUNTY, TENN.

| NAME | DESCRIPTION OF PROPERTY | | | | No. Acres Land or Town Lots | Value Acres Land or Town Lots Dollars | Value Pers'l Property Less $1,000 Dollars | Total Real, Personal and all Other Property Dollars | Poll Tax Dollars | COUNTY TAXES $ Cts. | Total County Taxes $ Cts. |
|---|---|---|---|---|---|---|---|---|---|---|---|
| | NORTH | SOUTH | EAST | WEST | | | | | | | |
| 1 Jackson, Paul | Critz | Dodson | Dodson | McGee | 50 | 600 | | 600 | 2.00 | 18 00 | 20 00 |
| 2 Jackson, R. W. | | | | | 50 | 1100 | | 1100 | 2.00 | 33 00 | 35 00 |
| 3 Johnson, P. E.Estate | Vaden | Crowder | Smithson | Johnson | 118 | 2400 | | 2400 | | | 72 00 |
| 4 | | | | | | | | | | | |
| 5 | | | | | | | | | | | |
| 6 King & Hughes (Steve & Tom) | Beard | Tomlin | Tomlin | Tomlin | 146 | 1500 | | 1500 | | | 45 00 |
| 7 King, Lillie | Cotton | West | Cotton | McGee | 20 | 300 | | 300 | | | 9 00 |
| 8 | | | | | | | | | | | |
| 9 | | | | | | | | | | | |
| 10 Ladd, James A. | Ladd | Nolen | Smithson | Rd. | 104 | 1900 | | 1900 | | | 57 00 |
| 11 Ladd, Joe H. | Rd. | Campbell | Green | Givens | 25 | 600 | | 600 | 2.00 | 18 00 | 20 00 |
| 12 Ladd, Leonard & Robert | Deason | Garner | Nevils | Rd. | 165 | 3200 | | 3200 | | | 96 00 |
| 13 Lillard, L. H. | Moseley | Rd. | Moseley | Bond | 63 | 700 | | 700 | | | 21 00 |
| 14 Lillard, O. C. | Rd. | Lillard | Chunn | Rd. | 174 | 3800 | | 3300 | | | 99 00 |
| 15 | | | | | | | | | | | |
| 16 | | | | | | | | | | | |
| 17 Marlin, W. S. | Hussey | McGee | Cotton | Hussey | 104 | 1400 | | 1400 | | | 42 00 |
| 18 Maxwell, J. M. | Glenn | Rd. | Haynes | Tomlin | 37 | 2300 | | | | | |
| 19 " " | Nevils | McGee | Smith | McGee | 80 | 700 | | 3000 | 2.00 | 90 00 | 92 00 |
| 20 | | | | | | | | | | | |
| 21 | | | | | | | | | | | |
| 22 | | | | | | | | | | | |
| | | | | | 1,136 | 20,000 | | 20,000 | 5.00 | | 608 00 |

# TAX BOOK, 1950, WILLIAMSON COUNTY, TENN.





| NAME | DESCRIPTION OF PROPERTY | | | | No. Acres Land or Town Lots | Value Acres Land or Town Lots Dollars | Value Pers'l Property Less $1,000 Dollars | Total Real, Personal and all Other Property Dollars | Poll Tax Dollars | COUNTY TAXES $ Cts. | Total County Taxes $ Cts. |
|---|---|---|---|---|---|---|---|---|---|---|---|
| | NORTH | SOUTH | EAST | WEST | | | | | | | |
| 1 Meeks, Roy G. | Ladd | Waddey | Rd. | Bennett | 78 | 900 | | | | | |
| 2 " " | Bennett | Garner | Neely | Tomlin | 43 | 700 | | | | | |
| 3 " " | Warren | Rd. | Rd. | King | 132 | 2500 | | | | | |
| 4 " " | Rd. | Bennett | Ladd | Tomlin | 43 | 700 | | | | | |
| 5 " " | King | Rd. | Warren | Smithson | 34 | 1500 | | 6300 | | | 189 00 |
| 6 McGee, J. E. | Ladd | Simmons | Rd. | Ladd | 20 | 500 | | | | | |
| 7 " " | Reynolds | Rd. | Simmons | Campbell | 55 | 1000 | | 1500 | 2.00 | 45 00 | 47 00 |
| 8 McGee, Sam F. | Glenn | " | Haynes | Tomlin | 196 | 5000 | | 5000 | | | 150 00 |
| 9 McMahon, J. R. | Rd. | Gee | Rd. | Gee | 67 | 1400 | | 1400 | 2.00 | 42 00 | 44 00 |
| 10 Moseley, Lee X. A | Lillard | Neely | Davis | Rd. | 107 | 2400 | | 2400 | | | 72 00 |
| 11 | | | | | | | | | | | |
| 12 | | | | | | | | | | | |
| 13 Nevils, W. W. estate | McGee | Rd. | Rd. | Harrison | 20 | 700 | | | | | |
| 14 " " | Boundaries unknown | | | | 1 | 100 | | 800 | | | 24 00 |
| 15 | | | | | | | | | | | |
| 16 Pate, Mrs. A. T. | Campbell | Simmons | Stephens | Rd. | 70 | 2200 | | | | | |
| 17 " " | Vaden | Poteete | Rd. | Johnson | 29 | 500 | | 2700 | | | 81 00 |
| 18 Poteete, Emory | Bennett | Johnson | Tomlin | Tomlin | 52 | 400 | | | | | |
| 19 " " | " | Poteete | Rd. | Johnson | 25 | 200 | | 600 | | | 18 00 |
| 20 Pratt, J. E. | Vaden | West | Parks | Tomlin | 200 | 3200 | | 3200 | | | 96 00 |
| 21 | | | | | | | | | | | |
| 22 | | | | | | | | | | | |
| | | | | | 1,172 | 23,900 | | 23,900 | 4.00 | | 721 00 |

# TAX BOOK, 1950, WILLIAMSON COUNTY, TENN.

| | NAME | DESCRIPTION OF PROPERTY | | | | No. Acres Land or Town Lots | Value Acres Land or Town Lots Dollars | Value Pers'l Property Less $1,000 Dollars | Total Real, Personal and all Other Property Dollars | Poll Tax Dollars | County Taxes $ | Cts. | Total County Taxes $ | Cts. |
|---|---|---|---|---|---|---|---|---|---|---|---|---|---|---|
| | | NORTH | SOUTH | EAST | WEST | | | | | | | | | |
| 1 | Robinson, Jimmy | Vaden | Gee | Gee | Rd. | 37 | 600 | | | | | | | |
| 2 | " " | Green | Rd. | Vaden | Hatcher | 105 | 2200 | | 2800 | 2.00 | 84 | 00 | 86 | 00 |
| 3 | | | | | | | | | | | | | | |
| 4 | | | | | | | | | | | | | | |
| 5 | Simmons, H. W. | Ladd | Nolen | McMahon | Rd. | 45 | 1000 | | 1000 | | | | 30 | 00 |
| 6 | Skinner, W. N. | Rd. | Hatcher | Green | Campbell | 39 | 700 | | 700 | | | | 21 | 00 |
| 7 | Sledge, Willie | Meeks | Robinson | Crafton | Heithcock | 29 | 300 | | 300 | | | | 9 | 00 |
| 8 | Sledge, W. D.& W. C. | River | Rd. | Akin | Ryan | 126 | 3000 | | 3000 | | | | 90 | 00 |
| 9 | Smithson, Mrs. Ben | Pratt | Johnson | Simmons | Rd. | 72 | 1400 | | 1400 | | | | 42 | 00 |
| 10 | Smithson, Escar | Rd. | Hall | Moseley | Ladd | 73 | 1400 | | | | | | | |
| 11 | " " | Johnson | Rd. | Smithson | Hayes | 76 | 1700 | | 3100 | | | | 93 | 00 |
| 12 | Smithson, L.H. | Lillard | " | Lillard | Rd. | 76 | 900 | | 900 | | | | 27 | 00 |
| 13 | Smithson, T. W. Est. | Johnson | Beard | West | Vaden | 254 | 7300 | | 7300 | | | | 219 | 00 |
| 14 | Spears, Mrs. Lela | King | Warren | Tomlin | King | 45 | 1000 | | | | | | | |
| 15 | " " | Store house at Peytonsville | | | | 1 | 300 | | | | | | | |
| 16 | " " | Ladd | Nolen | McMahon | Rd. | 63 | 1000 | | 2300 | | | | 69 | 00 |
| 17 | Stanfield, Shelby | Gibson | Gentry | Gee | Gee | 60 | 1300 | | 1300 | | | | 39 | 00 |
| 18 | | | | | | | | | | | | | | |
| 19 | | | | | | | | | | | | | | |
| 20 | | | | | | | | | | | | | | |
| 21 | | | | | | | | | | | | | | |
| 22 | | | | | | | | | | | | | | |
| | | | | | | 1,101 | 24,100 | | 24,100 | 2.00 | | | 725 | 00 |

# TAX BOOK, 1950, WILLIAMSON COUNTY, TENN.

| | NAME | DESCRIPTION OF PROPERTY | | | | No. Acres Land or Town Lots | Value Acres Land or Town Lots Dollars | Value Pers'l Property Less $1,000 Dollars | Total Real, Personal and all Other Property Dollars | Poll Tax Dollars | County Taxes $ | Cts. | Total County Taxes $ | Cts. |
|---|---|---|---|---|---|---|---|---|---|---|---|---|---|---|
| | | NORTH | SOUTH | EAST | WEST | | | | | | | | | |
| 1 | Tomlin, Mrs. Ben A. | House and lot | | Peytonsville | | 1 | 500 | | 500 | | | | 15 | 00 |
| 2 | Tomlin, H. D. | Johnson | Smithson | Rd. | Johnson | 47 | 1100 | | 1100 | | | | 33 | 00 |
| 3 | Tomlin, Johnnie | Rd. | Bennett | Bennett | McGee | 149 | 2100 | | 2100 | | | | 63 | 00 |
| 4 | Tomlin, Marvin | " | Tomlin | McGee | Church | 10 | 600 | | 600 | 2.00 | 18 | 00 | 20 | 00 |
| 5 | Tomlin, Reese | House and lot | | Peytonsville | | 1 | 400 | | 400 | | | | 12 | 00 |
| 6 | | | | | | | | | | | | | | |
| 7 | | | | | | | | | | | | | | |
| 8 | Vaden, A.L. | Vaden | Cotton | York | Hussey | 115 | 2500 | | 2500 | | | | 75 | 00 |
| 9 | " " | Rd. | Crowder | Smithson | Johnson | 26 | 2000 | | 4500 | | | | 135 | 00 |
| 10 | Vaden, W. W. | Dodson | Smithson | " | McGee | 112 | 1600 | | 1600 | 2.00 | 48 | 00 | 50 | 00 |
| 11 | Veach, Dennis | Ogilvie | Ogilvie | Haynes | McGee | 40 | 600 | | 600 | 2.00 | 18 | 00 | 20 | 00 |
| 12 | Veach, Mrs. Mollie | Garner | McGee | Waddey | Bennett | 46 | 500 | | 500 | | | | 15 | 00 |
| 13 | | | | | | | | | | | | | | |
| 14 | Waddey, J.L. | Alexander | Lillard | Woods | Rd. | 124 | 2300 | | 2300 | | | | 69 | 00 |
| 15 | Waddey, R. P. | Rd. | Moseley | Waddey | Veach | 205 | 5500 | 700 | 6200 | | | | 186 | 00 |
| 16 | Wallace, O. C. | River | Warren | West | Boxley | 85 | 4700 | | 4700 | | | | 141 | 00 |
| 17 | Waters, Albert | Green | Rd. | Waddey | Green | 41 | 2500 | | 2500 | | | | 75 | 00 |
| 18 | West, G. W. | Rd. | Boyd | Rd. | Wallace | 63 | 3000 | | 3000 | | | | 90 | 00 |
| 19 | Williams, W. L. | " | Buchanan | King | Smithson | 86 | 2500 | | 2500 | 2.00 | 75 | 00 | 77 | 00 |
| 20 | | | | | | | | | | | | | | |
| 21 | | | | | | | | | | | | | | |
| 22 | | | | | | | | | | | | | | |
| | | | | | | 1,151 | 32,400 | 700 | 33,100 | 8.00 | | | 1001 | 00 |

# TAX BOOK, 1950, WILLIAMSON COUNTY, TENN.

| | NAME | DESCRIPTION OF PROPERTY | | | | No. Acres Land or Town Lots | Value Acres Land or Town Lots Dollars | Value Pers'l Property Less $1,000 Dollars | Total Real, Personal and all Other Property Dollars | Poll Tax Dollars | COUNTY TAXES $ Cts. | Total County Taxes $ Cts. |
|---|---|---|---|---|---|---|---|---|---|---|---|---|
| | | NORTH | SOUTH | EAST | WEST | | | | | | | |
| 1 | York, C. D. | Reynolds | Pratt | Reynolds | Rd. | 146 | 3600 | | 3600 | | | 108 00 |
| 2 | York, Claude Estate | Boyd | Russell | Rd. | Johnson | 214 | 7000 | | 7000 | | | 210 00 |
| 3 | York, J. W. | York | Campbell | " | Cotton | 95 | 2500 | | 2500 | 2.00 | 75 00 | 77 00 |
| 4 | | | | | | | | | | | | |
| 5 | | | | | | | | | | | | |
| 6 | | | | | | | | | | | | |
| 7 | | | | | | | | | | | | |
| 8 | | | | | | | | | | | | |
| 9 | | | | | | | | | | | | |
| 10 | | | | | | | | | | | | |
| 11 | | | | | | | | | | | | |
| 12 | | | | | | | | | | | | |
| 13 | | | | | | | | | | | | |
| 14 | | | | | | | | | | | | |
| 15 | | | | | | | | | | | | |
| 16 | | | | | | | | | | | | |
| 17 | | | | | | | | | | | | |
| 18 | | | | | | | | | | | | |
| 19 | | | | | | | | | | | | |
| 20 | | | | | | | | | | | | |
| 21 | | | | | | | | | | | | |
| 22 | | | | | | 455 | 13,100 | | 13,100 | 2.00 | | 395 00 |

# TAX BOOK, 1950, WILLIAMSON COUNTY, TENN.

| | NAME Colored | DESCRIPTION OF PROPERTY | | | | No. Acres Land or Town Lots | Value Acres Land or Town Lots Dollars | Value Pers'l Property Less $1,000 Dollars | Total Real, Personal and all Other Property Dollars | Poll Tax Dollars | COUNTY TAXES $ Cts. | Total County Taxes $ Cts. |
|---|---|---|---|---|---|---|---|---|---|---|---|---|
| | | NORTH | SOUTH | EAST | WEST | | | | | | | |
| 1 | Crowder, Charlie | Thompson | Ladd | Gee | Vaden | 40 | 600 | | 600 | | | 18 00 |
| 2 | Crowder, Odelia | Hatcher | Vaden | Crowder | " | 19 | 400 | | 400 | | | 12 00 |
| 3 | Crowder, Tom | Vaden | Rd. | Smithson | Crowder | 10 | 300 | | 300 | | | 9 00 |
| 4 | Crowder, Will | Johnson | " | Crowder | Rd. | 20 | 400 | | 400 | | | 12 00 |
| 5 | | | | | | | | | | | | |
| 6 | | | | | | | | | | | | |
| 7 | Gentry, James M. | Meeks | Crafton | Crafton | Rd. | 38 | 1000 | | | | | |
| 8 | "        " | Rd. | Simmons | Hughes | " | 48 | 1100 | | 2100 | 2.00 | 63 00 | 65 00 |
| 9 | Gibson, Loss Est. | Gibson | Crowder | Gee | Gee | 10 | 300 | | 300 | | | 9 00 |
| 10 | | | | | | | | | | | | |
| 11 | | | | | | | | | | | | |
| 12 | Hayes, Bud Estate | McGee | Simmons | Lillard | Nevils | 12 | 300 | | 300 | | | 9 00 |
| 13 | | | | | | | | | | | | |
| 14 | Luster, Grant | Luster | Luster | Pk. | Luster | 2 | 300 | | 300 | | | 9 00 |
| 15 | | | | | | | | | | | | |
| 16 | Reynolds, Winnie | Hatcher | Vaden | Crowder | Vaden | 19 | 400 | | 400 | | | 12 00 |
| 17 | | | | | | | | | | | | |
| 18 | Smithson, John | Smithson | Nevils | Simmons | Smith | 10 | 200 | | 200 | | | 6 00 |
| 19 | Smithson, Oze, Est. | " | Beal | " | " | 20 | 300 | | 300 | | | 9 00 |
| 20 | Starnes, Minnie | Beal | Hughes | Gentry | Rd. | 14 | 200 | | 200 | | | 6 00 |
| 21 | | | | | | | | | | | | |
| 22 | | | | | | 262 | 5,800 | | 5,800 | 2.00 | | 176 00 |

NATHANIEL N., MARGARET KNOTT AND ELIJAH KNOTT SMITHSON POSE AT THEIR HOME IN THE HEART OF PEYTONSVILLE IN 1866. LATER, THE HOME OF THE SAM MCGEE FAMILY. TODAY THE HOME OF RONNY MANGRUM.

THE LOG HOME OF GARNER MCCONNICO JORDAN, AN EARLY CITIZEN OF PEYTONSVILLE, LOCATED ON COOL SPRINGS ROAD. LATER THE HOME OF MRS. WILLIE JOE BUFORD.

THE HOME OF JAMES GOSEY (1772-1854) AND REBECCA BOWER GOSEY (1785-1859) ON GOSEY HILL ROAD. ALSO, THEIR SON, MOSES GENTRY GOSEY CALLED THIS HOME. RECENTLY, THE HOME OF BILLY AND BARBARA PRATT NOLAND.

THE HOME OF GREGORY JOHNSON (1855), WILLIAM V. PARKS (1890), CLAUDE YORK, SR. (1918) AND WESLEY YORK FAMILIES ON GOSEY HILL ROAD.

THE HOME OF SAMUEL PRATT FAMILY ON GOSEY HILL ROAD.

THE HOME OF SPOTSWOOD H. AND MARY ANDREWS HATCHER AT THE
CORNER OF GOSEY HILL ROAD AND LONG LANE.

THE HENRY DAVID TOMLIN FAMILY HOME ON GOSEY HILL ROAD.

THE HOME OF T.G. GOSEY, BEN AND MAGGIE LEE SMITHSON, AND NOW THE
HOME OF JOHN W. HAM ON GOSEY HILL ROAD.

THE HENRY BEAL HOME ON TRINITY-PEYTONSVILLE ROAD.

THE HOME OF JOHN AND BETTY (BENNETT) BURGE ON TRINITY-PEYTONSVILLE ROAD.

THE HOME OF S.S. STARNES-DR. A.R. PINKSTON-JIM CROWELL ON TRINITY-PEYTONSVILLE ROAD.

THE HOME OF LELA WILLIAMS WARREN SPEARS ON PEYTONSVILLE ROAD. ALSO, MISS KATIE LOU GATLIN BOARDED HERE.

THE J.A. JOHNSON HOME ON GOSEY HILL ROAD NEAR CROWDER ROAD.

THE ESCAR SMITHSON HOME ON ARNO-PEYTONSVILLE ROAD.

# NOTABLE HOMES GONE BUT NOT FORGOTTEN
## OF THE 13TH DISTRICT

KNOWN AS THE OLD SMITHSON HOUSE AND THOUGHT TO HAVE BEEN
NEAR THE VILLAGE ON THE PEYTONSVILLE-TRINITY ROAD.

THE TURNEL LUNDY GREEN HARRISON HOME WAS LOCATED NEXT DOOR
TO THE METHODIST CHURCH AND THE VILLAGE BLACKSMITH SHOP,
ACROSS THE ROAD FROM THE CHURCH OF CHRIST.

THE THOMAS WALTER SMITHSON HOUSE ON PEYTONSVILLE ROAD.

THE WILLIAM JONES HOUSE ON PEYTONSVILLE-ARNO ROAD.

THE J.J. HOLLAND HOUSE ON COOL SPRINGS ROAD. L TO R: J.J. AND MARY HOLLAND, W.P. LADD, THOMAS W. SMITHSON AND STELLA (SMITHSON) LADD.

THE THOMAS MERRITT HOUSE ON PEYTONSVILLE ROAD BURNED IN 1982.

THE OLIVER C. LILLARD HOME NEAR THE PEYTONSVILLE-ARNO ROAD. O.C. LILLARD SERVED ON THE COUNTY QUARTERLY COURT FOR NEARLY 50-YEARS.

THE O.C. LILLARD HOUSE ON COOL SPRINGS ROAD WAS DESTROYED BY A TORNADO ON JANUARY 30, 1960.

THE THOMAS WALTER SMITHSON, THOMAS WADE SMITHSON, ELLA VADEN SMITHSON HOME, LATER BUD AND NADEEN SMITHSON. THIS HOME WAS MOVED TO BUCHANAN ROAD.

THE HOME OF EDWARD STANDING BEAR GOSEY ON GOSEY HILL ROAD.

**REV. CALUDIUS BUCHANAN**, a native of Williamson County, was born December 17, 1842. His father, Joseph Buchanan, was born in this State about 1809, and in 1936 wedded Martha Edminston, a native of Tennessee, born about 1809. To this union were born seven children, two of them of whom are yet living, our subject being one of them. The father died in 1876. Our subject's grandfather, John Buchanan, was born in Washington County, Va., in 1772, and married Margaret Edmondson in 1798; she was also a native of Virginia, born about 1774. They came to Tennessee about 1800 and purchased 200 acres of land in this district on what is known as the "Old Hightower Road." He died in 1820 and the grandmother in 1858. Our subject has followed agricultural pursuits the principal part of his life. In 1861 he enlisted in Company D., Twentieth Tennessee Regiment, was taken prisoner at Missionary Ridge, imprisoned at Rock Island, Ill., and retained there fifteen months. At the close of the war he returned home and in 1866 was married to Miss Dolly J. Smithson, a native of this State, born October 12, 1844, and the daughter of Sylvanus and Louisa Smithson, natives, respectively, of Virginia and Tennessee. The father was born about 1791 and served as a private in the late war; was wounded in the Cheat Mountain campaign. He died in 1872 and the mother in 1850. To our subject and wife were born six children: Josephine E., born September 11, 1867; M. Blanche, born December 29, 1869; William C., born August 10, 1871; John B., born July 24, 1874; Lillian M., born September 10, 1877, and Gerald M., born March 28, 1880. In January 1867, Mr. Buchanan moved to the farm upon which he is now living and in 1870 purchased it from his father. It contains 300 acres of medium land in a fair state of cultivation. In 1871 he obtained license to preach and has since been a local preacher. He is a member of the Masonic fraternity and is a Democrat in politics. He and his wife are devout members of the Methodist Episcopal Church South.

**MOSES G. GOSEY**, an old and a prominent citizen of this district, was born in Tennessee December 2, 1815. His father, James Gosey, was born in Virginia about 1770, and was married in 1798 to Rebecca Bowers, a native of Virginia, born about 1785. In 1801 they came to Tennessee, where the father followed the occupation of a farmer. He was a good, pious citizen, having joined the Methodist Episcopal Church at an early age. He died in 1856, and his widow followed in 1859. Our subject was united in marriage to Miss Mary A. Nevils in 1846. She was a native of this State, born August 12, 1824, and the daughter of Josiah and Sallie Beech Nevils. Our subject and wife became the parents of five children: James G., Sarah E., Mary T., Mattie L. and an infant not named. All have crossed the dark river into the valley of the shadow of death, and only two lived to be grown. In 1849 our subject began merchandising at Peytonsville and carried on a thriving business there until 1860. During the war he was very unfortunate, losing about $17,000 of hard-earned money. He lives on a farm of seventy-two acres on the edge of Peytonsville, and since the war has directed his attention to farming. He is a member of the Masonic fraternity, and he and wife are members of the Methodist Church Episcopal South.

**TURNEL LUNDY GREEN HARRISON** was born in Tennessee June 5, 1838. His father, Nathaniel Lundy Harrison, was born in Warren County, N.C., December 2, 1808, and came to Tennessee with his parents when quite young. He remained in this county many years and held the office of constable and deputy sheriff. He was a good neighbor, a kind father, and reared and educated his children to become useful men

and women. His home was in the Tenth District until 1843 when he moved to the Thirteenth. His death occurred November 21, 1885. Our subject's mother, Christina Knight, was born in Tennessee in 1812, and in the year 1832 was wedded to Nathaniel L. Harrison, by whom she became the mother of eleven children. Her death occurred in 1863. Our subject was united in marriage, in 1863, to Ella A. Martin, a native of this State, born in 1843, and the daughter of Benjamin F. and Jane D. Alston Martin. To her union with Mr. Harrison she became the mother of four children: Covoda, born in 1863, Modera, born 1865; Odo, born 1870, and Goldie, born 1877. Our subject followed agricultural pursuits until 1858, when he began merchandising in Nashville. In 1861 he enlisted in the Confederate service, was promoted to third lieutenant, and stood at his post of duty during the entire war. In 1865 he returned home and began blacksmithing in the village of Peytonsville, his present location. In 1881 he was elected justice of the peace. He and wife are members of the Christian Church, and he is a Democrat in politics.

**J.W.L. Nevils**, a leading citizen of Williamson County, was born in this State July 14, 1834. His father, Josiah Nevils, was born in Virginia in 1794, and the mother, Sallie Beech, was also born in Virginia, about 1809. They both came to Tennessee in the year 1821 and in 1823 were united in marriage. The father left his farm to fight in the War of 1812 and was in the memorable Battle of New Orleans. He died in 1854 and his wife in 1852. Our subject wedded Miss Ella G. Low in 1871. She was born in Tennessee September 13, 1851 and was the daughter of Gabriel and Vina H. Pinkston Yarbrough Low. To our subject and wife were born six children: John L., deceased, born in 1872; Augie V., born 1874; Josiah W., deceased, born in 1876; William W., born in 1877; Sallie M., born in 1880, and an infant not named. Our

subject engaged in the mercantile business in Maury County, Tenn., in 1856, and in 1861 closed out and enlisted in the Confederate Army, serving his country until the close of the war. One year after returning from the war he engaged again in the mercantile business in Peytonsville for about ten years, after which he sold out his stock of good and gave his undivided attention to farming. He has 104 acres of good land near Peytonsville. He is a member of the Masonic lodge, also of the I.O.O.F., and he and wife are worthy members of the Methodist Episcopal Church South. Mr. Nevils is a Democrat and in 1874 he was elected magistrate in this district.

**JOHN M. NEVILS**, sheriff of Williamson County, was born in Maury County, Tenn., October 3, 1835, son of Josiah and Sarah Beech Nevils, and of Dutch-English descent. Our subject was reared on the farm and secured a good practical education in the common schools. He followed the occupation of a farmer until the beginning of the late war, when he enlisted in the Confederate Army, Company B. Eleventh Tennessee Regiment, and served four years. In 1865 he engaged in merchandising in Nashville, but soon removed to Peytonsville, this county, and continued farming and merchandising. In 1868 he wedded Lydia A. Low, who died in 1878. In 1879 he wedded Alice Merritt, and to them were born two children: Robert H. and Edward M. Mr. Nevils is a member of the Masonic fraternity and the I.O.O.F. He has made one of the best sheriffs the county has ever had. He is a member of the Methodist Episcopal Church and is one of the prominent men of this county. Mrs. Nevils is a member of the Christian Church.

**NATHANIEL N. SMITHSON**, a respected citizen of Williamson County, was born in this State April 2, 1826. He received his education as the average country boy in the district schools. November 30, 1851, he was married to Miss Margaret K. Johnson, a native of Tennessee, born March 8, 1833, and the daughter of Jesse and Dolly Smithson Johnson. Our subject and

wife were blessed by an interesting family of ten children: James M., born in 1860; Dolly A., born in 1863; Martha P., born in 1865, Permelia (deceased), born in 1867; Mary E., born in 1879; Lydia in 1874, and Jesse W. (deceased), born in 1877. In 1870 our subject moved to his present location in the edge of Peytonsville, where he has a fine farm of 190 acres, besides this he has another farm of 400 acres in another part of the county. He is a mason, a staunch Democrat and a member of the Methodist Episcopal Church South. His wife is a member of the Baptist Church. Mr. Smithson is the son of Tandy S. and Ann Cheatham Smithson. Her father, a native of Virginia, was born in 1802, and died in 1873, and the mother was born in 1804.

**GEORGE W. SMITHSON**, of the firm Smithson, Kenneday, Hodge & Co., is a native of Lunnenburg County, Va., his birthday being

December 30, 1838, son of William G. and Mary Smithson, whose maiden name was Crenshaw. The parents were born in Virginia, the father in 1819 and the mother in 1820. The family of English extraction and came to Tennessee about 1840. There the mother of our subject died in 1846 and the father in 1852. Our subject lived on a farm until he reached the age of thirteen, when he began clerking in the store of Charles W. Smithson at Peytonsville, this county. He continued as clerk until 1859, when he engaged in this business for himself at Peytonsville in partnership with John C. Helms and remained in this business until 1862. He then enlisted in Capt. Ewing's company, First Battalion, Tennessee Cavalry. In 1865 he came to Franklin and engaged in the dry goods business and the same he now continues. From October 1863 to March 1865, he was cashier of the Farmers' National Bank, of Franklin. In the spring of 1865, he became a partner of the firm, Smithson, Kenneday, Hodge & Co, this is the most extensive dry goods store in Franklin and is doing a large trade. In 1871 he wedded Miss Sallie M. Henderson, daughter of Dr. Samuel Henderson of this county. Mr. and Mrs. Smithson were born four children: Janey, George H., Mary and Sallie, Mr. Smithson is a first-class citizen, a Democrat, a Royal Arch Mason, and his wife is a member of the Methodist Episcopal Church South.

## WILLIAM PARRISH ESTATE 1870

***Miscellaneous Records Volume 6***
**Louise Gillespie Lynch**
November 1870-William Parrish estate-John S. Parrish and W.C. Parrish are joint owners of a tract of land in the 13th District containing about 500 acres bounded on the north by William Stevens, Alexander Reid, William J. Smithson and Thomas Helm's land-on the west by Louis J. Beard, C.W. Mallory, originally the old Fleming tract-on the south by Sam Harris, S.W. Smithson, deceased, land on the east by William Neely, the old Garner Jordan land, N.L. Harrison and J.W.L. Nevils. The land descended to them from their father William Parrish and their grandmother Catherine Parrish. Dr. Alexander Reid is the administrator of the estate of William Parrish and the debts can be paid without a sale of the land. They want a division of the Loose Records 1907.

Louis J. Beard died July 4, 1906. He owned 2 tracts of land in the 13th District where he had been residing more than 50 years. The land was deeded to him by William Parrish in 1855. There was 115 acres in one tract and the second tract contained 12 ½ acres and was conveyed to him by John Overton in 1890. At the death of Louis, his daughter Etta Beard lived with him. His wife having died 6 or 7 years before. George Beard lived in another house on the 115-acre tract.

Edna Hawkins, another daughter, was living on the 12 ½ acre trace with her two small children. Her husband, Dave, had left her. Etta Beard later went to live with her brother Alex Beard. Owen, Mosley, and Company purchased the land at the sheriff's sale in 1899. Louis J. Beard was an old man at the time of the sale, about 72 or 73 years old. He lived about 5 ½ years after the time of the sale. The heirs are: George Beard, W.H.S. Beard, L.J. Beard, Jr., William Ivy and wife Mary Ivy, Richard Beard, Edna Beard, Charlie Beard, Etta Beard, Porter Hartley and wife E.F. Hartley, William Tomlin and wife Agnes Tomlin, Charles Hinson, and wife Adeline Hinson, Lee Robinson and wife Lizzie Robinson, Robert Jackson and wife Annie Johnson, William Ivey and John Ivy, J.L. Beard and Ewing Heithcock and wife Bettie Ann Heithcock.

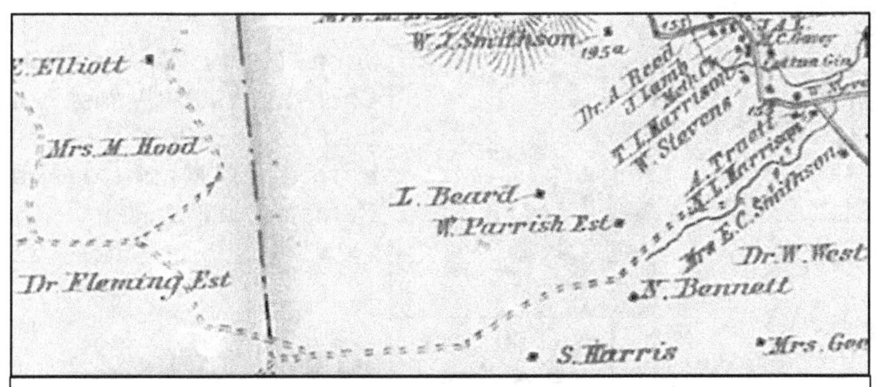



THE 1878 BEERS MAP LOCATES THE WILLIAM PARRISH ESTATE. THE DASH LINE IS THE HARPETH-PEYTONSVILLE ROAD TODAY. MRS. E.C. SMITHSON WOULD BE THE S.W. SMITHSON PLACE. TODAY, THIS WOULD BE THE OLD MEEKS FARM. NOTICE THAT THE LOUIS BEARD FARM WAS NEXT TO THE WILLIAM PARRISH ESTATE.

## SAMUEL S. STARNES ESTATE 1848

***Miscellaneous Records Volume 8***
**Louise Gillespie Lynch**
1848-James W. Starnes, Lycurgus H. Mosley and wife Mary A., Peter G. Mosley, and wife Catharine M., Allison Treadwell and wife Rebecca E., Nancy P. Starnes, Samuel S. Starnes, John D. Starnes and Ebenezer Starnes, (last four minors by guardian Lycurgus H. Mosley), Nancy T., Samuel S., John D., and Ebenezer Starnes are the owners of the following tracts of land lying on Big Harpeth River; tract containing 314 acres adjoining the lands of John Starnes, James Price and others and conveyed to Samuel S. Starnes, deceased. (who with their father) by Mordicia Pillow; a tract adjoining the other land containing 87 acres and conveyed to Samuel S. Starnes by the Clerk and Master of Chancery Court in Franklin; 1 tract containing 221 ¾ acres adjoining the lands of Crafton and others and conveyed to said Samuel S. Starnes by Dennis M. Crafton, Exr. Of Daniel Wilkes deceased out of this tract is excepted a tract containing 147 11/16 acres allotted to Catharine M. Mosley; a tract containing about 216 acres adjoining the lands formerly owned by the heirs of Edward Breathitt and the lands of John Starnes conveyed to Samuel S. Starnes by Elisha Davis out of which lands are excepted two tracts containing 119 ¼ acres adjoining the lands of Richard H. Rudder and conveyed to their father by Reese and Lewis Corzine. The other 1/7 is owned by their brother, Shubal Starnes who recently died intestate leaving heirs: Nancy P., Samuel S., John D., Ebenezer, James W. Starnes, Catharine M. Mosley and Rebecca E. Treadwell. L.H. Mosley was appointed Administrator of the estate. There is a sufficiency of estate without resorting to his land to settle his debts. The last-mentioned tract of land cannot be divided without destroying the value of the land and should be sold and the proceeds divided. The land has been rented out and much waste has been committed. The rent on the land is less than the interest.

April 1848, Deposition of Richard W. Robinson-I am acquainted with the lands owned by the heirs of Dr. Samuel S. Starnes: the Pillow place, the Radford place, the Wilkes place, the Davis place and the Corzine place. I think it would be in the best interest of the minors for the land to be sold.

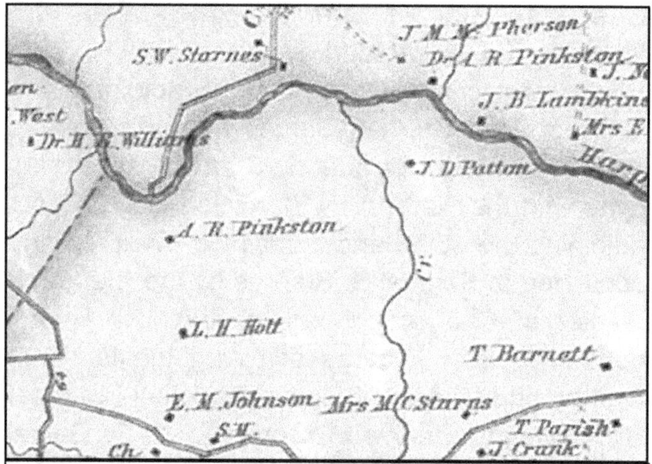

THE SAMUEL S. STARNES PLACE APPEARS TO BE MAINLY THE JIM CROWELL PLACE ON PEYTONSVILLE-TRINITY ROAD. ON THE 1878 MAP, THE SAMUEL S. STARNES' ESTATE WOULD BE LOCATED AROUND DR. A.R. PINKSTON'S FARM, WHICH LATER BECAME THE JIM CROWELL PLACE. THE MRS. M.C. STARNES WOULD BE THE RICHARD RUDDER FARM ON MEEKS ROAD, ALONG HURRICANE CREEK.

# THE JOHN CRUNK FAMILY OF THE ARNO COMMUNITY

**Taken in part from an article by Linda Lillard Cotton in *College Grove Williamson County History & Families* 2011.**

John Henry Crunk born June 2, 1876, married Annie Bell Graves, born Nov. 19, 1887, on Dec. 20, 1906. They lived in the Arno community. John was a dairy farmer and raised tobacco to pay the bills. He would kill hogs around Thanksgiving, and in the spring would always plant a garden for his family.

Annie was a housewife, who raised chickens to eat and eggs to sell for spending money. She was a good cook and would carry food to anyone sick in the community. She was a very good seamstress and made clothes for her family.

John liked to square dance and would go dancing most Saturday nights. They reared eight children on the farm and attended Wesley Chapel United Methodist Church at Arno.

Julia Myrtle Crunk was born April 12, 1911 and died May 11, 1911. The other children are as follows: Mary Gertrude Crunk West Jordan was born Sept. 23, 1906 and died July 14, 1985. Howard Perkins Crunk was born Dec. 25, 1908 and died June 12, 1994. Ruby Estelle Crunk Wood was born Sept. 20, 1912 and died Jan. 23, 1991.

Annie Bell Graves Lillard was born June 12, 1914 and died May 20, 2001. John Henry Crunk, Jr. was born March 29, 1916 and died Feb. 11, 1975. Walter Eugene Crunk was born July 2, 1918 and died Feb. 11, 1978, Robert Herbert Crunk was born Feb. 29, 1920 and died Sept. 27, 1923.

JOHN HENRY AND ANNIE BELL (GRAVES) CRUNK

John Henry Crunk died Sept 13, 1956. Annie Bell died Nov. 7, 1945. They are buried at Mount Hope Cemetery in Franklin.

RUBY (CRUNK) WOOD, CATHERINE (CRUNK) JEAN, ANNIE (CRUNK) LILLARD, MARY (CRUNK) JORDAN, HOWARD, GENE, JIM WILL, HERBERT AND JOHNNY CRUNK

# THE MERRITT FAMILY OF THE 13TH DISTRICT

**In part taken from Jerry W. Cook's article in** *College Grove Williamson County, Tennessee History & Families* **2011.**

John Applewhite Merritt was the son of Thomas Merritt, born Feb. 18, 1770, and died in Williamson County on July 6, 1845, and Rebecca Applewhite, born July 24, 1773, and died in Williamson County on Dec. 24, 1863.

John A. Merritt was married to Ann D. Burton, the daughter of Peter Burton, in Williamson County on Aug. 19, 1830. John and Ann were landowners and resided on a 262-acre farm on Hurricane Creek in the 13th Civil District. They resided in a large two-story log house that stood until 1984, when it burned to the ground while being restored. At that time, it was owned by the McGee family.

John was killed on the early morning of Aug. 23, 1853, when he was struck by lightning, and was buried in the garden behind his house where several of his younger children lay buried. There are no tombstones to be found in this graveyard today.

Ann gave birth to 11 children, but only five daughters survived to adulthood. After the death of their father, their mother died the next year and was buried by his side in the garden. John and Ann owned a large amount of property when they died, and all this was put up for sale.

The daughters of John Applewhite Merritt and Ann D. (Burton) Merritt follow: Rebecca Jane Merritt was born July 9, 1831, and died Oct. 5, 1859, in Williamson County. She was married to William R. Roberts on June 24, 1858. This union resulted in the birth of an infant child born July 1, 1859 and died Oct. 3, 1859.

Susan Elizabeth Merritt was born in Williamson County on Oct. 15, 1832, and died on Sept. 25, 1864, with her burial in Mt. Hope Cemetery. Susan was married to Alpheus Truett in Williamson County on Dec. 1, 1853, as his second wife, he being the son of Henry M. Truett and Sarah Clampett. Alpheus Truett was born in Hickman County on May 17, 1823 and died in 1898. Mr. Truett came to Williamson County during the 1840s and here began the operation of a nursey business, just north of Franklin, on the Nashville Pike. Near his greenhouse, he built a large, two-story white frame antebellum house, which still stands today. The Truett House was used as the headquarters for Gen. John M. Schofield during the Battle of Franklin. Born to Alpheus and Susan E. (Merritt) were five known children. The 1878 Beers map shows Alpheus Truett owning land in the middle of the village of Peytonsville.

Mary Katharine Merritt, daughter of John and Ann Merritt, was born in Williamson County on April 23, 1838 and died at College Grove on June 31, 1908. She was married to William Patton Demonbreun.

Frances Alice "Fannie" Merritt was born in Williamson County on Jan. 23, 1840, and died at the home of her sister, Sarah Ann Merritt Demonbreun, at College Grove on May 7, 1907. Fannie was married to Monroe D. Williams on Dec. 11, 1867, he being born in Williamson County in May 5, 1839, and died in the same county on March 10, 1898. Born to this union was one son, Walter J. Williams, born Sept 17, 1868, and died Dec. 13, 1869. Fannie and Monroe were buried in the Jesse Williams burying ground beside their infant son.

Sarah Ann "Sallie" Merritt was born in Williamson County on April 15, 1842 and died at College Grove on Jan. 17, 1919. Sallie was married to John Forsyshe Demonbreun of College Grove.

JOHN F. AND SARAH ANN (MERRITT) DEMONBREUN

MARY ANN (MERRITT) DEMONBREUN

# THOMAS AND DOLL (SMITHSON) HAMM OF THE RUDDERVILLE COMMUNITY

**Taken in part from an article written by Joan Ham Veach in *College Grove Williamson County History & Families* 2011.**

On Sept. 3, 1941, Thomas Lavender Hamm of Rudderville and Bennie Thelma 'Doll" Smithson of Arno were married in Franklin, TN. After a honeymoon in Chattanooga, they returned to Rudderville to live on Meek Road with my grandparents, John and Maggie Lee Ham, where Daddy helped with a dairy farm with my

grandfather and Uncle John Ham, Jr., known as Toad, Jr to most.

In February of 1942, my dad was drafted in the U.S. Army. He went to basic training and was later stationed in Richmond, VA. After a while, my mother joined him in Richmond and worked at Miller & Rhodes as a seamstress. Later my dad was sent to India and my mother came back to Tennessee.

In January 1946, my father was discharged, and we returned to the dairy farm on Meek Road. My great grandfather and grandmother lived with my Uncle Toad and Aunt Willie Lee and cousins Alvin, J.W. (Bubba) and Joyce lived in another house on the farm. My great grandfather, Joe Ham, passed away in 1949.

My grandfather, John Ham, Sr., remarried later and moved to Columbia, TN. The rest of the family remained on Meek Road and worked the farm and milked cows until 1956. My Daddy and uncle sold that farm at auction and Howard Smithson bought it. Part of it was later sold to the county and Page High School was built there.

My Uncle John Ham, Jr. bought the J.H. Akin farm across the way on Arno Road in Rudderville. Daddy and Mamma bought the Covington-Hopkins place owned by Mr. And Mrs. James E. Cooke, Jr. and Mr. and Mrs. R.M. Kennedy, heirs of James E. Cooke on Covington-Eudailey Road. At that time, the place was rented to C.C. Still on a 50-50 share crop basis for the year 1956. We moved from Meek Road in Rudderville in a one and one-half ton Studebaker truck and a wagon with a team of mules. That was the first time I actually felt I was an only child because I no longer was with my three cousins.

Once we moved to what had been the Hopkins place, we milked cows as Grade B instead of Grade A. I went to the barn with my Daddy every morning before school and every afternoon after school. In addition to barn chores, I was responsible for bringing in wood to be used for heat and after my mother started working at W.T. Grant's in Franklin, I had to feed and water the chickens and gather the eggs as well. I would also start supper and she would finish up when she got home from work, while I was helping Daddy with barn chores. We raised dairy calves, hogs and sheep and had mules and a horse. Our crops consisted of burley tobacco, hay and corn. We had a garden every year and sometimes grew strawberries, sweet potatoes and peanuts.

In later years. Mama went to work at Frank's Department Store on Main Street in Franklin as the alteration lady. She worked there for approximately 20 years. Daddy served as a county road commissioner when Mr. Mack Hatcher was the road superintendent under the leadership of Wilburn Kelly and Robert Ring.

Our house was more than 100 years old and was in the book of historical homes in Williamson County. There was a log house across the road. Daddy tore down the log house and built a granary in that spot. Several people in the community came and got some of the sandstone rocks from the chimney of that log house. There was also a log smokehouse where we kept our meat a few years until Daddy tore it down and built a tool shed with a smokehouse on the back.

In February 1963, my step-grandmother passed away and my grandfather moved back in with us that May, the week I graduated from high school. He later went to live with my Uncle Toad and Aunt Willie Lee until his death in October 1989 at the age of 96.

DOLL (SMITHSON) AND THOMAS HAM

W.F. COVINGTON-THOMAS HAM HOME ON EUDAILEY-COVINGTON ROAD

**The next section is the family history from the early settlers of the 13th District to present time. There may be omissions and a few errors, but this was an undertaking from the heart. Also, we have tried to protect the identity of living folk.**

# MICHAEL LONG
## 1755-1832

### LONG FAMILY

## FAMILY HISTORY OF THE 13TH DISTRICT

### HUSBAND'S PARENTS
**Jakob Long**  |  **Judith Baruchmeyer**
1734 - 1821  |  1730 - 1768

### WIFE'S PARENTS
**Michael Kinard**  |  **Catherine Swittenberg**
1754 - 1839  |  1756 - 1800

### HUSBAND
**Michael Long**
**BIRTH:** 1755, Newberry, District, SC
**DEATH:** 18 Apr. 1832, Peytonsville, TN

### WIFE
**Catherine Kinard**
**BIRTH:** 1775, North Carolina
**DEATH:** After Nov. 1850, Lauderdale Co. TN

### CHILDREN

**Mary Ann Long**
Daughter
**BIRTH:** 1794
**DEATH:** 1856

**George W. Long**
Son
**BIRTH:** 16 Oct. 1797
**DEATH:** 21 Aug. 1879

**Elizabeth Long**
Daughter
**BIRTH:** 1800
**DEATH:** 1865

**James Long**
Son
**BIRTH:** 1801
**DEATH:** Unknown

**Sarah "Sally" Long**
Daughter
**BIRTH:** 4 Dec. 1804
**DEATH:** 3 Aug. 1854

**Susan J. Long**
Daughter
**BIRTH:** 2 Mar. 1808
**DEATH:** 15 Feb. 1864

**Rebecca Long**
Daughter
**BIRTH:** 2 Mar. 1808
**DEATH:** 15 Feb. 1864

**Caroline Long**
Daughter
**BIRTH:** 8 Mar. 1813
**DEATH:** 14 Sep. 1889

## WILL OF MICHAEL LONG

"In the name of God amen. I Michael Long of the county of Williamson and State of Tennessee knowing that life is uncertain and knowing that the young and old are both subject to death and believing that agreeable to the cause of nature that I can't live much longer and being in my proper mind and senses, I make this my last will and testament.

"1st item: my will is that my just debts and burial expenses be paid first.

"2nd item: my will is that my Caty Long have the use of my land and plantation where I now live also I leave her all my horses except three and I leave her also my cattle and oxen, sheep and hogs and all my household and kitchen furniture, my looms and wheels and all my corn, meat, wheat, oats, and tubs and all my light casks and vessels belonging to my distillery. And she is to have all the whiskey that is on hand and also all of the money that is on hand and all the debts that is due me during her natural life except seven hundred fifty dollars which George Long owes me.

"3rd item: my will is that my daughter, Rebecca Long, have one bed and bed clothing and one comfoot bedstead and one young horse and one cow.

"4th item: my will is that Carolina Long my daughter have one bed and bed clothing and comfoot bedstead and one young horse and one cow.

"5th item: my will is that my son James Long have after the death of my wife, Caty Long the plantation and the land where I now live and also all my blacksmith tools and one bedstead and bed clothing and a young horse.

"6th item: My will is my six daughters: Mary Salsbury, Elizabeth Priest, Susan Priest, Sally Quinn, Rebecca Long and Caroline Long have seven hundred and fifty dollars equally divided between them whenever it is collected off of George Long also these six daughters after the death of my wife Caty Long to have all property that I have left to my wife Caty Long divided equally between them except the land and plantation where I now live and if it should not be convenient to divide it then let it be sold on twelve months credit and the money be equally divided between them.

# WILLIAM KENNEDY
# 1755-1853

## KENNEDY FAMILY

### HUSBAND'S PARENTS
**Unknown    Unknown**

### WIFE'S PARENTS
**Unknown    Unknown**

### HUSBAND
**William Kennedy**
**BIRTH:** 13 Apr. 1755, Culpepper Co. VA
**DEATH:** 1853, Williamson Co. TN

### WIFE
**Elizabeth Pursell**
**BIRTH:** 1769, NJ
**DEATH:** 3 July 1841, Williamson Co. TN

### CHILDREN

| | |
|---|---|
| **Sarah Ann Kennedy**<br>**Daughter** | **BIRTH:** 1802<br>**DEATH:** 18 Sep. 1871 |
| **Mary Ann Kennedy**<br>**Daughter** | **BIRTH:** 1804<br>**DEATH:** 2 Sep. 1877 |
| **Rachel Kennedy**<br>**Daughter** | **BIRTH:** 1805<br>**DEATH:** Dec. 1870 |
| **Celia Kennedy**<br>**Daughter** | **BIRTH:** 1805<br>**DEATH:** 1879 |
| **Elizabeth Kennedy**<br>**Daughter** | **BIRTH:** 1808<br>**DEATH:** 1850 |
| **Nancy Maria Kennedy**<br>**Daughter** | **BIRTH:** 1812<br>**DEATH:** 2 Sep. 1877 |

## HIS LIFE

William Kennedy was born on April 13, 1755, in Culpepper, Virginia. He was living there when he was drafted into Captain Lewis Yancey's Company during the Revolutionary War. They marched to a ford on the Rappahnannock River toward Fredericksburg. Before arriving there, orders were received that they were not needed. They marched back home and were discharged. This tour was for two months. He again entered services in 1781, in Captain Robert Pollard's Company and Colonel James Slaughter's Regiment. They marched from Culpepper Courthouse through Fredricksburg, crossing James River at Sandy Point. They met the British forces there and were pursued to Petersburg where they engaged in battle. This was the first battle William Kennedy was in. They joined Lafayette and marched down the north side of the James River, eight or nine miles below Richmond under the command of Lafayette where the Americans were encamped. Kennedy, with a guard of about 120 men, under Joseph James of Fauquire County, Virginia, was sent to Chesterfield. While on the engagement, Kennedy and about 60 other men were taken prisoners and sent to Norfolk. He remained there four months and ten days. He was taken prisoner in May of 1781 and liberated in the latter part of September. He described his sufferings in the horrible prison as "perfectly intolerable." Their only food for the greater part of the time being bad "horse-beef" with water once a day and sometimes not that. The hot weather, close confinements and bad food soon caused the death of most of the prisoners, only seven surviving to be exchanged. William Kennedy was in such weak condition that he fell by the roadside on his way home and was discovered and relieved by some passing soldiers.

William moved to Lincoln County, North Carolina in 1786. He married, Elizabeth Pursell in Greene County, Tennessee on July 25, 1796, when he was 41-years old. In 1818 they moved to Williamson County, Tennessee. In 1826, he deeded 50-acres of land to Rachel Kennedy. He was paying taxes on 72-acres of land on McCrory's Creek. In May 1852, there was an article stating that even though he was over 90-years of age, he still made his yearly walk to Nashville, a distance of more than 25-miles, to receive his yearly pension. William Kennedy died in 1853 intestate at the impressive age of 98. The remainder of his land was sold to Daniel Sledge and Octavias Hatcher. He is said to have been buried on his land in the Arno community.

---

# JOHN D. SECREST
# 1758-1847

## SECREST FAMILY

### HUSBAND'S PARENTS

**Jacob Secrest**      **Jeanette Barbara Simms**
**1734 - 1821**          **1730 - 1768**

### WIFE'S PARENTS

**Robert Lewis**      **Martha Tomberlin**
1714 - 1784            1736 - 1810

### HUSBAND
**John D Secrest**
BIRTH: 2 Apr. 1758, Culpepper Co. VA
DEATH: 30 Nov. 1847, Peytonsville, TN

### WIFE
**Sabra Jeanette Lewis**
BIRTH: 1769 in Mecklenburg Co, NC
DEATH: 2 Nov. 1837 in Peytonsville, TN

## CHILDREN

| | |
|---|---|
| **Martha Secrest** Daughter | BIRTH: 20 Nov. 1787 <br> DEATH: 4 Jun. 1871 |
| **Isaac Secrest** Son | BIRTH: 16 July 1792 <br> DEATH: 18 July 1864 |
| **Barbara Secrest** Daughter | BIRTH: 1794 <br> DEATH: Bet. 1850-1858 |
| **Tabitha Secrest** Daughter | BIRTH: 4 Apr. 1795 <br> DEATH: 8 July 1854 |
| **John Secrest. Jr.** Son | BIRTH: 16 May 1796 <br> DEATH: 29 Sep. 1835 |
| **Matilda Secrest** Daughter | BIRTH: 21 Feb. 1800 <br> DEATH: 18 July 1859 |
| **Jane Secrest** Daughter | BIRTH: 22 Jan. 1802 <br> DEATH: 19 Oct. 1888 |
| **Tyree G Secrest** Son | BIRTH 1810 <br> DEATH: 1876 |

## HIS LIFE

In March 1780, John volunteered for service in Captain Neal Morrison's Company when he was only 22. The Company was marched to Colonel Hogan's Regiment and then on to Six Mile Creek and on to Waxhaw Creek. The British were only about 15 miles from from their camp, so the regiment spent its time patrolling and observing the British. John's three-month tour expired and he was given a discharge.

Upon returning home, John volunteered in Captain Polk's Company of horse troops where he served as scout until December, 1780. The Tories in Mecklenburg and adjoining counties were ravaging the country. John fought in several skirmishes with the Tories, as far away as Camden, South Carolina.

While John was in Captain Foster's Scouting Company, they saw several skirmishes with the Tories. On one occasion John received a rifle ball in his right breast which remained there the rest of his life. He continued serving in scouting parties until Cornwallis marched his forces toward Yorktown. Later, John returned to Wilmington and heard the news of Cornwallis's defeat. He was discharged in October, 1781.

John Secrest married Sabra Jeanette Lewis (1769-1837) in 1786 in Mecklenburg County. They had eight children in 23-years. In 1818 when he moved with his family to Williamson County, Tennessee where he was one of the earliest settlers of the area.

John D. Secrest died on November 30, 1847, in Peytonsville, Williamson County, Tennessee. He lived a long life of 89-years and was buried in the Secrest Family Cemetery at Peytonsville, in the Thirteenth District of Williamson County, Tennessee.

The obituary of John Secrest appeared in the *Western Weekly Review*, December, 1847:

Died - at his residence near Peytonsville, in Williamson County, Tennessee on Tuesday, 30th November. Mr. John Secrest aged about 90 years. The deceased was an old and respected citizen of this county and was a gallant soldier of the Revolutionary struggle. He lived and died respected and esteemed by his many friends, relatives and acquaintances.

### WILL OF JOHN SECREST

December term 1847,
Williamson County TN

In the name of God, Amen.

I JOHN SECREST of the County of Williamson and State of Tenn I make and publish this my last Will and Testament in manner and form following, to wit.

First I commend my body to God who first gave it life and direct that the same be decently buried and the expense thereof paid by my executor hereinafter named out of the first money that shall come unto his hands, and that all my just debts be paid in the same manner.

Secondly I will and direct that all my lands the same amounting to about three hundred and eighty one and 3/4 acres, be divided into seven shares or portions,
one of which shares or portions I give, devise and bequeath to my daughter MARTHA LANEY
one to my daughter BARBARA GRAY
one to my son ISAAC SECREST
one to my daughter MATILDA SMITHSON
one to my daughter JANE LIGGATT
one to my son TYRE G. SECREST
Third it is my will and desire that my executor sell all my perishable property and that the proceeds of such sale as well as all the rest and residue of my estate of very kind of description  be divided unto seven shares after the payment of my debts and funeral expenses and the expenses of executing this will, and that each of my said children have one share thereof except my daughter TABITHA RAY whose share thereof is hereby given to said ISAAC SECREST as her Trustee upon the same trusts and conditions and in the same manner as her share of the land. And whereas I have heretofore given to my beloved son TYREE G. SECREST the sum of nine hundred dollars for the purchase of a tract of land I will  and direct that be account for that amount as an advancement, and that the same be deducted out of his share of my estate Lastly I do nominate and appoint my son ISAAC SECREST my executor

In Witness of all which I have subscribed my name and affixed my seal to this my last will and testament hereby revoking all other wills by me heretofore made, on this fourth day of November 1847

John SECREST his mark

Witnessed by:
H. Smithson, Thomas Helm, John Andrews

# DANIEL CRENSHAW
## 1760-1831

### CRENSHAW FAMILY

#### HUSBAND'S PARENTS
**Cornelius Crenshaw**     **Martisha Winn**
1739 - 1785                1740 - 1798

#### WIFE'S PARENTS
**James Jennings**     **Philadelphia Bruce**
1737 - 1795            1741 - ?

#### HUSBAND
**Daniel Crenshaw**
**BIRTH:** 1760, Lunenburg Co. VA
**DEATH:** 15 Sep. 1831, Peytonsville, TN

#### WIFE
**Nancy Ann Jennings**
**BIRTH:** 9 Oct. 1772, Lunenburg Co. VA
**DEATH:** 11 Dec. 1860, Peytonsville, TN

### CHILDREN

| | |
|---|---|
| **Cornelius Crenshaw** Son | **BIRTH:** 12 May 1790 **DEATH:** 1817 |
| **Joseph Crenshaw** Son | **BIRTH:** 1793 **DEATH:** 1818 |
| **Martha Patsy** Daughter | **BIRTH:** 25 Oct. 1794 **DEATH:** 1850 |
| **Mary J.** Daughter | **BIRTH:** 25 Oct. 1794 **DEATH:** 14 Apr. 1875 |
| **Daniel Crenshaw Jr.** Son | **BIRTH:** 1800 **DEATH:** Unknown |
| **James Jefferson** Crenshaw-Son | **BIRTH:** 1800 **DEATH:** 29 Jan. 1870 |
| **Chesteen 'Chester'** Crenshaw-Son | **BIRTH:** 1811 **DEATH:** Unknown |

### HIS LIFE

Daniel Crenshaw was born in 1760, in Lunenburg Co, Virginia. He served in the Virginia Line as a private during the Revolutionary War. He served one six-month tour and a second three-month tour. He participated in the Battle of Guilford County Courthouse. His commanding officers were Capt. Joseph Winn and Gen. Nathaniel Green.

Daniel Crenshaw married, Nancy Jennings on July 2, 1789 in Lunenburg County, Virginia. They resided there for many years before moving to Williamson County, Tennessee.

Daniel died September 15, 1831 and was buried in the Crenshaw Family Cemetery in Peytonsville, Tennessee. It is interesting to note that this cemetery was re-located to Williamson Memorial Gardens when I-840 came through Peytonsville in 1998.

# JAMES BOYD
## 1768-1821

### BOYD FAMILY

#### HUSBAND'S PARENTS
**James Boyd**     **Martha Burns**
1729 - 1784        1735 - 1790

#### WIFE'S PARENTS
**Nicholas Gentry Sr.**     **Elizabeth P. Gibson**
1740 - 1782                 1751 - 1830

#### HUSBAND
**James Boyd**
**BIRTH:** 1768, Craven Co. SC
**DEATH:** 24 May 1821, Williamson Co. TN

#### WIFE
**Nancy Mary Gentry**
**BIRTH:** 1776, Greenwood, SC
**DEATH:** 24 May 1828, Williamson Co. TN

| | |
|---|---|
| **Mary Polly Boyd**<br>**Daughter** | **BIRTH:** 27 Apr. 1795<br>**DEATH:** 1850 |
| **Abner Monroe Boyd**<br>**Son** | **BIRTH:** 8 Nov. 1796<br>**DEATH:** 26 May 1854 |
| **Elizabeth Boyd**<br>**Daughter** | **BIRTH:** 27 July 1798<br>**DEATH:** 25 Apr. 1875 |
| **George G. Boyd**<br>**Son** | **BIRTH:** 1800<br>**DEATH:** 27 Sep. 1841 |
| **Sinai Boyd**<br>**Daughter** | **BIRTH:** 1802<br>**DEATH:** 18 June 1831 |
| **John G. Boyd**<br>**Son** | **BIRTH:** 1804<br>**DEATH:** 21 Mar. 1854 |
| **Nancy Boyd**<br>**Daughter** | **BIRTH:** 1806<br>**DEATH:** 26 Jan. 1830 |
| **James Washington Boyd-Son** | **BIRTH:** 1808<br>**DEATH:** 30 May 1847 |
| **Nicholas H. Boyd**<br>**Son** | **BIRTH:** 2 Nov. 1813<br>**DEATH:** 5 Mar. 1894 |
| **Miria Boyd**<br>**Daughter** | **BIRTH:** 30 Oct. 1814<br>**DEATH:** 23 Sep. 1892 |

# THE LIFE OF A FOUNDER OF THE CUMBERLAND SETTLEMENTS

James Boyd was born in 1768 in Craven County, South Carolina. By the time he was age 11, he was on a great flotilla on a boat called "Adventure" with a captain named, John Donelson. This journey was a grueling four-months long from Fort Patrick Henry on the Holston River to the French Salt Springs on the Cumberland River. The fleet took its departure on Dec. 22, 1779. There were 30 flatboats loaded with 200 people when they left Fort Patrick Henry. The largest boat "Adventure" held about 30 people including Donelson's 12-year old daughter Rachel Donelson, who would later become the wife of the seventh President, Andrew Jackson. What an adventure for a young boy to experience.

Another group went by land and were led by James Robertson. Their journey took them through the Cumberland Gap, Kentucky and finally into Nashville. While Robertson's journey didn't have many mishaps, Donelson's was wrought with unimaginable misfortunes.

Their journey as you could say, struck a snag (literally). They found themselves run aground and stuck on ice. They had to overwinter there until Feb. 27, when their boats could finally move again.

The first death was that of an African American man on March 4 from frostbite. During the four-month voyage, the pioneers suffered attacks from Native Americans, a smallpox outbreak, hunger, exhaustion, extreme cold, swift currents, and treacherous shoals.

The cargo of the Adventure consisted of the personal effects of the passengers on board and those who had gone by land with Robertson. Among them were the wife and five children of James ROBERTSON, Robert CARTWRIGHT and family, and Colonel DONELSON'S family. The names of other persons who came with this fleet are as follows: John DONELSON, Jr., son of Colonel DONELSON, Benjamin PORTER, Hugh ROGAN, James MCCAIN, Isaac NEELY, John COTTON, Jonathan JENNINGS, William CRUTCHFIELD, John BOYD, Isaac RENFROE, John and Solomon TURPIN, Francis ARMSTRONG, John MONTGOMERY, Isaac LANIER, Daniel DUNHAM, John COCKRILL, John CAFFREY, Thomas HUTCHINS, Benjamin BELEW, John GIBSON, Hugh and Thomas HENRY, Frank HANEY, Russell GOWER, Daniel CHAMBERS, David GWINN, M. ROUNDSEVER, and MESSRS. MAXWELL, STUART, PAYNE and JOHNS, also Mrs. Mary PURNELL and Mrs. Mary HENRY, and their respective families.

Their journey ended on April 24, 1780, Donelson's party had traveled a thousand miles and were finally reunited with family and friends at the Big Salt Lick (now Nashville). Within a week of Donelson's arrival, Henderson prepared the Cumberland Compact, of which Donelson was the fifth signer. At least 33 of the settlers had died or had been captured along the way.

The community that they started is today known as Nashville, named for Francis Nash, a Brigadier General in the American Revolutionary War.

James Boyd married Nancy Mary Gentry (1776-1828) at Fort Nashboro, in 1794 when he was 26 years old. By 1805 they would be living in Williamson County, Tennessee. In 1819, James purchased land from John Donelson in Williamson County which the deed is recorded in Book F-Page 54. This may have been their homestead on Harpeth Lick Road (now known as Peytonsville Road). This road went from Franklin to Shelbyville.

### WILL OF JAMES BOYD

I James Boyd of Williamson County & state of Tennessee do make this my will in the first place I will & bequeath to my Son John G. Boyd the sum of five hundred dollars to be furnished to him as he may need them for the purpose of purchasing books & paying for tuition.
Secondly I will & bequeath to my beloved wife Nancy Boyd the balance of my estate both real and personal to insure to her use & benefit during her widowhood and in case she never marry, then I will & bequeath the same to her during her natural life with a request, that she give to each of her children as they shall Marry a sum not exceeding that which has been given to my Daughter Polly, or Elizabeth who have already married. Thirdly, at the happening of either of the above contingencies to say, the marriage or death of my wife Nancy Boyd, it is my will & desire that my estate of every kind be equally divided amongst my children. Share & share alike having reference to the portions which have already been received or may hereafter be received by any of the children when they shall marry and allowing the five hundred Dollars above bequeathed to John G. Boyd as an extra bequest to him.

Lastly I appoint my sons Abner Boyd and John G. Boyd executors of this my will without security witnessed my hand & seal this 21st day of March 1821

Done in presence of us: Tho J Hardeman, Nathan W. ?, Samuel Pratt

James Boyd "Seal"

## CLEMENT SMITHSON
## 1768-1814

### SMITHSON FAMILY

#### HUSBAND'S PARENTS
**John S. Smithson      Drusilla Ann Walker**
1739 - 1784            1744 - 1811

#### WIFE'S PARENTS
**John Pettus      Susannah Winston**
1736 - 1799      1737 - 1821

#### HUSBAND
**Clement Smithson**
BIRTH: 10 Nov. 1768, Lunenberg Co. VA
DEATH: 24 Sep. 1814, Peytonsville, TN

#### WIFE
**Nancy D. Pettus**
BIRTH: 7 Dec. 1772, Charlotte, VA
DEATH: 27 Apr. 1863, Peytonsville, TN

#### CHILDREN

| | |
|---|---|
| **Susan T. Smithson** Daughter | BIRTH: 11 Nov. 1794 DEATH: 9 Aug. 1855 |

| Drucilla Wade<br>Smithson-Daughter | **BIRTH:** 13 Oct. 1796<br>**DEATH:** 3 Apr. 1872 |
| --- | --- |

**Drucilla Wade**
**Smithson-Daughter**
BIRTH: 13 Oct. 1796
DEATH: 3 Apr. 1872

**Sylvanus Wright**
**Smithson-Son**
BIRTH: 12 Dec. 1798
DEATH: 15 Mar. 1872

**Martha D. Smithson**
**Daughter**
BIRTH: 11 Nov. 1800
DEATH: 3 June 1846

**Sarah B. Smithson**
**Daughter**
BIRTH: 25 May 1803
DEATH: 4 Mar. 1825

**Clement Smithson, Jr.**
**Son**
BIRTH: 10 Oct. 1805
DEATH: 21 June 1871

**John Pettus Smithson**
**Son**
BIRTH: 8 Aug. 1808
DEATH: 26 Mar. 1855

**Horatio Sharp**
**Smithson-Son**
BIRTH: 22 Jan. 1810
DEATH: 18 June 1900

**William Overton**
**Smithson-Son**
BIRTH: 8 Feb. 1812
DEATH: 5 Mar. 1885

## HIS LIFE

When Clement Smithson was born on November 10, 1768, in Lunenburg County, Virginia, his father, John was 29 and his mother, Drusilla was 24. He married Nancy D. Pettus (1772-1863) on December 18, 1792 in Lunenburg County, Virginia. They had nine children in 17 years. He died on September 24, 1814, in Peytonsville, Williamson County, Tennessee.

# SAMUEL PETTUS SHELBURNE
# 1769-1838

## SHELBURNE FAMILY

### HUSBAND'S FAMILY
**Rev. James Shelburne    Virginia A. Petrus**
1738 - 1820                     1748 - 1831

### HUSBAND
**Samuel Pettus Shelburne**
**BIRTH:** 4 Feb. 1769, Lunenburg Co. VA
**DEATH:** 9 Aug. 1838, Lauderdale Co. AL

### 1ST WIFE
**Sarah Pamplin**
**BIRTH:** 1770, Lunenburg, VA
**DEATH:** 1804, Williamson Co. TN

### 2ND WIFE
**Mary Polly Browder**
**BIRTH:** 1773, James City, VA
**DEATH:** 25 Apr. 1825

### 3RD WIFE
**Peggy Hardin**
**BIRTH:** ABT 1775, James City, VA
**DEATH:** 9 Mar. 1844

### CHILDREN OF SAMUEL AND SARAH

**Pettus Shelburne**
**Son**
BIRTH: 27 July 1787
DEATH: 1864

**Samuel P. Shelburne**
**Son**
BIRTH: 1 Mar. 1797
DEATH: 1865

### CHILDREN OF SAMUEL AND PEGGY

**Mary Polly Shelburne**
**Daughter**
BIRTH: 1807
DEATH: Unknown

**Anne Pettus Shelburne**
**Daughter**
BIRTH: 1808
DEATH: 1860

**Jeremiah F.C.**
**Shelburne-Son**
BIRTH: 1814
DEATH: 1815

**Mary H Shelburne**
**Daughter**
BIRTH: 1816
DEATH: 1817

**Nancy Taylor Shelburne**
**Daughter**
BIRTH: 1821
DEATH: 21 Jan. 1887

**Thomas Riley**
**Shelburne-Son**
BIRTH: 1822
DEATH: 20 Mar. 1870

| Margaret Shelburne<br>Daughter | BIRTH: 1827<br>DEATH: 27 Oct. 1903 |
| --- | --- |

| Silas Shelburne<br>Son | BIRTH: Unknown<br>DEATH: Unknown |

| James Shelburne<br>Son | BIRTH: Unknown<br>DEATH: Unknown |

| John P. Shelburne<br>Son | BIRTH: Unknown<br>DEATH: Unknown |

## HIS LIFE

When Samuel Pettus Shelburne was born on February 4, 1769, in Lunenburg County, Virginia, his father, James was 30 and his mother, Virginia was 21. He was married three times. He died on August 9, 1838, in Lauderdale, Alabama at the age of 69.

# THOMAS MERRITT
# 1770-1857

### MERRITT FAMILY

### HUSBAND'S PARENTS
**James Merritt**    **Mary Merritt**
1743 - 1837    1754 - 1830

### WIFE'S PARENTS
**Henry Applewhite**    **Anne Harris**
1735 - 1783    1738 - 1795

### HUSBAND
**Thomas Merritt**
BIRTH: 18 Feb. 1770, Tarboro, NC
DEATH: 6 July 1857, Peytonsville, TN

### WIFE
**Rebecca W. Applewhite**
BIRTH: 24 June 1773, Southampton, VA
DEATH: 24, Dec. 1863, Peytonsville, TN

### CHILDREN

| Nancy Merritt<br>Daughter | BIRTH: 23 Mar. 1800<br>DEATH: 27 June 1891 |
| --- | --- |

| Jane Merritt<br>Daughter | BIRTH: 15 Feb. 1802<br>DEATH: Unknown |

| Henry J. Merritt<br>Son | BIRTH: 23 Dec. 1803<br>DEATH: 22 June 1873 |

| John A. Merritt<br>Son | BIRTH: 1806<br>DEATH: 1853 |

| Bennett Barnam<br>Merritt-Son | BIRTH: 23 Nov. 1808<br>DEATH: 3 July 1900 |

| Susan Merritt<br>Daughter | BIRTH: 3 Apr. 1810<br>DEATH: 1900 |

| Harvey Milton Merritt<br>Son | BIRTH: 8 Apr. 1812<br>DEATH: 31 July 1887 |

| Narcissa Merritt<br>Daughter | BIRTH: 6 Aug. 1816<br>DEATH: 14 Oct. 1908 |

| Amanda F. Merritt<br>Daughter | BIRTH: 1818<br>DEATH: Unknown |

| Margaret Merritt<br>Daughter | BIRTH: 1819<br>DEATH: Unknown |

## HIS LIFE

When Thomas Merritt was born on February 18, 1770, in Tarboro, North Carolina, his father, James was 26 and his mother, Mary was 15. He married Rebecca W. Applewhite on June 20, 1799, in Nash, North Carolina. They had 10 children in 19-years. He died on July 6, 1857, in Williamson County, Tennessee when he was 87-years old. He was buried in the Merritt Cemetery in Peytonsville, Tennessee.

From the probate of the Estate of Thomas Merritt 1857: Thomas Merritt departed this life in Williamson County in 1857 leaving a will. He bequeathed his entire estate to his widow, Rebecca Merritt for her lifetime and then to go to their children and grandchildren. Thomas left children: Nancy Moore wife of Alexander Moore; Jane Johnson wife of David Johnson; Susan McConnico wife of Lemuel B. McConnico, Narcissa Johnson wife of James Johnson;

Amanda Moulton wife of Thomas J. Moulton, Henry J. Merritt, Bennett B. Merritt and Harvey M. Merritt and his grandchildren: Rebecca Susan, Mary Francis and Sarah Merritt. The said Sarah has married to Alpheus Truett. Thomas owned a tract of land on which he resided containing about 180 acres and personal property. Since the death of Thomas Merritt, the dwelling house and most of the other houses on the tract of land and household furniture has been destroyed by fire. Due to her old age, Rebecca says it is impossible for her to rebuild and dwell on the tract of land. She is 85 years old and thinks it is best to sell the land and not resume housekeeping. Rebecca, Susan, Mary Frances and Sarah are the daughters of a deceased son, John A. Merritt.

# JAMES E. GOSEY
# 1772-1854

## GOSEY FAMILY

### HUSBAND'S PARENTS
**Aaron Gosey**    **Susannah Wallace**
1735 - 1806        1726 - 1793

### WIFE'S PARENTS
**Unknown**    **Unknown**

### HUSBAND
**James McGuire**
**BIRTH:** 11 Feb. 1772, Lunenburg Co. VA
**DEATH:** 3 Oct. 1854, Peytonsville, TN

### WIFE
**Rebecca Bowers**
**BIRTH:** 1783, Lunenburg Co. VA
**DEATH:** 1859, Peytonsville, TN

### CHILDREN

**Claiborne Gosey**    **BIRTH:** 9 Mar. 1802
**Son**                **DEATH:** Unknown

**Elizabeth Gosey**    **BIRTH:** 9 Mar. 1802
**Daughter**           **DEATH:** 29 June 1838

**Mary Ann Gosey**     **BIRTH:** ABT 1810
**Daughter**           **DEATH:** 1859

**John Roberts Gosey** **BIRTH:** ABT 1813
**Son**                **DEATH:** ABT 1847

**Moses Gentry Gosey** **BIRTH:** 2 Dec. 1815
**Son**                **DEATH:** ABT 1903

**Edward 'Standing**   **BIRTH:** 8 Sep. 1820
**Bear' Gosey-Son**    **DEATH:** 20 Feb. 1887

## HIS LIFE

When James E. Gosey was born on February 11, 1772 in Lunenburg County, Virginia, his father, Aaron was 37 and his mother, Susannah was 46. He married Rebecca Bowers on January 20, 1800 in his hometown of Lunenburg County, Virginia. They had six children in 18-years. He died on October 3, 1854 in Peytonsville, Williamson County, Tennessee. He lived a long life of 82-years and was buried in the Gosey Cemetery on Gosey Hill Road in Peytonsville.

# DAVID PINKSTON
# 1773-1851

## PINKSTON FAMILY

### HUSBAND'S PARENTS
**William Pinkston**   **Mary Ann Polk**
1733 - 1815           1735 - 1828

### 1ST WIFE'S PARENTS
**William Pennington**   **Druscillia A. Smithson**
1765 - 1806             1767 - 1824

### 2ND WIFE'S PARENTS
**Ephraim Andrews**    **Stacy Humphress**
1761 - ?              1767 - 1824

## HUSBAND
### David Pinkston
**BIRTH:** 17 Dec. 1773, Rowan Co. NC
**DEATH:** 24 Feb. 1851  Peytonsville, TN

## 1ST WIFE
### Elizabeth Pennington
**BIRTH:** 12 July 1786, Surry Co. VA
**DEATH:** 1821, Williamson Co. TN

## 2ND WIFE
### Frances Needham Andrews
**BIRTH:** 31 Mar. 1792
**DEATH:** 1850, Peytonsville, TN

## CHILDREN OF DAVID AND ELIZABETH

**Nancy Howard Pinkston-Daughter**
BIRTH: 27 May 1804
DEATH: 1851

**Polly T. Pinkston Daughter**
BIRTH: 8 Feb. 1806
DEATH: 1851

**William R. Pinkston Son**
BIRTH: 16 Aug. 1807
DEATH: 7 Feb. 1875

**Benjamin Pinkston Son**
BIRTH: 18 Feb. 1810
DEATH: Unknown

**Rebecca Pinkston Daughter**
BIRTH: 27 Aug. 1812
DEATH: 1847

**David Pinkston Jr. Son**
BIRTH: 7 July 1814
DEATH: 1892

**Lavinia Howard Pinkston-Daughter**
BIRTH: 13 June 1820
DEATH: 11 May 1893

## CHILDREN OF DAVID AND FRANCES

**Andrew Jackson Pinkston-Son**
BIRTH: 13 Sep. 1822
DEATH: BEF 1880

**Thomas Needham Pinkston-Son**
BIRTH: 2 June 1824/25
DEATH: Unknown

**George Washington Pinkston-Son**
BIRTH: 9 Feb. 1824
DEATH: 2 Dec. 1881

**Alexander Rufus Pinkston-Son**
BIRTH: 25 May 1826
DEATH: 1900

**Tennessee America Pinkston-Daughter**
BIRTH: 26 Aug. 1828
DEATH: Unknown

**Ephram Turner Pinkston-Son**
BIRTH: 12 July 1830
DEATH: ABT 1862

## HIS LIFE

When David Pinkston was born on December 17, 1773 in Rowan County, North Carolina, his father, William was 40 and his mother, Mary was 38. He was living in the 13 colonies at one of the most important turning points in American history —the signing of the Declaration of Independence.

David married Elizabeth Pennington and they had seven children together. After Elizabeth died (maybe in childbirth), he married, Frances Needham Andrews and they had six children. He died on February 24, 1851 in Peytonsville, Williamson County, Tennessee at the age of 77.

# NATHANIEL B. SMITHSON
# 1773-1859

## SMITHSON FAMILY

### HUSBAND'S PARENTS
**John S. Smithson**     **Drusilla Ann Walker**
1739 - 1784                    1744 - 1811

### WIFE'S PARENTS
**Daniel Cheatham**     **Agnes Robertson**
1746 - 1815                    1749 - 1815

## HUSBAND
### Nathaniel B. Smithson
**BIRTH:** 16 May 1773, Lunenburg Co. VA
**DEATH:** 3 Aug. 1859, Peytonsville, TN

WIFE

**Mary Polly Pauline Cheatham**
BIRTH: 12 Oct. 1777, Lunenburg Co. VA
DEATH: 16 May 1850, Peytonsville, TN

## CHILDREN

| | |
|---|---|
| **Samuel Cheatham Smithson-Son** | BIRTH: 16 Oct. 1799<br>DEATH: 26 Oct. 1837 |
| **Tandy S. Smithson Son** | BIRTH: 17 Jan. 1801<br>DEATH: 26 May 1873 |
| **Charlotte Smithson Daughter** | BIRTH: 1805<br>DEATH: 22 Oct. 1877 |
| **Martha W. Smithson Daughter** | BIRTH: 1806<br>DEATH: 1880 |
| **Catherine K. Smithson-Daughter** | BIRTH: 1811<br>DEATH: 1870 |
| **Charles W. Smithson Son** | BIRTH: 1813<br>DEATH: 1890 |
| **Nathaniel B. Smithson-Son** | BIRTH: 23 Oct. 1814<br>DEATH: 18 Apr. 1894 |
| **William J. Smithson Son** | BIRTH: 1817<br>DEATH: 1880 |
| **Coleman G. Smithson Son** | BIRTH: 26 Mar. 1819<br>DEATH: 24 Oct. 1888 |
| **Mary Smithson Daughter** | BIRTH: 7 June 1822<br>DEATH: 1 Dec. 1882 |

## HIS LIFE

When Nathaniel B. Smithson was born on May 16, 1773 in Lunenburg County, Virginia, his father, John was 34 and his mother, Drusilla was 29. He married Mary Pauline "Polly" Cheatham on March 30, 1797 in Lunenburg County, Virginia. They had ten children in 22 years.

Nathaniel and wife, Mary Polly arrived in Williamson County, Tennessee around 1811. According to family history, there were about two-hundred friends and family traveling together.

Nathaniel B. Smithson died on August 3, 1859 in Peytonsville, Williamson County, Tennessee when he was 86-years old.

The following is a story that Nathaniel B. Smithson, Sr, handed down from generation to generation. This story was forwarded by Frank W. Smithson of Nashville, TN.

Nathaniel was born 16 May, 1773 to Drucilla Anne Walker Smithson, daughter of Captain Sylvanus Walker and wife of John S. Smithson, in Lunenburg County, Virginia. He was the third of five sons and he grew up with two sisters. The 30th of May 1797 was a bright day for Nathaniel. On that day, he was married to Mary Pauline Cheatham. They shared six sons and four daughters. The first two sons, Samuel Cheatham (1799) and Tandy Sylvanus (1801) came over the mountains with their parents riding horses on lonely forest trails, but with a party of some two hundred friends and kinsmen. There were five brothers and two sisters riding in the party and carried between them were Revolutionary War veterans' land grants of some 4,800 acres. Some of these grants came from being heirs of John S. Smithson who died in service of the Continental Forces. Some they earned themselves. Others were purchased for them by a grandfather and grandmother, Francis Marion Smithson and Sarah Smithson. There were no wagons or buggies because there were no roads. Each adult family member rode a horse and led other horses with children aboard. Still other horses were used as pack horses. They came in late spring in order to have grass enough for the four hundred horses as they traveled. One party stopped in Cannon County, Tennessee. Three came to Williamson, one to Maury and one to Giles County. Nathaniel B. and Mary settled in Williamson County where eight more children were born. Family and friends helped build a five-room log house by a spring at Peytonsville in six busy days, upon arrival in 1803. Brick houses were built in 1819 and 1830 near the store at the Peytonsville crossroads. Nathaniel B. died August 3, 1859 at the age of eighty-six and is buried in the family cemetery beside Mary and together with twenty of their descendants.

# JOHN SMITHSON
# 1777-1837

## SMITHSON FAMILY

### HUSBAND'S PARENTS
**John S. Smithson**      **Drusilla Ann Walker**
1739 - 1784                      1744 - 1811

### WIFE'S PARENTS
**Richard Knott**      **Margaret ?**
1745 - 1820                1742 - ?

### HUSBAND
**John Smithson**
**BIRTH:** 1777, Lunenburg Co. VA
**DEATH:** 12 Sep. 1837, Peytonsville, TN

### WIFE
**Elizabeth G. "Betsy" Knott**
**BIRTH:** 1775, Lunenburg Co. VA
**DEATH:** 29 Jan. 1839, Peytonsville, TN

### CHILDREN

| | |
|---|---|
| **Louisa Abney Smithson-Daughter** | **BIRTH:** Mar. 1802<br>**DEATH:** 1850 |
| **Benjamin Smithson** Son | **BIRTH:** 1803<br>**DEATH:** 25 Mar. 1861 |
| **Charles N. Smithson** Son | **BIRTH:** 10 Oct. 1806<br>**DEATH:** 1890 |
| **Richard K. Smithson** Son | **BIRTH:** 20 Jan. 1809<br>**DEATH:** ABT 1836 |
| **Sylvanus W. Smithson-Son** | **BIRTH:** 8 Aug. 1810<br>**DEATH:** 15 Mar. 1872 |
| **Dolly Smithson** Daughter | **BIRTH:** ABT 1812<br>**DEATH:** ABT 1884 |

### HIS LIFE

When John Smithson was born in 1777 in Lunenburg County, Virginia, his father, John was 38 and his mother Drusilla was 33. He married Elizabeth G. "Betsy" Knott in 1801 in his hometown. They had six children in 10-years.

John and his family arrived in Williamson County, Tennessee around 1811. According to family history there were about two-hundred family and friends traveling together. (See story about Nathaniel B. Smithson, John's brother, in previous story).

# JAMES MCGUIRE
# 1782-1870

## MCGUIRE FAMILY

### HUSBAND'S PARENTS
**Thomas Spencer McGuire**      **Mary Dobbins**
1740 - 1802                              1753 - 1843

### WIFE'S PARENTS
**James M. McCutcheon**  **Martha Patterson**
1757 - 1836                        1758 - 1852

### HUSBAND
**James McGuire**
**BIRTH:** 1782, North Carolina
**DEATH:** 1870, Peytonsville, TN

## WIFE
### Rachel Cannada McCutchan
**BIRTH:** ABT 1792, KY
**DEATH:** 1877, Peytonsville, TN

### CHILDREN

| | |
|---|---|
| **Thomas McGuire** Son | **BIRTH:** 8 Nov. 1811 **DEATH:** 20 June 1879 |
| **Elizabeth C. McGuire** Daughter | **BIRTH:** 1812 **DEATH:** 26 Jan. 1883 |
| **Rebecca McGuire** Daughter | **BIRTH:** 1822 **DEATH:** Unknown |
| **Rachel McGuire** Daughter | **BIRTH:** 1824 **DEATH:** Unknown |
| **George McGuire** Son | **BIRTH:** 28 Apr. 1827 **DEATH:** 18 May 1864 |
| **John White McGuire** Son | **BIRTH:** 1828 **DEATH:** Unknown |
| **William A. McGuire** Son | **BIRTH:** Jan. 1832 **DEATH:** 10 June 1911 |
| **Samuel B. (Sammi) McGuire-Son** | **BIRTH:** 1835 **DEATH:** 12 Jan. 1862 |

## HIS LIFE

When James McGuire was born in 1782 in North Carolina, his father, Thomas Spencer McGuire was 42 and his mother, Mary Elizabeth was 29. He married Rachel Cannada McCutchan on November 22, 1810 in Williamson County, Tennessee. They had eight children in 24-years. He died in 1870 in Peytonsville, Williamson County, Tennessee at the age of 88.

# NELSON W. GEE
## 1784-1870

### GEE FAMILY

### HUSBAND'S PARENTS

| Henry Gee | Martha Waller |
|---|---|
| 1760 - 1820 | 1760 - 1820 |

### WIFE'S PARENTS

| James Byars | Sarah Campbell |
|---|---|
| 1739 - 1799 | 1769 - 1799 |

## HUSBAND
### Nelson W. Gee
**BIRTH:** 1784, Lunenburg Co. VA
**DEATH:** 14 Feb. 1854, Peytonsville, TN

## WIFE
### Catherine Byars
**BIRTH:** ABT 1784, Lunenburg Co. VA
**DEATH:** 14 Feb. 1859, Peytonsville, TN

### CHILDREN

| | |
|---|---|
| **Theodorick J. Gee** Son | **BIRTH:** ABT 1812 **DEATH:** ABT 1859 |
| **Martha L. Gee** Daughter | **BIRTH:** ABT 1815 **DEATH:** Unknown |
| **Sarah C. Gee** Daughter | **BIRTH:** ABT 1820 **DEATH:** AFT 1910 |
| **Thomas H. Gee** Son | **BIRTH:** ABT 1825 **DEATH:** Unknown |
| **Drury Gee** Son | **BIRTH:** 15 Dec. 1827 **DEATH:** 24 Oct. 1901 |
| **George William Gee** Son | **BIRTH:** 8 Sep. 1820 **DEATH:** ABT 1858 |
| **Elizabeth C. Gee** Daughter | **BIRTH:** 28 Feb. 1830 **DEATH:** 28 Mar. 1900 |

## HIS LIFE

When Nelson W. Gee was born in 1784 in Lunenburg County, Virginia his father, Henry, was 24 and his mother, Martha was 24. He married Catherine Byars on December 15, 1811 in his hometown. They had seven children in 18-years.

On July 3, 1813, Nelson had enlisted for service in the War of 1812. He was a part of Captain James Neblett's Company of Virginia Militia. This war claimed the lives of 15,000 American soldiers. He was discharged on January 7, 1814.

Nelson W. Gee died on February 14, 1859 in Peytonsville, Williamson County, Tennessee at the age of 75.

---

# THOMAS HELM
# 1784-1863

### HELM FAMILY

#### HUSBAND'S PARENTS
**John Steele Helm**     **Mary McAlister**
1741 - 1826             1749 - 1824

#### WIFE'S PARENTS
**Jacob Carl**     **Phebe Beadle**
1766 - 1845        1768 - 1842

#### HUSBAND
**Thomas Helm**
**BIRTH:** 6 Sep. 1784, Campbell Co. VA
**DEATH:** 11 May 1863, Peytonsville, TN

#### WIFE
**Elizabeth Carl**
**BIRTH:** 8 Mar. 1800, Dutchess, NY
**DEATH:** 4 Dec. 1855, Williamson Co. TN

#### CHILDREN

**John Carl Helm**      **BIRTH:** 29 Nov. 1825
**Son**                 **DEATH:** 3 Nov. 1862

### HIS LIFE

When Thomas Helm was born on September 6, 1784, in Campbell County, Virginia his father, John was 43 and his mother, Mary was 35. He married Elizabeth Carl on February 17, 1825 in Williamson County, Tennessee. They had one

child during their marriage. He died on May 11, 1863, in Williamson County, Tennessee at the age of 78.

---

# BARTHOLOMEW
# CROWDER
# 1785-1854

### CROWDER FAMILY

#### HUSBAND'S PARENTS
**Bartholomew Crowder IV**   **Martha Johnson**
1745 - 1828                  1750 - 1795

#### WIFE'S PARENTS
**James Thompson**     **Elizabeth Bishop**
1755 - 1794            1755 - ?

#### HUSBAND
**Bartholomew Crowder**
**BIRTH:** 1785, Lunenburg Co. VA
**DEATH:** Jan. 1854, Peytonsville, TN

#### WIFE
**Jane Collier Thompson**
**BIRTH:** 1785, Lunenburg Co. VA
**DEATH:** Peytonsville, TN

#### CHILDREN

**Elizabeth R. Crowder**   **BIRTH:** 1809
**Daughter**               **DEATH:** Unknown

**Martha Crowder**         **BIRTH:** 1813
**Daughter**               **DEATH:** Unknown

**John J. Crowder**        **BIRTH:** 1821
**Son**                    **DEATH:** Unknown

**Louisa Crowder**         **BIRTH:** Unknown
**Daughter**               **DEATH:** Unknown

**Mary A. Crowder**        **BIRTH:** Unknown
**Daughter**               **DEATH:** Unknown

**Lucy A. Crowder**        **BIRTH:** Unknown

Daughter                    DEATH: Unknown

## HIS LIFE

When Bartholomew Crowder was born in 1785, in Lunenburg County, Virginia, his father, Bartholomew was 40 and his mother, Martha was 35. He married Jane Collier Thompson on November 25, 1805, in Brunswick, Virginia. They had six children in 12-years. He died in January, 1854, in Williamson County, Tennessee at the age of 69.

# ROBERT GRAY
# 1787-1873

## GRAY FAMILY

### HUSBAND'S PARENTS
**Robert Gray**        **Mary Polly Yarborugh**
1745 - 1829             1766 - 1878

### 1ST WIFE'S PARENTS
**Father Unknown    Mother Unknown**

### 2ND WIFE'S PARENTS
**Jonas Meadow Holland  Theodocia Beck**
1756 - ?                    1770 - 1840

### HUSBAND
**Robert Gray Jr.**
**BIRTH:** 18 Sep. 1787, Mt. Eden, KY
**DEATH:** 7 Apr. 1873, Peytonsville, TN

### 1ST WIFE
**Polly McClain**
**BIRTH:** 1790
**DEATH:** 1820, Mt. Eden, Shelby Co. KY

### 2ND WIFE
**Patsey Martha Holland**
**BIRTH:** 1800, Virginia
**DEATH:** ABT 1876, Peytonsville, TN

## CHILDREN OF ROBERT AND POLLY

**Mary Gray**          **BIRTH:** 1810
**Daughter**           **DEATH:** Unknown

**James Gray**         **BIRTH:** ABT 1813
**Son**                **DEATH:** 25 Nov. 1887

**Buford T. Gray**     **BIRTH:** ABT 1816
**Son**                **DEATH:** ABT 1903

## CHILDREN OF ROBERT AND PATSEY MARTHA

**William M. Gray**    **BIRTH:** Dec. 1822
**Son**                **DEATH:** 6 Apr. 1909

**Polly Gray**         **BIRTH:** 1823
**Daughter**           **DEATH:** 1848

**Jonas Gray**         **BIRTH:** 29 May 1825
**Son**                **DEATH**: 10 Dec. 1903

**Anderson J. Gray**   **BIRTH:** 5 Mar. 1827
**Son**                **DEATH:** 4 Aug. 1910

**Joel A. Gray**       **BIRTH:** 23 Nov. 1828
**Son**                **DEATH:** 14 Dec. 1884

**Samuel Thrower Gray** **BIRTH:** ABT 1830
**Daughter**           **DEATH:** 28 June 1906

**Sarah Sallie Gray**  **BIRTH:** 20 Mar. 1832
**Daughter**           **DEATH:** Unknown

**Francsis Theadocia** **BIRTH:** 12 Mar. 1835
**Gray-Daughter**      **DEATH:** 14 May 1917

**Robert D. Gray**     **BIRTH:** Aug. 1837
**Son**                **DEATH:** 27 Apr. 1905

**America Turner Gray** **BIRTH:** 12 Feb. 1839
**Daughter**           **DEATH:** 28 Dec. 1902

## HIS LIFE

When Robert Gray was born in 1787 in Eden, Kentucky his father, Robert was 42 and his mother, Mary was 21. He was married two times and had six daughters and seven sons. He died on April 7, 1873 in Peytonsville, Williamson County, Tennessee at the age of 86.

---

# ALLEN FREDERICK NICHOLS
## 1787-1848

### NICHOLS FAMILY

#### HUSBAND'S PARENTS
**George Nichols**     **Elizabeth Heathcock**
1755 - 1800              1765 - 1804

#### WIFE'S PARENTS
**John Shaffer**     **Magdalina Eichelberge**
**1774 - 1859**       **1775 - 1812**

#### HUSBAND
**Allen Frederick Nichols**
**BIRTH:** 1787, Newberry, SC
**DEATH:** 1848, Peytonsville, TN

#### WIFE
**Eva Shaffer**
**BIRTH:** 1795, Newberry, SC
**DEATH:** 1787, Peytonsville, TN

#### CHILDREN

**Frederick Shaffer Nichols-Son**     **BIRTH:** 7 Sep. 1834
                                       **DEATH:** 24 May 1896

**Mary J.L. Nichols Daughter**     **BIRTH:** 1838
                                    **DEATH:** Unknown

### HIS LIFE

When Allen Frederick Nichols was born in 1787, his father, George was 32 and his mother, Elizabeth was 22. He married Eva Shaffer in 1810 in Newberry, South Carolina. They had two children during their marriage.

Banks shuttered their doors and unemployment skyrocketed when Allen Frederick Nichols lived in Tennessee during the economic depression that became known as the Panic of 1837.

Allen Frederick Nichols died in 1848, in Peytonsville, Tennessee at the age of 61.

---

# PETTUS SHELBURNE
## 1787-1864

### SHELBURNE FAMILY

#### HUSBAND'S PARENTS
**Samuel Pettus Shelburne**   **Sarah Pamplin**
1769 - 1838                    1770 - 1804

#### WIFE'S PARENTS
**Daniel Crenshaw**   **Nancy Ann Jennings**
1768 - 1814            1772 - 1863

#### HUSBAND
**Pettus Shelburne**
**BIRTH:** 27 July 1787, Lunenburg Co. VA
**DEATH:** 1864, Peytonsville, TN

#### WIFE
**Mary Jennings Crenshaw**
**BIRTH:** 25 Oct. 1794, Lunenburg Co. VA
**DEATH:** 14 Apr. 1875, Peytonsville, TN

#### CHILDREN

**Mary S. Shelburne Daughter**     **BIRTH:** 1810
                                    **DEATH:** 1885

**Elizabeth Shelburne Daughter**     **BIRTH:** 1812
                                      **DEATH:** 1843

**Thomas Shelburne Son**     **BIRTH:** 1812
                              **DEATH:** Unknown

**Ruth Shelburne Daughter**     **BIRTH:** 1813
                                 **DEATH:** Unknown

**Cephas Shelburne Son**     **BIRTH:** 1816
                              **DEATH:** Unknown

### HIS LIFE

When Pettus Shelburne was born on July 27, 1787, in Lunenburg County, Virginia, his father, Samuel was 18 and his mother, Sarah was 17. He married Mary Jennings Crenshaw on December 6, 1810, in Williamson County, Tennessee. They had five children together. He died in 1864, in Williamson County at the age of 77.

# CLEMENT S. PENNINGTON
## 1790-1861

### PENNINGTON FAMILY

### HUSBAND'S PARENTS
**William Pennington**   **Druscillia Smithson**
1765 - 1806                         1767 - 1824

### WIFE'S PARENTS
**Clement Smithson**   **Nancy D. Pettus**
1768 - 1814                      1772 - 1863

### HUSBAND
**Clement S. Pennington**
**BIRTH:** 1790, Lunenburg Co. VA
**DEATH:** 1861, Peytonsville, TN

### WIFE
**Susan T. Smithson**
**BIRTH:** 11 Nov. 1794 Lunenburg Co, VA
**DEATH:** 9 Aug. 1855, Peytonsville, TN

### CHILDREN

**William S. Pennington** **BIRTH:** ABT 1821
**Son**                                  **DEATH:** Unknown

**Clement S.**                  **BIRTH:** 1823
**Pennington-Son**       **DEATH:** 1854

**David Pennington**    **BIRTH:** 1826
**Son**                                **DEATH:** Unknown

**Martha J. Pennington** **BIRTH:** 15 Mar. 1828
**Daughter**                       **DEATH:** 15 June 1916

**Charles W.**                  **BIRTH:** 1831
**Pennington-Son**       **DEATH:** BEF 1900

**Nancy Pennington**  **BIRTH:** 1833
**Daughter**                    **DEATH:** 30 Mar. 1850
**Martha Pennington**  **BIRTH:** 1 Mar. 1836
**Daughter**                     **DEATH:** 15 June 1916

**John Alexander**         **BIRTH:** 1839
**Pennington-Son**       **DEATH:** 2 July 1886

### HIS LIFE

When Clement S. Pennington was born in 1790 in Lunenburg County, Virginia his father, William was 25 and his mother, Druscillia was 23. He married Susan T. Smithson on January 6, 1817 in Peytonsville, Williamson County, Tennessee. They had seven children in 18-years. He died in Peytonsville in 1861, at the age of 71.

# SAMUEL PRATT
## 1791-1854

### PRATT FAMILY

### HUSBAND'S PARENTS
**Father Unknown**   **Mother Unknown**

### 1ST WIFE'S PARENTS
**James Boyd**      **Nancy Mary Gentry**
1768 - 1821              1776 - 1828

### 2ND WIFE'S PARENTS
**Father Unknown**   **Mother Unknown**

### HUSBAND
**Samuel Pratt**
**BIRTH:** 18 May 1791, Virginia
**DEATH:** 31 Mar. 1854, Davidson Co. TN

### 1ST WIFE
**Mary Polly Boyd**
**BIRTH:** 27 Apr. 1795, Fort Nashboro, Davidson Co. TN

**DEATH:** 1850, Davidson Co. TN

## 2ND WIFE
**Melinda Ann Short Burnett**
**BIRTH:** 1800, NC
**DEATH:** Unknown

## CHILDREN OF SAMUEL AND MARY POLLY

| | |
|---|---|
| **Nancy G. Pratt** <br> Daughter | **BIRTH:** 1816 <br> **DEATH:** 1871 |
| **James Harvey Pratt** <br> Son | **BIRTH:** 14 July 1818 <br> **DEATH:** 1879 |
| **Abner Boyd Pratt** <br> Son | **BIRTH:** 20 Mar. 1820 <br> **DEATH:** 6 Mar. 1902 |
| **Susan Elizabeth Pratt** <br> Daughter | **BIRTH:** 23 Dec. 1821 <br> **DEATH:** 1 Jan. 1903 |
| **Samuel Houston Pratt** <br> Son | **BIRTH:** 27 Sep. 1823 <br> **DEATH:** BEF 1900 |
| **John W. Pratt** <br> Son | **BIRTH:** 25 Jan. 1825 <br> **DEATH:** 6 May 1870 |
| **Mary Louisa Pratt** <br> Daughter | **BIRTH:** 4 Apr. 1827 <br> **DEATH:** AFT 1900 |
| **George Washington** <br> **Pratt-Son** | **BIRTH:** 6 July 1829 <br> **DEATH:** 8 Mar. 1903 |
| **Eliza Tennessee Pratt** <br> Daughter | **BIRTH:** ABT 1833 <br> **DEATH:** 22 May 1913 |
| **Martha Virginia Pratt** <br> Daughter | **BIRTH:** 27 Mar. 1836 <br> **DEATH:** 12 Apr. 1915 |
| **Cornelia Ann Pratt** <br> Daughter | **BIRTH:** 10 Mar. 1838 <br> **DEATH:** Unknown |
| **Caroline G. Pratt** <br> Daughter | **BIRTH:** 4 Sep. 1841 <br> **DEATH:** 16 Sep. 1841 |

## HIS LIFE

Samuel Pratt was born on May 18, 1791 in Virginia. Samuel joined the military to serve in the War of 1812 when he was 21-years old. He was a private of Captain Davis Mason's Company of Tennessee Militia. The regiment's assignment was to fight and destroy the Creek Indians. The regiment consisted of 400 men. They marched from Fayetteville, Tennessee to Huntsville, Alabama and on to Fort Strother which was a stockade fort at Ten Islands in the Mississippi Territory, in what is today St. Clair County, Alabama. The regiment was stationed there after the Battle of Talladega. Colonel William Pillow, Lieutenant Joseph Mason and Captain David Mason were the officers. Samuel was paid 87 cents per day as a private. He entered into service on August 18, 1813, and served until May 21, 1814 when he was honorably discharged. This war claimed the lives of 15,000 American soldiers.

Samuel Pratt married Mary Polly Boyd (1795-1850) on Harpeth Lick Road (later became Peytonsville Road), in Williamson County, Tennessee on September 7, 1814, when he was 23-years old. They had 12 children. By 1836, Samuel and his family had moved to Otter Creek Road, Davidson County, Tennessee. Mary Polly passed away in 1850 in Davidson County, Tennessee at the age of 55. They had been married for 36-years.

The third child of Samuel and Polly was Abner Boyd Pratt. Abner and his offspring would hold the Pratt lands until the death of his grandchildren, Elsworth and Carrie Bush. They bequeathed the last twenty-five acres to the Trevecca Nazarene College. The college would sell the land to the state of Tennessee and one of the last remaining parcels of the of the Pratt land progression would become a part of the Radnor Lake State Natural Area. This parcel is documented as 40 DV 172 by Division of Archaeology, and includes the Pratt Cemetery. The Pratt Cemetery contains about fifteen graves.

Samuel married Melinda Ann Short Burnett

(1800-?) in Williamson County, Tennessee on October 19, 1852 when he was 61-years old.

Samuel Pratt died on March 31, 1854, in Davidson County, Tennessee when he was 62-years old. He is buried in the Pratt Cemetery on the Otter Creek family farm.

# WILLIAM SAMUEL HATCHER
# 1793-1866

## HATCHER FAMILY

### HUSBAND'S PARENTS
**Elijah Hatcher**    **Sarah Haile**
1749 - 1829    1755 - 1810

### WIFE'S PARENTS
**William Rucker Sr.**    **Sarah North**
1760 - 1826    1762 - 1845

### HUSBAND
**William Samuel Hatcher**
BIRTH: 20 June 1793, Bedford Co. VA
DEATH: 31 May 1866, Williamson Co. TN

### WIFE
**Lucy Rucker**
BIRTH: 17 Oct. 1797, Bedford Co. VA
DEATH: 27 Aug. 1884, Williamson Co. TN

### CHILDREN

| | | |
|---|---|---|
| **Octavius Claiborne Hatcher-Son** | BIRTH: 29 Dec. 1816 | DEATH: 21 June 1856 |
| **John Rucker Hatcher Son** | BIRTH: 26 Oct. 1818 | DEATH: 12 June 1857 |
| **Margaret Susan Hatcher-Daughter** | BIRTH: 17 Aug. 1820 | DEATH: 5 Feb. 1889 |
| **William H. Hatcher Son** | BIRTH: 9 Oct. 1822 | DEATH: 8 June 1843 |
| **Bernard McKendree Hatcher-Son** | BIRTH: 1824 | DEATH: 11 July 1898 |
| **Sarah Ann Hatcher Daughter** | BIRTH: 15 May 1827 | DEATH: 21 Mar. 1879 |
| **Thomas Logwood Hatcher-Son** | BIRTH: 2 Mar. 1828 | DEATH: 8 Jan. 1904 |
| **Lucy North Hatcher Daughter** | BIRTH: 21 Aug. 1830 | DEATH: 7 Oct. 1907 |
| **Henry Spotswood Hatcher-Son** | BIRTH: 29 Nov. 1831 | DEATH: 3 Aug. 1891 |
| **Edith J. Hatcher Daughter** | BIRTH: 20 Apr. 1834 | DEATH: 20 June 1834 |
| **Abram Woolridge Hatcher-Son** | BIRTH: 24 Apr. 1835 | DEATH: 28 Apr. 1902 |
| **Elizabeth Jane Hatcher-Daughter** | BIRTH: 13 Nov. 1839 | DEATH: 28 Apr. 1919 |

## HIS LIFE

When William Samuel Hatcher was born on June 20, 1793, in Bedford County, Virginia, his father, Elijah was 44 and his mother, Sarah was 38. William enlisted in the military for the War of 1812, on September 1, 1814, when he was 21-years old.

William married Lucy Rucker (1797-1884) in Bedford County, Virginia on December 18, 1815, when he was 22-years old. By 1820 they were living in Williamson County, Tennessee. They had 12 children in 22-years. William Samuel Hatcher died on May 31, 1866, in Williamson County, Tennessee when he was 72-years old.

# JOSIAH NEVILS
# 1794-1854

## NEVILS FAMILY

**HUSBAND'S PARENTS**
George Washington Nevils     Sarah Foster
1760 - 1816                  1766 - 1861

**WIFE'S PARENTS**
**Father Unknown    Mother Unknown**

**HUSBAND**
**Josiah Nevils**
**BIRTH:** 1794, Charlotte Court House, VA
**DEATH:** 1854, Peytonsville, TN

**WIFE**
**Sarah Beech**
**BIRTH:** ABT 1801, VA
**DEATH:** 21 Feb. 1882, Peytonsville, TN

**CHILDREN**

| | |
|---|---|
| **Mary A. Nevils** Daughter | **BIRTH:** 12 Aug. 1823 **DEATH:** 26 Aug. 1896 |
| **Martha Nevils** Daughter | **BIRTH:** 1830 **DEATH:** Unknown |
| **John M. Nevils** Son | **BIRTH:** 1832 **DEATH:** 1900 |
| **J. W. L. Nevils** Son | **BIRTH:** 14 July 1834 **DEATH:** 11 July 1893 |
| **Ann E. Nevils** Daughter | **BIRTH:** 1839 **DEATH:** 1839 |
| **Virginia Nevils** Daughter | **BIRTH:** 1841 **DEATH:** 1861 |
| **Catherine Nevils** Daughter | **BIRTH:** 1849 **DEATH:** 1861 |

**HIS LIFE**

When Josiah Nevils was born in 1794, in Charlotte Court House, Virginia, his father, George was 34 and his mother, Sarah was 28. He married Sarah B. Beech on June 21, 1821, in Williamson County, Tennessee. They had seven children in 26-years. He died in 1854, in Williamson County, Tennessee at the age of 60.

# ANDREW B. PARKS
## 1794-1870

**PARKS FAMILY**

**HUSBAND'S PARENTS**
John Uriah Parks     Rachel Johnson
1750 - 1822          1753 - 1834

**1ST WIFE'S PARENTS**
James Neely     Sarah Sanders
1775 - 1835     1798 - ?

**2ND WIFE'S PARENTS**
James P. Barnett     Margaret Gibson
1783 - 1828          1791 - 1873

**HUSBAND**
**Andrew B. Parks**
**BIRTH:** 20 Mar. 1794, Wilkes Co. NC
**DEATH:** 18 Sep. 1870, Peytonsville, TN

**1ST WIFE**
**Rhoda Ann Neely**
**BIRTH:** ABT. 1803
**DEATH:** 19 Sep. 1843, Franklin, TN

**2ND WIFE**
**Elizabeth Gibson Barnett**
**BIRTH:** 22 Mar. 1815, Peytonsville, TN
**DEATH:** 18 Feb. 1901, Peytonsville, TN

**CHILDREN OF ANDREW AND RHODA**

| | |
|---|---|
| **Sarah Jane Parks** Daughter | **BIRTH:** 10 July 1822 **DEATH:** 31 July 1892 |
| **Steven Sanders Neely Parks-Son** | **BIRTH:** 5 Apr. 1824 **DEATH:** 24 Jan. 1858 |
| **John Washington Parks-Son** | **BIRTH:** 15 Jun. 1828 **DEATH:** 19 Dec. 1873 |

| **John B. Parks**<br>Son | **BIRTH:** 30 Mar. 1830<br>**DEATH:** 19 Dec. 1873 |
| --- | --- |
| **James Adams Parks**<br>Son | **BIRTH:** 30 Mar. 1830<br>**DEATH:** 5 July 1873 |
| **Mary Elizabeth**<br>**Sanders Parks-Dau.** | **BIRTH:** 25 May 1833<br>**DEATH**: 18 Mar. 1874 |
| **Andrew Baker Parks**<br>Son | **BIRTH:** 12 Mar. 1835<br>**DEATH:** 5 July 1864 |
| **Susan Frances Parks**<br>Daughter | **BIRTH:** 30 Mar. 1836<br>**DEATH:** 1837 |
| **William Flack Parks**<br>Son | **BIRTH:** 28 July 1838<br>**DEATH:** 29 July 1842 |
| **Thomas D. Parks**<br>Son | **BIRTH:** 28 Jan. 1841<br>**DEATH:** 14 Feb. 1842 |
| **Brice A. Parks**<br>Son | **BIRTH:** 18 Mar. 1843<br>**DEATH:** 30 July 1843 |

### CHILDREN OF ANDREW AND ELIZABETH

| **Sophronia A. Parks**<br>Daughter | **BIRTH:** ABT. 1846<br>**DEATH:** 12 Mar. 1846 |
| --- | --- |
| **Margaret Rachel**<br>**Parks-Daughter** | **BIRTH:** 1848<br>**DEATH:** Unknown |
| **Joe Bennett Parks**<br>Son | **BIRTH:** ABT. 1850<br>**DEATH:** 17 Feb. 1906 |

### HIS LIFE

When Andrew B. Parks was born in 1794 in Wilkes County, North Carolina, his father, John was 44 and his mother, Rachel was 41. He served in the military during the War of 1812. By 1820 his family was living in Williamson County, Tennessee.

Andrew married Rhoda Ann Neely (1803-1843) on April 30, 1821, when he was 27-years old and they had 11 children together. When his wife Rhoda Ann passed away on September 19, 1843 at the age of 40, they had been married for 22-years. He then married, Elizabeth Gibson Barnett (1815-1901) in Peytonsville, Tennessee on November 22, 1845 when he was 51-years old. Andrew and Elizabeth had three children together. Andrew B. Parks died on September 18, 1870, in Peytonsville, Tennessee when he was 76-years old.

# GEORGE B. LONG
# 1797-1879

## LONG FAMILY

### HUSBAND'S PARENTS
**Michael Long**    **Catherine Kinard**
1755 - 1832      1775 - 1850

### WIFE'S PARENTS
**James E. Gosey**    **Rebecca Bowers**
1772 - 1854      1783 - 1859

### HUSBAND
**George B. Long**
**BIRTH:** 16 Oct. 1797, South Carolina
**DEATH:** 21 Aug. 1879, Williamson Co. TN

### WIFE
**Elizabeth Gosey**
**BIRTH:** 9 Mar. 1802, Lunenburg Co. VA
**DEATH:** 29 June 1838, Peytonsville, TN

### CHILDREN

| **Josiah Long**<br>Son | **BIRTH:** 1823<br>**DEATH:** BET. 1850-60 |
| --- | --- |
| **Martha J. Long**<br>Daughter | **BIRTH:** 9 Sep. 1824<br>**DEATH:** 4 Jan. 1907 |
| **Mary Long**<br>Daughter | **BIRTH:** 13 Sep. 1826<br>**DEATH:** 27 Sep. 1852 |
| **James M. Long**<br>Son | **BIRTH:** 26 Feb. 1830<br>**DEATH:** 26 Aug. 1891 |

| Harriet Elizabeth Long-Daughter | BIRTH: 1835<br>DEATH: Unknown |
|---|---|

## HIS LIFE

When George B. Long was born on October 16, 1797, in South Carolina, his father, Michael was 42 and his mother Catherine was 22. He married Elizabeth Gosey on March 14, 1822 in Williamson County, Tennessee. They had five children in 12-years. He died on August 21, 1879 in Williamson County, Tennessee at the age of 81.

# SAMUEL STEAGALL
# 1798-1873

## STEAGALL FAMILY

### HUSBAND'S PARENTS
**Rolfe R. Stegall**    **Susanna Lafoon**
1767 - 1850    1757 - 1828

### WIFE'S PARENTS
**Henry Gee**    **Martha Waller**
1760 - 1820    1760 - 1820

### HUSBAND
**Samuel Steagall**
BIRTH: 22 May 1798, Lunenburg Co. VA
DEATH: 22 Oct. 1873, Peytonsville, TN

### WIFE
**Nancy Gee**
BIRTH: 11 Aug. 1801, Lunenburg Co. VA
DEATH: 9 Aug. 1856, Peytonsville, TN

### CHILDREN

| Elizabeth A. Steagall Daughter | BIRTH: 1822<br>DEATH: AFT. 1870 |
|---|---|
| Henry W. Steagall Son (died at Shiloh) | BIRTH: 1827<br>DEATH: Apr. 1862 |
| Martha C. Steagall Daughter | BIRTH: 1829<br>DEATH: 1856 |

| Julia C. Steagall Daughter | BIRTH: 1832<br>DEATH: Unknown |
|---|---|
| Lucy A. Steagall Daughter | BIRTH: Dec. 1835<br>DEATH: AFT. 1900 |
| Mary L. Steagall Daughter | BIRTH: 1837<br>DEATH: Unknown |
| Thomas R. Steagall Son | BIRTH: 1840<br>DEATH: Unknown |
| William M. Steagall Son | BIRTH: 1843<br>DEATH: 1860 |

## HIS LIFE

When Samuel Steagall was born on May 22, 1798, in Lunenburg County, Virginia, his father, Rolfe was 31 and his mother, Susanna was 41. He married Nancy Gee on January 8, 1821, in Lunenburg County, Virginia. Sometime between 1822 and 1827, he moved with his family to Williamson County, Tennessee. Samuel and Nancy had eight children in 21-years. He died on October 22, 1873, in Peytonsville, Tennessee at the age of 75. He is buried in the Steagall cemetery.

# SAMUEL CHEATHAM
# SMITHSON
# 1799-1837

## SMITHSON FAMILY

### HUSBAND'S PARENTS
**Nathaniel B. Smithson**    **Mary P. Cheatham**
1773 - 1859    1777 - 1850

### WIFE'S PARENTS
**John D. Secrest**    **Sabra Jeanette Lewis**
1758 - 1847    1769 - 1837

### HUSBAND
**Samuel Cheatham Smithson**

**BIRTH:** 16 Oct. 1799, Lunenburg Co. VA
**DEATH:** 26 Oct. 1837, Peytonsville, TN

### WIFE
**Matilda Secrest**
**BIRTH:** 21 Feb. 1800, Mecklenburg, VA
**DEATH:** 18 July 1859, Peytonsville, TN

### CHILDREN

| | |
|---|---|
| **Mary "Jane" Smithson-Daughter** | **BIRTH:** 12 Oct. 1821 **DEATH:** 1904 |
| **Minerva Smithson Daughter** | **BIRTH:** 19 Dec. 1823 **DEATH:** Unknown |
| **Elizabeth G. Smithson Daughter** | **BIRTH:** 14 Feb. 1826 **DEATH:** 27 July 1850 |
| **John S. Smithson Son** | **BIRTH:** 9 Nov. 1828 **DEATH:** Unknown |
| **Samuel Cheatham Smithson-Son** | **BIRTH:** 19 Feb. 1833 **DEATH:** 23 Aug. 1887 |
| **Nathaniel "Nat" Green Smithson-Son** | **BIRTH:** 19 Aug. 1835 **DEATH:** 1 Nov. 1898 |

### HIS LIFE

When Samuel Cheatham Smithson was born on October 16, 1799, in Lunenburg County, Virginia, his father, Nathaniel was 26 and his mother, Mary was 22. Samuel married Matilda Secrest in Williamson County, Tennessee on December 7, 1818, when he was 19-years old and they had six children together.

# GEORGE G. BOYD
# 1800-1841

## BOYD FAMILY

### HUSBAND'S PARENTS
**James Boyd**      **Nancy Mary Gentry**
1768 - 1821      1776 - 1828

### WIFE'S PARENTS
**Freeman Walker    Polly Toone**
1765 - 1835

### HUSBAND
**George G. Boyd**
**BIRTH:** 1800, Davidson Co. TN
**DEATH:** 27 Sep. 1841, Williamson Co. TN

### WIFE
**Martha Ann Walker**
**BIRTH:** 4 July 1800, VA **DEATH:** TN

### CHILDREN

| | |
|---|---|
| **Martha J. Boyd Daughter** | **BIRTH:** 1820 **DEATH:** 1848 |
| **Mary Elizabeth Boyd Daughter** | **BIRTH:** 1822 **DEATH:** 22 Jan. 1883 |
| **Caroline Tennessee Boyd-Daughter** | **BIRTH:** 1825 **DEATH:** 22 Jun. 1913 |
| **Ann A. Boyd Daughter** | **BIRTH:** 1835 **DEATH:** Unknown |
| **George Washington Boyd-Son** | **BIRTH:** 29 Apr. 1837 **DEATH:** 24 Jan. 1927 |
| **Abner V. Boyd Son** | **BIRTH:** 1840 **DEATH:** Feb. 1881 |

### HIS LIFE

When George G. Boyd was born in 1800, in Fort Nashboro, Davidson County, Tennessee, his father, James was 32 and his mother, Nancy was 24. He married Martha Walker in Williamson County, Tennessee on February 20, 1821 when he was 21-years old. They had six children together. George died on September 27, 1841, in Williamson County, Tennessee at the age of 41.

# TANDY S. SMITHSON
## 1801-1873

### SMITHSON FAMILY

#### HUSBAND'S PARENTS
**Nathaniel B. Smithson**   **Mary P. Cheatham**
1773 - 1859                 1777 - 1850

#### WIFE'S PARENTS
**Father Unknown**   **Mother Unknown**

#### HUSBAND
**Tandy S. Smithson**
**BIRTH:** 17 Jan. 1801, Lunenburg Co. VA
**DEATH:** 26 May 1873, Williamson Co. TN

#### WIFE
**Ann Calvert**
**BIRTH:** 3 May 1804, GA
**DEATH:** 17 May, 1888, Peytonsville, TN

#### CHILDREN

| | | |
|---|---|---|
| **Parmelia W. Smithson** **Daughter** | **BIRTH:** 17 June 1824 **DEATH:** 20 Feb. 1873 | |
| **Nathaniel Nicholas Smithson-Son** | **BIRTH:** 20 Apr. 1826 **DEATH:** 10 Apr. 1896 | |

### HIS LIFE

When Tandy S. Smithson was born on January 17, 1801, in Lunenburg County, Virginia, his father, Nathaniel was 27 and his mother, Mary was 23. He married Ann Calvert on March 27, 1823, in Maury County, Tennessee. They had two children during their marriage. He died on May 26, 1873, in Peytonsville, Tennessee at the age of 72 and was buried in Bethesda, Tennessee.

# JOHN D. LILLARD
## 1802-1864

### LILLARD FAMILY

#### HUSBAND'S PARENTS
**Morgan Lillard**   **Abbie Howard**
1770 - 1825          1780 - ?

#### WIFE'S PARENTS
**Father Unknown**   **Mother Unknown**

#### HUSBAND
**John D. Lillard**
**BIRTH:** 1802, Rockingham, NC
**DEATH:** 1864, Williamson Co. TN

#### WIFE
**Rachel Jarrell**
**BIRTH:** 1801, VA
**DEATH:** Dec. 1864, Williamson Co. TN

#### CHILDREN

| | |
|---|---|
| **Edmond Lillard** **Son** | **BIRTH:** ABT 1828 **DEATH:** 1870 |
| **Sarah Elizabeth Lillard-Daughter** | **BIRTH:** 20 Jan. 1829 **DEATH:** 9 Feb. 1914 |
| **J. Lillard** **Son** | **BIRTH:** 1834 **DEATH:** 1865 |
| **Nancy Ellen Lillard** **Daughter** | **BIRTH:** ABT 1837 **DEATH:** BEF 1947 |
| **Harriett Virginia Lillard-Daughter** | **BIRTH:** 1840 **DEATH:** 2 Sep. 1893 |
| **Moses C.D. Lillard** **Son** | **BIRTH:** 1841 **DEATH:** Unknown |
| **Frances Marian Lillard-Daughter** | **BIRTH:** 1841 **DEATH:** 1865 |
| **Monroe Claiborne Lillard-Son** | **BIRTH:** 1844 **DEATH:** 1891 |

## HIS LIFE

When John D. Lillard was born in 1802, in Rockingham, North Carolina his father, Morgan was 32 and his mother, Abbie was 22. He married Rachel Jarrell on February 2, 1828 in his hometown. They had eight children in 19-years. He died in 1864 in Williamson County, Tennessee at the age of 62.

# GARNER MCCONNICO JORDAN
## 1803-1900

### JORDAN FAMILY

#### HUSBAND'S PARENTS
**Archibald Jordan**    **Elizabeth "Betsy" Walker**
1770 - 1835      1774 - 1832

#### 1ST WIFE'S PARENTS
**Peter Burton**    **Rebecca Guinn**
1754 - 1834      1758 - 1830

#### 2ND WIFE'S PARENTS
**Thomas Grainger Stephens**   **Sarah Miller**
1750 - 1836      1757 - 1846

#### HUSBAND
**Garner McConnico Jordan**
**BIRTH:** 1803, Williamson Co. TN
**DEATH:** 1900, Williamson Co. TN

#### 1ST WIFE
**Rebecca G. Burton**
**BIRTH:** 4 June 1806, Stokes Co. NC
**DEATH:** 12 Feb. 1839, Peytonsville, TN

#### 2ND WIFE
**Mary M. Stephens**
**BIRTH:** 4 Aug. 1805, TN
**DEATH:** 8 Aug. 1873, Peytonsville, TN

### CHILDREN OF GARNER AND REBECCA

| | |
|---|---|
| **Elizabeth W. Jordan** Daughter | **BIRTH:** 27 Jan. 1827 **DEATH:** 1 Dec. 1853 |
| **Rebecca G. Jordan** Daughter | **BIRTH:** 1829 **DEATH:** Unknown |
| **Sarah J. Jordan** Daughter | **BIRTH:** 1830 **DEATH:** 1897 |
| **Ann Eliza** Daughter | **BIRTH:** 1835 **DEATH:** Unkknown |
| **Susan Jordan** Daughter | **BIRTH:** 1837 **DEATH:** Unknown |
| **Garner McConnico Jordan Jr.-Son** | **BIRTH:** 23 Nov. 1838 **DEATH:** 27 Dec. 1908 |

### HIS LIFE

When Garner McConnico Jordan was born in 1803, in Williamson County, Tennessee his father, Archibald was 33 and his mother, Elizabeth was 29. He married Rebecca G. Burton on December 20, 1824, and they had six children together. After the death of Rebecca on February 12, 1839, he married Mary M. Stephens on October 20, 1839, in Williamson County, Tennessee. He died in 1900 in his hometown at the impressive age of 97.

# JESSE J. JOHNSON
## 1804-1866

### JOHNSON FAMILY

#### HUSBAND'S PARENTS
**Benjamin Johnson**    **Mary McDonough**
1780 - 1821      1783 - 1856

#### WIFE'S PARENTS
**John Smithson**    **Elizabeth G. "Betsy" Knott**
1777 - 1837      1775 - 1839

## HUSBAND
### Jesse J. Johnson
**BIRTH:** 1804, Brunswick Co. VA
**DEATH:** 1866, Williamson Co. TN

## WIFE
### Dolly Smithson
**BIRTH:** ABT 1812, Williamson Co. TN
**DEATH:** ABT 1884, Williamson Co. TN

## CHILDREN

| | |
|---|---|
| **William L. Johnson**<br>Son | **BIRTH:** July 1829<br>**DEATH:** AFT 1880 |
| **John Asa Johnson**<br>Son | **BIRTH:** 20 Feb. 1831<br>**DEATH:** 2 Oct. 1910 |
| **Margaret Knott**<br>**Johnson-Daughter** | **BIRTH:** 8 Mar. 1833<br>**DEATH:** 1880 |
| **Mary Jane Johnson**<br>Daughter | **BIRTH:** 5 May 1837<br>**DEATH:** 24 Aug. 1867 |
| **Adeline V. Johnson**<br>Daughter | **BIRTH:** ABT 1839<br>**DEATH:** AFT 1900 |
| **Martha Parilee**<br>**Johnson-Daughter** | **BIRTH:** ABT 1840<br>**DEATH:** 7 Aug. 1910 |
| **Dolly Johnson**<br>Daughter | **BIRTH:** 1841<br>**DEATH:** Unknown |
| **L.L. Johnson**<br>Son | **BIRTH:** 1843<br>**DEATH:** Unknown |
| **Sylvanius Wade**<br>**Johnson-Son** | **BIRTH:** 24 Apr. 1844<br>**DEATH:** 26 Apr. 1920 |
| **Lucy Johnson**<br>Daughter | **BIRTH:** 1846<br>**DEATH:** Unknown |
| **Bettie E. Johnson**<br>Daughter | **BIRTH:** 17 Jun. 1847<br>**DEATH:** 7 Jan. 1929 |
| **Benjamin Monroe**<br>**Johnson-Son** | **BIRTH:** 7 Mar. 1850<br>**DEATH:** 19 Sep. 1904 |
| **Gregory Johnson**<br>Son | **BIRTH:** 1855<br>**DEATH:** Unknown |

## HIS LIFE

When Jesse J. Johnson was born in 1804, in Brunswick County, Virginia his father, Benjamin was 24 and his mother, Mary was 21. He married Dolly Smithson on October 8, 1828, in Williamson County, Tennessee. They had 13 children in 26-years. He died in 1866, in Peytonsville, Tennessee at the age of 62.

# WILLIAM HENRY VADEN JR.
## 1804-1885

### VADEN FAMILY

### HUSBAND'S PARENTS
**William Henry Vaden Sr.**     **Catherine Moseley**
1782 - 1845                     1780 - 1820

### WIFE'S PARENTS
**Nathaniel B. Smithson**   **Mary P. Cheatham**
1773 - 1859                 1777 - 1850

## HUSBAND
### William Henry Vaden Jr.
**BIRTH:** 1804, Williamson Co, TN
**DEATH:** Jan. 1885, Williamson Co, TN

## WIFE
### Martha W. Smithson
**BIRTH:** 1806, Lunenburg Co, VA
**DEATH:** 1880, Williamson Co, TN

## CHILDREN

| | |
|---|---|
| **Charles W. Vaden**<br>Son | **BIRTH:** ABT 1834<br>**DEATH:** Unknown |
| **Mary E. Vaden**<br>Daughter | **BIRTH:** 1835<br>**DEATH:** BEF 1865 |
| **Catherine K. Vaden**<br>Daughter | **BIRTH:** 1838<br>**DEATH:** Unknown |

| Martha Vaden<br>Daughter | BIRTH: 1841<br>DEATH: Unknown |
|---|---|
| Nathaniel Bedford<br>Vaden-Son | BIRTH: 1844<br>DEATH: 20 Jan. 1927 |

## HIS LIFE

William Henry Vaden Jr. was born in 1804 in Georgia. He married Martha W. Smithson on April 27, 1832 in Williamson County, Tennessee. They had five children in 11-years. He died in January 1885 in Peytonsville, Tennessee at the age of 81-years old.

# DANIEL SLEDGE
## 1804-1873

### SLEDGE FAMILY

**HUSBAND'S PARENTS**

| John Lewis Sledge | Cinthia L. Sammons |
|---|---|
| 1772 - 1823 | 1771 - 1840 |

**WIFE'S PARENTS**

| William Kennedy | Elizabeth Pursell |
|---|---|
| 1755 - 1853 | 1769 - 1841 |

**HUSBAND**
**Daniel Sledge**
**BIRTH:** 1804, NC
**DEATH:** 17 June 1873, Peytonsville, TN

**WIFE**
**Celia Kennedy**
**BIRTH:** 1805, TN
**DEATH:** 1879, Peytonsville, TN

### HIS LIFE

When Daniel Sledge was born in 1804, in North Carolina, his father, John was 32 and his mother, Cinthia was 33. He married Celia Kennedy on December 15, 1824, in Williamson County, Tennessee. He died on June 17, 1873, in Peytonsville, Tennessee at the age of 69.

Records of the Cool Springs Primitive Baptist Church show, "Daniel Sledge received by experience" in September 1844. The records also have an entry, "Daniel Sledge departed this life 17 June, 1873.

Celia's estate sale took place in 1878. Buyers at the sale included: J.W. Sledge, W.O. Sledge, R. Sledge and Robt Sledge. A.W. Hatcher, Admin, filed final account 21 August, 1882, Williamson County. No record of any children.

# JOSEPH A. VADEN
## 1806-1850

### VADEN FAMILY

**HUSBAND'S PARENTS**

| William Henry Vaden Sr. | Catherine Moseley |
|---|---|
| 1782 - 1845 | 1780 - 1820 |

**WIFE'S PARENTS**

| Mark Wilson | Phoebe Gibson |
|---|---|
| 1771 - 1839 | 1780 - 1820 |

**HUSBAND**
**Joseph A. Vaden**
**BIRTH:** 1806, AL
**DEATH:** Apr. 1850, Lauderdale Co. AL

**WIFE**
**Catherine G. Wilson**
**BIRTH:** 1814, TN
**DEATH:** 4 Feb. 1873, Williamson Co. TN

### CHILDREN

| Mark Wilson Vaden<br>Son | BIRTH: 19 Apr,.1840<br>DEATH: 26 Jan. 1919 |
|---|---|

### HIS LIFE

When Joseph A. Vaden was born in 1806, in Alabama, his father, William was 24 and his mother, Catherine was 26. He married Catherine G. Wilson on September 27, 1838, in Williamson County, Tennessee. They had one child during their marriage. He died in April 1850, in Lauderdale County, Alabama at the age of 44.

# NATHANIEL LUNDY HARRISON
# 1808-1885

## HARRISON FAMILY

### HUSBAND'S PARENTS
**Nathaniel Harrison**     **Hixey Robertson**
1778 - 1852                       1780 - 1810

### 1ST WIFE'S PARENTS
**Samuel W. Knight**     **Sarah Wade Smithson**
1770 - 1850                       1774 - 1865

### 2ND WIFE'S PARENTS
**Unknown Father**     **Unknown Mother**

### HUSBAND
**Nathaniel Lundy Harrison**
**BIRTH:** 2 Dec. 1808, Warren Co. NC
**DEATH:** 21 Nov. 1885, Williamson Co. TN

### 1ST WIFE
**Christina T. Knight**
**BIRTH:** 15 Oct. 1811, Lunenburg Co, VA
**DEATH:** 4 Sep. 1862, Peytonsville, TN

### 2ND WIFE
**Martha E. Ozburne**
**BIRTH:** ABT 1825
**DEATH:** Unknown

## CHILDREN OF NATHANIEL AND CHRISTINA

| | |
|---|---|
| **Sarah Ann Frances Harrison-Daughter** | **BIRTH:** 15 Jan. 1832 <br> **Death:** 18 July 1876 |
| **Samuel Knight "SK" Harrison-Son** | **BIRTH:** 5 Mar. 1833 <br> **DEATH:** 7 Mar. 1889 |
| **Lydia E. Harrison Daughter** | **BIRTH:** 1834 <br> **DEATH:** 1860 |
| **Arabella Marion Harrison-Daughter** | **BIRTH:** 28 Nov. 1835 <br> **DEATH:** 8 Feb. 1904 |
| **Turnel Lundy Green Harrison-Son** | **BIRTH:** 5 Jun. 1838 <br> **DEATH:** 22 May 1918 |
| **William Henry "Tip" Harrison-Son** | **BIRTH:** 5 Sep. 1840 <br> **DEATH:** 24 July 1887 |
| **Susan T. Harrison Daughter** | **BIRTH:** 1843 <br> **DEATH:** 19 Feb. 1868 |
| **James Gentry Harrison-Son** | **BIRTH:** 26 Aug. 1845 <br> **DEATH:** 1877 |
| **Joseph Jones Harrison-Son** | **BIRTH:** 3 Oct. 1847 <br> **DEATH:** 13 Jan. 1919 |
| **Randal Lytle Harrison Son** | **BIRTH:** 18 Jan. 1851 <br> **DEATH:** 24 Oct. 1921 |
| **C.H. Harrison Son** | **BIRTH:** 1854 <br> **DEATH:** 1854 |

## HIS LIFE

When Nathaniel Lundy Harrison was born on December 2, 1808, his father, Nathaniel was 30 and his mother, Hixey was 28. He married Christina T. Knight on November 9, 1830, and they had 11 children together. After Christina's death in 1862, he married Martha E. Ozburne on December 12, 1865, in Williamson County, Tennessee. He died on November 21, 1885, in Peytonsville, at the age of 76.

In the Review and Journal, a local newspaper in Williamson County, Nov. 1885, Reid's Store correspondent gave a brief notice of the death of Nathaniel Lundy Harrison (1808-1885):

"When a good man and a good citizen dies something more than the mere announcement of his death is due to the honesty, integrity and virtues which are required to build up for himself an honored name, unaided by wealth and unassisted by high or aristocratic family influence. If our system of government had done nothing more than to give equal chances for a distinction to all men and to hold in veneration rather than those who but reflect this luster of a distinguished ancestry, it would merit the admiration and support of all true patriots. Nature alone had limited the ambition of every citizen of our free and happy country, and if she has endowed him with the wealth of energy and intellect he may aspire without presumption to the highest place in the gift of a free people. He who acts well his part in any spare to which nature had adopted him deserves the praise and esteem of his fellow citizens as much, and sometimes more, that others more richly endowed. The improvement of the one talent was as acceptable as that of him who "gained other five talents," and the same "willl done thou good and faithful servant" was applicable to the one as much as to the other.

Nathaniel Lundy Harrison in his lifetime well illustrated the truth of the above. For more than twenty-years he held offices in the county of Williamson as Constable and Deputy Sheriff. The duties of these offices are hard to discharge in a manner equally satisfactory to debtors and creditors, and it is said of having a tendency to harden the heart and render it callous to the appeals to humanity and deaf so the prayers of the poor and needy. If this is true, then indeed, Lundy Harrison must have been an exceptionally tender-hearted man, for his fellow man which found expression in a charity bounded only by his ability to follow up the dictates of his heart. His house was ever the home of a generous and profuse hospitality and the humblest beggar found a welcome as hearty as the most aristocratic visitor.

Sprung from revolutionary stock, he was born in Warren County, North Carolina, on the 2nd day of December 1808. At the age of 10, he came with his father to Williamson County, Tennessee and settled on the farm whereon Dr. Samuel Henderson resided a short time before his death. When quite young he intermarried with Christina Knight, a daughter of Samuel & Sarah Knight. Samuel Knight was an Englishman by birth; his wife, Sarah was born in Lunenburg County, VA., and the family immigrated to Tennessee in 1810, making their first home in the 13th district of Williamson County. The last years of her life she was an inmate of her daughter's (Mrs. Harrison) family whom she survived about three years. Mrs. Harrison dying in 1862 and her mother in 1865. Eleven children were born to N.L. and Christina Harrison, seven sons and four daughters, all of whom, with the exception of two, attained to adult age. This large family was raised and educated by their parents to become useful men and women.

N.L. Harrison was elected Constable of the 10th civil district of Williamson County about the year 1832, and held that office for several years. He was appointed deputy sheriff of the county first by James Hughes, holding office as long as Hughes held the office of Sheriff. Wiley B. White who succeeded Hughes also appointed Mr. Harrison as his deputy, and he continued to act as such during the entire term of office of W.W. White. Ill health finally compelled him to retire from public life. For nearly ten years he was afflicted with dropsy, and after lingering for many years, he died at the residence of his son, R.L. Harrison, on the 21st day of November 1885, in the 77th year of his age. Of him it may be truly said that he was a good father, a good husband, a good citizen and a good neighbor. His opportunities considered, we know of no one who has surpassed and but few who lay equaled him in the conscientious discharge of his every duty."

Nathaniel Lundy Harrison is buried in the Harrison Cemetery in the 14th District. At this writing it is located on the farm of Jimmy Robinson. There are several unmarked graves, three gravestones with no engraving.

Harrison, Christina, wife of N.L. Harrison, B. Oct. 15, 1811, D. Sept. 4, 1862.
Harrison, Infant of N.L Harrison, B. _____, D._____
Harrison, Nathaniel Lundy, B. Dec. 2, 1808, D. Nov. 21, 1885
Pate, Arabella T., daughter of Sarah Ann and T.W. Pate, B. Mar. 18, 1861, D. Dec. 3, 1861
Pate, Sarah Ann, wife of T.W. Pate, B. Jan. 15, 1833, D. July 18, 1876

NATHANIEL LUNDY
HARRISON

# GABRIEL R. LOW
## 1808-1882

### LOW FAMILY

**HUSBAND'S PARENTS**
**John H. Low**    **Lydia Cannon**
1770 - 1840       1760 - 1847

**WIFE'S PARENTS**
**David Pinkston    Frances Needham Andrews**
1773 - 1851           1792 - 1850

**HUSBAND**
**Gabriel R. Low**
**BIRTH:** 1808, SC
**DEATH:** 1882, Peytonsville, TN

**WIFE**
**Lavinia Howard Pinkston**
**BIRTH:** 13 June 1820, Williamson Co. TN
**DEATH:** 11 May 1893, Williamson Co. TN

**CHILDREN**

| | |
|---|---|
| **Lavinia F. Low** Daughter | **BIRTH:** 1841 **DEATH:** Unknown |
| **Viney Angeline Low** Daughter | **BIRTH:** 21 Aug. 1843 **DEATH:** 1878 |
| **Lydia Arabella Low** Daughter | **BIRTH:** 1848 **DEATH:** 1865 |
| **Sophronia Low** Daughter | **BIRTH:** 1850 **DEATH:** 1875 |
| **Ellen Gabriella Low** Daughter | **BIRTH:** 13 Sep. 1852 **DEATH:** 31 Oct. 1932 |
| **V.G. Low** Daughter | **BIRTH:** 1854 **DEATH:** Unknown |
| **Rebecca Low** Daughter | **BIRTH:** 1856 **DEATH:** Unknown |
| **Florence Low** Daughter | **BIRTH:** 1858 **DEATH:** Unknown |
| **Robert E. Low** Son | **BIRTH:** 9 Aug. 1863 **DEATH:** 28 Mar,.1935 |

**HIS LIFE**

Gabriel R. Low was born in 1808, in South Carolina. He married Lavinia H. Pinkston on March 21, 1839, in Williamson County, Tennessee. They had six children in 13-years. He died in 1882, in Peytonsville, Tennessee at the age of 74.

# CONRAD H. HICKS
# 1808-1881

## HICKS FAMILY

### HUSBAND'S PARENTS
**Unknown Father**   **Unknown Mother**

### 1ST WIFE'S PARENTS
**William Steger**   **Martha Davenport**
1785 - ?         1781 - 1840

### 2ND WIFE'S PARENTS
**Nathaniel B. Smithson**   **Mary Polly Cheatham**
1773 - 1859          1777 - 1850

## HUSBAND
**Conrad H. Hicks**
**BIRTH:** 6 Mar. 1808, Prussia, IA
**DEATH:** 1 Oct. 1881, Peytonsville, TN

## 1ST WIFE
**Mary Steger**
**BIRTH:** 4 June 1806, Stokes Co. NC
**DEATH:** 12 Feb. 1839, Peytonsville, TN

## 2ND WIFE
**Mary Smithson**
**BIRTH:** 7 June 1822, Williamson Co. TN
**DEATH:** 1 Dec. 1882, Williamson Co. TN

## CHILDREN OF CONRAD AND MARY STEGER

**Henry Richard Hicks**   **BIRTH:** 18 Mar. 1846
**Son**              **DEATH:** Unknown

**Mary Elizabeth Hicks**   **BIRTH:** 17 June 1848
**Daughter**           **DEATH:** Unknown

## CHILDREN OF CONRAD AND MARY SMITHSON

**Martha C. Hicks**   **BIRTH:** 3 June 1853
**Daughter**       **DEATH:** Unknown

**William H. Hicks**   **BIRTH:** 21 June 1855
**Son**            **DEATH:** Unknown

**John L. Hicks**   **BIRTH:** 11 Jan. 1857
**Son**          **DEATH:** 28 Oct. 1857

**Charles Thomas**   **BIRTH:** 28 Oct. 1858
**Hicks-Son**      **DEATH:** 14 Mar. 1950

## HIS LIFE

Conrad H. Hicks was born on March 6, 1808 in Prussia, Iowa. He married Mary A. Steger and they had two children together. Mary died February 12, 1839, in Peytonsville, Tennessee. He then married Mary Smithson and they had four children together. Conrad died on October 1, 1881, in Peytonsville, Tennessee at the age of 73.

# WILLIAM ANDREWS
## 1808-1860

### ANDREWS FAMILY

#### HUSBAND'S PARENTS
**James M. Andrews**     **Jane McGuire**
1780 - 1850                     1787 - ?

#### WIFE'S PARENTS
**Isham Matthews**     **Mary Baker Sims**
1782 - 1862                     1788 - 1865

#### HUSBAND
**William Andrews**
**BIRTH:** 14 Sep. 1808, Williamson Co. TN
**DEATH:** 28 Feb. 1860, Peytonsville, TN

#### WIFE
**Mary Pegram Matthews**
**BIRTH:** 10 Apr. 1812, Williamson Co. TN
**DEATH:** 25 July 1844, Williamson Co. TN

#### CHILDREN

| | |
|---|---|
| **Mary Jane Andrews** Daughter | **BIRTH:** 15 Mar. 1835 **DEATH:** 4 Oct. 1928 |
| **William Mortimer Andrews-Son** | **BIRTH:** 29 Sep. 1839 **DEATH:** 31 Dec. 1920 |
| **John Samuel Andrews-Son** | **BIRTH:** 3 Oct. 1841 **DEATH:** 22 Sep. 1863 |
| **Thomas E. Andrews-Son** | **BIRTH:** 24 Feb. 1844 **DEATH:** 25 July 1925 |

### HIS LIFE

William Andrews was born on September 14, 1808, in Williamson County, Tennessee. He married Mary Pegram Matthews on December 24, 1833. They had four children during their marriage.

William Andrews died on February 28, 1860 in Peytonsville, Tennessee at the age of 51. He was buried in the Andrews-Hatcher-Pollard Cemetery.

# GREGORY JOHNSON
## 1809-1887

### JOHNSON FAMILY

#### HUSBAND'S PARENTS
**Benjamin Johnson**     **Mary McDonough**
1780 - 1821                     1783 - 1856

#### WIFE'S PARENTS
**Elijah R. Corzine**     **Esther Sherrill**
1772 - ?                          1773 - 1830

#### HUSBAND
**Gregory Johnson**
**BIRTH:** 26 Oct. 1809, Brunswick Co. VA
**DEATH:** 24 Mar. 1887, Williamson Co. TN

#### WIFE
**Rachael M. Corzine**
**BIRTH:** 3 Jan. 1812, NC
**DEATH:** Unknown

#### CHILDREN

| | |
|---|---|
| **Eli M. Johnson** Son | **BIRTH:** 1834 **DEATH:** 9 May 1894 |
| **Elizabeth Ester Johnson-Daughter** | **BIRTH:** 4 Dec. 1836 **DEATH:** 23 Aug. 1918 |
| **William Lewis Johnson-Son** | **BIRTH:** 16 June 1840 **DEATH:** 1 Apr. 1908 |
| **Jesse Henderson Johnson-Son** | **BIRTH:** 6 Dec. 1842 **DEATH:** 27 Sep. 1914 |
| **Martha J. Johnson** Daughter | **BIRTH:** 5 Apr. 1845 **DEATH:** 20 May 1919 |
| **James Andrews Johnson-Son** | **BIRTH:** 24 Mar. 1848 **DEATH:** 26 Nov. 1938 |

Andrew Johnson
Son
**BIRTH:** 1851
**DEATH:** 14 June 1925

Sallie Johnson
Daughter
**BIRTH:** 1854
**DEATH:** 8 June 1935

## HIS LIFE

When Gregory Johnson was born on October 26, 1809, in Brunswick County, Virginia, his father, Benjamin was 29 and his mother, Mary was 26. He married Rachael M. Corzine on January 13, 1831, in Williamson County, Tennessee. They had eight children in 20-years. He died on March 24, 1887 at the age of 77. He was buried in the Johnson Cemetery in Nolensville, Tennessee.

# SYLVANUS W. SMITHSON
# 1810-1872

## SMITHSON FAMILY

### HUSBAND'S PARENTS
**John Smithson**      **Elizabeth G. "Betsy" Knott**
1777 - 1837            1775 - 1839

### 1ST WIFE'S PARENTS
**John B. Gibson**      **Jenny Jane Wilson**
1776 - 1824            1777 - 1824

### 2ND WIFE'S PARENTS
**Nelson W. Gee**      **Catherine Byars**
1784 - 1859            1792 - 1880

### HUSBAND
**Sylvanus W. Smithson**
**BIRTH:** 8 Aug. 1810, Lunenburg Co. VA
**DEATH:** 15 Mar. 1872, Peytonsville, TN

### 1ST WIFE
**Mary Jane Gibson**
**BIRTH:** 1820, Williamson Co. TN
**DEATH:** 27 Feb. 1862, Williamson Co. TN

### 2ND WIFE
**Elizabeth C. Gee**
**BIRTH:** 28 Feb, 1830, VA
**DEATH:** 28 Mar, 1900, Peytonsville, TN

## CHILDREN OF SYLVANUS AND MARY JANE

Patrick Gibson
Smithson-Son
**BIRTH:** 1 Nov. 1838
**DEATH:** 9 June 1897

James Polk
Smithson-Son
**BIRTH:** 8 Sep. 1840
**DEATH:** 12 Feb. 1902

Benjamin Franklin.
Smithson-Son
**BIRTH:** 4 June 1843
**DEATH:** 3 Mar. 1909

Sarah Catherine
Smithson-Daughter
**BIRTH:** 16 Oct. 1845
**DEATH:** 1896

William Parrish
Smithson-Son
**BIRTH:** 6 May. 1848
**DEATH:** 1 June 1876

John Wilson
Smithson-Son
**BIRTH:** 16 Mar. 1850
**DEATH:** Unknown

Alexander Reid
Smithson-Son
**BIRTH:** 16 Oct. 1845
**DEATH:** 1896

Joseph Wilson
Smithson-Son
**BIRTH:** 24 May 1856
**DEATH:** 1900

Richard Knott
Smithson-Son
**BIRTH:** 11 June 1859
**DEATH:** 5 Feb. 1923

## CHILDREN OF SYLVANUS AND ELIZABETH

Thomas Walter
Smithson-Son
**BIRTH:** 6 Apr. 1864
**DEATH:** 16 May 1926

## HIS LIFE

When Sylvanus W. Smithson was born on August 8, 1810, in Lunenburg County, Virginia, his father, John was 33 and his mother, Elizabeth was 35. He married Mary Jane Gibson and they had nine children together. Mary Jane died on February 27, 1862. Sylvanus then married Elizabeth C. Gee and they had one son together.

He died on March 15, 1872, in Peytonsville at the age of 61.

# ISAAC W.P. WEST
# 1812-1897

## WEST FAMILY

### HUSBAND'S PARENTS
**Father Unknown    Mother Unknown**

### 1ST WIFE'S PARENTS
**Father Unknown    Mother Unknown**

### 2ND WIFE'S PARENTS
**Father Unknown    Mother Unknown**

### HUSBAND
**Isaac W.P. West**
**BIRTH:** 1812, TN
**DEATH:** 14 May 1897, Peytonsville, TN

### 1ST WIFE
**Mary D. Price**
**BIRTH:** 1818, NC
**DEATH:** 1878

### 2ND WIFE
**Louisa F. "Lou" Faughender**
**BIRTH:** 1829, MO
**DEATH:** Unknown

### CHILDREN OF ISAAC AND MARY

| | |
|---|---|
| **Mary Elizabeth West** Daughter | **BIRTH:** 1836 **DEATH:** 1880 |
| **A.Z. West** Son | **BIRTH:** 1849 **DEATH:** Unknown |
| **Thomas West** Son | **BIRTH:** 1855 **DEATH:** Unknown |
| **George W. West** Son | **BIRTH:** 1859 **DEATH:** Unknown |
| **L.W. West** Son | **BIRTH:** 1860 **DEATH:** Unknown |
| **Maram A. West** Daughter | **BIRTH:** 1862 **DEATH:** Unknown |

## HIS LIFE

Isaac W.P. West was born in 1812, in Tennessee. He married Mary D. Price and they had six children together. Mary died in 1878 and Isaac married, Louisa F. "Lou" Faughender on September 3, 1878, in Williamson County, Tennessee. He died on May 14, 1897, at the age of 85.

# ROBERT SLEDGE
# 1813-1891

## SLEDGE FAMILY

### HUSBAND'S PARENTS
**John Lewis Sledge      Cinthia L. Gammons**
1772 - 1823              1771 - 1840

### WIFE'S PARENTS
**Nathaniel B. Smithson    Mary P. Cheatham**
1772 - 1859                1777 - 1850

### HUSBAND
**Robert Sledge**
**BIRTH:** 1813, Williamson Co. TN
**DEATH:** 14 Feb. 1891, Peytonsville, TN

### WIFE
**Catherine K. Smithson**
**BIRTH:** 1811, Williamson Co. TN
**DEATH:** 1870, Peytonsville, TN

### CHILDREN

| | |
|---|---|
| **Mary L. Sledge** Daughter | **BIRTH:** 1833 **DEATH:** Unknown |
| **John William Sledge** Son | **BIRTH:** 12 July 1837 **DEATH:** 29 Jan. 1908 |

| Nathaniel Sledge<br>Son | BIRTH: May 1838<br>DEATH: Apr. 1869 |
| --- | --- |

| Sarah E. Sledge<br>Daughter | BIRTH: July 1841<br>DEATH: AFT 1900 |

| Ann Eliza Sledge<br>Daughter | BIRTH: Aug. 1845<br>DEATH: Unknown |

| Robert Sledge<br>Son | BIRTH: Feb. 1853<br>DEATH: ABT 1920 |

| John Sledge<br>Son | BIRTH: 1864<br>DEATH: Unknown |

| Martha Sledge<br>Daughter | BIRTH: 1866<br>DEATH: 1920 |

## HIS LIFE

When Robert Sledge was born in 1813, in Williamson County, Tennessee, his father, John was 41 and his mother, Cinthia was 42. He married Catherine K. Smithson on March 28, 1833 in Williamson County, Tennessee. They had eight children in 33-years. He died on February 14, 1891 in Peytonsville, Tennessee at the age of 78.

# RICHARD B. CRUNK
# 1814-1871

## CRUNK FAMILY

### HUSBAND'S PARENTS
**John William Crunk    Elizabeth Letcher Scales**
1770 - 1850                1792 - 1819

### WIFE'S PARENTS
**Eleazar Hardeman      Elizabeth Foster**
1779 - 1841                1777 - 1843

### HUSBAND
**Richard B. Crunk**
BIRTH: 16 July 1814, Williamson Co. TN
DEATH: 1871, Peytonsville, TN

### WIFE
**Nancy L. Hardeman**
BIRTH: 8 Mar. 1817, TN
DEATH: 1868, Williamson Co. TN

### CHILDREN

| Mary S. Crunk<br>Daughter | BIRTH: 1837<br>DEATH: 1838 |
| --- | --- |

| Mary Susan Crunk<br>Daughter | BIRTH: May 1839<br>DEATH: June 1900 |

| Seth S. Crunk<br>Son | BIRTH: 1842<br>DEATH: June 1867 |

| John E. Crunk<br>Son | BIRTH: 1844<br>DEATH: Unknown |

| George N. Crunk<br>Son | BIRTH: Dec. 1845<br>DEATH: 1920 |

| Lydia H. Crunk<br>Daughter | BIRTH: 1846<br>DEATH: Unknown |

| John N.E. Crunk<br>Son | BIRTH: 1847<br>DEATH: 1848 |

| Richard P. Crunk<br>Son | BIRTH: 16 July 1814<br>DEATH: 1871 |

| William Henry Crunk<br>Son | BIRTH: 22 Aug. 1852<br>DEATH: 8 Nov. 1918 |

## HIS LIFE

When Richard B. Crunk was born on July 16, 1814, in Williamson County, Tennessee, his father, John was 44 and his mother, Elizabeth was 21. He married Nancy L. Hardeman on July 15, 1835, in Williamson County. They had nine children in 15-years. He died in 1871 in Peytonsville, Tennessee at the age of 57.

Richard willed a 230-acre property to his son. As of 2002, this property was still in the Crunk family name and is a part of the Land Trust of Tennessee. Under terms of the permanent easement, the property can continue to be used as a farm and passed down to the next generations in the Crunk family, but commercial development will not be permitted.

# MOSES GENTRY GOSEY
# 1815-1903

### GOSEY FAMILY

**HUSBAND'S PARENTS**
**James E. Gosey**     **Rebecca Bowers**
1772 - 1854     1783 - 1859

**WIFE'S PARENTS**
**Josiah Nevils**     **Sarah B. Beech**
1794 - 1854     1801 - 1882

### HUSBAND
**Moses Gentry Gosey**
**BIRTH:** 2 Dec. 1815, Williamson Co. TN
**DEATH:** 21 Jan. 1903, Peytonsville, TN

### WIFE
**Mary A. Nevils**
**BIRTH:** 12 Aug. 1823, Peytonsville, TN
**DEATH:** 26 Aug. 1896, Peytonsville, TN

### CHILDREN

**Gentry Gosey**     **BIRTH:** 1846
**Son**     **DEATH:** BEF 1860

**Sarah E. Gosey**     **BIRTH:** 1848
**Daughter**     **DEATH:** Unknown

**Mary I. Gosey**     **BIRTH:** 1849
**Daughter**     **DEATH:** Unknown

**Thomas Gosey**     **BIRTH:** 1849
**Son**     **DEATH:** 1865

**Mattie Lieu Gosey**     **BIRTH:** 16 Oct. 1853
**Daughter**     **DEATH:** 9 Apr. 1856

### HIS LIFE

Moses Gentry Gosey was born in Tennessee on December 2, 1815. His father, James Gosey, was born in Virginia about 1770, and was married in 1798 to Rebecca Bowers, a native of Virginia, born about 1785. In 1801 they came to Tennessee, where the father followed the occupation of farmer. He was a good, pious citizen, having joined the Methodist Episcopal Church at an early age. He died in 1854, and his widow followed in 1859. Our subject was united in marriage to, Mary A. Nevils in 1846. She was a native of Tennessee, born August 12, 1823, and the daughter of Josiah and Sallie Beech Nevils. Moses and wife became the parents of five children and an infant not named. Only two children lived to be grown. In 1849, Moses began merchandising at Peytonsville and carried on a thriving business there until 1860. During the war he was very unfortunate, losing about $17,000 of hard-earned money. After the war he farmed on 72-acres on the edge of Peytonsville. He was also a member of the Masonic fraternity.

Moses died on January 21, 1903, in Peytonsville and is buried in the Gosey Cemetery on Gosey Hill Road.

# JOHN WILSON GIBSON
# 1817-1870

### GIBSON FAMILY

**HUSBAND'S PARENTS**
**John B. Gibson**     **Jenny Jane Wilson**
1776 - 1824     1777 - 1824

**WIFE'S PARENTS**
**Robert Henry Lester**     **Martha P. Pennington**
1782 - 1851     1788 - 1860

### HUSBAND
**John Wilson Gibson**
**BIRTH:** 1817, Williamson Co. TN
**DEATH:** 1870, Peytonsville, TN

**Martha H. Lester**
BIRTH: 1815, VA
DEATH: 1869

## CHILDREN

| | |
|---|---|
| **Martha Jane Gibson** Daughter | BIRTH: 1841 DEATH: 1873 |
| **John H. Gibson** Son | BIRTH: 1842 DEATH: Unknown |
| **Mary A. Gibson** Daughter | BIRTH: 1844 DEATH: Unknown |
| **Sarah Elizabeth Gibson-Daughter** | BIRTH: 9 Jan. 1845 DEATH: 17 Sep. 1916 |
| **Susan Tennessee Gibson-Daughter** | BIRTH: 1 Feb. 1847 DEATH: 10 May 1913 |
| **Parmelia S. Gibson** Daughter | BIRTH: 1848 DEATH: Unknown |
| **Joseph Bryant Gibson-Son** | BIRTH: 12 Apr. 1855 DEATH: 16 Nov. 1904 |
| **Celia Gibson** Daughter | BIRTH: 30 July 1855 DEATH: 123 Feb. 1920 |
| **William L. Gibson** Son | BIRTH: 10 Oct. 1858 DEATH: 21 June 1931 |
| **Alice J. Gibson** Daughter | BIRTH: 8 June 1861 DEATH: 18 Dec. 1923 |

## HIS LIFE

When John Wilson Gibson was born in 1817 in Tennessee, his father, John was 41 and his mother, Jenny was 40. He married Martha H. Lester on December 31, 1840, in Williamson County, Tennessee. They had 10 children in 20-years. He died in 1870 at the age of 53.

# JAMES WELLBORN STARNES
# 1817-1863

## STARNES FAMILY

### HUSBAND'S PARENTS
**Samuel Scott Starnes MD   Nancy M. Wellborn**
1786 - 1841                          1797 - 1842

### WIFE'S PARENTS
**Richard H. Rudder      Mary G. Bostick**
1788 - 1852                    1797 - 1850

### HUSBAND
**James Wellborn Starnes**
BIRTH: 9 July 1817, Wilkes Co. NC
DEATH: 30 June 1863, Tullahoma, TN

### WIFE
**Mary Christina Rudder**
BIRTH: 1830, Franklin, TN
DEATH: 1904, Franklin, TN

## CHILDREN

| | |
|---|---|
| **Cora D. Starnes** Daughter | BIRTH: 7 Apr. 1850 DEATH: 9 May 1859 |
| **Henry M. Starnes** Son | BIRTH: 12 Nov. 1851 DEATH: 18 Jan. 1859 |
| **James Wellborn Starnes Jr.-Son** | BIRTH: 10 July 1853 DEATH: 16 Feb. 1894 |
| **Marian B. Starnes** Daughter | BIRTH: 12 Dec. 1860 DEATH: 19 Aug. 1863 |
| **William Rudder Starnes-Son** | BIRTH: 10 Aug. 1863 DEATH: 7 Aug. 1895 |

## HIS LIFE

James Starnes was the son of Dr. Samuel Scott and Nancy Matilda (Wellborn) Starnes. He was a prominent physician and planter from

Peytonsville. He was born in North Carolina on July 9, 1817, the eldest child of Dr. Samuel Scott and Nancy Matilda (Welborn) Starnes. The family moved to Tennessee when James was very young. The elder Starnes died in 1841, and his wife passed away a year later. James was the eldest of seven children, his siblings being Margaret (Mosely), Catherine (Mosely), Nancy Parthenia (Tullous), Samuel Scott, Jr., John E., and Ebenezer.

James was a graduate of Jefferson Seminary Medical School in Louisville, Ky. When the War with Mexico broke out, he enlisted and was made the chief surgeon of the First Tennessee Volunteer Regiment. Shortly before he left for the war, Starnes had an altercation with a neighbor, Thomas J. Hill, which led to Hill's violent attack on Starnes with a hickory stick. Though Starnes got the better of the fight, cutting Hill badly and laying him up for several months, the young soldier did suffer a broken arm and head wounds. With his right arm useless and in a sling, he was forced to learn to fire his pistol with his left hand and was said to have become an expert shot with either hand. Though Starnes was not large in physical stature, he more than made up for it in courage and determination.

After the war with Mexico, Dr. Starnes returned to Peytonsville. On April 4, 1849, he was married to Mary Christine Rudder and they had five children. Mary was born in Tennessee in 1830 and was the daughter of Richard and Mary Bostick Rudder, whose home was at Rudderville in the 13th District. While still in his 20s, Dr. Starnes had the responsibility of settling the enormous estates of his father and father-in-law. He and his wife inherited hundreds of acres of rich river bottom land, and, while they enjoyed a large degree of prosperity, they suffered many personal sorrows. The Starnes' two eldest children, Cora and Henry, had both died in 1859.

When the Civil War broke out James raised a company of cavalry in Williamson County, Tennessee. On the 28th of September, a second company of cavalry was assembled at John McGavock's Carnton plantation on the Lewisburg Pike. The soldiers adopted for their troop the simple name of "The Williamson County Cavalry." The formation of this new unit was formally announced in the Oct. 10 edition of Franklin's newspaper, *"The Western Weekly Review."*

"Another fine cavalry company was organized at this place last Saturday and mustered into the service. The following officers were elected: James W. Starnes, Captain; W.S. McLemore, 1st Lieutenant; Thomas F.P. Allison, 2nd Lieutenant, and T.L.G. Harrison 3rd Lieutenant. It numbers about 100 of the finest looking men we ever saw. Wo unto the Jenny that encounters this gallant band of Southern patriots for they will surely "bite" the dust."

Most of the men in Starnes' company were the sons of planters and farmers from the eastern Williamson County communities of Nolensville, Petersburg (Arrington), Triune, Peytonsville, College Grove, Bethesda and Mount Carmel (Duplex). As throughout the southern army, the soldiers were expected to provide their own weapons and horses. Because of this necessary policy, they were generally poorly armed. Most of the young men were equipped only with muzzle-loading, double-barreled shotguns; hunting guns they had brought from home. Some of the troopers also had pistols, but very few owned rifles or sabers. The command was much more fortunate when it came to their horses. The bluegrass region of Middle Tennessee was widely known for its fine bloodlines, and most of the troopers were well-mounted. In fact, the Confederate army's practice of requiring each man to supply his own horse helped to assure the soldiers of having a sound, healthy mount with which they were familiar. This was often not the case with the government issued stock in the Northern army.

All three of James Starnes' brothers served in the Confederate army. John was also a member of "The Williamson County Cavalry." Ebenezer enlisted in an artillery company and later served with General William H. "Red" Jackson's escort (Company A in the Seventh Tennessee Cavalry Regiment). He was killed in a fight at Franklin on April 10, 1863. Sam was in "The Williamson County Light Dragoons." Starnes' nephews, Samuel and Robert Mosely, were also members of Capt. Ewing's company.

At the time the company was formed, James and his wife, Mary had two living children, James Welborn, Jr., age eight, and Marian, age one-year. In addition to his 2,000+ acres in Williamson County, Starnes owned a substantial cotton plantation in the Mississippi Valley. His farm soon became so profitable that he abandoned his medical practice entirely and devoted himself full-time to his agricultural pursuits.

On October 30, 1861, 87 men mounted up and rode into Nashville, where they were mustered into Confederate service by Lt. Thomas W. Hunt.

He was later promoted to Colonel of the 4th Tennessee Cavalry, CSA. By 1863, Dr. Starnes was the commander of a brigade of Forrest's Cavalry and led it in action in Forrest's Brentwood Raid, in the fights around Franklin and the successful pursuit of Streight's raiders in Alabama.

On June 18, 1863, accompanied by Captain Daniel Fountain Wade, a fellow Williamson Countian, Colonel Starnes rode outside Tullahoma near Bobo's Crossroads on a reconnaissance tour. The pair drew the interest of many eyes for both men were well mounted, and while Colonel Starnes was in a plain suit of jeans, Captain Wade was in full Confederate uniform with the insignia of his rank. When sharpshooters got their range, Wade prudently suggested that they retire, but Starnes refused, saying Wade could leave if he was afraid. Stung by the remark, for he was a brave and true man, Wade stayed his ground. Almost immediately

Colonel Starnes was struck by a bullet that sent him reeling in the saddle. Despite the whine of Minie balls, Captain Wade took both bridles in one hand and started back toward Confederate lines supporting the sagging colonel with his other arm as the horses touched all the way.

As their friends assisted the pair from their mounts, Captain Wade fainted from pain, and seeing his bloody clothes, the men thought both officers were wounded. The wound Captain Wade had received at Fort Donelson had re-opened; his friends revived him by splashing his face with water dipped from a wagon rut.

Colonel Starnes, who was mortally wounded, died on June 30, 1863. Captain Wade and other friends placed his body in an ambulance and drove rapidly to Winchester where a casket was secured, and the men hastily buried their colonel. Then with the enemy at hand, they barely escaped capture before rejoining Bragg.

Later, Mrs. Starnes had her husband's body brought home for burial in the Rudder-Starnes-Boyd Cemetery. His imposing marker is surrounded by those of his family members on the crest of a lofty hill. With its monuments towering above the thick rock walls, this burial ground is one of the most beautiful and historic in Williamson County.

His obituary in the Chattanooga Daily Rebel stated in part:

"Many of his exploits are wholly unrecorded and numbers of them forgotten amid the confused turmoil of war, and its crowded canvass of events. After the most useful career as an independent commander, Col. Starnes was attached to the regular cavalry service, and gained a rare, though not noisy reputation in the service for courage, reliability and skill. Personally he was a man of unblemished character as a Christian and citizen. His manners were quiet and reserved, but respectful and kind. He was in the prime of life, and the vigor of experience. The tears of a bereaved family and the sorrow of a devoted band of comrades follow him to an early but hallowed grave. All honor his name."

To provide insight into the extent of Starnes' wealth, the 1860 tax records indicate he owned 1,583-acres in the 13th District (Peytonsville), valued at $47,460. The Starnes-Rudder property would have extended from McDaniel Road to Peytonsville-Trinity all the way to Westwood and back along Meek Road.

Colonel Starnes, a daring and venturesome leader, did not hesitate to attack forces many times his strength. It might be said he was careless of danger to the point of foolhardiness. His military tactics were in direct contrast to his personality when he was at home. Slight of build, he was quiet and reserved, with gentle hands and a sympathetic manner that made him beloved as a physician. In battle, at the head of his crack regiment of cavalry, his bold initiative was capable of spreading pandemonium in enemy ranks equal to that of Morgan the Raider.

Space does not allow a detailed discussion of Colonel Starnes' military career. Battles and promotions followed one another until, according to family tradition, his mind was put forward for the commission of brigadier-general. When he came home for short leave, Mrs. Starnes melted silver coins to make the stars for his uniform collar designating his new rank, but his death occurred before the commissions could clear the proper channels.

DR. JAMES WELLBORN
STARNES

# ALEXANDER REID M.D.
## 1818-1887

### REID FAMILY

**HUSBAND'S PARENTS**
**James Alexander Reid**   **Margaret Ardery**
1795 - 1876              1800 - 1841

**WIFE'S PARENTS**
**Isaac Benjamin Wilson**   **Catherine Hartley**
1798 - 1857               1799 - 1874

**HUSBAND**
**Alexander Reid M.D.**
**BIRTH:** 1818, Aryshire, Scotland
**DEATH:** 22 Sep. 1887, Ennis, TX

**WIFE**
**Sarah Jane Wilson**
**BIRTH:** 9 Jan. 1821, NC
**DEATH:** 31 July 1900, Ennis TX

**William Wallace Reid** BIRTH: 20 Feb. 1843
**Son** DEATH: 16 Jan. 1932

## HIS LIFE

When Alexander Reid was born in 1818, in Scotland, his father, James was 23 and his mother, Margaret was 18. He married Sarah Jane Wilson and they had one son. In October of 1881, Dr. Reid and about 60 friends and family from Peytonsville and College Grove set out on a wagon train to emigrate to Texas. This is taken from an article published in *The Nashville Tennessean.*

**Franklin**
**Wholesale Emigration from Williamson**
**From Our Regular Correspondent.**

Franklin, Oct. 13, 1881. —On Monday next a party of some sixty persons will emigrate from the Eastern part of the county to Texas. They live in the neighborhood of Peytonsville and College Grove, and some of the heads of families were land owners and the best of citizens. Contemplating the step for some time, they have turned their land and personal property into money, and go to add their muscle, money and energy to the development of the Lone Star State and the improvement of their own fortunes. Among the number are Dr. Alexander Reid, Thomas G. Pate and others, whose removal will be a great loss to their community and a great acquisition to the young empire State of the West. While we must deplore their departure, and can ill afford the loss to this State, the best wishes of their friends and neighbors will attend them. I hope the Bureau of Immigration, Statistics, etc., will be able, some day, to recruit our population from some source at least as fast as it emigrates. It is said that others will soon follow this party.

Dr. Alexander Reid died on September 22, 1887, in Ennis, Ellis County, Texas when he was 69-years old. He is buried in the Myrtle Cemetery.

# JOHN RUCKER HATCHER
# 1818-1857

## HATCHER FAMILY

### HUSBAND'S PARENTS
**William Samuel Hatcher    Lucy Rucker**
1793 - 1866                1797 - 1884

### WIFE'S PARENTS
**Julius Wooldridge Hatcher  Mary Polly White**
1794 - 1876                1801 - 1876

### HUSBAND
**John Rucker Hatcher**
BIRTH: 26 Oct. 1818, Bedford Co. VA
DEATH: 12 June 1857, Williamson Co. TN

### WIFE
**Matilda Spiers Hatcher**
BIRTH: 27 Mar. 1823, Bedford Co. VA
DEATH: 17 Apr. 1874, Williamson Co. TN

### CHILDREN

**Mary Catherine** BIRTH: 2 Mar. 1845
**Hatcher-Daughter** DEATH: 23 Mar. 1872

**William Henry Hatcher** BIRTH: 3 June 1846
**Son** DEATH: 25 Apr. 1915

**John Milton Hatcher** BIRTH: 12 June 1848
**Son** DEATH: 30 Dec. 1923

**Lucy Frances Hatcher** BIRTH: 16 June 1850
**Daughter** DEATH: 8 Jan. 1875

**Sarah Alice Hatcher** BIRTH: 10 Jan. 1852
**Daughter** DEATH: 11 May 1939

**Kate Hatcher** BIRTH: 1853
**Daughter** DEATH: Unknown

**Charles Anthony** BIRTH: 10 Feb. 1854
**Hatcher-Son** DEATH: 27 Mar. 1857

**Anna Wooldridge** BIRTH: 6 Nov. 1855
**Hatcher-Daughter** DEATH: 11 Apr. 1878

**Charles Allen Hatcher BIRTH:** 18 Nov. 1857
**Son**                              **DEATH:** 21 Dec. 1932

### HIS LIFE

When John Rucker Hatcher was born on October 26, 1818, in Bedford County, Virginia, his father, William was 25 and his mother, Lucy was 21. John was a Major in the Tennessee Militia.

He married Matilda Spiers Hatcher on January 18, 1844, in Williamson County, Tennessee. They had nine children in 12-years.

Note: John and Matilda were first cousins. John's father, William and Matilda's father, Julius Wooldridge Hatcher were brothers.

John bought 192-acres at Arno, Tennessee for $2,000. In 1852 he bought and adjoining 40-acres. (Williamson County Deed Book 5, p. 592 & Deed Book 5, p. 306). He built a home on the rise southwest of Hatcher Cemetery Hill and moved there in 1849. He and son, John Milton raised their families there.

John Rucker Hatcher died on June 12, 1857, in Williamson County at the age of 38 and is buried in the Hatcher Cemetery.

# COLEMAN G. SMITHSON
# 1819-1888

### SMITHSON FAMILY

#### HUSBAND'S PARENTS
**Nathaniel B. Smithson    Mary P. Cheatham**
1773 - 1859                         1777 - 1850

#### 1ST WIFE'S PARENTS
**Robert Henry Lester    Martha P. Pennington**
1782 - 1851                     1788 - 1860

#### 2ND WIFE'S PARENTS

**Abel James Creswell    Martha Frances White**
1815 - 1850                         1819 - 1850

### HUSBAND
**Coleman G. Smithson**
**BIRTH:** 26 Mar. 1819, Williamson Co. TN
**DEATH:** 24 Oct. 1888, Peytonsville, TN

### 1ST WIFE
**Celia Lester**
**BIRTH:** 1823, TN
**DEATH:** 1866, TN

### 2ND WIFE
**Mary Ann Creswell**
**BIRTH:** 1 Nov. 1841, Flat Creek, TN
**DEATH:** Oct. 1879, Peytonsville, TN

### CHILDREN OF COLEMAN AND CELIA

**James B. Smithson**    **BIRTH:** 5 Nov. 1844
**Son**                              **DEATH:** 3 Nov. 1919

**Mary A. Smithson**    **BIRTH:** 1848
**Daughter**                     **DEATH:** Unknown

### CHILDREN OF COLEMAN AND MARY ANN

**Celia E. Smithson**    **BIRTH:** July 1868
**Daughter**                   **DEATH:** 1900

**Sallie F. Smithson**    **BIRTH:** 1873
**Daughter**                    **DEATH:** Unknown

### HIS LIFE

When Coleman G. Smithson was born on March 26, 1819, in Williamson County, Tennessee, his father, Nathaniel was 45 and his mother, Mary was 41. He married Celia Lester and they had two children together. When Celia died in 1866, Coleman married, Mary Ann Creswell and they had two children together. Coleman G. Smithson died on October 24, 1888, in Peytonsville, Tennessee at the age of 69.

# EDWARD "STANDING BEAR" GOSEY
# 1820-1887

## GOSEY FAMILY

### HUSBAND'S PARENTS
**James E. Gosey**  **Rebecca Bowers**
1772 - 1854       1783 - 1859

### 1ST WIFE'S PARENTS
**Noah Butler Cotton**  **Elizabeth Conger**
1789 - 1859           1789 - 1879

### 2ND WIFE'S PARENTS
**Tandy S. Smithson**  **Ann Calvert**
1801 - 1873          1804 - 1888

### 3RD WIFE'S PARENTS
**Jesse J. Johnson**  **Dolly Smithson**
1804 - 1886         1812 - 1884

### HUSBAND
**Edward "Standing Bear" Gosey**
**BIRTH:** 8 Sep. 1820, Peytonsville, TN
**DEATH:** 20 Feb. 1887, Peytonsville, TN

### 1ST WIFE
**Talitha C. Cotton**
**BIRTH:** 1826, Sumner Co. TN
**DEATH:** 1851, Williamson Co. TN

### 2ND WIFE
**Parmelia W. Smithson**
**BIRTH:** 17 June 1824, Peytonsville, TN
**DEATH:** 20 Feb. 1873, Peytonsville, TN

### 3RD WIFE
**Adeline V. Johnson**
**BIRTH:** 1839, Peytonsville, TN
**DEATH:** AFT 1900

### CHILDREN OF EDWARD AND TALITHA

**Mary F. Gosey**
Daughter
**BIRTH:** 8 Jan. 1848
**DEATH:** 10 Nov. 1921

### CHILDREN OF EDWARD AND PARMELIA

**James Washington Gosey-Son**
**BIRTH:** Dec. 1854
**DEATH:** 15 Oct. 1897

**Thomas Charles Gosey-Son**
**BIRTH:** 27 Sep. 1856
**DEATH:** 17 Nov. 1876

**Tandy Burton Gosey Son**
**BIRTH:** 1865
**DEATH:** 1927

### CHILDREN OF EDWARD AND ADELINE

**Minnie Virginia Gosey**
Daughter
**BIRTH:** 14 Aug. 1875
**DEATH:** 17 Dec. 1928

## HIS LIFE

When Edward "Standing Bear" Gosey was born on September 8, 1820, in Williamson County, Tennessee, his father, James was 48 and his mother, Rebecca was 37. He was married three times and had three sons and two daughters. He died on February 20, 1887, in Peytonsville, Tennessee at the age of 66. He is buried in the Gosey Cemetery.

EDWARD S.B. GOSEY

# ANDREW WASHINGTON PARKS
## 1820-1872

### PARKS FAMILY

#### HUSBAND'S PARENTS
**John Parks**    **Susanna Neely**
1785 - 1850      1800 - 1873

#### 1ST WIFE'S PARENTS
**George G. Boyd**    **Martha Ann Walker**
1800 - 1841          1800 - ?

#### 2ND WIFE'S PARENTS
**Isham Matthews**    **Mary Baker Sims**
1782 - 1862          1788 - 1865

#### HUSBAND
**Andrew Washington Parks**
BIRTH: 3 May 1820, Williamson Co. TN
DEATH: Feb. 1872, Peytonsville, TN

#### 1ST WIFE
**Martha J. Boyd**
BIRTH: 1820, TN
DEATH: 1848, Williamson Co. TN

#### 2ND WIFE
**Nancy Caroline Matthews**
BIRTH: 7 Mar. 1822, Williamson Co. TN
DEATH: Unknown

#### CHILDREN OF ANDREW AND NANCY

| | |
|---|---|
| **Isham Matthews Parks-Son** | BIRTH: 9 Sep. 1850<br>DEATH: 1855 |
| **John Andrew Parks Son** | BIRTH: Jan. 1853<br>DEATH: 17 Nov, 1927 |
| **William Andrews Parks-Son** | BIRTH: 9 Apr. 1853<br>DEATH: 1931 |
| **Mary Arabella Parks Daughter** | BIRTH: 14 Feb. 1856<br>DEATH: 26 Dec. 1933 |

### HIS LIFE

When Andrew Washington Parks was born on May 3, 1820, in Williamson County, Tennessee, his father, John was 35 and his mother, Susanna was 20. He married Martha J. Boyd on December 23, 1847, and after her death in 1848, he married Nancy Caroline Matthews. Andrew and Nancy had four children together. He died in February 1872 in Peytonsville, Tennessee at the age of 51.

# THOMAS BURNETT
## 1821-1881

### BURNETT FAMILY

#### HUSBAND'S PARENTS
**William Burnett**    **Martha Jeffries**
1759 - 1844          1775 - 1848

#### WIFE'S PARENTS
**Father Unknown**    **Mother Unknown**

#### HUSBAND
**Thomas Burnett**
BIRTH: 1821, TN
DEATH: 20 Sep. 1881, TN

#### WIFE
**Elizabeth Jane Gray**
BIRTH: 1828, TN
DEATH: Unknown

#### CHILDREN

| | |
|---|---|
| **Alina Laura S. Burnett Daughter** | BIRTH: 1845<br>DEATH: 1881 |
| **Martha F. Burnett Daughter** | BIRTH: 2 Sep. 1847<br>DEATH: 30 July 1930 |

| | |
|---|---|
| **Adaline Burnett**<br>Daughter | **BIRTH:** 1 Aug. 1859<br>**DEATH:** 26 Mar. 1939 |
| **Eliza Jane Burnett**<br>Daughter | **BIRTH:** 10 June 1861<br>**DEATH:** 9 June 1936 |
| **Robert Burnett**<br>Son | **BIRTH:** 1866<br>**DEATH:** Unknown |
| **James Burnett**<br>Son | **BIRTH:** 1867<br>**DEATH:** Unknown |
| **Irene Burnett**<br>Daughter | **BIRTH:** Dec. 1869<br>**DEATH:** 1960 |

### HIS LIFE

When Thomas Burnett was born in 1821, in Tennessee, his father, William was 62 and his mother, Martha was 46. He married Elizabeth Jane Gray on December 19, 1843, in Rutherford County, Tennessee.

**Taken from his probate record in 1881:**

Thomas Burnett departed this life on 20 Sept. 1881 intestate leaving a widow, Eliza J. And heirs: Martha Ladd (wife of W.P. Ladd), James Burnett, Adaline (wife of W.C. Snell), Eliza J. Burnett, Robert Burnett and Irene Burnett and the children of a deceased daughter Lana (the wife of R.R. Wray): W.T., J.C. and Eliza R. Wray. The last three are minors and without guardian. W.C. Snell was appointed guardian. In October Term Thomas left a small personal estate that will be sufficient to pay all the debts. He owned a tract of land containing 327 acres in the 13th district on which he lived and the land was bounded by the lands of J.D. Patton, H.T. Parrish, Mrs. Crouch et al and small tract of land in Rutherford Co. in the 12th district containing 64 acres, a 50 acre tract of land in Bedford County. The dower has been allotted the widow consisting of 127 acres of the home tract including the mansion house. Thomas had made advancement to some of his children in his lifetime. The heirs want a division made.

Thomas and Elizabeth had seven children in 24-years. He was 60-years old at the time of his death.

---

# WILLIAM JONES
## 1822-1898

### JONES FAMILY

#### HUSBAND'S PARENTS
**Unknown Father    Unknown Mother**

#### 1ST WIFE'S PARENTS
**Samuel T. Edwards    Sarah Matthews**
Unknown Father        1805 - 1888

#### 2ND WIFE'S PARENTS
**Benjamin Franklin Martin    Jane D. Alston**
1820 - 1862                   1824 - 1906

#### HUSBAND
**William Jones**
**BIRTH:** 1822, KY
**DEATH:** June 1898, Peytonsville, TN

#### 1ST WIFE
**Anne E.P. Edwards**
**BIRTH:** 1829, TN
**DEATH:** 7 July 1880, TN

#### 2ND WIFE
**Mary Jane Martin**
**BIRTH:** 3 May 1851, Williamson Co. TN
**DEATH:** 9 Aug. 1936, Williamson Co. TN

#### CHILDREN OF WILLIAM AND ANNE

| | |
|---|---|
| **James C. Jones**<br>Son | **BIRTH:** 1844<br>**DEATH:** Unknown |
| **Martha Jones**<br>Daughter | **BIRTH:** 1846<br>**DEATH:** 1860 |
| **S. Ann E. Jones**<br>Daughter | **BIRTH:** 1848<br>**DEATH:** Unknown |

| **Martisia Tennessee Jones-Daughter** | **BIRTH:** 19 June 1851 **DEATH:** 15 Jan. 1921 |
|---|---|
| **Mattie A. Jones Daughter** | **BIRTH:** 1853 **DEATH:** 1878 |
| **John William Jones Son** | **BIRTH:** 1855 **DEATH:** Unknown |
| **S.J. Jones Son** | **BIRTH:** 1856 **DEATH:** BEF 1870 |
| **M.V. Jones Daughter** | **BIRTH:** 1860 **DEATH:** Unknown |
| **P. Girtrude Jones Son** | **BIRTH:** 1863 **DEATH:** Unknown |

## HIS LIFE

William Jones was born in 1822, in Kentucky. He married Anne E.P. Edwards on December 22, 1842, and they had nine children together. After Anne's death on July 7, 1880, he married, Mary Jane Martin on September 13, 1881, in Williamson County, Tennessee. He died in June 1898, at the age of 76.

WILLIAM JONES, MARY JANE (MARTIN), DAISY AND E.K. SMITHSON

# JOSEPH ALEXANDER BENNETT
## 1824-1904

### BENNETT FAMILY

#### HUSBAND'S PARENTS
**Alexander Bennett**      **Rebecca Yarborough**
1776 - 1830                      1792 - 1850

#### WIFE'S PARENTS
**John McGee**      **Elizabeth Rogers**
1790 - 1860          1791 - 1848

### HUSBAND
**Joseph Alexander Bennett**
**BIRTH:** 2 Sep. 1824, Williamson Co. TN
**DEATH:** 7 Feb. 1904, Peytonsville, TN

### WIFE
**Martha Susan McGee**
**BIRTH:** 10 Mar. 1827, Williamson Co. TN
**DEATH:** 3 June 1896, Williamson Co. TN

### CHILDREN

| **Anna Loretta Bennett Daughter** | **BIRTH:** 20 Feb. 1844 **DEATH:** 17 Apr. 1914 |
|---|---|
| **Nancy Jane Bennett Daughter** | **BIRTH:** 1 Feb. 1847 **DEATH:** 27 Mar. 1880 |
| **William Alexander Bennett-Son** | **BIRTH:** 29 June 1849 **DEATH:** 22 July 1852 |
| **John Reece Bennett Son** | **BIRTH:** 22 Jan. 1851 **DEATH:** 13 Mar. 1941 |
| **Joseph James Bennett-Son** | **BIRTH:** 22 Feb. 1853 **DEATH:** 26 May 1933 |
| **Sennie Ophelia Bennett-Daughter** | **BIRTH:** 23 July 1855 **DEATH:** 13 Jan. 1939 |
| **Elizabeth Caroline Bennett-Daughter** | **BIRTH:** 1 Sep. 1857 **DEATH:** 20 July 1927 |

**Susan Emey Bennett**
**Daughter**
BIRTH: 26 Aug. 1860
DEATH: 1962

**Mary Elizabeth**
**Bennett-Daughter**
BIRTH: 18 Nov. 1862
DEATH: 3 June 1885

**Bedford Forest**
**Bennett-Daughter**
BIRTH: 1 Mar. 1865
DEATH: 22 Mar. 1883

**Israel Washington**
**Bennett-Son**
BIRTH: 27 Jan. 1868
DEATH: 24 Apr. 1939

## HIS LIFE

Joseph Alexander Bennett was born September 2, 1824, in Williamson County, Tennessee. He married Martha Susan McGee on March 29, 1843, when he was 19-years old. They had 12 children together.

Joseph had two narrow escapes from death in accidents, one when the railroad was being built at Thompson's Station and again in digging a well at the old Anderson place. At the latter he was blown upward a distance of 40-feet, having an almost miraculous escape from death.

Joseph Bennett died on Sunday, February 7, 1904 at the home of his nephew, Will McGee near Harpeth. He is buried in the family cemetery.

# JOHN CARL HELM
# 1825-1862

## HELM FAMILY

### HUSBAND'S PARENTS
**Thomas Helm     Elizabeth Helm**
1784 - 1863          1800 - 1855

### WIFE'S PARENTS
**Henry J. Merritt     Rebecca Newsom**
1803 - 1873          1808 - 1870

## HUSBAND
### John Carl Helm
BIRTH: 29 Nov. 1825, Williamson Co. TN
DEATH: 11 Mar. 1862

## WIFE
### Mary Louise Merritt
BIRTH: 7 Oct. 1832, TN
DEATH: 19 July 1903, Williamson Co. TN

## CHILDREN

**Mary A. Helm**
**Daughter**
BIRTH: 3 Sep. 1853
DEATH: 24 Feb. 1886

**Sarah Elizabeth Helm**
**Daughter**
BIRTH: 6 Oct. 1855
DEATH: 24 June 1940

**John Thomas Helm**
**Son**
BIRTH: 15 Mar. 1857
DEATH: 19 Jan. 1912

**Walter Henry Helm**
**Son**
BIRTH: 28 Sep. 1858
DEATH: 1898

**Ella Helm**
**Daughter**
BIRTH: 23 May 1861
DEATH: 25 June 1934

## HIS LIFE

When John Carl Helm was born on November 29, 1825, in Williamson County, Tennessee, his father, Thomas was 41 and his mother, Elizabeth was 25. He married Mary Louise Merritt on July 26, 1852, in Peytonsville, Tennessee. They had five children during their marriage. He died on March 11, 1862, at the age of 36 and was buried in Nashville, Tennessee.

# NATHANIEL NICHOLAS
# SMITHSON
# 1826-1896

## SMITHSON FAMILY

**Tandy S. Smithson    Ann Calvert**
1801 - 1873    1804 - 1888

**WIFE'S PARENTS**

**Jesse J. Johnson    Dolly Smithson**
1804 - 1866    1812 - 1884

**HUSBAND**
**Nathaniel Nicholas Smithson**
**BIRTH:** 20 Apr. 1826, Williamson Co. TN
**DEATH:** 10 Apr. 1896, Peytonsville, TN

**WIFE**
**Margaret Knott Johnson**
**BIRTH:** 8 Mar. 1833, Peytonsville, TN
**DEATH:** 1880, Peytonsville, TN

**CHILDREN**

| | |
|---|---|
| **James M. Smithson**<br>Son | **BIRTH:** 20 Dec. 1852<br>**DEATH:** 4 Aug. 1920 |
| **Joseph P. Smithson**<br>Son | **BIRTH:** 29 Dec. 1855<br>**DEATH:** 18 Apr. 1889 |
| **Tandy S. Smithson**<br>Son | **BIRTH:** 9 Nov. 1857<br>**DEATH:** 12 July 1884 |
| **Elijah Knott Smithson**<br>Son | **BIRTH:** 14 May 1860<br>**DEATH:** 1 Nov. 1941 |
| **Dolly Ann Smithson**<br>Daughter | **BIRTH:** 11 Jan. 1863<br>**DEATH:** 3 Jan. 1907 |
| **Martha Parilee**<br>**Smithson-Daughter** | **BIRTH:** 27 Mar. 1865<br>**DEATH:** 10 Sep. 1943 |
| **Permelia Ada**<br>**Smithson-Daughter** | **BIRTH:** 23 May 1867<br>**DEATH:** 3 July 1884 |
| **Mary E. Smithson**<br>Daughter | **BIRTH:** 28 Apr. 1870<br>**DEATH:** 15 Nov. 1953 |
| **Lydia Ophelia**<br>Daughter | **BIRTH:** Feb. 1875<br>**DEATH:** 24 Nov. 1954 |
| **Jesse W. Smithson**<br>Son | **BIRTH:** 18 Nov. 1877<br>**DEATH:** 8 Jan. 1878 |

## HIS LIFE

Taken from: *The Goodspeed Histories of Maury, Williamson, Rutherford, Wilson, Bedford, & Marshall Counties of Tennessee. Originally published in 1886, reprinted 1971. pg. 1009.*

Nathaniel N. Smithson, a respected citizen of Williamson County, was born in this State April 20, 1826. He received his education as the average country boy in the district schools. November 30, 1851, he was married to Miss Margaret K. Johnson, a native of Tennessee, born March 8, 1833, and the daughter of Jesse and Dolly (Smithson) Johnson. Our subject and wife were blessed by an interesting family of ten children: James M. born in 1852; Dolly A., born in 1863; Martha P., born in 1865, and Elijah K., born in 1860; Mary E., born in 1870; Lydia O., born in 1875, and Jesse W. (deceased), born in 1877. In 1870 our subject moved to his present location in the edge of Peytonsville, where he has a fine farm of 190 acres; besides this he has another farm of 400 acres in another part of the county. He is a Mason, a staunch Democrat and a member of the Methodist Episcopal Church South. His wife is a member of the Baptist Church. Mr. Smithson is the son of Tandy S. and Ann (Calvert) Smithson. Her father, a native of Virginia, was born in 1804, and died in 1866, and the mother was born in 1804.

Nathaniel Nicholas Smithson died on April 10, 1896, in Peytonsville, Tennessee at the age of 69. He is buried in Bethesda, Tennessee in the Hargrove-Smithson Cemetery.

# JAMES LUCAS GEE
## 1828-1896

### GEE FAMILY

**HUSBAND'S PARENTS**
**William Oliver Gee**   **Nancy Knott**
1800 - 1840          1804 - 1880

**WIFE'S PARENTS**
**Clement Smithson Jr.   Mary Ann Smithson**
1805 - 1871          1809 - 1869

### HUSBAND
**James Lucas Gee**
BIRTH: 1828, Williamson Co. TN
DEATH: 1896, Peytonsville, TN

### WIFE
**Sarah Ann Smithson**
BIRTH: 11 Sep. 1843, Williamson Co. TN
DEATH: 26 Dec. 1915, Peytonsville, TN

### CHILDREN

**Frank Lavender Gee**   BIRTH: 1 Nov. 1874
Son                      DEATH: 22 June 1940

**Ola Mai Gee**          BIRTH: 17 Dec. 1877
Daughter                 DEATH: 14 Sep. 1943

**James Larry Gee**      BIRTH: 7 July 1880
Son                      DEATH: 7 Feb. 1947

**Leslie Orell Gee**     BIRTH: 3 Apr. 1883
Son                      DEATH: 3 Oct. 1970

### HIS LIFE

When James Lucas Gee was born in 1828, in Williamson County, Tennessee, his father, William was 28 and his mother, Nancy was 24. He married Sarah Ann Smithson on December 30, 1872, in Marshall County, Tennessee. They had four children during their marriage. He died in 1896, in Peytonsville, Tennessee at the age of 68.

# GEORGE WASHINGTON KING
## 1828-1914

### KING FAMILY

**HUSBAND'S PARENTS**
**Allen Green King**   **Catherine Brown**
1791 - 1870          1791 - 1843

**WIFE'S PARENTS**
**Henry Roberts**   **Elizabeth Ray**
1800 - 1865          1795 - 1860

### HUSBAND
**George Washington King**
BIRTH: 3 Aug. 1828, Guiliford Co. NC
DEATH: 7 Feb. 1914, Peytonsville, TN

### WIFE
**Nancy Lethia Roberts**
BIRTH: 6 June 1837, Coffee Co. TN

**DEATH:** 8 June 1911, Peytonsville, TN

## CHILDREN

| | |
|---|---|
| **George Marion King**<br>**Son** | **BIRTH:** 30 July 1857<br>**DEATH:** 7 Oct. 1945 |
| **Martha E. King**<br>**Daughter** | **BIRTH:** 1861<br>**DEATH:** Unknown |
| **Nancy Jane King**<br>**Daughter** | **BIRTH:** Nov. 1862<br>**DEATH:** 14 Aug. 1956 |
| **George Thomas King**<br>**Son** | **BIRTH:** 11 Feb. 1866<br>**DEATH:** 14 Feb. 1959 |
| **William Robert King**<br>**Son** | **BIRTH:** 2 Apr. 1867<br>**DEATH:** 24 Mar. 1956 |
| **Mary Ada King**<br>**Daughter** | **BIRTH:** 4 July 1868<br>**DEATH:** Feb. 1966 |
| **Sarah Catherine King**<br>**Daughter** | **BIRTH:** 27 Feb. 1873<br>**DEATH:** 26 Apr. 1927 |
| **James Watson King**<br>**Son** | **BIRTH:** 21 Oct. 1874<br>**DEATH:** 12 Oct. 1940 |
| **Samuel Moses King**<br>**Son** | **BIRTH:** 15 Dec. 1875<br>**DEATH:** 1 Nov. 1949 |
| **Melissa "Lissie" Ann King-Daughter** | **BIRTH:** 14 Aug. 1876<br>**DEATH:** 7 Feb. 1923 |

## HIS LIFE

When George Washington King was born on August 3, 1828, in Guilford County, North Carolina, his father, Allen was 37 and his mother, Catherine was 37. He married Nancy Lethia Roberts on October 28, 1858, in Coffee County, Tennessee.

George joined the 11th Cavalry Partisan Rangers which was an independent cavalry unit that fought for the South. They were irregular soldiers who fought guerrilla warfare, making surprise raids behind the lines of the invading enemy. For the most part, they were volunteers who elected their own officers and provided their own horses, weapons, and other equipage. They frequently provided vital information and services to the Confederate Army, as well as destroying enemy lines of supply and communication. Two companies of Major Daniel W. Holman's Battalion of Partisan Rangers were raised in Giles County, in September and October, 1862. Captain Andrew R. Gordon raised a company of 160 men and Captain James Rivers raised a company of 100 men. After a recommendation from General Robert E. Lee, the law authorizing Partisan Rangers was abolished and almost all Partisan Rangers were required to join the regular Confederate Army. Holman's Battalion was no exception. "On the 20th of February, 1863, the battalion against the wishes of every man composing it, was taken to form a part of the Eleventh Tennessee Cavalry, and from that time till the close of the war its history is identified with the history of that regiment." Holman's Battalion had served as Partisan Rangers for only four months. General Nathan Bedford Forrest issued orders at Columbia, Tennessee, on February 20, 1863, forming the Eleventh Tennessee Cavalry, composed of 11 companies, including Gordon's and Rivers' companies of Holman's Battalion. (Film Number: M231 roll 24). Tennessee Cavalry (Holman's) Overview: 11th Cavalry Regiment was organized in February, 1863, by consolidating Holman's and part of Douglass' Tennessee Cavalry Battalion plus other companies. It was assigned to Forrest's, Humes', J.B. Biffle's and Dibrell's Brigade. The regiment took an active part in the conflicts at Brentwood and Chickamauga, then was involved in the Atlanta Campaign and Hood's operations in Tennessee. During January, 1865, it was consolidated with the 10th Tennessee Cavalry Regiment and in May contained 30 officers and 280 men. Serving in Alabama, it surrendered with the Department of Alabama, Mississippi, and East Louisiana. The field officers were Colonels James H. Edmondson and Daniel W. Holman, Lieutenant Colonel Jacob T. Martin, and Major Chatham Coffee.

George and his wife had 10 children in 22-years. He died on February 7, 1914, in Peytonsville, Tennessee at the age of 85. He was buried in the King Cemetery in Peytonsville.

**George Washington King**
1828-1914
Co E 1st TN Inf. US

# WILLIAM PARRISH
# 1828-1865

### PARRISH FAMILY

### HUSBAND'S PARENTS
**Elijah R. Parrish**    **Catherine Gibson**
1798 - 1840        1792 - 1870

### WIFE'S PARENTS
**Michael B. Kinnard**   **Adaline Bird McConnico**
1797 - 1847        1805 - 1853

### HUSBAND
**William Parrish**
**BIRTH:** 1828, Williamson Co. TN
**DEATH:** 1865, Peytonsville, TN

### WIFE
**Susan C. Kinnard**
**BIRTH:** 1836, TN
**DEATH:** BEF 1860, TN

### CHILDREN

**John S. Parrish**      **BIRTH:** 1853
Son      **DEATH:** Unknown

**Elijah R. Parrish**      **BIRTH:** 1855
Son      **DEATH:** Unknown

**William C. Parrish**      **BIRTH:** 1858
Son      **DEATH:** Unknown

### HIS LIFE

When William Parrish was born in 1828, in Williamson County, Tennessee, his father, Elijah was 30 and his mother, Catherine was 36. He married Susan C. Kinnard on December 18, 1851, and they had three children during their marriage.

**Taken from a Probate record of 1870:**
John S. Parrish and W.C. Parrish are joint owners of a tract of land in the 13th District containing about 500 acres bounded on the north by William Stevens, Alexr. Reid, William J. Smithson and Thomas Helm's land - on the west by Louis J. Beard, C.W. Mallory originally the old Fleming tract - on the south by Sam Harris, S.W. Smithson Dec'd. Land - on the east by William Neely the old Garner Jordan land, N.L. Harrison and J.W.L. Nevils. The land descended to them from their father William Parrish and their grandmother Catherine Parrish. Dr. Alexander Reid is the Admr. of the estate of William Parrish the debts can be paid without a sale of the land. They want a division of the land.

William Parrish died in 1865, in Williamson County, Tennessee at the age of 37.

# THOMAS LOGWOOD HATCHER
# 1828-1904

## HATCHER FAMILY

### HUSBAND'S PARENTS
**William Samuel Hatcher**     **Lucy Rucker**
1793 - 1866                    1797 - 1884

### 1ST WIFE'S PARENTS
**Joseph D. Pollard**     **Martha Patsy Nicholson**
1785 - 1839               1789 - 1852

### 2ND WIFE'S PARENTS
**Anthony Clinton Lavender**  **Paralee Sprott**
1804 - 1854                   1815 - 1897

### HUSBAND
**Thomas Logwood Hatcher**
BIRTH: 2 Mar. 1828, Williamson Co. TN
DEATH: 8 Jan. 1904, Williamson Co. TN

### 1ST WIFE
**Mary Jane Pollard**
BIRTH: 20 Jan. 1832, Williamson County, TN
DEATH: 7 July 1880, TN

### 2ND WIFE
**Emiline E. Lavender**
BIRTH: 4 Aug. 1841, Williamson Co. TN
DEATH: 24 June 1909, Williamson Co. TN

### CHILDREN OF THOMAS AND MARY

| | |
|---|---|
| **Martha Burnette Hatcher-Daughter** | BIRTH: 29 Sep. 1853<br>DEATH: 23 Sep. 1930 |
| **Octavius Alphonzo Hatcher-Son** | BIRTH: 5 Jan. 1857<br>DEATH: 8 June 1950 |
| **George William Hatcher-Son** | BIRTH: 1858<br>DEATH: 11 Oct. 1865 |
| **Lucy Elizabeth "Ella" Hatcher-Daughter** | BIRTH: 13 Mar. 1861<br>DEATH: 7 Sep. 1910 |
| **J. R. Hatcher Son** | BIRTH: 1865<br>DEATH: Unknown |
| **Thomas Robert Hatcher-Son** | BIRTH: 1865<br>DEATH: 7 Sep. 1960 |

### CHILDREN OF THOMAS AND EMILINE

| | |
|---|---|
| **Ora May Hatcher Daughter** | BIRTH: 17 Mar. 1873<br>DEATH: 29 Aug. 1946 |
| **John Lavender Hatcher-Son** | BIRTH: 7 Aug. 1876<br>DEATH: 29 Jan. 1963 |

### HIS LIFE

When Thomas Logwood Hatcher was born on March 2, 1828, in Williamson County, Tennessee, his father, William was 34 and his mother, Lucy was 30. He married Mary Jane Pollard and they had six children together. After Mary's death on July 7, 1880, he then married, Emiline E. Lavender and they had two children together. He died on January 8, 1904, in Peytonsville, Tennessee at the age of 75. He is buried in the Hatcher Cemetery.

# WILLIAM JOEL "JOLLIE" PETWAY
# 1828-1908

## PETWAY FAMILY

### HUSBAND'S PARENTS
**John S. Petway**     **Mary M. Stephens**
1803 - 1832            1805 - 1873

### WIFE'S PARENTS
**William Burns**     **Keturah N. Burns**
1800 - 1873           1802 - 1862

### HUSBAND
**William Joel "Jollie" Petway**
BIRTH: 6 Sep. 1828, Williamson Co. TN

**DEATH:** 3 Feb, 1908, TN

### WIFE
**Mary Elizabeth Burns**
**BIRTH:** 25 Sep. 1829, Williamson Co. TN
**DEATH:** 28 Dec. 1908, Franklin, TN

### CHILDREN

| | |
|---|---|
| **John Thomas**<br>Son | **BIRTH:** 17 Oct. 1851<br>**DEATH:** 23 Aug. 1927 |
| **William Burns Petway**<br>Son | **BIRTH:** 9 Sep. 1855<br>**DEATH:** 9 June 1910 |
| **Joseph Oliver Petway**<br>Son | **BIRTH:** 1859<br>**DEATH:** 16 Apr. 1940 |
| **Walter Petway**<br>Son | **BIRTH:** 30 May. 1866<br>**DEATH:** 18 July 1947 |

### HIS LIFE

When William Joel "Jollie" Petway was born on September 6, 1828, in Franklin, Tennessee, his father, John was 24 and his mother, Mary was 23. He married Myra Elizabeth Burns on January 15, 1851, in Williamson County, Tennessee. They had four children in 14-years. He died on February 3, 1908, at the age of 79. He is buried in the Mount Hope Cemetery.

# JAMES M. LONG
# 1830-1891

### LONG FAMILY

### HUSBAND'S PARENTS
| **George B. Long** | **Elizabeth Gosey** |
|---|---|
| 1797 - 1879 | 1802 - 1838 |

### WIFE'S PARENTS
| **Nathaniel Lundy Harrison** | **Christina T. Knight** |
|---|---|
| 1808 - 1885 | 1811 - 1862 |

### HUSBAND
**James M. Long**
**BIRTH:** 26 Feb. 1830, Peytonsville, TN
**DEATH:** 26 Aug. 1891, College Grove, TN

### WIFE
**Arabella M. Harrison**
**BIRTH:** 28 Nov. 1835, Peytonsville, TN
**DEATH:** 8 Feb. 1904, Peytonsville, TN

| | |
|---|---|
| **Mattie Bruce Long**<br>Daughter | **BIRTH:** 10 Dec. 1855<br>**DEATH:** 13 Apr. 1905 |
| **George W. Long**<br>Son | **BIRTH:** 25 Aug. 1857<br>**DEATH:** 4 Apr. 1932 |
| **James M. Long**<br>Son | **BIRTH:** 23 May 1859<br>**DEATH:** 1913 |
| **Robert Henry Long**<br>Son | **BIRTH:** 15 June 1861<br>**DEATH:** 3 Sep. 1908 |
| **Mary Inez Long**<br>Daughter | **BIRTH:** 10 July 1863<br>**DEATH:** 24 Mar. 1956 |
| **Walter A. Long**<br>Son | **BIRTH:** Sep. 1865<br>**DEATH:** 3 Sep. 1937 |
| **Thomas Long**<br>Son | **BIRTH:** 18 Jan. 1868<br>**DEATH:** Unknown |
| **Leslie Long**<br>Daughter | **BIRTH:** 8 Jan. 1870<br>**DEATH:** Unknown |
| **Wallace Gentry Long**<br>Son | **BIRTH:** 1872<br>**DEATH:** 1945 |
| **Perkins P. Long**<br>Son | **BIRTH:** 18 Aug. 1874<br>**DEATH:** Unknown |

## HIS LIFE

When James M. Long was born on February 26, 1830, his father, George was 32 and his mother, Margaret was 28. He married Arabella M. Harrison on March 17, 1853, in Williamson County, Tennessee. They had 10 children in 18-years. He died on August 26, 1891, in College Grove, Tennessee at the age of 61. He was buried in Rutherford County, Tennessee.

# JOHN ASA JOHNSON
# 1831-1910

## JOHNSON FAMILY

### HUSBAND'S PARENTS
**Jesse J. Johnson**     **Dolly Smithson**
1804 - 1866                    1812 - 1884

### 1ST WIFE'S PARENTS
**William Henry Vaden**   **Martha W. Smithson**
1804 - 1855                          1806 - 1880

### 2ND WIFE'S PARENTS
**John Wilson Gibson**     **Martha H. Lester**
1817 - 1870                         1815 - 1869

### 3RD WIFE'S PARENTS
Unknown Father     Unknown Mother

### HUSBAND
**John Asa Johnson**
**BIRTH:** 20 Feb. 1831, Peytonsville, TN
**DEATH:** 2 Oct. 1910, Peytonsville, TN

### 1ST WIFE
**Mary E. Vaden**
**BIRTH:** 1835, TN
**DEATH:** 1865, Williamson Co. TN

### 2ND WIFE
**Martha Jane Gibson**
**BIRTH:** 1841, TN
**DEATH:** 1873, Peytonsville, TN

### 3RD WIFE
**Margaret Elizabeth "Maggie" Smith**
**BIRTH:** 1842
**DEATH:** 1900

### CHILDREN OF JOHN AND MARY

| | |
|---|---|
| **M.L. Johnson**<br>Daughter | **BIRTH:** 1859<br>**DEATH:** Unknown |
| **Mary Elizabeth**<br>Johnson-Daughter | **BIRTH:** 15 Dec. 1861<br>**DEATH:** 8 Apr. 1936 |

### CHILDREN OF JOHN AND MARTHA

| | |
|---|---|
| **Patrick G. Johnson**<br>Son | **BIRTH:** July 1865<br>**DEATH:** 3 May 1943 |

| Martha Ida Johnson | BIRTH: 1 Apr. 1868 |
| Daughter | DEATH: 30 Sep. 1929 |

| William Wilson | BIRTH: 4 Feb. 1870 |
| Johnson-Son | DEATH: 23 Dec. 1941 |

| Eula Johnson | BIRTH: 4 Mar. 1872 |
| Daughter | DEATH: Unknown |

| Beulah B. Johnson | BIRTH: 4 Mar. 1872 |
| Daughter | DEATH: 21 Dec. 1955 |

### CHILDREN OF JOHN AND MAGGIE

| Joseph Parks | BIRTH: 20 Nov. 1876 |
| Johnson-Son | DEATH: 20 Dec. 1952 |

| Jessie Lula Johnson | BIRTH: 15 Sep. 1879 |
| Daughter | DEATH: Feb. 1968 |

### HIS LIFE

When John Asa Johnson was born on February 20, 1831, in Williamson County, Tennessee, his father, Jesse was 27 and his mother, Dolly was 19. He was married three times and had three sons and six daughters. He died on October 2, 1910, in Peytonsville, Tennessee at the age of 79.

# SPOTSWOOD HENRY HATCHER
# 1831-1891

### HATCHER FAMILY

### HUSBAND'S PARENTS

**William Samuel Hatcher**     **Lucy Rucker**
1793 - 1866                    1797 - 1884

### WIFE'S PARENTS

**William Andrews**     **Mary Pegram Matthews**
1808 - 1860             1812 - 1844

### HUSBAND
**Spotswood Henry Hatcher**

BIRTH: 29 Nov. 1831, Williamson Co. TN
DEATH: 3 Aug. 1891, Peytonsville, TN

### WIFE
**Mary Jane Andrews**
BIRTH: 15 Mar. 1835, Williamson Co. TN
DEATH: 4 Oct. 1928, Peytonsville, TN

### CHILDREN

| J.W. Hatcher | BIRTH: 1856 |
| Son | DEATH: Unknown |

| Henry T. Hatcher | BIRTH: July 1861 |
| Son | DEATH: Unknown |

| Samuel A. Hatcher | BIRTH: 31 May 1866 |
| Son | DEATH: 23 Dec. 1944 |

| Sallie Minerva | BIRTH: 17 Aug. 1868 |
| Hatcher-Daughter | DEATH: 5 Mar. 1944 |

| Nannie Lou Hatcher | BIRTH: 9 Dec. 1872 |
| Daughter | DEATH: 26 Aug. 1964 |

| Mary E. Hatcher | BIRTH: June 1879 |
| Daughter | DEATH: Unknown |

### HIS LIFE

When Spotswood Henry Hatcher was born on November 29, 1831, in Williamson County, Tennessee, his father, William was 38 and his mother, Lucy was 34. He married Mary Jane Andrews on November 29, 1854 in Peytonsville, Tennessee.

Spotswood and his brother, Abe were members of Company A, 45th Tennessee Infantry Regiment in the Civil War. Spotswood enlisted at McMinnville, Tennessee on December 19, 1862. His brother Abe (Abraham Woldridge Hatcher) mustered in at Camp Trousdale on December 17, 1861 and he was promoted to Fifth Sergeant on May 19, 1862.

During Spotswood's time in the war, he wrote his wife, Mary Jane Andrews, beautiful, insightful letters that are still kept by the family.

**This is a Civil War letter, still in possession of the family:**

July 8, 1864
River Camp near Chatahoocha

My dear wife,

I have just heard of an opportunity of sending you a few lines and I gladly embrace it. I will be hurried and can't write much and the shells are flying and bursting around us, continually. Mary, there is no use in trying to give you a description of what we have passed through since the 10th of May. We have been under arms most of the time, and most of the time in hearing of the balls and shells. Abe and I have both come out unhurt so far, and I earnestly pray that God in much much mercy may continue to spare us. We are both in excellent health and have been most of the time. I might say all the time, for neither of us has been unwell as to leave the company, nothing more than a cold or a headache. Our company has been quite unlucky. We have lost three killed dead and one in the company that is consolidated with us, and Capt. Wilson now seriously, if not mortally wounded. I very much fear that he will never recover. The killed are: F C Russel, E A Williams, from Rutherford County and O C Wilson.

Mary, I am staying here trying to do my duty, not because I do not dread fighting or that I willfully stay away from you and my sweet little children, or I can tell you I would not pass through again what we have experienced in the last two months for all the wealth of the world. Yet, there may be just as bad in store for us, and doubtless many of us will yet fall victim to this cruel war.

I greatly desire to be spared to return to my family in peace (it may be my desire is too great). I want to live and die in peace at home with loved ones around. I want to be spared to lead my children to the rock that is higher than I. To instruct them and influence them to yield submissively to the will of God and obey his commandments. I think sometimes that I am not really afraid of death, but I very much dread death on the hands of men. I prefer falling into the hands of my maker, and I thank and praise his name that He has spared me thus far.

I received a letter from my niece, M C H, last week which I was very glad to get, and it was a very nice letter indeed - and Abe one from M P H, but neither of them paid one word about mine or Abe's family. I have heard nothing direct from you since Gray was here. I don't know anything about how you are making out, but I hope and pray that you may not suffer.

Mary, don't distress yourself about me but turn your attention to your children, and if I should never be permitted to return to you again, try to raise them right and instill the right principles within. Mary, don't think because I warn you in almost every letter about the children that I have not full confidence in you as a Christian and as a faithful parent, for I believe you will try to do your duty. But there is so much wickedness and careless negligence in the land and so many dying without any hope in Christ or opportunity without being at all concerned, that I want it deeply and forcibly, and lastingly impressed upon their minds the necessity of a Godly life of trusting in the atoning merits of the blood of Christ - of making it their aim in life to give God the praise and last obtain an admittance in Heaven, impress upon their minds that worldly honor and possessions are not lasting and not so much to be desired.

I have written you by flag of truce and otherwise but don't know whether you have received them or not. John Waddy was wounded on the 15th of May, and it is thought he is dead. George Greeman has been killed.

Jordon of the 20th was wounded and is dead. Bob Fleming has lost his leg. W Price has lost his left arm (I think it was his left). I tried to hear from Rowlett but have not had a chance to hear from him yet. I have forgotten the number of his regiment. George McConnico was slightly wounded in the hand.

Give my love and respect to all my friends and especially my parents and to you and my dear sweet little children - and to Mira, Julian and the children. And if we never meet on earth again, God grant that we may meet in that better land where all is joy and peace. Write every chance and continue to pray for us.

Your husband,
S H Hatcher

(Give my heart felt love to my dear, yes dear sisters, Sallie and Bet). Charley Davis as well.

Spotswood Henry Hatcher and his wife, Mary Jane Andrews had six children in 23-years. He died on August 3, 1891, in Peytonsville, Tennessee at the age of 59.

# CHARLES W. PENNINGTON
## 1831-1900

PENNINGTON FAMILY



**Clement S. Pennington**     **Susan T. Smithson**
1790 - 1861                          1794 - 1855

**WIFE'S PARENTS**
**Robert Sledge**     **Catherine K. Smithson**
1813 - 1891                  1811 - 1870

**HUSBAND**
**Charles W. Pennington**
**BIRTH:** 1831, Williamson Co. TN
**DEATH:** 1900, Peytonsville, TN

**WIFE**
**Sarah E. Sledge**
**BIRTH:** July 1841, Peytonsville, TN
**DEATH:** 1900

**CHILDREN**

| | |
|---|---|
| **Susan C. Pennington** Daughter | **BIRTH:** 1866 **DEATH:** Unknown |
| **Ellen T. Pennington** Daughter | **BIRTH:** 1868 **DEATH:** Unknown |
| **John N. Pennington** Son | **BIRTH:** 24 Sep. 1869 **DEATH:** 16 July 1952 |
| **Nora E. Pennington** Daughter | **BIRTH:** 8 Mar. 1874 **DEATH:** 23 Aug. 1942 |
| **Lean T. Pennington** Daughter | **BIRTH:** 1875 **DEATH:** Unknown |
| **Charles R. Pennington-Son** | **BIRTH:** 1878 **DEATH:** Unknown |
| **Bettie Wade Pennington-Daughter** | **BIRTH:** 9 Sep. 1883 **DEATH:** 14 Sep. 1960 |

**HIS LIFE**

When Charles W. Pennington was born in 1831, in Williamson County, Tennessee, his father, Clement was 41 and his mother, Susan was 37. He married Sarah E. Sledge on January 28, 1864, in Peytonsville, Tennessee. They had seven children in 17-years. He died in 1900 in

Williamson County, Tennessee when he was 69-years old.

## GEORGE F. LESTER
## 1831-1900

### LESTER FAMILY

**HUSBAND'S PARENTS**
**Samuel Lester**     **Priscilla Allen**
1808 - ?             1814 - 1874

**WIFE'S PARENTS**
**John S. Allen**     **Lucinda Wiley**
1813 - ?             1816 - 1875

**HUSBAND**
**George F. Lester**
BIRTH: 1831, Williamson Co. TN
DEATH: 1900, Dallas, TX

**WIFE**
**Mary Allen**
BIRTH: 1837, TN
DEATH: 1900, Williamson Co. TN

### CHILDREN

| | |
|---|---|
| **Lucinda Lester**<br>Daughter | BIRTH: 1856<br>DEATH: Unknown |
| **Henry Lester**<br>Son | BIRTH: Oct, 1858<br>DEATH: Unknown |
| **Maggie Lester**<br>Daughter | BIRTH: 1860<br>DEATH: Unknown |
| **John Lester**<br>Son | BIRTH: May 1865<br>DEATH: Unknown |
| **William Lester**<br>Son | BIRTH: 1867<br>DEATH: 1880 |
| **Oliver Lester**<br>Son | BIRTH: 1870<br>DEATH: 1953 |

| | |
|---|---|
| **David Silas Lester**<br>Son | BIRTH: 26 Jan. 1876<br>DEATH: 21 Mar. 1960 |

### HIS LIFE

George F. Lester was born in 1831, in Tennessee. He married Mary Allen on November 3, 1853, in Williamson County, Tennessee. They had seven children in 20-years. He died in 1900 at the age of 69.

## HENRY FORD
## 1831-1920

### FORD FAMILY

**HUSBAND'S PARENTS**
**John Ford**     **Polly Corlett**
1800 - 1849     1790 - 1848

**WIFE'S PARENTS**
**Josiah S. Jackson**     **Martha Bridgeman**
1783 - 1870             1802 - 1870

**HUSBAND**
**Henry Ford**
BIRTH: 1831, Rowan Co. NC
DEATH: 29 Mar. 1920, Peytonsville, TN

**WIFE**
**Sarah E. Jackson**
BIRTH: 8 Jan. 1834, Williamson Co. TN
DEATH: 8 Jan. 1907, Williamson Co. TN

### CHILDREN

| | |
|---|---|
| **Martha Emma Ford**<br>Daughter | BIRTH: 4 July 1855<br>DEATH: 3 Oct. 1907 |
| **Mary E. Ford**<br>Daughter | BIRTH: 1859<br>DEATH: 1865 |
| **Henry Buell Ford**<br>Son | BIRTH: 16 Mar. 1862<br>DEATH: 31 Jan. 1933 |

| John P. Ford<br>Son | **BIRTH:** 11 Dec. 1865<br>**DEATH:** 8 Oct. 1949 |
| --- | --- |
| James T. Ford<br>Son | **BIRTH:** 9 Feb. 1867<br>**DEATH:** 7 Mar. 1931 |
| Amanda Ford<br>Daughter | **BIRTH:** Feb. 1869<br>**DEATH:** 22 Aug. 1952 |
| Robert Ford<br>Son | **BIRTH:** 24 Dec. 1873<br>**DEATH:** 16 Nov. 1875 |
| William Gilln Ford<br>Son | **BIRTH:** 15 May 1874<br>**DEATH:** 31 Jan. 1964 |
| Jesse Munro Ford<br>Son | **BIRTH:** Oct. 1876<br>**DEATH:** 26 Apr. 1913 |

## HIS LIFE

When Henry Ford was born in 1831, in Rowan County, North Carolina, his father, John was 31 and his mother, Polly was 41. He married Sarah E. Jackson on November 29, 1853, in Williamson County, Tennessee.

When the Civil War broke out, Henry joined the 32nd Regiment, Tennessee, Infantry, Company D, Edmond C. Cook's Company of Tennessee Volunteers, CSA on November 2, 1861.

Henry and Sarah had nine children in 21-years. He died on March 29, 1920, in Peytonsville, Tennessee at the age of 89 and was buried in the Barnett Cemetery.

**HENRY FORD**

# JOHN M. NEVILS
# 1832-1900

### NEVILS FAMILY

**HUSBAND'S PARENTS**
**Josiah Nevils**    **Sarah B. Beech**
1794 - 1854      1801 - 1882

**WIFE'S PARENTS**
**Gabriel R. Low**    **Lavinia Howard Pinkston**
1808 - 1882      1820 - 1893

**HUSBAND**
**John M. Nevils**
**BIRTH:** 3 Oct. 1832, Maury Co. TN
**DEATH:** 1900, Williamson Co. TN

**WIFE**
**Lydia Arabella Low**
**BIRTH:** 1848, TN
**DEATH:** 1878, Williamson Co. TN

| | |
|---|---|
| **Richard Nevils** **Son** | **BIRTH:** 1869 **DEATH:** Unknown |
| **Robert Howard** **Emmet Nevils-Son** | **BIRTH:** 13 Apr. 1872 **DEATH:** 19 Dec. 1915 |
| **Edward Marshall** **Nevils-Son** | **BIRTH:** 12 July 1875 **DEATH:** 28 Oct. 1970 |

## HIS LIFE

When John M. Nevils was born on October 3, 1832, in Maury County, Tennessee, his father, Josiah was 38 and his mother, Sarah was 31. He married Lydia Arabella Low and they had three children together. After Lydia's death in 1878, he then married, Alice Merritt on March 17, 1879.

**Taken from *The Goodspeed History*:**
John M. Nevils, sheriff of Williamson County, was born in Maury County, Tenn., October 3, 1832, son of Josiah and Sarah Beech Nevils, and of Dutch-English descent. Our subject was reared on the farm and secured a good practical education in the common schools. He followed the occupation of a farmer until the beginning of the late war, when he enlisted in the Confederate Army, Company B. Eleventh Tennessee Regiment, and served four years. In 1865 he engaged in merchandising in Nashville, but soon removed to Peytonsville, this county, and continued farming and merchandising. In 1868 he wedded Lydia A. Low, who died in 1878. In 1879 he wedded Alice Merritt. Mr. Nevils is a member of the Masonic fraternity and the I.O.O.F. He has made one of the best sheriffs the county has ever had. He is a member of the Methodist Episcopal Church and is one of the prominent men of this county. Mrs. Nevils is a member of the Christian Church.

John M. Nevils died in 1900, in Williamson County, Tennessee at the age of 68.

# J.W.L. NEVILS
## 1834-1893

### NEVILS FAMILY

**HUSBAND'S PARENTS**
**Josiah Nevils    Sarah B. Beech**
1794 - 1854        1801 - 1882

**WIFE'S PARENTS**
**Gabriel R. Low   Lavinia Howard Pinkston**
1808 - 1882        1820 - 1893

**HUSBAND**
**J.W.L. Nevils**
**BIRTH:** 14 July 1834, TN
**DEATH:** 11 July 1893, Franklin, TN

**WIFE**
**Ellen Gabella Low**
**BIRTH:** 13 Sep. 1852, Arno, Tennessee
**DEATH:** 31 Oct. 1932, Nashville, TN

### CHILDREN

| | |
|---|---|
| **John Nevils** **Son** | **BIRTH:** 1871 **DEATH:** 1871 |
| **Joe Nevils** **Son** | **BIRTH:** 1872 **DEATH:** 1872 |
| **Augie Virginia Nevils** **Daughter** | **BIRTH:** 23 Apr. 1874 **DEATH:** 21 Oct. 1954 |
| **William "Willie" W.** **Nevils-Son** | **BIRTH:** 12 Dec. 1877 **DEATH:** 20 Jan. 1948 |
| **Sallie May Nevils** **Daughter** | **BIRTH:** 28 July 1880 **DEATH:** 29 Nov. 1903 |
| **Julia Mildred Nevils** **Daughter** | **BIRTH:** 1884 **DEATH:** 1884 |
| **Robie F. Nevils** **Daughter** | **BIRTH:** Mar. 1887 **DEATH:** 18 Jan. 1939 |

| | |
|---|---|
| **Watt Ella Nevils**<br>Daughter | **BIRTH:** 23 Aug, 1893<br>**DEATH:** Nov, 1966 |

## HIS LIFE

When J.W.L. Nevils was born on July 14, 1834, in Tennessee, his father, Josiah was 40 and his mother, Sarah was 33.

The following was taken from *The Goodspeed History*:

J.W.L. Nevils, a leading citizen of Williamson County, was born in this State July 14, 1834. His father, Josiah Nevils, was born in Virginia in 1794, and the mother, Sarah Beech, was also born in Virginia, about 1801. They both came to Tennessee in the year 1821 and in 1823 were united in marriage. The father left his farm to fight in the war of 1812 and was in the memorable Battle of New Orleans. He died in 1854 and his wife in 1882. Our subject wed Miss Ella G. Low in 1871. She was born in Tennessee September 13, 1852 and was the daughter of Gabriel and Vina H. Pinkston Yarbrough Low. To our subject and wife were born six children: John L., deceased, born in 1872; Augie V., born 1874; Josiah W., deceased, born in 1872; William W., born in 1877; Sallie M., born in 1880, and an infant not named. Our subject engaged in the mercantile business in Maury County, Tenn., in 1856, and in 1861 closed out and enlisted in the Confederate Army, serving his country until the close of the war. One year after returning from the war he engaged again in the mercantile business in Peytonsville for about ten years, after which he sold out his stock of goods and gave his undivided attention to farming. He has 104 acres of good land near Peytonsville. He is a member of the Masonic lodge, also of the I.O.O.F., and he and wife are worthy members of the Methodist Episcopal Church South. Mr. Nevils is a Democrat and in 1874 he was elected magistrate in this district.

J.W.L. and Ellen had eight children in 22-years. He died on July 11, 1893, in Franklin, Tennessee, at the age of 58.

# FREDERICK SHAFFER NICHOLS
# 1834-1896

### NICHOLS FAMILY

### HUSBAND'S PARENTS
| | |
|---|---|
| **Allen Frederick Nichols** | **Eva Shaffer** |
| 1787 - 1848 | 1795 - 1878 |

### WIFE'S PARENTS
| | |
|---|---|
| **William L. Neely** | **Elizabeth Blackwell** |
| 1804 - 1878 | 1813 - 1875 |

### HUSBAND
**Frederick Shaffer Nichols**
**BIRTH:** 7 Sep. 1834, Williamson Co. TN
**DEATH:** 24 May 1896, Kerr Co. TX

### WIFE
**Sarah Elizabeth Neely**
**BIRTH:** 6 July 1833, Williamson Co. TN
**DEATH:** 16 Mar. 1906, Kerr Co. TX

### CHILDREN

| | |
|---|---|
| **Madora Nichols**<br>Daughter | **BIRTH:** 1857<br>**DEATH:** Unknown |
| **William A. Nichols**<br>Son | **BIRTH:** 1860<br>**DEATH:** Unknown |
| **Sarah A. Nichols**<br>Daughter | **BIRTH:** 1861<br>**DEATH:** Unknown |
| **Emma F. Nichols**<br>Daughter | **BIRTH:** 1864<br>**DEATH:** Unknown |
| **John Frederick**<br>**Nichols-Son** | **BIRTH:** 11 Feb. 1866<br>**DEATH:** 12 Nov. 1950 |
| **Josephine Catherine**<br>**Nichols-Daughter** | **BIRTH:** 18 Mar. 1867<br>**DEATH:** 27 Feb. 1931 |
| **Cora Nichols**<br>Daughter | **BIRTH:** 1874<br>**DEATH:** Unknown |

## HIS LIFE

When Frederick Shaffer Nichols was born on September 7, 1834, in Williamson County, Tennessee, his father, Allen was 47 and his mother, Eva was 39. He married Sarah Elizabeth Neely on September 7, 1854, in Peytonsville, Tennessee. They had seven children in 17-years. He died on May 24, 1896, in Kerr County, Texas, at the age of 61. He was buried in Ingram, Texas.

FREDERICK SHAFFER NICHOLS

## GEORGE GARNER KINNARD
### 1834-1900

### KINNARD FAMILY

#### HUSBAND'S PARENTS
**Michael B. Kinnard**   **Adaline Bird McConnico**
1797 - 1847                  1805 - 1853

#### WIFE'S PARENTS
**William Covington   Margaret W. Demonbreun**
1813 - 1897                  1820 - 1897

#### HUSBAND
**George Garner Kinnard**
**BIRTH:** 20 May 1834, TN
**DEATH:** 1900, TN

#### WIFE
**Mary Jane Covington**
**BIRTH:** 25 Sep. 1838, Williamson Co. TN
**DEATH:** 27 Feb. 1922, College Grove, TN

#### CHILDREN

| | |
|---|---|
| **Michael G. Kinnard** Son | **BIRTH:** Nov. 1857 **DEATH:** Unknown |
| **Gabriel Cannon Kinnard-Son** | **BIRTH:** 11 Sep. 1860 **DEATH:** 17 Oct. 1931 |

## HIS LIFE

When George Garner Kinnard was born on May 20, 1834, in Tennessee, his father, Michael was 36 and his mother, Adaline was 28. He married,Mary Jane Covington on June 6, 1855, in Williamson County, Tennessee. They had two children during their marriage. He died in 1900, in Peytonsville, Tennessee at the age of 66.

## BRITTON MARION MEEK
### 1834-1919

### MEEK FAMILY

#### HUSBAND'S PARENTS
**Blaney Meek**   **Rebecca Davis**
1795 - 1850          1808 - 1862

#### WIFE'S PARENTS
**Aaron Jennings   Isabella Richardson**
1813 - 1862              1816 - 1902

#### HUSBAND

## Britton Marion Meek
**BIRTH:** 26 Mar. 1834, Augusta, GA
**DEATH:** 7 Oct. 1919, Peytonsville, TN

### WIFE
## Caroline Jennings
**BIRTH:** 10 June 1838, Edgefield, SC
**DEATH:** 18 Feb. 1920, Peytonsville, TN

### CHILDREN

| | |
|---|---|
| **Charles Meek** <br> Son | **BIRTH:** 1 Sep. 1857 <br> **DEATH:** 28 Nov. 1927 |
| **Celoma Ann Meek** <br> Daughter | **BIRTH:** 11 Mar. 1859 <br> **DEATH:** 15 Mar. 1879 |
| **Emma Dora Meek** <br> Daughter | **BIRTH:** 15 Aug. 1861 <br> **DEATH:** 27 Aug. 1941 |
| **Josephine Virginia Meek-Daughter** | **BIRTH:** 10 July 1864 <br> **DEATH:** 6 Aug. 1925 |
| **William Meek** <br> Son | **BIRTH:** 3 Sep. 1867 <br> **DEATH:** 25 July 1957 |
| **Thomas Richard Meek-Son** | **BIRTH:** 15 Feb. 1870 <br> **DEATH:** 26 July 1957 |
| **James Aaron Meek** <br> Son | **BIRTH:** 28 May. 1872 <br> **DEATH:** 23 Apr. 1950 |
| **Britton Marion Meek** <br> Son | **BIRTH:** 6 Sep. 1874 <br> **DEATH:** 26 Feb. 1926 |
| **Fannie Estella Meek** <br> Daughter | **BIRTH:** 23 May. 1877 <br> **DEATH:** 11 Feb. 1949 |
| **Walter Blanney Meek** <br> Son | **BIRTH:** 1 Nov. 1879 <br> **DEATH:** Aug. 1964 |

### HIS LIFE

When Britton Marion Meek was born on March 26, 1834, in Augusta, Georgia, his father, Blaney was 39 and his mother, Rebecca was 26. He married Caroline Jennings on November 6, 1856, in Tallapoosa, Alabama.

During the Civil War, he served as a Private and later a Corporal in Company A, "The Tallapoosa Rifles," 1st Alabama Infantry Regiment. He was captured at Port Hudson, Louisiana on July 9, 1863. He was exchanged and captured again at Nashville, Tennessee on December 15, 1864. He was held prisoner until the end of the war.

Britton and Caroline had ten children in 22-years. He died on October 7, 1919, in Peytonsville, Tennessee at the age of 85. He is buried in the Cool Springs Cemetery.

# ABRAM WOOLRIDGE HATCHER
# 1835-1902

### HATCHER FAMILY

### HUSBAND'S PARENTS
**William Samuel Hatcher**   **Lucy Rucker**
1793 - 1866                   1797 - 1884

### 1ST WIFE'S PARENTS
**Eli Dodson**   **Elizabeth Fitzgerald**
1803 - 1877      1806 - 1850

**George W. Chriesman**     **Jane Sprott**
1801 - 1868     1817 - 1881

## HUSBAND
**Abram Woolridge Hatcher**
**BIRTH:** 24 Apr. 1835, Peytonsville, TN
**DEATH:** 28 Apr. 1902, Peytonsville, TN

## 1ST WIFE
**Mary Susan Dodson**
**BIRTH:** 23 June 1842, TN
**DEATH:** 2 Sep. 1865, Williamson Co. TN

## 2ND WIFE
**Martha Elizabeth Chriesman**
**BIRTH:** 27 Dec. 1844, TN
**DEATH:** 20 July 1912, Arno, TN

## CHILDREN OF ABRAM AND MARY

**John Ernest**
**Hatcher-Son**
**BIRTH:** 11 July 1859
**DEATH:** 22 Oct. 1925

**William Dodson**
**Hatcher-Son**
**BIRTH:** 14 May 1861
**DEATH:** 27 Sep. 1911

## CHILDREN OF ABRAM AND MARTHA

**Mary Susan Hatcher**
**Daughter**
**BIRTH:** 13 Apr. 1870
**DEATH:** 3 Feb. 1934

**James Chriesman**
**Hatcher-Son**
**BIRTH:** 1872
**DEATH:** 31 Dec. 1929

**Charles Woolridge**
**Hatcher-Son**
**BIRTH:** 21 July 1873
**DEATH:** 1 Nov. 1914

**Lucy Jane Hatcher**
**Daughter**
**BIRTH:** 8 July 1875
**DEATH:** 10 Jan. 1945

**Sarah Alice Hatcher**
**Daughter**
**BIRTH:** 14 Aug. 1877
**DEATH:** 15 Sep. 1940

**Elizabeth Ruth**
**Hatcher-Daughter**
**BIRTH:** 7 Mar. 1880
**DEATH:** 5 Feb. 1932

**Madeline Lowry**
**Hatcher-Daughter**
**BIRTH:** 31 Oct. 1882
**DEATH:** 11 Apr. 1953

**George Abram**
**Hatcher-Son**
**BIRTH:** 21 June 1885
**DEATH:** 16 Mar. 1974

## HIS LIFE

When Abram Woolridge Hatcher was born on April 24, 1835, in Peytonsville, Tennessee, his father, William was 41 and his mother, Lucy was 37. He married Mary Susan Dodson in Williamson County, Tennessee on October 12, 1858. They had two children together before she died on September 2, 1865. He then married, Martha Elizabeth Chriesman on March 26, 1868, when he was 32-years old. They had eight children together. He died on April 28, 1902, in Peytonsville, Tennessee at the age of 67. He was buried in the Mt. Hope Cemetery in Franklin, Tennessee.

MARTHA (CHRIESMAN) AND
ABRAM WOOLRIDGE HATCHER

# GEORGE WASHINGTON BOYD
## 1837-1927

### BOYD FAMILY

**HUSBAND'S PARENTS**
**George G. Boyd**    **Martha Ann Walker**
1800 - 1841    1800 - ?

**WIFE'S PARENTS**
**Timothy Terrell**    **Nancy W. Dodson**
1810 - 1859    1818 - 1846

**HUSBAND**
**George Washington Boyd**
**BIRTH:** 29 Apr. 1837, Peytonsville, TN
**DEATH:** 24 Jan. 1927, Peytonsville, TN

**WIFE**
**Sarah R. Terrell**
**BIRTH:** 18 Aug. 1838, Franklin, TN
**DEATH:** 1906

### CHILDREN

| | |
|---|---|
| **James Abner Boyd** Son | **BIRTH:** 7 Oct. 1862 **DEATH:** 20 Nov. 1918 |
| **John Wesley Boyd** Son | **BIRTH:** 8 Apr. 1864 **DEATH:** 8 May. 1923 |
| **Martha Ann Boyd** Daughter | **BIRTH:** 7 Jun. 1872 **DEATH:** 25 Oct. 1948 |
| **Margaret Boyd** Daughter | **BIRTH:** Apr. 1874 **DEATH:** 1963 |
| **Oscar C. Boyd** Son | **BIRTH:** Jun. 1879 **DEATH:** 13 Feb. 1934 |

### HIS LIFE

When George Washington Boyd was born on April 29, 1837, in Tennessee, his father George was 37 and his mother, Martha was 36. George, a private, fought for the Confederacy during the Civil War. He married, Sarah R. Terrell on October 13, 1861, in Williamson County, Tennessee. They had five children in 16-years. He died on January 24, 1927, at the age of 89. He is buried in the Mount Hope Cemetery in Franklin, Tennessee.

# ROBERT D. GRAY
## 1837-1905

### GRAY FAMILY

**HUSBAND'S PARENTS**
**Robert Gray**    **Patsey Martha Holland**
1787 - 1873    1800 - 1876

**WIFE'S PARENTS**
**Richard B. Crunk**    **Nancy L. Hardeman**
1814-1871    1817-1868

**HUSBAND**
**Robert Gray**
**BIRTH:** Aug. 1837, Peytonsville, TN
**DEATH:** 27 Apr. 1905, Peytonsville, TN

**WIFE**
**Mary Susan Crunk**
**BIRTH:** May 1839, Peytonsville, TN
**DEATH:** 1900, Peytonsville TN

### CHILDREN

| | |
|---|---|
| **Mary R. Gray** Daughter | **BIRTH:** 1863 **DEATH:** Unknown |
| **Sarah E. Gray** Daughter | **BIRTH:** 1867 **DEATH:** Unknown |
| **Richard T. Gray** Son | **BIRTH:** 17 Oct. 1867 **DEATH:** 21 Mar. 1917 |
| **W.H. Gray** Son | **BIRTH:** 1869 **DEATH:** 1880 |
| **Liddie L. Gray** Daughter | **BIRTH:** 1872 **DEATH:** Unknown |

| Martha Mattie J. Gray<br>Daughter | BIRTH: 10 July 1875<br>DEATH: 25 Apr. 1915 |
| --- | --- |
| Susan Gray<br>Daughter | BIRTH: 1878<br>DEATH: Unknown |
| Gertrude Gray<br>Daughter | BIRTH: 1882<br>DEATH: Unknown |
| Jonas E. Gray<br>Son | BIRTH: 27 Jan. 1884<br>DEATH: Unknown |
| Arthur E. Gray<br>Son | BIRTH: 14 Sep. 1890<br>DEATH: Unknown |

### HIS LIFE

When Robert D. Gray was born in August, 1837, in Peytonsville, Tennessee, his father, Robert was 50 and his mother, Patsey was 37. He married Mary Susan Crunk on October 4, 1860, in Peytonsville. They had ten children in 26-years. He died on April 27, 1905, in Peytonsville, Tennessee at the age of 67.

ROBERT D. GRAY

# GEORGE WASHINGTON SMITHSON
# 1838-1900

## SMITHSON FAMILY

### HUSBAND'S PARENTS
**William G. Smithson**     **Mary A.E. Crenshaw**
1819 - 1852                         1820 - 1846

### WIFE'S PARENTS
**Samuel Henderson M.D.  Rachel Hughes**
1804 - 1884                         1818 - 1858

### HUSBAND
**George Washington Smithson**
BIRTH: 30 Dec. 1838, Lunenburg Co. VA
DEATH: 1 Oct. 1900, Franklin, TN

### WIFE
**Sarah Martin Henderson**
BIRTH: 14 Sep. 1847, Williamson Co. TN
DEATH: 26 Oct. 1899, Franklin, TN

### CHILDREN

| Janie Smithson<br>Daughter | BIRTH: 30 Jan. 1873<br>DEATH: 6 May 1952 |
| --- | --- |
| George Henderson<br>Smithson-Son | BIRTH: 23 Sep. 1874<br>DEATH: 18 Mar. 1958 |
| Mary S. Smithson<br>Daughter | BIRTH: 1876<br>DEATH: 6 May 1952 |
| Sallie Martin<br>Smithson-Daughter | BIRTH: 27 Apr. 1878<br>DEATH: 15 Oct. 1966 |

### HIS LIFE

When George Washington Smithson was born on December 30, 1838, in Lunenburg County, Virginia, his father, William was 19 and his mother, Mary was 18.

George lived on a farm until he reached the age of thirteen. He then began clerking in the store of Charles W. Smithson at Peytonsville, Tennessee. He continued to clerk until 1859, he went into business for himself at Peytonsville in a partnership with John C. Helms. He remained in this business until 1861. He then enlisted in Captain Ewing's Company, First Battalion, Tennessee Cavalry. He enrolled on May 28, 1861 in Franklin, Tennessee.

In 1865, George opened a dry goods business in Franklin. In the spring of 1865, he became a partner of the firm, Smithson, Kennedy, Hodge & Co. This was the most extensive dry goods store in Franklin at the time.

On February 9, 1871, George married, Sallie Martin Henderson in Franklin. They had 4 children during their marriage. He died on October 1, 1900, in Franklin at the age of 61. He was buried in Mount Hope Cemetery in Franklin, Tennessee.

# TURNEL LUNDY GREEN HARRISON
## 1838-1918

### HARRISON FAMILY

**HUSBAND'S PARENTS**

**Nathaniel Lundy Harrison**  **Christina T. Knight**
1808 - 1885                 1811 - 1862

**WIFE'S PARENTS**

**Benjamin Franklin Martin**  **Jane D. Alston**
1820 - 1862                 1824 - 1906

### HUSBAND
**Turnel Lundy Green Harrison**
**BIRTH:** 5 June 1838, Peytonsville, TN
**DEATH:** 22 May 1918, Davidson Co. TN

### WIFE
**Ellen Augusta Martin**
**BIRTH:** 13 Feb. 1842, Williamson Co. TN
**DEATH:** 21 Apr. 1898

### CHILDREN

| | |
|---|---|
| **Covoda Harrison** Daughter | **BIRTH:** 22 Oct. 1863 **DEATH:** 2 Feb. 1907 |
| **Modera Harrison** Daughter | **BIRTH:** 22 May 1865 **DEATH:** 22 May 1914 |
| **Odora "Oudo" Harrison-Daughter** | **BIRTH:** 1871 **DEATH:** 28 May 1899 |
| **Goldie G. Harrison** Son | **BIRTH:** 19 Aug. 1877 **DEATH:** 9 Dec. 1900 |

### HIS LIFE

When Turnel Lundy Green Harrison was born on June 5, 1838, in Peytonsville, Tennessee, his father, Nathaniel was 29 and his mother, Christina was 26. He was raised in the Peytonsville area and worked on his father's farm until 1858, when he entered into merchandising in Nashville.

Turnel enlisted in the Civil War at Nashville, Tennessee on October 30, 1861. He was elected Third Lieutenant of Company F, 4th Tennessee Cavalry and promoted to Second Lieutenant in place of, T.F.P. Allison on December 11, 1861. He received a saber wound in the thigh at Altamont in April 1862. He resigned his commission and withdrew from service on May 26, 1862.

Turnel married, Ellen Augusta Martin on January 13, 1863 in Peytonsville. They had four children in 13-years. He died on May 22, 1918, in Davidson County, Tennessee at the age of 79.

Turnel Lundy Green Harrison
1838-1918
3rd Lt. Co F 4th TN Cavalry

# THOMAS GEORGE PATE

## 1838-1921

PATE FAMILY

**HUSBAND'S PARENTS**
**Thomas Pate    Martha E.H. Beatty**
1799 - 1872    1800 - 1847

**1ST WIFE'S PARENTS**
**Gabriel R. Low    Lavinia Howard Pinkston**
1808 - 1882    1820 - 1893

**2ND WIFE'S PARENTS**
**James K.P. Rucker    Virginia M.E. Pearce**
1844 - 1888    1849 - 1913

**HUSBAND**
**Thomas George Pate**
BIRTH: 7 Jan. 1838, Peytonsville, TN
DEATH: 8 Feb. 1921, Mineral Wells, TX

**1ST WIFE**
**Viney Angeline Low**
BIRTH: 21 Aug. 1843, Williamson Co. TN
DEATH: Sep. 1879, Williamson Co. TN

**2ND WIFE**
**Lou Eugenia Rucker**
BIRTH: 16 Oct. 1870, Ripley, MS
DEATH: 8 Apr. 1959, Mineral Wells, TX

**CHILDREN OF THOMAS GEORGE AND VINEY**

| | |
|---|---|
| **William David Pate** Son | BIRTH: 1867 DEATH: 20 Jan. 1907 |
| **Gebreella Pate** Daughter | BIRTH: 1869 DEATH: Unknown |
| **Josie Pate** Son | BIRTH: 1872 DEATH: Unknown |
| **Robert Pate** Son | BIRTH: 1874 DEATH: Unknown |
| **Thomas George Pate Jr.-Son** | BIRTH: 27 Jan. 1877 DEATH: 12 Aug. 1956 |

**CHILDREN OF THOMAS GEORGE AND Lou**

| Sarah Virginia Pate | **BIRTH:** 30 Jun. 1900 |
| Daughter | **DEATH:** 10 May 1976 |

### HIS LIFE

When Thomas George Pate was born on January 7, 1838, in Peytonsville, Tennessee, his father, Thomas was 39 and his mother, Martha was 38.

He served in the 20th Tennessee Infantry in the Civil War. After the War he married, Viney Angeline Low on October 24, 1865, in Peytonsville, Tennessee. They had five children together. Viney died in 1879.

Sometime after 1881, Thomas George and a group of people from Peytonsville and College Grove set out on a journey to relocate to Texas. There was about 60 people in the party. On July 12, 1898, Thomas George married, Lou Eugenia Rucker in Palo Pinto, Texas, when he was 60-years old.

Thomas George Pate served as postmaster of Boyce, Texas for 32-years and a merchant for 56-years in that same town. He was also a Master of No. 900, Masonic Lodge for some period. He died on February 8, 1921, in Mineral Wells, Texas when he was 83-years old.

THOMAS GEORGE PATE

# WILLIAM LEWIS JOHNSON
## 1840-1908

### JOHNSON FAMILY

#### HUSBAND'S PARENTS

| **Gregory Johnson** | **Rachael M. Corzine** |
| 1809 - 1887 | 1812 - ? |

#### WIFE'S PARENTS

| **John S. Allen** | **Lucinda Wiley** |
| 1813 - ? | 1816 - 1875 |

#### HUSBAND
**William Lewis Johnson**
**BIRTH:** 16 June 1840, Peytonsville, TN
**DEATH:** 1 Apr. 1908. Nashville, TN

#### WIFE
**Elizabeth Allen**
**BIRTH:** 1843
**DEATH:** 10 May 1922, Nashville, TN

### CHILDREN

| Ella Rachel Johnson | **BIRTH:** 1866 |
| Daughter | **DEATH:** Unknown |

| Lucinda Virginia | **BIRTH:** 25 Oct. 1868 |
| Johnson-Daughter | **DEATH:** 23 Feb. 1935 |

| Walter Lee Johnson | **BIRTH:** 20 Mar. 1871 |
| Son | **DEATH:** 21 Nov. 1944 |

| Cora Johnson | **BIRTH:** 1875 |
| Daughter | **DEATH:** Unknown |

| Richard Johnson | **BIRTH:** 1877 |
| Son | **DEATH:** Unknown |

| Muray M. Johnson | **BIRTH:** Nov. 1881 |
| Son | **DEATH:** 7 Dec. 1951 |

### HIS LIFE

When William Lewis Johnson was born on June 16, 1840, in Williamson County, Tennessee, his father, Gregory was 30 and his mother, Rachael was 28. He married, Elizabeth Allen on October 10, 1864, in Peytonsville, Tennessee. They had six children in 15-years. He died on April 1, 1908, in Nashville, Tennessee at the age of 67.

# MARK WILSON VADEN
## 1840-1919

### VADEN FAMILY

#### HUSBAND'S PARENTS
**Joseph A. Vaden**   **Catherine G. Wilson**
1806 - 1850       1814 - 1873

#### WIFE'S PARENTS
**Gregory Johnson**   **Rachael M. Corzine**
1809 - 1887       1812 - ?

#### HUSBAND
**Mark Wilson Vaden**
BIRTH: 19 Apr. 1840, Peytonsville, TN
DEATH: 26 Jan. 1919, Peytonsville, TN

#### WIFE
**Martha J. Johnson**
BIRTH: 5 Apr. 1845, Peytonsville, TN
DEATH: 20 May 1919, Peytonsville TN

### CHILDREN

| | | |
|---|---|---|
| **Joseph Vaden** Son | BIRTH: June 1867 | DEATH: 21 Dec. 1920 |
| **James M. Vaden** Son | BIRTH: 1869 | DEATH: 1912 |
| **William Edgar Vaden** Son | BIRTH: 1872 | DEATH: 22 Oct. 1934 |
| **Alva Lee Vaden** Son | BIRTH: 24 May 1874 | DEATH: 31 Jan. 1954 |
| **John Henry Vaden** Son | BIRTH: 1876 | DEATH: 1940 |
| **Ely Howard Vaden** Son | BIRTH: 1877 | DEATH: 2 Aug. 1940 |
| **Blanche M. Vaden** Daughter | BIRTH: 21 Apr. 1882 | DEATH: 10 Sep. 1943 |

### HIS LIFE

When Mark Wilson Vaden was born on April 19, 1840, in Williamson County, Tennessee, his father, Joseph was 34 and his mother, Catherine was 26.

When the Civil War broke out, Mark went to Alabama where his parents once lived to join the Confederate Army. He became the 2nd Corporal, Company I, 27th Alabama Infantry Regiment.

Mark married Martha J. Johnson on September 13, 1866, in Peytonsville, Tennessee. They had seven children in 14-years. He died on January 26, 1919, in Peytonsville at the age of 78. He is buried in the Mount Hope Cemetery in Franklin, Tennessee.

MARK WILSON VADEN

# THOMAS ALEXANDER "ECK" DAVIS
## 1840-1919

### DAVIS FAMILY

**HUSBAND'S PARENTS**

**John Davis**    **Rachel Greer**
1795 - 1848      1800 - 1858

**WIFE'S PARENTS**

**David Ransom Ray**    **Catherine J. Whitten**
1808 - 1867             1815 - 1868

### HUSBAND
**Thomas Alexander "Eck" Davis**
**BIRTH:** 25 Jan. 1840, Tallapoosa, AL
**DEATH:** 17 Jan. 1919, Peytonsville, TN

### WIFE
**Nancy Elizabeth Ray**
**BIRTH:** 3 Dec. 1841, Meriwether Co. GA
**DEATH:** 29 Jan. 1925, Peytonsville, TN

### CHILDREN

| | |
|---|---|
| **Margaret Elizabeth Davis-Daughter** | **BIRTH:** 19 Jan. 1868 <br> **DEATH:** 24 Oct. 1874 |
| **William Early Davis Son** | **BIRTH:** 20 Nov. 1870 <br> **DEATH:** 27 Aug. 1945 |
| **Jonah D. Davis Son** | **BIRTH:** 1 Oct. 1873 <br> **DEATH:** 30 Oct. 1880 |
| **Florence Rebecca Davis-Daughter** | **BIRTH:** 25 Feb. 1874 <br> **DEATH:** 1933 |
| **Greer Jordan Davis Daughter** | **BIRTH:** 19 Jan. 1879 <br> **DEATH:** 13 Jun. 1926 |
| **Lucy Thomas Davis Daughter** | **BIRTH:** 8 July 1882 <br> **DEATH:** 25 Sep. 1969 |

### HIS LIFE

When Thomas Alexander "Eck" Davis was born on January 25, 1840, in Tallapoosa, Alabama his father, John was 45 and his mother, Rachel was 40.

In 1860, Thomas "Eck" was living with his brother John Daniel Davis and his family in Tallapoosa County, Alabama. He was a soldier in the Civil War in Alabama. He married Nancy Elizabeth Ray on December 29, 1866. Nancy had two children from her previous marriage. Her first husband, John Ransom Franklin Farrow died in an unknown location in the Civil War. By 1873, they were living in Tennessee along with other Tallapoosa County, Alabama families, namely the Bill Ray family, the Mathis family, Adairs, Kings and Meek.

Eck and Nancy had six children in 14-years. He died on January 17, 1919, in Williamson County, Tennessee at the age of 78. He is buried in the Cool Springs Cemetery in Peytonsville, Tennessee.

THOMAS ALEXANDER "ECK" DAVIS

# JESSE HENDERSON JOHNSON
## 1842-1914

### JOHNSON FAMILY

#### HUSBAND'S PARENTS
**Gregory Johnson**      **Rachael M. Corzine**
1809 - 1887                    1812 - 1888

#### 1ST WIFE'S PARENTS
**Hillary I. Harvey**      **Elizabeth P. Williams**
1826 - 1904                    1827 - 1877

#### 2ND WIFE'S PARENTS
**John Blythe Sprott**      **Sarah E. Crutcher**
1826 - 1897                    1831 - 1878

#### HUSBAND
**Jesse Henderson Johnson**
BIRTH: 6 Dec. 1842, Williamson Co, TN
DEATH: 27 Sep. 1914, Peytonsville, TN

#### 1ST WIFE
**Mary Elizabeth Harvey**
BIRTH: 1 Oct. 1848, TN
DEATH: 27 Oct. 1876, TN

#### 2ND WIFE
**Ophelia Zorilda Sprott**
BIRTH: 14 June 1851, Williamson Co. TN
DEATH: 22 Aug. 1917, Williamson Co. TN

#### CHILDREN OF JESSE AND MARY

**Fannie K. Johnson**
Daughter
BIRTH: 31 Oct. 1866
DEATH: 2 Nov. 1936

**Leander H. Johnson**
Son
BIRTH: 20 Feb. 1871
DEATH: 25 June 1926

**Callie E. Johnson**
Daughter
BIRTH: 16 Oct. 1876
DEATH: 12 Dec. 1939

### CHILDREN OF JESSE AND OPHELIA

**Mary V. Johnson**
Daughter
BIRTH: 22 Aug. 1882
DEATH: 28 May 1946

**Nancy Johnson**
Daughter
BIRTH: Aug. 1883
DEATH: BEF 1900

**Albert Johnson**
Son
BIRTH: 5 Aug. 1885
DEATH: 28 Apr. 1928

**John G. Johnson**
Son
BIRTH: 23 Jan. 1887
DEATH: Unknown

**Perry Evans Johnson**
Son
BIRTH: 21 Sep. 1888
DEATH: 14 June 1939

**James Andry Pink Johnson-Son**
BIRTH: Abt 1894
DEATH: 9 Feb. 1934

### HIS LIFE

When Jesse Henderson Johnson was born on December 6, 1842, in Williamson County, Tennessee, his father, Gregory was 33 and his mother, Rachael was 30. He married Mary Elizabeth Harvey and they had three children together. He then married Ophelia Zorilda Sprott and they had six children together. He died on September 27, 1914, in Williamson County at the age of 71. He was buried in Mount Hope Cemetery in Franklin, Tennessee.

# BENJAMIN FRANKLIN SMITHSON
## 1843-1909

### SMITHSON FAMILY

#### HUSBAND'S PARENTS
**Sylvanus W. Smithson**      **Mary Jane Gibson**
1810 - 1872                          1820 - 1862

#### WIFE'S PARENTS
**Andrew Washington Parks**      **Martha J. Boyd**

1820 - 1872                    1820 - 1848

## HUSBAND
**Benjamin Franklin Smithson**
**BIRTH:** 4 June 1843, Peytonsville, TN
**DEATH:** 3 Mar. 1909, Peytonsville, TN

## WIFE
**Martha Susan Parks**
**BIRTH:** 1849, TN
**DEATH:** 3 July 1937, Williamson Co. TN

## CHILDREN

| | |
|---|---|
| **William Henry Smithson-Son** | **BIRTH:** 6 Aug. 1870<br>**DEATH:** 24 Mar. 1942 |
| **Minnie S. Smithson** Daughter | **BIRTH:** 1872<br>**DEATH:** Unknown |
| **Mary Smithson** Daughter | **BIRTH:** 1873<br>**DEATH:** Unknown |
| **Mamie Gertrude Smithson-Daughter** | **BIRTH:** 11 Mar. 1874<br>**DEATH:** 1 Dec. 1939 |
| **Sylvanus Andrew Smithson-Son** | **BIRTH:** 24 Oct. 1879<br>**DEATH:** 4 Dec. 1947 |
| **Van Smithson** Son | **BIRTH:** 16 Nov. 1885<br>**DEATH:** 23 June 1950 |

## HIS LIFE

When Benjamin Franklin Smithson was born on June 4, 1843, in Peytonsville, Tennessee, his father Sylvanus was 32 and his mother, Mary was 23.

Benjamin served in the Civil War as 4th Sargent, Company D, 20th Tennessee Infantry Regiment. He enlisted on May 27, 1861.

After the War he married, Martha Susan Parks on October 15, 1868, in Peytonsville, Tennessee. They had six children in 15-years. He died on March 3, 1909, in Peytonsville at the age of 65 and was buried in the Gibson Cemetery in Peytonsville.

BENJAMIN FRANKLIN
SMITHSON

# MONROE CLAIBORNE LILLARD
# 1844-1891

## LILLARD FAMILY

### HUSBAND'S PARENTS
**John D. Lillard**      **Rachel Jarrell**
1802 - 1864              1801 - 1864

### 1ST WIFE'S PARENTS
**Robert Bigger**      **Elizabeth Price**
1819 - 1855              1815 - ?

### 2ND WIFE'S PARENTS
**James S. Hay**      **Elizabeth Holland**
1805 - ?                    ? - ?

### HUSBAND
**Monroe Claiborne Lillard**
**BIRTH:** 1844, Williamson Co. TN
**DEATH:** 1891, Peytonsville, TN

### 1ST WIFE

**Cynthia A. Bigger**
BIRTH: 1844, TN
DEATH: 1870, Williamson Co. TN

### 2ND WIFE
**Mary Penny Hay**
BIRTH: 24 Apr. 1847, Williamson Co. TN
DEATH: 24 Sep. 1917, Williamson Co. TN

### CHILDREN OF MONROE AND CYNTHIA

| Sarah Lillard | BIRTH: 1864 |
| Daughter | DEATH: Unknown |

### CHILDREN OF MONROE AND MARY

| Oliver C. Lillard | BIRTH: 15 Sep. 1873 |
| Son | DEATH: 7 Mar. 1953 |
| Johnnie S. Lillard | BIRTH: 1876 |
| Son | DEATH: Unknown |
| Richard M. Lillard | BIRTH: 1878 |
| Son | DEATH: 26 Oct. 1940 |
| Lemuel Hamilton Lillard-Son | BIRTH: 23 Dec. 1880 |
| | DEATH: 8 Feb. 1935 |

### HIS LIFE

When Monroe Claiborne Lillard was born in 1844, in Williamson County, Tennessee, his father, John was 42 and his mother, Rachel was 43. He married Cynthia A. Bigger on January 3, 1863. They had one child. When she died in 1870, he married, Mary Penny Hay on November 3, 1870. They had four children together. He died in 1891, in Peytonsville, Tennessee at the age of 47.

# JOHN E. CRUNK
## 1844-1904

### CRUNK FAMILY

### HUSBAND'S PARENTS
| Richard B. Crunk | Nancy L. Hardeman |
| 1814 - 1871 | 1817 - 1868 |

### WIFE'S PARENTS
| Holcomb P. Harvey | Martha A. Elliott |
| 1820 - 1885 | 1820 - 1884 |

### HUSBAND
**John E. Crunk**
BIRTH: 4 Oct. 1844, Williamson Co. TN
DEATH: 17 Aug. 1904, Peytonsville, TN

### WIFE
**Mary E. Harvey**
BIRTH: ABT 1847, TN
DEATH: 2 Oct. 1910, Williamson Co. TN

### CHILDREN

| William P. Crunk | BIRTH: 27 Aug. 1867 |
| Son | DEATH: 26 June 1941 |
| Samuel Crunk | BIRTH: 1870 |
| Daughter | DEATH: BEF 1880 |
| Zula Myrtle Crunk | BIRTH: 8 July 1870 |
| Daughter | DEATH: 31 Oct. 1906 |
| John Henry Crunk | BIRTH: 6 June 1876 |
| Son | DEATH: 13 June 1956 |
| Harvey Perkins Crunk | BIRTH: 1879 |
| Son | DEATH: 1912 |

### HIS LIFE

When John E. Crunk was born on October 4, 1844 in Williamson County, Tennessee, his father Richard was 30 and his mother Nancy was 27. He married Mary E. Harvey on August 2, 1867 in Peytonsville. They had five children in 12-years. He died on August 17, 1904, in Williamson County at the age of 59.

## NATHANIEL BEDFORD VADEN
## 1844-1927

### VADEN FAMILY

#### HUSBAND'S PARENTS
**William Henry Vaden**     **Martha W. Smithson**
1804 - 1885                 1806 - 1880

#### WIFE'S PARENTS
**John Wilson Gibson**     **Martha H. Lester**
1817 - 1870                1815 - 1869

#### HUSBAND
**Nathaniel Bedford Vaden**
**BIRTH:** Feb. 1844, Williamson Co. TN
**DEATH:** 20 Jan. 1927, Peytonsville, TN

#### WIFE
**Susan Tennessee Gibson**
**BIRTH:** 1 Feb. 1847, TN
**DEATH:** 10 May 1913, TN

#### CHILDREN

**Charles Wilson Vaden** **BIRTH:** 7 Aug. 1869
Son                      **DEATH:** 16 June 1935

**Martha Virginia Vaden** **BIRTH:** May 1873
Daughter                  **DEATH:** 27 Jan. 1927

**William H. Vaden** **BIRTH:** 21 June 1877
Son                  **DEATH:** 15 June 1940

**Ella Vaden** **BIRTH:** 27 Aug. 1879
Daughter       **DEATH:** 29 May 1952

**Alice Vaden** **BIRTH:** July 1884
Daughter        **DEATH:** 13 Apr. 1972

**Sarah Lou Vaden** **BIRTH:** 25 Jan. 1889
Daughter            **DEATH:** 5 June 1943

### HIS LIFE

When Nathaniel Bedford Vaden was born in February 1844, in Peytonsville, Tennessee, his father, William was 40 and his mother, Martha was 38. He married Susan Tennessee Gibson on October 18, 1868, in Peytonsville. They had six children in 19-years. He died on January 20, 1927, in Peytonsville at the age of 82. He is buried in the Vaden Family Cemetery in Peytonsville.

## WILLIAM PRICE LADD
## 1847-1915

### LADD FAMILY

#### HUSBAND'S PARENTS
**Joseph H. Ladd**     **Emily C. Waggoner**
1816 - 1910            1826 - ?

#### WIFE'S PARENTS
**Thomas Burnett**     **Elizabeth Jane Gray**
1821 - 1881            1828 - ?

#### HUSBAND
**William Price Ladd**
**BIRTH:** 17 Feb. 1847, Williamson Co. TN
**DEATH:** 20 Jan. 1915, Peytonsville, TN

#### WIFE
**Martha F. Burnett**
**BIRTH:** 2 Sep. 1847, Williamson Co. TN
**DEATH:** 30 July 1930, Williamson Co. TN

#### CHILDREN

**Thomas B. Ladd** **BIRTH:** Dec. 1875
Son                **DEATH:** 28 Feb. 1957

**Josie Emma Ladd** **BIRTH:** 5 May 1876
Daughter            **DEATH:** 18 Sep. 1945

**William Price Ladd Jr.** **BIRTH:** 28 June 1877
Son                        **DEATH:** 24 May 1964

**Edgar Ladd** **BIRTH:** 30 July 1878
Son            **DEATH:** 30 July 1879

| Elmer Ladd<br>Son | **BIRTH:** 30 July 1878<br>**DEATH:** 30 July 1879 |
| --- | --- |
| Robert N. Ladd<br>Son | **BIRTH:** 24 Dec. 1879<br>**DEATH:** 12 Sep. 1953 |
| Thornton Ladd<br>Son | **BIRTH:** Feb. 1882<br>**DEATH:** Unknown |
| Leonard Lee Ladd<br>Son | **BIRTH:** 4 Sep. 1883<br>**DEATH:** 8 July 1949 |

## HIS LIFE

When William Price Ladd was born on February 17, 1847, in Williamson County, Tennessee, his father, Joseph was 30 and his mother, Emily was 21. He married Martha F. Burnett on February 26, 1874, in Williamson County, Tennessee. They had eight children during their marriage.

William died on January 20, 1915, in Peytonsville, Tennessee at the age of 67. He is buried in the Ladd Cemetery.

# JOSEPH JONES HARRISON
# 1847-1915

### HARRISON FAMILY

### HUSBAND'S PARENTS
**Nathaniel Lundy Harrison**  **Christina T. Knight**
1808 - 1885                 1811 - 1862

### WIFE'S PARENTS
**Henry W. Stegall**    **Elizabeth C. Gee**
1827 - 1862            1830 - 1900

### HUSBAND
**Joseph Jones Harrison**
**BIRTH:** 3 Oct. 1847, Peytonsville, TN
**DEATH:** 13 Jan. 1919, Williamson Co, TN

### WIFE
**Mary Catherine Stegall**
**BIRTH:** 12 Feb. 1860, Peytonsville, TN
**DEATH:** 20 Dec. 1934, Franklin, TN

### CHILDREN

| Nathaniel Henry<br>Harrison-Son | **BIRTH:** 1878<br>**DEATH:** Unknown |
| --- | --- |
| Era M. Harrison<br>Daughter | **BIRTH:** ABT 1880<br>**DEATH:** 1940 |
| Modie Wallace<br>Harrison-Son | **BIRTH:** 27 Dec. 1894<br>**DEATH:** 24 Nov. 1949 |

### HIS LIFE

When Joseph Jones Harrison was born on October 3, 1847, in Peytonsville, Tennessee, his father, Nathaniel was 38 and his mother, Christina was 35.

Joseph joined his brothers in battle during the Civil War. He enlisted on June 1, 1863, in Murfreesboro, Tennessee with Company D, 25th

Tennessee Infantry Regiment as a Teamster. He was captured near Drewry's Bluff in Virginia on May 16, 1864, and exchanged on October 11, 1864. He spent time in the dreaded prison of Point Lookout, Maryland which was the largest and one of the worst Union prisoner-of-war camps. It was located at the extreme tip of St. Mary's County, on the long, low, and barren peninsula where the Potomac River joins Chesapeake Bay. At one time this Union prison held 20,000 prisoners, because it was so close to the battlefields on the Eastern Theater. He was at sometime transferred to Elmira, New York, known to the Confederates as "Hellmira," the notorious Civil War prison camp on the banks of the Chemung River.

Joseph married, Mary Catherine Stegall on October 31, 1876, in Peytonsville, Tennessee. They had three children in 16-years. He died on January 13, 1919, in Williamson County, Tennessee at the age of 71. He is buried in Mount Hope Cemetery in Franklin, Tennessee.

# BRICE HUGHES
## 1847-1915

### HUGHES FAMILY

### HUSBAND'S PARENTS
**Father Unknown    Mother Unknown**

### WIFE'S PARENTS
**Father Unknown    Mother Unknown**

### HUSBAND
**Brice Hughes**
**BIRTH:** Nov. 1847, Williamson Co. TN
**DEATH:** 1915, Williamson Co. TN

### WIFE
**Mary Thornton**
**BIRTH:** 1839, TN
**DEATH:** 1900, Williamson Co. TN

### CHILDREN

| | |
|---|---|
| **Sandy Hughes** <br> Son | **BIRTH:** 1869 <br> **DEATH:** 3 Oct. 1948 |
| **Brice William Hughes** <br> Son | **BIRTH:** Oct. 1870 <br> **DEATH:** 19 May 1930 |
| **Mary Jane Hughes** <br> Daughter | **BIRTH:** Aug. 1873 <br> **DEATH:** 11 Feb. 1925 |
| **Eula Hughes** <br> Son | **BIRTH:** Oct. 1875 <br> **DEATH:** 4 May 1928 |
| **James H. Hughes** <br> Son | **BIRTH:** 1876 <br> **DEATH:** Unknown |
| **Sallie M. Hughes** <br> Daughter | **BIRTH:** Oct. 1876 <br> **DEATH:** 1906 |
| **Winnie E. Hughes** <br> Daughter | **BIRTH:** 1878 <br> **DEATH:** Unknown |
| **Eliza Hughes** <br> Daughter | **BIRTH:** 9 July 1884 <br> **DEATH:** 19 Nov. 1951 |

Brice Hughes was born in November, 1847, in Williamson County, Tennessee. He married, Mary Thornton about 1869. They had four sons and four daughters between 1869 and 1884. Brice died in 1915, in Williamson County, Tennessee when he was 68-years old.

# JOHN MILTON HATCHER
# 1848-1923

### HATCHER FAMILY

### HUSBAND'S PARENTS
**John Rucker Hatcher   Matilda Spiers Hatcher**
1818 - 1857                      1823 - 1874

### 1ST WIFE'S PARENTS
**George W. Chriesman     Jane Spratt**
1801 - 1868               1817 - 1881

### 2ND WIFE'S PARENTS
**John Smith Battle    Martha Elizabeth Gant**
1832 - 1906               1835 - 1916

### HUSBAND
**John Milton Hatcher**
**BIRTH:** 12 June 1848, Williamson Co. TN
**DEATH:** 30 Dec. 1923, Williamson Co. TN

### 1ST WIFE
**Sarah Ruth Chriesman**
**BIRTH:** 19 Aug. 1852, Williamson Co. TN
**DEATH:** 24 Sep. 1882, Williamson Co. TN

### 2ND WIFE
**Willie Mayo Battle**
**BIRTH:** 8 Dec. 1858, Williamson Co. TN
**DEATH:** 24 Sep. 1917, Williamson Co. TN

### CHILDREN OF JOHN AND SARAH

| | |
|---|---|
| **Milton Chriesman Hatcher-Son** | **BIRTH:** 14 Aug. 1875 <br> **DEATH:** 27 Dec. 1956 |
| **Edgar White Hatcher** Son | **BIRTH:** 3 Jan. 1878 <br> **DEATH:** 5 Sep. 1960 |
| **John Rucker Hatcher** Son | **BIRTH:** 8 Nov. 1879 <br> **DEATH:** 2 July 1880 |
| **Andrew Charles Hatcher-Son** | **BIRTH:** 15 July 1881 <br> **DEATH:** 2 May 1914 |

### CHILDREN OF JOHN AND WILLIE

| | |
|---|---|
| **Ben Gant Hatcher** Son | **BIRTH:** 12 Feb. 1886 <br> **DEATH:** 14 Apr. 1889 |
| **Alice Ruth Hatcher** Daughter | **BIRTH:** 25 Apr. 1887 <br> **DEATH:** 23 Mar. 1972 |
| **Jessie Mae Hatcher** Daughter | **BIRTH:** 25 Mar. 1889 <br> **DEATH:** 14 Nov. 1917 |
| **Kathleen Hatcher** Daughter | **BIRTH:** 1891 <br> **DEATH:** 1892 |
| **James Battle Hatcher** Son | **BIRTH:** 31 July 1892 <br> **DEATH:** 9 Aug. 1982 |
| **John William Hatcher** Son | **BIRTH:** 1895 <br> **DEATH:** Unknown |

### HIS LIFE

When John Milton Hatcher was born on June 12, 1848, in Williamson County, Tennessee, his father, John was 29 and his mother, Matilda was 25. He married Sarah Ruth Chriesman on September 24, 1874. They had four children together. Sarah died on September 24, 1882, at the age of 30. John then married, Willie Mayo Battle on July 29, 1884, when he was 36-years old and they had six children.

John Milton Hatcher died on December 30, 1923, in Peytonsville at the age of 75. He is buried in the Hatcher Cemetery.

# WASH SMITHSON
## 1848-?

WASH SMITHSON

### SMITHSON FAMILY

#### HUSBAND'S PARENTS
**Father Unknown**    **Mother Unknown**

#### WIFE'S PARENTS
**Father Unknown**    **Mother Unknown**

#### HUSBAND
**Wash Smithson**
**BIRTH:** May, 1848, TN
**DEATH:** Williamson Co. TN

#### WIFE
**Susan Beal**
**BIRTH:** 1948, TN
**DEATH:** Williamson Co. TN

### CHILDREN

**Mattie Smithson**
**Daughter**
**BIRTH:** June 1884
**DEATH:** Unknown

**John Smithson**
**Son**
**BIRTH:** 24 May 1885
**DEATH:** 30 Nov. 1964

**Ozie Lee Smithson**
**Son**
**BIRTH:** 1 June 1888
**DEATH:** 27 Apr. 1930

**Parthonea Smithson**
**Daughter**
**BIRTH:** Nov. 1889
**DEATH:** 27 May 1910

### HIS LIFE

Wash Smithson was born in May, 1848, in Tennessee. He married Susan Beal on April 21, 1879, in Williamson County, Tennessee. They had four children during their marriage. He died in Williamson County.

# DAVID MONROE TOMLIN
## 1848-1933

### TOMLIN FAMILY

#### HUSBAND'S PARENTS
**David Monroe Tomlin**    **Alice Ella Graham**
1796 - 1884                1797 - 1886

#### WIFE'S PARENTS
**Henry Ford**    **Sarah E. Jackson**
1831 - 1920       1834 - 1907

#### HUSBAND
**David Monroe Tomlin**
**BIRTH:** 26 Oct. 1848, Williamson Co. TN
**DEATH:** 2 Feb. 1933, Peytonsville, TN

#### WIFE
**Martha Emma Ford**
**BIRTH:** 4 July 1855, Williamson Co. TN
**DEATH:** 3 Oct. 1907, Williamson Co. TN

CHILDREN

| | |
|---|---|
| **Henretta Tomlin** <br> Daughter | **BIRTH:** Sep. 1872 <br> **DEATH:** 13 Sep. 1928 |
| **Sallie B. Tomlin** <br> Daughter | **BIRTH:** 1875 <br> **DEATH:** 18 Sep. 1945 |
| **Sarah Tomlin** <br> Daughter | **BIRTH:** 1877 <br> **DEATH:** 1900 |
| **Charles David Tomlin** <br> Son | **BIRTH:** 1 June 1879 <br> **DEATH:** 1 July 1954 |
| **Rebecca Tomlin** <br> Daughter | **BIRTH:** 1882 <br> **DEATH:** Unknown |
| **Robert Claud "Bob" Tomlin-Son** | **BIRTH:** 13 Aug. 1885 <br> **DEATH:** 8 Nov. 1935 |
| **Ophelia Elizabeth Tomlin-Daughter** | **BIRTH:** 20 Aug. 1886 <br> **DEATH:** 20 Apr. 1939 |
| **Emma J. Tomlin** <br> Daughter | **BIRTH:** Mar. 1892 <br> **DEATH:** Unknown |
| **Irene Tomlin** <br> Daughter | **BIRTH:** 15 Mar. 1892 <br> **DEATH:** 26 Jan. 1951 |

## HIS LIFE

When David Monroe Tomlin was born on October 26, 1848, in Williamson County, Tennessee, his father, David was 52 and his mother, Alice was 51. During the Civil War, David joined the troops of Company G, 12th Tennessee US Cavalry.

David married Martha Emma Ford on April 5, 1872, in Peytonsville, Tennessee. They had nine children in 19-years. He died on February 2, 1933, in Williamson County, Tennessee at the age of 84. He was buried in the Cool Springs Baptist Church Cemetery in Peytonsville.

DAVID MONROE TOMLIN

# HENRY BEAL
# 1850-1911

BEAL FAMILY

**HUSBAND'S PARENTS**

| Richard H. Beal Jr. | Mary A.C. Moore |
|---|---|
| 1825 - 1910 | 1829 - 1884 |

**WIFE'S PARENTS**

| White Parrish | Martha Parrish |
|---|---|
| 1825 - ? | ? - ? |

HUSBAND
**Henry Beal**
**BIRTH:** Nov. 1850, Williamson Co. TN
**DEATH:** 3 Mar. 1911, Peytonsville, TN

WIFE
**Cornelia Parrish**
**BIRTH:** Dec. 1852, Williamson Co. TN
**DEATH:** 3 Aug. 1928, Williamson Co. TN

CHILDREN

| | |
|---|---|
| **William Henry Beal**<br>Son | **BIRTH:** 1874<br>**DEATH:** 17 Aug. 1950 |
| **Adaline Beal**<br>Daughter | **BIRTH:** 1875<br>**DEATH:** Unknown |
| **Tilton Beal**<br>Son | **BIRTH:** 25 May 1879<br>**DEATH:** 8 Apr. 1953 |
| **Hattie Beal**<br>Daughter | **BIRTH:** Nov. 1882<br>**DEATH:** 14 Mar. 1938 |
| **John Beal**<br>Son | **BIRTH:** 17 May 1883<br>**DEATH:** 29 Sep. 1958 |
| **Minnie Beal**<br>Daughter | **BIRTH:** Oct, 1883<br>**DEATH:** 13 June 1953 |
| **Johnie Beal**<br>Son | **BIRTH:** Dec. 1887<br>**DEATH:** Unknown |
| **Mary White Beal**<br>Daughter | **BIRTH:** 1 Apr. 1889<br>**DEATH:** Feb. 1968 |

### HIS LIFE

When Henry Beal was born in November, 1850, his father, Richard was 25 and his mother, Mary was 21. He married Cornelia Parrish on January 31, 1874, in Peytonsville, Tennessee. They had eight children in 15-years. He died on March 3, 1911, in Williamson County, Tennessee at the age of 60.

HENRY AND CORNELIA (PARRISH) BEAL

# JOSEPH "JOE" BENNETT PARKS
## 1850-1906

### PARKS FAMILY

#### HUSBAND'S PARENTS
**Andrew B. Parks**     **Elizabeth Gibson Barnett**
1793 - 1870                    1815 - 1901

#### WIFE'S PARENTS
**John Henry Sweeney**     **Mary Jane Johnson**
1828 - 1901                    1837 - 1876

#### HUSBAND
**Joseph "Joe" Bennett Parks**
**BIRTH:** 1850, Peytonsville, TN
**DEATH:** 17 Feb. 1906, Peytonsville, TN

#### WIFE
**Addie Ophelia F. Sweeney**
**BIRTH:** 31 Mar. 1858, TN
**DEATH:** 24 Jun. 1887, Peytonsville, TN

#### CHILDREN

| | |
|---|---|
| **Walter J. Parks**<br>Son | **BIRTH:** 8 Oct. 1878<br>**DEATH:** 13 Jul. 1955 |
| **Estelle Ophelia Parks**<br>Daughter | **BIRTH:** 27 Nov. 1879<br>**DEATH:** 1 Dec. 1961 |
| **Mary Elizabeth Parks**<br>Daughter | **BIRTH:** May, 1882<br>**DEATH:** 21 Sep. 1974 |
| **Andrew Magnus**<br>**Parks-Son** | **BIRTH:** 2 Aug,.1886<br>**DEATH:** 12 Oct. 1886 |

### HIS LIFE

When Joseph "Joe" Bennett Parks was born in 1850, in Williamson County, Tennessee, his father, Andrew was 56 and his mother, Elizabeth was 35. He married Addie Ophelia F. Sweeney on December 19, 1877, in Williamson County, Tennessee. They had four children during their marriage. He died on February 17, 1906, in Peytonsville, Tennessee at the age of 56.

# JOHN REECE BENNETT
# 1851-1941

### BENNETT FAMILY

### HUSBAND'S PARENTS
**Joseph Alexander Bennett  Martha S. McGee**
1824 - 1904                  1827 - 1896

### WIFE'S PARENTS
**Paul C. Garner     Martha Ann Rice**
1815 - 1860         1816 - 1880

### HUSBAND
**John Reece Bennett**
BIRTH: 22 Jan, 1851, Peytonsville, TN
DEATH: 13 Mar, 1941, Williamson Co. TN

### WIFE
**Martha Ann Garner**
BIRTH: 18 Aug, 1854, Williamson Co. TN
DEATH: 25 Feb, 1929, Williamson Co. TN

### CHILDREN

**Cora Ann Bennett**
Daughter
BIRTH: 4 Mar. 1878
DEATH: May 1973

**William Wright Bennett-Son**
BIRTH: Feb. 1881
DEATH: 9 May 1970

**Forest G. "Hood" Bennett-Son**
BIRTH: May 1883
DEATH: 1964

**James Morris Bennett** Son
BIRTH: 1884
DEATH: Unknown

**Dicus "Dyke" David Bennett-Son**
BIRTH: 28 Jan. 1886
DEATH: Jun. 1976

**Mattie Sue Bennett** Daughter
BIRTH: 9 Sep. 1886
DEATH: 10 May 1967

**Kelly Bennett** Son
BIRTH: 18 Aug. 1889
DEATH: 1979

**Pidgen Bennett** Daughter
BIRTH: Sep. 1890
DEATH: Unknown

**Joseph Bennett** Son
BIRTH: 9 Feb. 1893
DEATH: 22 Jan. 1958

### HIS LIFE

When John Reece Bennett was born on January 22, 1851, in Williamson County, Tennessee, his father, Joseph was 25 and his mother, Martha was 22. He married Martha Ann Garner on October 2, 1873, in Williamson County. They had nine children in 14-years. He died on March 13, 1941, in Peytonsville, Tennessee at the age of 90.

JOHN REECE BENNETT

212

# WILLIAM HENRY CRUNK
# 1852-1918

## CRUNK FAMILY

### HUSBAND'S PARENTS
**Richard B. Crunk**  **Nancy L. Hardeman**
1814 - 1871          1817 - 1868

### WIFE'S PARENTS
**Thomas A. Tanner**  **Harriet J. Russell**
1827 - 1895          1828 - ?

### HUSBAND
**William Henry Crunk**
**BIRTH:** 22 Aug. 1852, Peytonsville, TN
**DEATH:** 8 Nov. 1918, Williamson Co. TN

### WIFE
**Mary Elizabeth Tanner**
**BIRTH:** 3 June 1851, TN
**DEATH:** 15 Mar. 1926, Nashville, TN

### CHILDREN

| | |
|---|---|
| **Richard Thomas Crunk-Son** | **BIRTH:** 28 Apr. 1872 <br> **DEATH:** 4 Feb. 1930 |
| **Mary Ellen Crunk** Daughter | **BIRTH:** Oct. 1875 <br> **DEATH:** 7 Nov. 1932 |
| **Nora Jane Crunk** Daughter | **BIRTH:** 25 Feb. 1878 <br> **DEATH:** 16 Aug. 1968 |
| **Martha Louise Crunk** Daughter | **BIRTH:** 10 Jan. 1879 <br> **DEATH:** 20 July 1958 |
| **Susan "Susie" Lee Crunk-Daughter** | **BIRTH:** 5 Mar. 1886 <br> **DEATH:** June 1976 |
| **William Henry Crunk Jr.-Son** | **BIRTH:** 2 Jan. 1890 <br> **DEATH:** 20 Sep. 1958 |
| **Georgie Anna Crunk** Daughter | **BIRTH:** June 1896 <br> **DEATH:** 16 Feb. 1926 |

| | |
|---|---|
| **James Albert Crunk** Son | **BIRTH:** 26 Feb. 1909 <br> **DEATH:** 14 July 1981 |

## HIS LIFE

When William Henry Crunk was born on August 22, 1852, in Peytonsville, Tennessee, his father, Richard was 38 and his mother, Nancy was 35. He married Mary Elizabeth Tanner on August 12, 1871, in Peytonsville, Tennessee. They had eight children in 36-years. He died on November 8, 1918, in Peytonsville at the age of 66. He is buried in the Crunk-Ryan Cemetery in College Grove, Tennessee.

# WILLIAM OBIDIAH "OBE"
# SIMMONS
# 1852-1939

## SIMMONS FAMILY

### HUSBAND'S PARENTS
**James Henry Simmons**  **Rebecca E. Hill**
1825 - 1881              1813 - 1870

### WIFE'S PARENTS
**James Byrd Spann**  **Sarah Rebecca McCrary**
1816 - 1889          1820 - 1884

### HUSBAND
**William Obidiah Simmons**
**BIRTH:** 17 Nov. 1852, Williamson Co. TN
**DEATH:** 30 Apr. 1939, Peytonsville, TN

### WIFE
**Margaret "Maggie" A. Spann**
**BIRTH:** 27 Aug. 1857, TN
**DEATH:** 6 Oct. 1933, Peytonsville, TN

### CHILDREN

| | |
|---|---|
| **Sarah Rebecca Simmons-Daughter** | **BIRTH:** 3 Feb. 1882 <br> **DEATH:** 7 July 1882 |

| **William Oscar Simmons**-Son | **BIRTH:** 8 Aug. 1883 <br> **DEATH:** 10 Mar. 1943 |
|---|---|
| **Henry W. Simmons** Son | **BIRTH:** 5 Feb. 1885 <br> **DEATH:** Mar. 1971 |
| **Mary A. Simmons** Daughter | **BIRTH:** 7 Sep. 1886 <br> **DEATH:** 5 Oct. 1924 |
| **Ophelia F. Simmons** Daughter | **BIRTH:** 11 Nov. 1888 <br> **DEATH:** July 1967 |
| **Lillie Simmons** Daughter | **BIRTH:** 5 Oct. 1890 <br> **DEATH:** 22 Dec. 1946 |
| **James Robert Simmons**-Son | **BIRTH:** 2 Jan. 1895 <br> **DEATH:** 12 Feb. 1941 |
| **Lula Simmons** Daughter | **BIRTH:** 8 Jan. 1895 <br> **DEATH:** 21 Oct. 1929 |
| **Annice S. Simmons** Daughter | **BIRTH:** July 1897 <br> **DEATH:** Unknown |
| **Mike Garner Simmons** Son | **BIRTH:** 21 Dec. 1899 <br> **DEATH:** 22 Mar. 1968 |
| **Albert Simmons** Son | **BIRTH:** 1907 <br> **DEATH:** Unknown |

## HIS LIFE

When William Obidiah "Obe" Simmons was born on November 17, 1852, in Peytonsville, Tennessee, his father, James was 27 and his mother, Rebecca was 39. He married Margaret A. Spann and they had 11 children together. He died on April 30, 1939, in Peytonsville at the age of 86. He is buried in the Simmons Cemetery in Peytonsville.

OSCAR, MIKE, SALLY, ROBERT, LILLY, OBE AND OPHELIA SIMMONS

# MARTIN CROWDER
# 1853-1915

### CROWDER FAMILY

**HUSBAND'S PARENTS**

| Charles Crowder | Elizabeth Crowder |
|---|---|
| 1826 - 1898 | 1834 - ? |

**WIFE'S PARENTS**

| Jim Gibson | Philis Parrish |
|---|---|
| 1830 - ? | 1830 - ? |

**HUSBAND**
**Martin Crowder**
**BIRTH:** Aug. 1853, Peytonsville, TN
**DEATH:** 1915, Peytonsville, TN

## WIFE
**Anna Gibson**
**BIRTH:** Nov. 1851, Peytonsville, TN
**DEATH:** 24 Feb. 1926, Peytonsville, TN

### CHILDREN

| | |
|---|---|
| **Henry Crowder**<br>Son | **BIRTH:** 6 June 1879<br>**DEATH:** 25 Aug. 1939 |
| **Matilda Crowder**<br>Daughter | **BIRTH:** Oct. 1880<br>**DEATH:** 9 Nov. 1950 |
| **Charlie Crowder**<br>Son | **BIRTH:** 26 Nov. 1885<br>**DEATH:** May 1961 |
| **Willie Crowder**<br>Son | **BIRTH:** 1886<br>**DEATH:** Unknown |
| **Laura Bell Crowder**<br>Daughter | **BIRTH:** Mar. 1887<br>**DEATH:** 1961 |
| **William M. Crowder**<br>Son | **BIRTH:** 26 June 1888<br>**DEATH:** Oct. 1963 |
| **Jonnie Crowder**<br>Son | **BIRTH:** 10 Aug. 1894<br>**DEATH:** 19 Jan. 1952 |
| **John Crowder**<br>Son | **BIRTH:** 1896<br>**DEATH:** Unknown |
| **Odelia Crowder**<br>Son | **BIRTH:** 2 May 1896<br>**DEATH:** Nov. 1972 |
| **Thomas "Tom"**<br>**Crowder-Son** | **BIRTH:** 2 July 1898<br>**DEATH:** 2 Aug. 1966 |
| **Clarence Hine**<br>**Crowder-Son** | **BIRTH:** 23 Feb. 1900<br>**DEATH:** 14 Mar. 1933 |

### HIS LIFE

When Martin Crowder was born in August, 1853, in Williamson County, Tennessee, his father, Charles was 27 and his mother, Elizabeth was 19. He married Anna Gibson on May 19, 1875, in Peytonsville, Tennessee. They had 11 children in 20-years. He died in 1915 in Williamson County, Tennessee at the age of 62.

Many may remember the 1967 hit song, *"Everlasting Love"* sung by a Franklin native, Robert Knight. Robert's first roots grew in the Westwood community. Robert Peebles Knight descended from Martin and Ann Gibson Crowder's son Henry and his wife Sallie Hughes Crowder. Sallie Hughes Crowder came from another 13th District (Peytonsville) family, of Brice and Eliza Hughes.

MARTIN CROWDER

# ELIJAH TOMLIN
## 1853-1934

### TOMLIN FAMILY

#### HUSBAND'S PARENTS
| George Tomlin | Mary E. Mangrum |
|---|---|
| 1830 - 1875 | 1834 - 1875 |

#### 1ST WIFE'S PARENTS
| Joseph A. Bennett | Martha Susan McGee |
|---|---|
| 1824 - 1904 | 1827 - 1896 |

**2ND WIFE'S PARENTS**

| Henry Balam Hay | Sarah E.J. Litton |
|---|---|
| 1838 - 1920 | 1841 - 1866 |

## HUSBAND
**Elijah Tomlin**
**BIRTH:** 20 Mar. 1853, Peytonsville, TN
**DEATH:** 26 Feb. 1934, Peytonsville, TN

## 1ST WIFE
**Mary Elizabeth Bennett**
**BIRTH:** 18 Nov. 1862, TN
**DEATH:** 3 June 1885, Williamson Co. TN

## 2ND WIFE
**Nancy Elizabeth Hay**
**BIRTH:** 27 Aug. 1862, TN
**DEATH:** 18 Sep. 1947, Williamson Co. TN

## CHILDREN OF ELIJAH AND MARY

| Sennie E. Tomlin Daughter | **BIRTH:** 10 Nov. 1877 **DEATH:** 14 Dec. 1929 |
|---|---|
| Marry Ellen Tomlin Daughter | **BIRTH:** 16 Sep. 1878 **DEATH:** 22 Feb. 1914 |

## CHILDREN OF ELIJAH AND NANCY

| Henry Balam Tomlin Son | **BIRTH:** 18 Nov. 1885 **DEATH:** 2 Oct. 1968 |
|---|---|
| Richard A. Tomlin Son | **BIRTH:** 19 Nov. 1886 **DEATH:** 27 June 1931 |
| John Wesley Tomlin Son | **BIRTH:** 14 Mar. 1889 **DEATH:** 22 May 1951 |
| Julius Burton Tomlin Son | **BIRTH:** 8 Jan. 1891 **DEATH:** May 1973 |
| Irene Tomlin Daughter | **BIRTH:** Jan. 1894 **DEATH:** 1982 |
| Ora J. Tomlin Daughter | **BIRTH:** 2 Feb. 1895 **DEATH:** 8 May 1942 |

## HIS LIFE

When Elijah Tomlin was born on March 20, 1853, in Williamson County, Tennessee, his father George was 23 and his mother Mary was 18. He married Mary Elizabeth Bennett and they had two children together. He then married Nancy Elizabeth "Lizzie" Hay and they had six children. He died on February 26, 1934 in Williamson County at the age of 81.

NANCY ELIZABETH "LIZZY" (HAY), ELIJAH TOMLIN AND THEIR KIDS

# JOHN ABNER TOMLIN
# 1855-1944

## TOMLIN FAMILY

### HUSBAND'S PARENTS

| Charles Tomlin | Martha Mangrum |
|---|---|
| 1823 - 1880 | 1830 - 1880 |

### WIFE'S PARENTS

| Benjamin F. Tucker | Melissa J. Pritchett |
|---|---|
| 1823 - 1900 | 1822 - 1900 |

### HUSBAND
**John Abner Tomlin**
**BIRTH:** 30 Aug. 1855, Williamson Co. TN
**DEATH:** 5 Jan. 1944, College Grove, TN

**WIFE**
**Sarah Elizabeth Tucker**
BIRTH: 10 Aug. 1853, Williamson Co. TN
DEATH: 10 Mar. 1912, Peytonsville, TN

CHILDREN

| | |
|---|---|
| **Charles William Tomlin-Son** | BIRTH: 5 Dec. 1878<br>DEATH: 1930 |
| **Martha Jane Tomlin Daughter** | BIRTH: Feb. 1880<br>DEATH: 21 Mar. 1956 |
| **John Andrew Tomlin Son** | BIRTH: 10 Dec. 1882<br>DEATH: 19 Oct. 1924 |
| **Minerva E. Tomlin Daughter** | BIRTH: 1 Dec. 1884<br>DEATH: 30 Jan. 1932 |
| **Rosie "Tennie" Tomlin-Daughter** | BIRTH: 15 Oct. 1888<br>DEATH: 2 Jan. 1941 |
| **Sophia Alice Tomlin Daughter** | BIRTH: 8 Nov. 1893<br>DEATH: 14 Jan. 1972 |

HIS LIFE

When John Abner Tomlin was born on August 30, 1855, in Williamson County, Tennessee, his father, Charles was 32 and his mother, Martha was 25. He married Sarah Elizabeth Tucker on January 17, 1877, in Peytonsville, Tennessee. They had six children in 14-years. He died on January 5, 1944, at the age of 88.

# CHARLES MEEK
# 1857-1917

MEEK FAMILY

HUSBAND'S PARENTS

| Britton Marion Meek | Caroline Jennings |
|---|---|
| 1834 - 1919 | 1838 - 1920 |

**WIFE'S PARENTS**

| Isaac Jasper Gillispie | Nancy J. Mincy |
|---|---|
| 1833 - 1900 | 1827 - 1862 |

HUSBAND
**Charles Meek**
BIRTH: 1 Sep. 1857, Tallapoosa, AL
DEATH: 28 Nov. 1917, Peytonsville, TN

WIFE
**Mary Ann Gillispie**
BIRTH: 21 Nov. 1859, Williamson Co. TN
DEATH: 16 Jan. 1891, Williamson Co. TN

CHILDREN

| | |
|---|---|
| **Carrie M. Meek Daughter** | BIRTH: 1882<br>DEATH: AFT 1930 |
| **Josephine V. Meek Daughter** | BIRTH: 21 May 1886<br>DEATH: 3 Aug. 1957 |
| **Mary Ann Meek Daughter** | BIRTH: 4 Jan. 1888<br>DEATH: 12 June 1891 |
| **Charles Benjamin Meek-Son** | BIRTH: 9 Aug. 1890<br>DEATH: 19 May 1946 |

HIS LIFE

When Charles Meek was born on September 1, 1857, in Tallapoosa, Alabama, his father, Britton was 23 and his mother, Caroline was 19. After the Civil War, his family migrated to Tennessee with other families who also settled in the area namely the Bill Ray family, the Mathis family, Adairs, Kings and Meek family.

Charles married, Mary Ann Gillispie on December 16, 1880, in Williamson County, Tennessee. They had four children during their marriage. He died on November 28, 1917, in Williamson County at the age of 60. He was buried in the Meek Cemetery in Peytonsville, Tennessee.

# JOHN FRANKLIN MCGEE
# 1857-1944

### MCGEE FAMILY

#### HUSBAND'S PARENTS
**John Ruce McGee**   **Elizabeth Ann Poteete**
1829 - 1899        1836 - 1910

#### WIFE'S PARENTS
**James T. Truett**   **Parilee Daniels**
1836 - 1865       1839 - 1916

#### HUSBAND
**John Franklin McGee**
**BIRTH:** 22 Aug. 1857, Hickman Co. TN
**DEATH:** 30 Dec. 1944, Franklin, TN

#### WIFE
**Mary Elizabeth Truett**
**BIRTH:** 7 June 1859, Williamson Co. TN
**DEATH:** 28 Jan. 1941, Williamson Co. TN

#### CHILDREN

| | |
|---|---|
| **Mary Ella McGee** Daughter | **BIRTH:** 27 Jan. 1876 **DEATH:** 9 Sep. 1966 |
| **Sarah Elizabeth McGee-Daughter** | **BIRTH:** 7 June 1877 **DEATH:** 8 June 1970 |
| **Allen Reece McGee** Son | **BIRTH:** 25 May 1879 **DEATH:** 27 Nov. 1952 |
| **John L. McGee** Son | **BIRTH:** 21 Nov. 1880 **DEATH:** 27 May 1946 |
| **Seanny Angielline McGee-Daughter** | **BIRTH:** 13 June 1883 **DEATH:** 23 Nov. 1902 |
| **Martha Jane McGee** Daughter | **BIRTH:** 14 Nov. 1885 **DEATH:** 2 Feb. 1982 |
| **James Lighthall McGee-Son** | **BIRTH:** 14 June 1888 **DEATH:** 3 Oct. 1918 |
| **Daisy Ann McGee** Daughter | **BIRTH:** 2 Aug. 1890 **DEATH:** 2 Nov. 1984 |
| **Sam Fleming McGee** Son | **BIRTH:** 1 May 1894 **DEATH:** 21 Aug. 1975 |
| **David Kirkland McGee** Son | **BIRTH:** 4 Nov. 1899 **DEATH:** 24 Oct. 1983 |

### HIS LIFE

**John Franklin McGee, September 21, 1944:**
Inheritance of good qualities is a wonderful thing just as that of bad qualities is a dire calamity. John F. McGee who celebrated his 87th birthday on August 22, inherited the love of music and the talent to compose it from his father, John R. McGee, as did his six brothers and sisters. This gift was in turn inherited by his ten children, many of his 41 grandchildren and 52 great-grandchildren. Even Harry Guffee, Jr., two-years old starts to pat his foot as soon as someone begins playing the banjo.

As a very young boy Mr. McGee remembers playing the banjo with his father and it was not long before he was able to compose pieces and this he kept up until recent years. His children play exceptionally well the piano, guitar, fiddle and there isn't an instrument that they can not play. His son, Allen, played the fiddle as a cowboy in Oklahoma for several years. Sam and Kirk are famous comedians, appearing over a Nashville radio station for the past 18 years.

At his recent birthday celebration Mr. McGee had with him all of his children, except John Mack, who was unable to attend due to illness, many of the second and third generation to enjoy the good things to eat prepared by his daughter, Sallie, who keeps house for him since his wife's death on January 28, 1941. To her dishes the other members brought baskets of food to add to the picnic lunch. In the afternoon Sam and Kirk brought forth their musical instruments, some of the grandchildren did likewise, and placed Mr. McGee's trusted old fiddle on his knees asking him to select the tune. He began playing "Trouble among the Cattle" followed by "Leather Britches" and, Sunday though it was, some of the youngest members began keeping time, patting their feet and hands and the smaller ones moved in rhythmic swing to the music.

Of Mr. McGee's ten children-five girls and five boys-eight are living. A son, James Lighthall, died of pneumonia at the age of 30 in France during World War One, and afterward his body was returned to be interred in the family cemetery near the home. His daughter, Angeline, who married John L. Hood, a Spanish-American War veteran, died several years ago. The others make their home in Williamson County. Ella, the oldest child and is now 68, married James R. Poteete and they make their home near Franklin; Allen, who never left the family roof until after he was 25 with his wife and children live on an adjoining farm of 236 acres close enough to see that the father has plenty of wood and other necessities. Janie married Bert Guffee, and their son, Dr. Harry, is a first lieutenant in the Army Medical Corps, and after receiving instruction is ready for overseas duty, where John Mack's son, Herman, has been serving for four years with the navy. Daisy and her husband, Walter L. Hood, live in the Bethesda community, while the two

youngest, Sam and Kirk, are here today and there tomorrow, but they have lovely homes in the same neighborhood as their father. The boys are all farmers and the girls married farmers.

Mr. McGee was born in Hickman County, son of John R. and Betsy Ann Poteete McGee, and is one of seven children who grew up on a farm with cotton picking, corn and tobacco raising as his pastime from the time he was five years old until he was grown. The two-room log house in which he was born was chinked and daubed making it warm in winter and as for summer they stayed in it so seldom, except when they were asleep, they took no note of its comfort. Besides being a farmer his father was also a rock mason and some of the fences he built along Duck River are still standing so well was the work done.

The family moved to Maury County during the Civil War, and then came during the Civil War to Williamson County, settling in the community where Mr. McGee now lives and he attended school under the late William Cowles. He was considered the best speller in school and when the time came for the Friday afternoon spelling matches, using the old blue back speller, he was the first one chosen.

He says he remembers when he was a boy his father never made over $200 a year and on this fed and clothed his family, none of them ever went hungry or without comfortable clothing though he does recollect that in summer they wore next to nothing.

When Mr. McGee reached the ripe age of 18 he married Mary Elizabeth Truett, 16, daughter of James Truett, who was killed in Alabama during the Civil War while fighting in the Northern Army. The wedding took place in his father's home with Esq. Gid Radcliffe performing the double ceremony where his uncle, Brice Poteete, and Caroline Benton, were the other couple. A large number of friends and relatives assembled to witness the marriage rites and enjoy the bountiful supper, which included everything from barbecue to cake.

He and his wife lived for two years with his parents then went to Texas planted a crop but, not liking the climate returned before harvesting time. There was so much typhoid fever in that section he considered it too much of a risk to run for their two children. They went back to the same community from which they moved, locating on the Dr. Sam Fleming farm. In the latter part of the last century he bought a farm containing 150 acres and here in a two-story frame house his family completed their upbringing and gradually left for homes of their own. Here, too, he still holds the reins and what he says is law, for he reared his children to say "yes, sir" and "no, sir" along with other titles of respect and this they continue to do.

Among Mr. McGee's treasures is a prize he won in a fiddler's contest held several years ago in King's Garage in Franklin. In this performance he was holding his fiddle in the usual manner playing a very lively tune before his audience could wink an eye the fiddle was being held by one hand at his back and he was playing with the other, making the change without missing a note. He has several other trophies but seems to treasure this one the most.

A member of the Primitive Baptist Church at Cool Springs, Mr. McGee never misses a foot-washing service or an association. He never belonged to a secret order though his sons, Albert, John Mack and Sam, are members of the Masonic Lodge at Bethesda.

Mr. McGee reads without glasses, retains his teeth, his five and a half feet in height has decreased somewhat, due to the natural giving way to the infirmities for age, and his 125 normal weight is now slightly over a hundred. But he still holds to his grit and steady nerves. Only a few months ago he had a carbuncle to develop on his throat where the scar is still angry looking. His grandson, Dr. Harry Guffee, made ready to

lance it and, as the patient refused to take an anesthetic, said, "Grandpa, this is going to hurt, and if you move it will be worse." The old man braced himself, folded his arms tightly across his thin chest, looked his grandson in the eye and said, "Go ahead, son, I'm ready. If you don't flinch I won't for I trust you." The operation was soon over and as the kind old man looked at his grandson he said, "Son, I believe it was harder on your nerves than mine." Harry replied, "You remember the time you took me behind the woodshed to whip me and said it hurt you worse than it did me? I didn't believe you then, but I do now."

Thomas Paine summed up men such as Mr. McGee when he said, "I love the man that can smile in trouble, that can gather strength from distress, and grow brave by reflection. "Tis the business of little minds to shrink, but he whose heart is firm, and whose conscience approves his conduct, will pursue his principles unto death."

**Quotes from conversations with Maggie Virginia (McGee) Smithson, submitted by Harriet Jane (Smithson) Cantrell:**

Remembering Grandpa (John F.) and Grandma (Mary E.) McGee.

"Grandma always swept the yard". No grass grew. "She had rose bushes along the fence".

"She made grape wine and grape jelly. She would make tea cakes (sugar cookies) by the dishpan full. They were good. They had sugar on the top. People traveling through would stop to eat. They claimed she made the best cornbread."

"Mammy (mother) showed me how to quilt. Aunt Nettie, Mammy's sister, sewed for people. She brought scraps out there (from Nashville). I pieced my first quilt, when I was 12. It was a string quilt. Some people now call it a crazy quilt. You cut up paper in squares and sew the pieces starting at the corner. Grandma helped me. She said, "Anyone that young wanted to learn she would help.' I was the youngest she said she had ever seen." "Grandma, like Aunt Janie, was always neat and well-dressed."

"Grandpa had a big orchard and a cider mill. He sold apples by the wagon load and sold cider for 10 cents a gallon. He would keep apples in the cellar on the shelves." "We'd take our pans to the orchard to peel and slice the apples and take the apples to the house to dry."

"We'd put a gallon of milk in the log spring house to be cool for supper."

"Uncle Dave Macon (from the Grand Ole Opry) would come and stay two or three days. Grandpa, Uncle Kirk, and Uncle Sam would make music with him."

**Memories from Allene (Hood) Hazelwood:**

Mama (Daisy) and Aunt Janie had this joke about the bowl. They always knew what Grandma would give them for Christmas—it was always a small vegetable bowl.

We always like big dinners (reunions)—there were so many people, so much food, and we always had music. Jimmy D. Bennett would bring his family in the wagon.

I wouldn't ever want to spend the night in that house where Grandpa and Grandma lived because Mama said that you could hear things and see things. It could be Grandpa. One time Mama and Aunt Janie went up there to stay with Grandma because she was sick. They went outside the dining room door onto the porch to go to the bedroom and they saw a big white thing. They were so scared. Then they found out it was a white-faced cow. Mama told us about noises that they could hear there. I don't know if they were real or not but I wouldn't want to spend the night there. I told Virginia about it and

she just laughed. I don't know how she was able to spend the night there by herself.

**Notes from conversations with Allene Hazelwood and Mabel Hood, sisters and granddaughters of John Franklin and Elizabeth (Truitt) McGee, November 16, 1999.**

Allene and Mabel: We always celebrated 7-days of Christmas. We would go to Grandma's on Christmas Day. After that we would go to Uncle Allen's, Sam's, John's, Aunt Janie's, etc.; and they would come to our house.

Mabel: On Christmas Eve, me and Mama (Daisy) would cook 7 cakes. That was always the dessert—cake and ambrosia. You know what ambrosia is don't you? It's oranges cut up with coconut mixed with it.

Mabel: Everybody drank out of the same dipper. In the winter, Grandma kept a jug of milk with a lid on it near the fire on the hearth so it would clabber. (Once clabbered, it was churned and the butter removed. The remainder was used for cooking or drinking.)

John Franklin McGee died on December 30, 1944, in Franklin, Tennessee when he was 87-years old. He was buried in the Poteete Cemetery in Williamson County.

1ST ROW-MARTHA, JOHN F., MARY E., ALLEN, 2ND ROW-DAISY, SAM, KIRK, JOHN L., MARY ELLEN AND SALLIE MCGEE

# G. MARION "STEVE" KING
## 1857-1945

### KING FAMILY

#### HUSBAND'S PARENTS
**George Washington King   Nancy L. Roberts**
1828 - 1914                        1837 - 1911

#### WIFE'S PARENTS
**Gilly James Skinner    Mary Matilda Crick**
1822 - 1857                     1826 - 1868

#### HUSBAND
**G. Marion King**
BIRTH: 30 July 1857, Coffee Co. TN
DEATH: 7 Oct. 1945, Peytonsville, TN

#### WIFE
**Tennessee "Tennie" Skinner**
BIRTH: 20 July 1858, Bedford Co. TN
DEATH: 27 Jan. 1942, Thompson's Station, TN

#### CHILDREN

| | |
|---|---|
| **Norbie C. King** Son | BIRTH: June 1890 DEATH: ABT 1967 |
| **Ercelle King** Daughter | BIRTH: 1891 DEATH: 17 Oct. 1979 |

### HIS LIFE

G. Marion "Steve" King spent the greater part of his life as a blacksmith. On the day he was 14-years old, he nailed on a shoe and the victim was a sorrel mare belonging to Tom Knott, a stove repair man. When he reached his eightieth birthday he shod seven mules, fitting and nailing on 28 shoes. He had been known to put on as many as sixty-four horseshoes in one day in his younger years.

Being the oldest of ten children, he had little time to discuss with his parents what he should do with his life, nor did they have much leisure to listen had he done so. He was born July 30, 1857, in Coffee County, near Manchester. He quit school in the third grade to devote all his time to helping his father make a living, which he continued to do until he was 23-years old.

December 20, 1882, G. Marion married, Tennessee "Tennie" Skinner. They had two children together. They lived happily together for nearly 60-years, rarely being separated for longer than a week. After Tennie's death, their daughter, Ercelle and her family came to live with her father.

G. Marion King died on October 7, 1945, in Peytonsville, Tennessee when he was 88-years old. He was buried in the King Cemetery in Peytonsville.

STANDING L-R: GEORGE T., JAMES WATSON, SAMUEL MOSES, SEATED L-R: GEORGE W., NANCY, G. MARION, WILLIAM KING

# JOHN THOMAS HELM
## 1857-1912

### HELM FAMILY

**John Carl Helm**    **Mary Louise Merritt**
1825 - 1862      1832 - 1903

**WIFE'S PARENTS**
**Nathaniel N. Smithson**    **Margaret K. Johnson**
1826 - 1896      1833 - 1880

## HUSBAND
**John Thomas Helm**
**BIRTH:** 15 Mar. 1857, Williamson Co. TN
**DEATH:** 19 Jan. 1912, Williamson Co. TN

## WIFE
**Dolly Ann Smithson**
**BIRTH:** 11 Jan. 1863, Williamson Co. TN
**DEATH:** 3 Jan. 1907, Williamson Co. TN

## CHILDREN

| | |
|---|---|
| **Monte L. Helm** Son | **BIRTH:** 17 Mar. 1886   **DEATH:** 12 Aug. 1904 |
| **Ada Helm** Daughter | **BIRTH:** 12 Aug. 1888   **DEATH:** 20 Apr. 1972 |
| **Jessie B. Helm** Son | **BIRTH:** 31 May 1891   **DEATH:** 9 Nov. 1907 |
| **Baby Helm** Daughter | **BIRTH:** 17 Dec. 1893   **DEATH:** 19 Dec. 1893 |
| **Ethel Mai Helm** Daughter | **BIRTH:** 26 Dec. 1894   **DEATH:** 15 Oct. 1966 |
| **J. Wallace Helm** Son | **BIRTH:** 1896   **DEATH:** 1969 |
| **Walter Henry Helm** Son | **BIRTH:** 20 Nov. 1898   **DEATH:** 30 Jan. 1967 |
| **Margaret Louise Helm** Daughter | **BIRTH:** 31 May 1902   **DEATH:** 16 Apr. 1951 |
| **John Thomas Helm** Son | **BIRTH:** 28 Dec. 1906   **DEATH:** 16 Nov. 1961 |

## HIS LIFE

When John Thomas Helm was born on March 15, 1857, in Williamson County, Tennessee, his father, John was 31 and his mother, Mary was 24. He married Dolly Ann Smithson in 1885, in Peytonsville, Tennessee. They had nine children in 20-years. He died on January 19, 1912, in Williamson County, Tennessee at the age of 54. He was buried in the Mount Hope Cemetery in Franklin, Tennessee.

# LEWIS JACKSON BEARD JR.
## 1859-1943

### BEARD FAMILY

**HUSBAND'S PARENTS**
**Lewis J. Beard Sr.**    **Elizabeth A. Heathcock**
1827 - 1906      1835 - 1900

**1ST WIFE'S PARENTS**
**George Young**    **Emeline Heathcock**
1830 - 1870      1829 - ?

**2ND WIFE'S PARENTS**
**George Young**    **Emeline Heathcock**
1830 - 1870      1829 - ?

## HUSBAND
**Lewis Jackson Beard Jr.**
**BIRTH:** 17 Dec. 1859, Peytonsville, TN
**DEATH:** 24 Jan. 1943, Peytonsville, TN

## 1ST WIFE
**Amanda E. Young**
**BIRTH:** 1861, Williamson Co. TN
**DEATH:** 1893, Williamson Co. TN

## 2ND WIFE
**Mary Lucinda Young**
**BIRTH:** Oct. 1858, Williamson Co. TN
**DEATH:** 14 Dec. 1932, Williamson Co. TN

## CHILDREN OF LEWIS AND AMANDA

**Walter B. Beard**  
**Son**  
BIRTH: 8 Mar. 1882  
DEATH: 22 Oct. 1961

## CHILDREN OF LEWIS AND MARY

**George Fred Beard**  
**Son**  
BIRTH: 15 Dec. 1900  
DEATH: 1 Dec. 1935

### HIS LIFE

When Lewis Jackson Beard was born on December 17, 1859, in Williamson County, Tennessee, his father, Lewis was 32 and his mother, Elizabeth was 24. He married Amanda E. Young and they had one son together. Amanda died 1893. Lewis then married Amanda's sister, Mary Lucinda Young. They had one son together. Mary Lucinda passed away on December 14, 1932.

Lewis Jackson Beard Jr. died on January 24, 1943. He owned two tracts of land in Peytonsville, Tennessee. The land was deeded to him by, William Parrish in 1855. There was 115-acres in one tract and the second contained 12.5-acres, deeded to him by John Overton in 1890. Owen, Mosley and Company purchased the land at the sheriff's sale in 1899. Lewis lived about 5.5-years after the sale.

He was buried in the Beard Cemetery in Peytonsville, Tennessee.

# JAMES HENRY GRAVES
# 1860-1928

### GRAVES FAMILY

#### HUSBAND'S PARENTS
**Joseph L. Graves**    **Amanda Vaughan**  
1830 - 1920          1825 - ?

#### WIFE'S PARENTS
**Joseph H. Ladd**    **Emily Waggoner**  
1816 - 1910          1820 - 1880

#### HUSBAND
**James Henry Graves**  
BIRTH: 26 Apr. 1860, Peytonsville, TN  
DEATH: 16 Sep. 1928, Peytonsville, TN

#### WIFE
**Laura Gertrude Ladd**  
BIRTH: 3 Jan., 1860, TN  
DEATH: 24 Jan., 1932, Nashville, TN

#### CHILDREN

**Josie May Graves**  
**Daughter**  
BIRTH: 9 Oct. 1884  
DEATH: 29 Jan. 1918

**John Thomas Graves**  
**Son**  
BIRTH: 9 Apr. 1886  
DEATH: 26 Sep. 1942

**Annie Belle Graves**  
**Daughter**  
BIRTH: 19 Nov. 1887  
DEATH: 7 Nov. 1945

**William Rufus Graves**  
**Son**  
BIRTH: 24 Oct. 1889  
DEATH: 2 Nov. 1932

**Robert L. Graves**  
**Son**  
BIRTH: 1893  
DEATH: Unknown

**James Elmer Graves**  
**Son**  
BIRTH: 11 June 1894  
DEATH: 11 Dec. 1958

**Henry Eugene Graves**  
**Son**  
BIRTH: 28 Sep. 1896  
DEATH: 3 Apr. 1962

**Mattie Gertrude Graves-Daughter**  
BIRTH: 29 Sep. 1898  
DEATH: Sep. 1978

**Ethel Estelle Graves**  
**Daughter**  
BIRTH: 27 Dec. 1902  
DEATH: 29 Apr. 1958

### HIS LIFE

When James Henry Graves was born on April 26, 1860, in Peytonsville, Tennessee, his father, Joseph was 30 and his mother, Amanda was 35. He married Laura Gertrude Ladd on December 24, 1883, in Williamson County, Tennessee.

They had nine children in 18-years. He died on September 16, 1928, in Williamson County, Tennessee at the age of 68. He was buried in the Mount Hope Cemetery in Franklin, Tennessee.

The following is his obituary:
The funeral of James Henry Graves whose death occurred Sunday evening at 6:30 o'clock at his home at Arno, was conducted from the Wesley Chapel Methodist church Tuesday afternoon at 2 o'clock by Rev. H.E. Baker.

Mr. Graves' death which was very sudden came as a shock to his relatives and friends. He was a christian gentleman and was highly respected in his community. He took an active interest in the business and social affairs of the neighborhood and was an active member of the Wesley Chapel Methodist church.

The deceased is survived by his wife, Mrs. Laura Ladd Graves and the following children: Mrs. J.L. Hatcher and J.T. Graves of Detroit, Mich., W.R., R.L., J.E., and H.E. Graves of Nashville, Mrs. J.H. Crunk and Mrs. D.M. Lillard of Arno. One sister, Mrs. Phoebe Ferguson also survives him.

The Honorary pall-bearers were John McMahon, J.N. Akin, W.T. Lewis, T.A. Hickman, F.M. Maxwell, T.R. Meek, G.C. Kinnard and M.W. Patton.

Friends serving as active pall-bearers were Escar Smithson, C.R. Pennington, O.C. Lillard, J.W. West, C.R. Wood and W.A. Smithson.

Interment took place in Mt. Hope cemetery. Regen, Bethurum & Padgett were in charge.

LAURA (LADD) AND JAMES HENRY GRAVES

# ELIJAH K. SMITHSON
# 1860-1941

### SMITHSON FAMILY

### HUSBAND'S PARENTS
**Nathaniel N. Smithson   Margaret K. Johnson**
1826 - 1896                     1833 - 1880

### WIFE'S PARENTS
**Rufus Gaden Moore     Mary Jane Martin**
1842 - ?                          1851 - 1936

### HUSBAND
**Elijah K. Smithson**
**BIRTH:** 14 May 1860, Peytonsville, TN
**DEATH:** 1 Nov. 1941, Franklin, TN

### WIFE
**Daisy Jane Moore**
**BIRTH:** 26 Dec. 1873, AL
**DEATH:** 9 Aug. 1944, Nashville, TN

## CHILDREN

| | |
|---|---|
| **Ellen Smithson** | **BIRTH:** 6 Dec. 1899 |
| **Daughter** | **DEATH:** 13 Dec. 1974 |
| | |
| **Frank Woodward** | **BIRTH:** 26 June 1897 |
| **Smithson-Son** | **DEATH:** 16 June 1938 |

## HIS LIFE

### Who's Who Williamson County: S-Z
### Esq. E.K. Smithson, May 12, 1938

Esq. E.K. Smithson has answered "here" at the meeting of the Williamson County Court for the past 42 years except for a very short break once caused by changing the boundary line between the 13th and the 21st civil districts but at the next election he was reinstated. Esq. Stockett, another longtime squire, and he have seen many changes take place in all these years but the greatest revelation is the newly modernized courthouse. He closes his eyes in the present courtroom and tries to visualize the old one but The complete renovation has entirely wiped from his mind the old setting.

The fair-minded squire was born nearly 78 years ago, twelve miles east of town on the Murfreesboro Road, one of ten children, five girls and five boys, born to Nathaniel and Margaret Johnson Smithson, but only four of them can answer "here" today, Mrs. G.C. Kinnard, of Franklin; Mrs. Mary Graham, of Memphis; Mrs. J.G. Vaden, of Rocky Mount, N.C., and the subject of this sketch. He was born in the times when little boys wore dresses until they were ready for school and the change to trousers was a great event. He was taught at home by his mother until he was using the second grade reader, could write a legible hand and knew the multiplication tables. When he entered school at 9 he wore his first pair of trousers and his very first pair of shoes. Up to that time he had learned to do much about the farm and one of his accomplishments was picking as much as 100 pounds of cotton in a day. He filled quills for his mother to weave the cloth, which she dyed with bark and copperas to make the children's clothing.

His educational advantages were limited to the elementary grades but life has been a great professor and taught him much more in a number of ways than those possessing many lettered degrees. His only recollection of the Civil War was standing in the yard as a very small child with his mother and listening to the battle at Murfreesboro. He wonders sometimes if he really remembers it or is it only his mother's oft repeated account of the battle.

Esq. Smithson says the greater part of the work done on his parents' 700-acre farm was by the five sons as his father was an invalid but certainly knew how to have it done and did the directing while the oldest boy, Jim, was the leader. He says breaking young mules and horses fell to his lot and he could ride anything from a Texas pony to a purebred, sitting in the saddle like a professional. For 32 years he owned and operated a general store at Arno under his own name, selling goods to and buying produce from the neighbors for miles around. Nine years ago he sold the business which now operates under the name of Culbertson & Jordan but retains the property. He owns two farms, lives on one of 171 acres and has a tenant on the other 100 acres but superintends both.

When Esq. Smithson was a young man there was a little girl, Daisy Moore, daughter of a neighbor, whom he held on his knee, told stories to and made a great pet of. He told her he was going to wait for her to grow up before he looked for a wife. True to his word, when he was 35 years of age and she 20 they were married. Though there was a disparity in age the union has been a happy one and for 44 years they have lived in the 10-room frame house, bare of all modern conveniences except running water. They do not even have a radio for he formed a distaste for it when in the days of gramophones one ran day and night in his store. Now any sound akin to one grates on his nerves. They have two children, Frank Woodard Smithson, his wife and son, live in Louisville; Mrs. W.T. Cotton with her husband and two children make their home in Nashville. A granddaughter, Mary Blanche Smithson, 15, and a sophomore in College Grove High School, lives with her grandparents.

For many years Esq. Smithson has been a member of the Methodist Church at Wesley Chapel and for the past 40 years has served as a steward. Outside of being a member of the Democratic Party he has never belonged to any organization.

The squire, besides operating both farms, is a grower of Jersey cattle, having now a herd of 30 with 25 of them milk cows and sells whole milk to the dairy. He has a flock of 60 Southdown sheep but raises only enough hogs for home consumption. His principal crops are corn and tobacco. Last year he made close to $3,000 on tobacco alone but this year's crop was considerably less. His wife has a flock of 250 Barred Rock chickens and he says she loves these better than she does her husband and children. She hatches most of her brood but sometimes busy with additional day-old chicks to supplement her hatch. She is an active member of the Arno Demonstration Club and the Woman's Missionary Society at Wesley Chapel. Her hobby is fishing and her home is the gathering place of all the kin, her cooking being a strong drawing card.

Twelve years ago, Esq. Smithson was in an automobile accident leaving him with a bad left knee and for months he walked with the aid of crutches. On March 13, 1935, while he and his wife were returning from Nashville a truck ran into them on the Jackson Highway completely demolishing his car and landing them both in the hospital. His left arm became paralyzed and a diabetic condition arose making it necessary to amputate the great toe on his left foot. Two months later the foot was removed at the ankle. He spent several months in Protestant Hospital tenderly cared for by a nurse, Sara Frost, a Williamson County girl, who was at his service at a moment's notice.

With the aid of crutches-and he owns three pairs-and a cork leg he is able to go about his daily affairs thankful things are as well with him as they are. He does not spend his time bemoaning his lot in life but does whatever his hands find to do with a light heart and happy smile. He does not like to be waited upon and takes great pride in doing for others. He claims happiness is only the feeling we experience when we are too busy to be miserable, so he keeps busy.

Elijah K. Smithson died on November 1, 1941, in Franklin, Tennessee, at the age of 81. He was buried in the Mount Hope Cemetery in Franklin, Tennessee.

The following is his obituary taken from the *Nashville Banner*.

### Elijah Smithson Dies at Franklin

Franklin, Tenn, Nov. 3—(Special)—Funeral services for Elijah K. Smithson, 81, who died unexpectedly Saturday afternoon at 5 o'clock at his home in Franklin, will be held at the First Methodist Church here this afternoon at 2 o'clock.

The Rev. R.S. Lee and the Rev. Paul F. Lanius will officiate. The burial will be in Mt. Hope Cemetery here.

Mr. Smithson was born in Williamson County near Peytonsville. His parents were the late Nathaniel Smithson and Mrs. Margaret Johnson Smithson. He was educated in the county schools. Mr. Smithson married Miss Daisy Moore of this county. He engaged in farming and the general merchandise business at Peytonsville successfully for many years.

His health becoming broken one year ago, he moved into Franklin to reside, erecting a home here at Myles Manor on the Nashville Highway, to which he moved last June.

He was a member for more than thirty years of the Williamson County Court and a leader in the prohibition movement here several years ago. He was a member of the Wesley Chapel Methodist Church, and a steward for a period of years in the congregation.

He is survived by his wife, Mrs. Daisy Moore Smithson; one daughter, Mrs. Will T. Cotton of Nashville and three sisters, Mrs. G.C. Kinnard of Franklin, Mrs. Mary Graham of Memphis, and Mrs. Ophilia Vaden of Asheville, N.C.

ELIJAH K. AND DAISY
(MOORE) SMITHSON

# THOMAS WALTER
SMITHSON
1864-1926

## SMITHSON FAMILY

**HUSBAND'S PARENTS**
**Sylvanus W. Smithson   Elizabeth C. Gee**
1810 - 1872                1830 - 1900

**1ST WIFE'S PARENTS**
**Turnel L.G. Harrison   Ellen A. Martin**
1838 - 1918               1842 - 1898

**2ND WIFE'S PARENTS**
**Nathaniel Bedford Vaden   Susan T. Gibson**
1844 - 1927                  1847 - 1913

**HUSBAND**
**Thomas Walter Smithson**
**BIRTH:** 6 April, 1864, Peytonsville, TN
**DEATH:** 16 May 1926, Peytonsville, TN

**1ST WIFE**
**Covoda Harrison**
**BIRTH:** 22 Oct. 1863, Williamson Co. TN
**DEATH:** 2 Feb. 1907, Williamson Co. TN

**2ND WIFE**
**Ella Vaden**
**BIRTH:** 27 Aug. 1879, TN
**DEATH:** 29 May 1952, Peytonsville, TN

**CHILDREN OF THOMAS AND COVODA**

| | |
|---|---|
| **Stella Green Smithson-Daughter** | **BIRTH:** 26 Dec. 1886  **DEATH:** 23 Mar. 1959 |

**CHILDREN OF THOMAS AND ELLA**

| | |
|---|---|
| **Thomas Wade Smithson-Son** | **BIRTH:** 16 Mar. 1910  **DEATH:** 30 Jan. 1960 |

**HIS LIFE**

When Thomas Walter Smithson was born on April 6, 1864, in Peytonsville, Tennessee, his father, Sylvanus was 53 and his mother, Elizabeth was 34. He married Covoda Harrison on December 21, 1885, in Williamson County, Tennessee. They had one child during their marriage. Covoda died on February 2, 1907. Thomas then married, Ella Vaden on December

17, 1908, when he was 44-years old. Thomas and Ella had one son together. He died on May 16, 1926, in Peytonsville at the age of 62. He was buried in the Mount Hope Cemetery in Franklin, Tennessee.

**His obituary:**
*The Tennessean*, Mon, May 17, 1926

SMITHSON—Died at his home, 7.5 miles east of Franklin at 8:25 a.m., May 16, 1926. Thomas W. Smithson, survuved by his wife, Mrs. Ella Davis Smithson, and the following children: Mrs. Stella S. Ladd, Thomas W. Smithson Jr; one sister, Mrs. J.J. Harrison of Franklin; one brother, J.W. Smithson of Dallas, Texas; five grandchildren. Funeral services at his home 3 p.m. this (Monday) afternoon, May 17, conducted by Elder F. W. Smith. Active Pallbearers—Dr. J.B. Core, Dr. R.F. Cowles, Dan Riley, R.P. Waddey, Joe Price, D. Robert, J.F. Stockett, Mack Southall, J.O. Petway, Joe Mays. Interment Mt. Hope cemetery, Franklin. Regen & Cotton, funeral directors.

THOMAS, COVODA
(HARRISON) AND THEIR
DAUGHTER, STELLA
SMITHSON

# JOHN WESLEY BOYD
# 1864-1923

## BOYD FAMILY

### HUSBAND'S PARENTS
**George Washington Boyd     Sarah R. Terrell**
1837 - 1927                     1838 - 1906

### WIFE'S PARENTS
**John Raleigh Dodson     Rebecca H. Baugh**
1830 - 1910                     1836 - 1880

### HUSBAND
**John Wesley Boyd**
**BIRTH:** 8 Apr. 1864, Peytonsville, TN
**DEATH:** 8 May, 1923, Peytonsville, TN

### WIFE
**Francis Henrietta Dodson**
**BIRTH:** 27 Aug. 1864, TN
**DEATH:** 27 July 1912, Williamson Co. TN

### CHILDREN

| | |
|---|---|
| **Johnnie D. Boyd** <br> **Daughter** | **BIRTH:** 24 Aug. 1903 <br> **DEATH:** 2 Oct. 1970 |
| **James Oscar Boyd** <br> **Son** | **BIRTH:** 20 Sep. 1905 <br> **DEATH:** 6 Feb. 1989 |
| **Timothy Terrell Boyd** <br> **Son** | **BIRTH:** 4 July 1908 <br> **DEATH:** 23 May 1958 |

## HIS LIFE

When John Wesley Boyd was born on April 8, 1864, in Williamson County, Tennessee, his father, George was 26 and his mother, Sarah was 25. He married, Francis Henrietta Dodson on June 27, 1901, in Davidson County, Tennessee. They had three children during their marriage. He died on May 8, 1923, in Peytonsville, Tennessee. He was buried in Mount Hope Cemetery in Franklin, Tennessee.

JOHN WESLEY AND FRANCIS
(DODSON) BOYD

# GRANT LUSTER
# 1864-1931

## LUSTER FAMILY

### HUSBAND'S PARENTS
**Nelson Luster**    **Elizabeth Betsey Walter**
1834 - 1909      1842 - ?

### 1ST WIFE'S PARENTS
**Matt Patton**    **Patsy Patton**
1827 - ?      1840 - ?

### 2ND WIFE'S PARENTS
**Anderson Jones**    **Fannie Mathis**
1855 - 1949      1860 - 1924

## HUSBAND
**Grant Luster, Sr.**
**BIRTH:** 1864, Williamson Co. TN
**DEATH:** 20 Jan., 1931, Williamson Co. TN

## 1ST WIFE
**Anna Patton**
**BIRTH:** May 1865, TN
**DEATH:** 1915, Williamson Co. TN

## 2ND WIFE
**Sallie N. Jones**
**BIRTH:** 8 Apr. 1889, Williamson Co. TN
**DEATH:** Williamson Co, TN

## CHILDREN OF GRANT AND ANNA

| | |
|---|---|
| **Alex Luster** Son | **BIRTH:** Nov. 1889 **DEATH:** Unknown |
| **Grant Luster, Jr.** Son | **BIRTH:** 27 Nov. 1896 **DEATH:** 27 Apr. 1981 |
| **Jennie Luster** Daughter | **BIRTH:** Unknown **DEATH:** Unknown |
| **Mattie Luster** Daughter | **BIRTH:** 1900 **DEATH:** 4 July 1934 |

## HIS LIFE

When Grant Luster was born in 1864, in Williamson County, Tennessee, his father, Nelson was 30 and his mother, Elizabeth was 22.

Nelson Luster, Grant's father was born a slave in October, 1834. His father was born in North Carolina and his mother was a Virginia native. In 1870, Nelson Luster and his wife, Betsey, were living in the 21st District of Williamson County with their four children, aged four-months to eight-years. They were likely sharecroppers.

Their second son, Grant Luster, Sr., born in May 1864, purchased a farm of just over 80-acres southeast of the county seat of Franklin in the Arno-College Grove area in November 1906, from Henry Graves. Luster and his first wife,

Anna, born in May 1865, had four children, Grant Jr., Alex, Jennie and Mattie. They were living on the acreage in 1910, where Luster's occupation was listed as "general farmer." After Anna's death, Grant Luster Sr., married Sallie Jones in 1920. Nelson Luster II, the son of Grant Luster, Jr., carries the name of his ancestor and owns the farm today. His son, Anthony W. Luster, observes that "Families of the past, while working with hand tools and beasts of burden seemed closer knit than perhaps today, but the legacy, the heritage, and the bond of the land still continues."

Grant Luster died on January 20, 1931, at the age of 67.

# WILLIAM SAMUEL MARLIN
# 1866-1952

## MARLIN FAMILY

### HUSBAND'S PARENTS
**Joseph Bonapart Marlin**   **Sallie E. Grimes**
1839 - 1921                  1849 - 1870

### WIFE'S PARENTS
**George Marion Johnson**   **Elizabeth M. West**
1834 - 1916                 1840 - 1911

### HUSBAND
**William Samuel Marlin**
**BIRTH:** 8 Apr. 1866, Williamson Co. TN
**DEATH:** 13 July 1952, Peytonsville, TN

### WIFE
**Matilda Elizabeth Johnson**
**BIRTH:** 14 Feb. 1873, Williamson Co. TN
**DEATH:** 24 Nov. 1947, Peytonsville, TN

### CHILDREN

**Martha Ann Marlin**
**Daughter**
**BIRTH:** 29 Aug. 1889
**DEATH:** 25 Sep. 1960

**Jo Anna Marlin**
**Daughter**
**BIRTH:** 27 Aug. 1892
**DEATH:** 24 Dec. 1965

**William Jasper Marlin**
**Son**
**BIRTH:** 23 May 1895
**DEATH:** 30 Aug. 1962

**Lula E. Marlin**
**Daughter**
**BIRTH:** Oct. 1897
**DEATH:** 13 May 1986

**Fannie Wade Marlin**
**Daughter**
**BIRTH:** 30 Apr. 1901
**DEATH:** 31 July 1998

**James Taylor Marlin**
**Son**
**BIRTH:** 10 Mar. 1903
**DEATH:** 26 Aug. 1973

**Fleming Marlin**
**Son**
**BIRTH:** 25 June 1905
**DEATH:** 6 Sep. 1988

**Asalyn Marlin**
**Daughter**
**BIRTH:** 1909
**DEATH:** Jan. 1976

**Jerry Marlin**
**Son**
**BIRTH:** 22 Mar. 1910
**DEATH:** 22 Jan. 1972

**Bessie Marlin**
**Daughter**
**BIRTH:** 22 Jan. 1912
**DEATH:** 18 Oct. 2005

**Elizabeth Estelle Marlin-Daughter**
**BIRTH:** 18 Apr. 1914
**DEATH:** 13 Aug. 1994

## HIS LIFE

When William Samuel Marlin was born on April 8, 1866, in Williamson County, Tennessee, his father, Joseph was 27 and his mother, Sallie was 17. He married Matilda Elizabeth Johnson on November 4, 1888, in Peytonsville, Tennessee. They had 11 children in 24-years. He died on July 13, 1952, at the age of 86. He was buried in the Mount Hope Cemetery in Franklin, Tennessee

MATILDA (JOHNSON) AND
WILLIAM SAMUEL MARLIN

# FRANK MOORER HOUSER
## 1866-1961

### HOUSER FAMILY

#### HUSBAND'S PARENTS
**Andrew John Houser**   **Mary Jane Pooser**
1835 - 1907              1835 - 1870

#### WIFE'S PARENTS
**Henry Spotswood Hatcher**   **Mary J. Andrews**
1831 - 1891                   1835 - 1928

#### HUSBAND
**Frank Moorer Houser**
**BIRTH:** 14 Jan. 1866, Perry, GA
**DEATH:** 1961, Peytonsville, TN

#### WIFE
**Nannie Lou Hatcher**
**BIRTH:** 9 Dec. 1872, Peytonsville, TN
**DEATH:** 26 Aug. 1964, Peytonsville, TN

### CHILDREN

**Elizabeth Underwood**   **BIRTH:** 28 Sep. 1905
**Houser-Daughter**       **DEATH:** 24 Feb. 2003

### HIS LIFE

When Frank Moorer Houser was born on January 14, 1866, in Perry, Georgia, his father, Andrew was 30 and his mother, Mary was 30. He married Nannie Lou Hatcher on April 9, 1913, in Williamson County, Tennessee. They fostered one child, Elizabeth Houser.

The Houser home on Gosey Hill Road, was named "Bethany" by Frank. He placed the name on a board which hung over that of Lazarus and his sisters, Mary and Martha, open to all who are in need of shelter. The five rooms, screened in side porch and other porches were comfortably furnished. Electricity with accompanying conveniences lightened the household duties. Though Jack was 85-years old, he still gardened, milked a cow and gathered eggs from his flock of White Leghorns. He brought the eggs to Franklin to sell. When asked what kind they were he answered, "Fresh and fine," and that caused Rainey Lunn to nickname him, "Fresh and Fine," which followed him through all his years.

Frank Moorer Houser died in 1961, in Williamson County, Tennessee when he was 95-years old. He was buried in Mount Hope Cemetery in Franklin, Tennessee.

NANNIE LOU (HATCHER) AND FRANK
MOORER HOUSER

# RICHARD T. GRAY
## 1867-1917

### GRAY FAMILY

**HUSBAND'S PARENTS**
**Robert D. Gray**     **Mary Susan Crunk**
1837 - 1905          1839 - 1900

**WIFE'S PARENTS**
**B.H. Hall**   **Nancy Johnson**
1842 - ?       1845 - ?

**HUSBAND**
**Richard T. Gray**
**BIRTH:** 17 Oct. 1867, Peytonsville, TN
**DEATH:** 21 Mar. 1917, Franklin, TN

**WIFE**
**Sadie L. Hall**
**BIRTH:** 16 Apr. 1873, TX
**DEATH:** 10 Sep. 1937, Columbia, TN

### CHILDREN

**Ethel Gray**          **BIRTH:** Nov. 1898
**Daughter**            **DEATH:** 11 July 1955

### HIS LIFE

When Richard T. Gray was born on October 17, 1867, in Williamson County, Tennessee, his father, Robert was 30 and his mother, Mary was 28. He married Sadie L. Hall on February 2, 1893, in Peytonsville, Tennessee. They had one child during their marriage.

Richard T. Gray was sheriff of Williamson County and died in office on March 21, 1917, in Franklin, Tennessee when he was 49.

**The following is his obituary:**
**Richard T. Gray**
**Sheriff of Williamson County**
**Dies After Long Illness.**

Franklin, Tenn., March 21, —Richard T. Gray, sheriff of Williamson County, died at 5:15 o'clock today at his home on Bridge Street, after a lingering illness. The funeral services will be held at the residence at 10:30 o'clock tomorrow morning and will be conducted by Rev. W.S. Taylor and Rev. Felix W. Johnston. The remains will be taken to Rudderville and interred in the family burying ground at 2 p.m.

Mr. Gray is survived by his wife and one daughter, Mrs. Padgett. He had a great many friends and was highly esteemed by the community. He faithfully performed the duties of his office, and even after being confined to his bed, continued to direct the affairs of the county that came to the office of sheriff.

The following friends will serve as pall-bearers: Joe E. Lunn, John R. Grigsby, J.H. Truett and Ed Holt.

Honorary—Judge H.D. Jefferson, R.A. Gooch, Joe Mays, Claude Lavender, R.S. Owen and Ben Taylor.

RICHARD T., SADIE (HALL) AND DAUGHTER, ETHEL GRAY

❨❩

# ENOCH RUSHING CHEST
## 1867-1943

### CHEST FAMILY

**HUSBAND'S PARENTS**
**Fredrick Chest**    **Mary J. Sampson**
1836 - 1876             1847 - 1888

**WIFE'S PARENTS**
**William Lafayette McCall   Nancy Marilda Irvin**
1842 - 1926                           1842 - 1889

**HUSBAND**
**Enoch Rushing Chest**
**BIRTH:** 14 Dec. 1867, Williamson Co. TN
**DEATH:** 9 Jan. 1943, Franklin, TN

**WIFE**
**Annah Laura McCall**
**BIRTH:** 30 Nov. 1867, Bethesda, Tennessee
**DEATH:** 24 Feb. 1959, Nashville, TN

### CHILDREN

**Herschal Ovel Chest**    **BIRTH:** 4 Feb. 1892
**Son**                    **DEATH:** 30 Jan. 1957

**Roy Otis Chest**         **BIRTH:** 31 May 1894
**Son**                    **DEATH:** 1960

**William Orman Chest**    **BIRTH:** 28 Jan. 1897
**Son**                    **DEATH:** 23 Dec. 1918

**Fredrick Osie Chest**    **BIRTH:** 24 July 1899
**Son**                    **DEATH:** July 1976

**Elbert Olney Chest**     **BIRTH:** 3 June 1903
**Son**                    **DEATH:** Feb. 1986

### HIS LIFE

When Enoch Rushing Chest was born on December 14, 1867, in Williamson County, Tennessee, his father, Fredrick was 31 and his mother, Mary was 20. He married, Annah Laura McCall on September 26, 1889, in Peytonsville, Tennessee. They had five children in 11-years.

The village of Peytonsville didn't seem to have a public school until 1896 when School Directors B.M. Meek, G.M. Smithson, and Robert Gray received a deed of 2.5-acres from George W. and Nancy King for a school near the Peytonsville Church of Christ. Enoch R. Chest may have been the first teacher in this building since he lived nearby and gave the right-of-way and use of his well in 1898.

Enoch Rushing Chest died on January 9, 1943, in Franklin, Tennessee at the age of 75. He was buried in the Mt. Olivet Cemetery in Nashville, Tennessee.

**The following is his obituary:**
***The Tennessean*, 10 Jan, 1943, Sun**

CHEST—At his home on the Liberty Road, one mile from Franklin, Saturday morning at 12:15 o'clock. Enoch Rushing Chest, 73 years of age. Survived by his wife, Mrs. Laura McCall Chest; four sons, H.O. Chest and T.O. Chest of Nashville, R.O. Chest of Fayetteville and E.O. Chest of Franklin. The remains are at the residence as above. Funeral services will be conducted from the Franklin Nazarene Church Monday morning at 10 o'clock by Rev. H.H. Wise and Rev. W.M. Greathouse. Pallbearers will please serve as follows: Honorary: Williamson County Board of Education, W.P. Scales, F. J. Page, R.L. Johnson, Dr. W.J. Polk, Active: S. L. Tucker, Earl Martin, S.A. Smithson, D.B. Graham, T.C. Young and J.F. West. Interment Mt. Olivet Cemetery W.J. Bethurum & Son, funeral directors. Franklin, Tenn.

# WILLIAM ALBERT DODD
# 1868-1943

## DODD FAMILY

### HUSBAND'S PARENTS
**Albert Marcus Dodd**   **Hamite E. Sullivan**
1844 - 1918          1843 - 1929

### WIFE'S PARENTS
**Jerry Owen**   **Aletha Finley**
1817 - ?       1821 - ?

### HUSBAND
**William Albert Dodd**
BIRTH: 26 May 1868, Cannon Co. TN
DEATH: 3 Dec. 1943, Peytonsville, TN

### WIFE
**Anna Elizabeth "Lizzie" Owen**
BIRTH: 16 May, 1867, Cannon Co. TN
DEATH: 27 Nov. 1953, Peytonsville, TN

## CHILDREN

**Lena Dodd**
Daughter
BIRTH: 25 Feb. 1894
DEATH: 2 Feb. 1963

**William Bryan Dodd**
Son
BIRTH: 5 Nov. 1896
DEATH: 28 June 1978

**Albert O. Dodd**
Son
BIRTH: Jan. 1899
DEATH: Unknown

**John R. Dodd**
Son
BIRTH: 1902
DEATH: Unknown

**Maggie Florence Dodd-Daughter**
BIRTH: 1905
DEATH: Unknown

**Cyrus Graham Dodd**
Son
BIRTH: 16 Nov. 1907
DEATH: 13 Jan. 1975

## HIS LIFE

When William Albert Dodd was born on May 26, 1868, in Cannon County, Tennessee, his father, Albert was 23 and his mother, Hamite was 25. He married, Anna Elizabeth "Lizzie" Owen on October 12, 1890, in Peytonsville, Tennessee. They had six children in 14-years.

William Albert Dodd died on December 3, 1943, in Peytonsville, Tennessee at the age of 75. He was buried in Mount Hope Cemetery in Franklin, Tennessee.

# THOMAS SHERIDAN
# WILLIAMS
# 1868-1918

## WILLIAMS FAMILY

### HUSBAND'S PARENTS
**Samuel Henry Williams**   **Martha H. Smithson**
1839 - 1885            1844 - 1897

### WIFE'S PARENTS
**James William Graham**   **Elizabeth Jane Day**
1830 - 1885            1844 - 1916

HUSBAND<br>
Thomas Sheridan Williams<br>
BIRTH: 15 Dec. 1868, Williamson Co. TN<br>
DEATH: 9 Dec. 1918, Peytonsville, TN

WIFE<br>
Susanna A. Graham<br>
BIRTH: 22 Dec. 1873, TN<br>
DEATH: 16 June 1904, Williamson Co. TN

CHILDREN

| | |
|---|---|
| **Bessie Alta Williams** Daughter | **BIRTH:** 15 Sep. 1892 <br> **DEATH:** 3 Dec. 1918 |
| **Marvin Henry Williams-Son** | **BIRTH:** 10 June 1894 <br> **DEATH:** 10 Nov. 1963 |
| **Lela Maud Williams** Daughter | **BIRTH:** 2 Mar. 1896 <br> **DEATH:** 27 Nov. 1975 |
| **Bertha Eugenia Williams-Daughter** | **BIRTH:** 8 Feb. 1900 <br> **DEATH:** 10 June 1975 |
| **Waverly "Doc" Laban Williams-Son** | **BIRTH:** 19 Oct. 1901 <br> **DEATH:** May 1975 |

HIS LIFE

When Thomas Sheridan Williams was born on December 15, 1868, in Williamson County, Tennessee, his father, Samuel was 29 and his mother, Martha was 24. He married, Susanna A. Graham on December 27, 1891, in Williamson County. They had five children during their marriage. He died on December 9, 1918, in Peytonsville, Tennessee at the age of 49.

━━━⌣━━━

SAMUEL HOUSTON PRATT<br>
1868-1904

PRATT FAMILY

HUSBAND'S PARENTS<br>
George Washington Pratt   Elizabeth O. Akin<br>
1829 - 1903         1837 - 1893

WIFE'S PARENTS<br>
Newton J. Wood   Rebecca Ann Giles<br>
1836 - 1903       1837 - 1910

HUSBAND<br>
Samuel Houston Pratt<br>
BIRTH: 15 Mar., 1868, Williamson Co, TN<br>
DEATH: 13 Oct. 1904, Peytonsville, TN

WIFE<br>
Mary Frances Wood<br>
BIRTH: 31 Aug. 1876, Williamson Co, TN<br>
DEATH: 28 Jan. 1942, Franklin, TN

CHILDREN

| | |
|---|---|
| **Clarence H. Pratt** Son | **BIRTH:** 1896 <br> **DEATH:** 15 Nov. 1974 |
| **John Edward Pratt** Son | **BIRTH:** 7 Dec. 1897 <br> **DEATH:** 9 Feb. 1977 |
| **Will Pratt** Son | **BIRTH:** 28 Feb. 1900 <br> **DEATH:** 14 Dec.1913 |
| **Sadie Florence Pratt** Daughter | **BIRTH:** 21 July 1902 <br> **DEATH:** 26 Aug. 1980 |
| **Sammie Lou Pratt** Daughter | **BIRTH:** 14 Oct. 1904 <br> **DEATH:** 8 Aug. 1906 |

HIS LIFE

When Samuel Houston Pratt was born on March 15, 1868, in Williamson County, Tennessee, his father, George was 38 and his mother, Elizabeth was 31. He married, Mary Frances Wood on January 19, 1892, in Peytonsville, Tennessee. They had five children during their marriage. Samuel died on his farm in Peytonsville on October 13, 1904, at the age of 36. He was buried in the Pratt Cemetery in Peytonsville.

# JOHN TYLER GENTRY
# 1868-1958

## GENTRY FAMILY

### HUSBAND'S PARENTS
**Edmon Gentry**     **Jane Morton**
1832 - ?              1828 - ?

### 1ST WIFE'S PARENTS
**Turner Thompson**     **Sallie Crofton**
1855 - ?                 1860 - ?

### 2ND WIFE'S PARENTS
**James Cunningham**     **Mattie Hendon**
1870 - 1937              1881 - 1945

### HUSBAND
**John Tyler Gentry**
**BIRTH:** 15 Nov. 1868, Lewisburg, TN
**DEATH:** 2 May 1958, Peytonsville, TN

### 1ST WIFE
**Josephine Thompson**
**BIRTH:** 16 Oct. 1877, Williamson Co. TN
**DEATH:** 30 Sep. 1928, Peytonsville, TN

### 2ND WIFE
**Jimmie Cunningham**
**BIRTH:** 14 Feb. 1902, TN
**DEATH:** 8 Oct. 1983, Franklin, TN

### CHILDREN OF JOHN AND JOSEPHINE

| | |
|---|---|
| **Homer Gentry** Son | **BIRTH:** Dec. 1898 <br> **DEATH:** 14 Aug. 1973 |
| **Annie Louise Gentry** Daughter | **BIRTH:** 1901 <br> **DEATH:** 1933 |
| **Sophronia B. Gentry** Daughter | **BIRTH:** 1901 <br> **DEATH:** Apr. 1985 |
| **William Edward Gentry-Son** | **BIRTH:** 16 Aug. 1904 <br> **DEATH:** 1 Oct. 1978 |
| **Mittie Gentry** Daughter | **BIRTH:** 9 Feb. 1905 <br> **DEATH:** 7 Oct. 1957 |
| **James Monroe Gentry** Son | **BIRTH:** 24 July 1908 <br> **DEATH:** 15 Jan. 1981 |
| **Gertrude Gentry** Daughter | **BIRTH:** 1913 <br> **DEATH:** 22 Apr. 1992 |
| **Gutin Gentry** Daughter | **BIRTH:** 1915 <br> **DEATH:** Unknown |
| **Howard Tyler Gentry** Son | **BIRTH:** 27 Dec. 1919 <br> **DEATH:** 26 Feb. 1992 |

### HIS LIFE

When John Tyler Gentry was born on November 15, 1868, in Lewisburg, Tennessee, his father, Edmon was 36 and his mother, Jane was 40. He married, Josephine Thompson on January 20, 1897 and they had nine children together. Josephine passed away on September 30, 1928, at the age of 50. They had been married 31-years. John married, Jimmie Cunningham on

January 28, 1931, when he was 62-years old. He died on May 2, 1958, in Williamson County, Tennessee at the age of 89.

JOHN TYLER GENTRY

# CHARLES WILSON VADEN
## 1869-1935

### VADEN FAMILY

#### HUSBAND'S PARENTS
**Nathaniel Bedford Vaden**  **Susan T. Gibson**
1844 - 1927                  1847 - 1913

#### WIFE'S PARENTS
**Charles W. Pennington**  **Sarah E. Sledge**
1831 - 1900                1841 - 1900

#### HUSBAND
**Charles Wilson Vaden**
**BIRTH:** 7 Aug. 1869, Peytonsville, TN
**DEATH:** 16 June 1935, Peytonsville, TN

### WIFE
**Nora E. Pennington**
**BIRTH:** 8 Mar. 1874, Peytonsville, TN
**DEATH:** 23 Aug. 1942, Peytonsville, TN

### CHILDREN

**Annie Ophelia Vaden**  **BIRTH:** 31 Dec. 1895
**Daughter**             **DEATH:** 1930

**Ada Vaden**  **BIRTH:** Sep. 1899
**Daughter**   **DEATH:** 1993

**Lera Mae Vaden**  **BIRTH:** 30 July 1903
**Daughter**        **DEATH:** 30 Aug. 1962

**Walter Wilson Vaden**  **BIRTH:** 7 Mar. 1913
**Son**                  **DEATH:** 30 Apr. 1980

### HIS LIFE

When Charles Wilson Vaden was born on August 7, 1869, in Peytonsville, Tennessee, his father, Nathaniel was 25 and his mother, Susan was 22. He married, Nora E. Pennington on January 13, 1892, in Peytonsville. They had four children in 17-years. He died on June 16, 1935, in Peytonsville at the age of 65.

NORA (PENNINGTON), CHARLES WILSON AND DAUGHTER, LERA MAE VADEN

# CLAUDE YORK
# 1869-1947

## YORK FAMILY

### HUSBAND'S PARENTS
**John Wesley York**      **Margaret R. Chrisman**
1840 - 1907              1845 - 1919

### WIFE'S PARENTS
**James W. Stevens**   **Nancy Nannie Westbrook**
1828 - 1915                1832 - 1916

### HUSBAND
**Claud York**
**BIRTH:** 12 Sep. 1869, Williamson Co. TN
**DEATH:** 28 Apr. 1947, Peytonsville, TN

### WIFE
**Josephine Stevens**
**BIRTH:** 10 Dec. 1872, TN
**DEATH:** 15 Jan. 1956, Williamson Co. TN

### CHILDREN

**Claude Douglas York**   **BIRTH:** 2 Mar. 1898
Son                       **DEATH:** Oct. 1980

**Beulah**                **BIRTH:** 24 July 1899
Daughter                  **DEATH:** 12 May 1977

**Beale Webster York**    **BIRTH:** 10 June 1901
Son                       **DEATH:** 20 Feb. 1974

**Pauline L. York**       **BIRTH:** 27 Dec. 1903
Daughter                  **DEATH:** 26 Mar. 2001

**Joseph Wesley York**    **BIRTH:** 2 June 1909
Son                       **DEATH:** 28 Dec. 1997

### HIS LIFE

When Claude York was born on September 12, 1869, in Nolensville, Tennessee, his father, John was 29 and his mother, Margaret was 24. He married, Josephine Stevens on April 7, 1897, in Williamson County, Tennessee. They had five

CLAUD AND JOSEPHINE
(STEVENS) YORK

# BRICE WILLIAM HUGHES
# 1870-1930

## HUGHES FAMILY

### HUSBAND'S PARENTS
**Brice Hughes**      **Mary Thornton**
1847 - 1915          1839 - 1900

### WIFE'S PARENTS
**Rufus Carter**      **Millie Buchanan**
1850 - ?             1848 - 1928

### HUSBAND
**Brice William Hughes**
**BIRTH:** Oct. 1870, Peytonsville, TN
**DEATH:** 19 May 1930, Peytonsville, TN

## WIFE
**Ruthie A. Carter**
**BIRTH:** 1878, TN
**DEATH:** Unknown

### CHILDREN

| | |
|---|---|
| **Millie E. Hughes** Daughter | **BIRTH:** 1903 **DEATH:** Unknown |
| **Fannie Lee Hughes** Daughter | **BIRTH:** 21 June 1904 **DEATH:** 20 Dec. 1945 |
| **Cassie M. Hughes** Daughter | **BIRTH:** 1905 **DEATH:** Unknown |
| **Rufus B. Hughes** Son | **BIRTH:** 1908 **DEATH:** Unknown |
| **Annie P. Hughes** Daughter | **BIRTH:** **1910** **DEATH:** Unknown |
| **Elnora Hughes** Daughter | **BIRTH:** 1915 **DEATH:** Unknown |
| **Elmer Hughes** Son | **BIRTH:** 1915 **DEATH:** Unknown |
| **Louise Hughes** Daughter | **BIRTH:** 1920 **DEATH:** Unknown |
| **Ruth Hughes** Daughter | **BIRTH:** 1923 **DEATH:** |

### HIS LIFE

When Brice William Hughes was born in October, 1870, in Williamson County, Tennessee his father, Brice was 22 and his mother, Mary was 31. He married, Ruthie A. Carter on September 5, 1900, in Williamson County. They had nine children in 20-years. He died on May 19, 1930, in Peytonsville, Tennessee at the age of 59. He was buried in the Westwood Cemetery in Peytonsville.

# THOMAS RICHARD "DICK" MEEK
# 1870-1957

### MEEK FAMILY

#### HUSBAND'S PARENTS
**Britton Marion Meek**      **Caroline Jennings**
1834 - 1919                          1838 - 1920

#### WIFE'S PARENTS
**John C. Smithson**      **Tennessee V. Gilliam**
1839 - 1896                       1848 - 1873

### HUSBAND
**Thomas Richard "Dick" Meek**
**BIRTH:** 15 Feb. 1870, Williamson Co. TN
**DEATH:** 26 July 1957, Davidson Co. TN

### WIFE
**Lena Allen Smithson**
**BIRTH:** 27 Oct. 1872, Gibson Co. TN
**DEATH:** 2 July 1913, Peytonsville, TN

### CHILDREN

| | |
|---|---|
| **Roy Gilliam Meek** Son | **BIRTH:** 10 Mar. 1895 **DEATH:** 13 Nov. 1967 |
| **Dixie Lorene Meek** Daughter | **BIRTH:** 18 Dec. 1896 **DEATH:** 4 July 1978 |
| **Addie Louise Meek** Daughter | **BIRTH:** 6 June 1902 **DEATH:** 9 Jan. 1968 |
| **Nell Caroline Meek** Daughter | **BIRTH:** 11 Sep. 1910 **DEATH:** 28 Apr. 2006 |

### HIS LIFE

When Thomas Richard "Dick" Meek was born on February 15, 1870, in Williamson County, Tennessee, his father, Britton was 35 and his mother, Caroline was 31. He married Lena Allen Smithson on September 19, 1893, in Peytonsville, Tennessee. They had four children in 15-years. He died on July 26, 1957, in Davidson County, Tennessee at the age of 87. He was buried in The Cool Springs Cemetery in Peytonsville.

# WILLIAM EARLY DAVIS
# 1870-1945

### DAVIS FAMILY

### HUSBAND'S PARENTS
**Thomas Alexander Davis**  **Nancy E. Ray**
1840 - 1919                 1841 - 1925

### WIFE'S PARENTS
**Reese Alexander Mills**  **Margaret F. Mills**
1859 - 1929                1866 - 1944

### HUSBAND
**William Early Davis**
**BIRTH:** 20 Nov. 1870, Tallapoosa, AL
**DEATH:** 27 Aug. 1945, Peytonsville, TN

### WIFE
**Lillie Mills**
**BIRTH:** 1895, Williamson Co. TN
**DEATH:** 1989, Peytonsville, TN

### CHILDREN

| | |
|---|---|
| **Mary Elizabeth Davis** Daughter | **BIRTH:** 9 June 1911 **DEATH:** 1 Oct. 1999 |
| **Margaret Florence Davis-Daughter** | **BIRTH:** 31 July 1912 **DEATH:** 9 Feb. 1980 |
| **Eugene Jonah Davis** Son | **BIRTH:** 25 Aug. 1914 **DEATH:** 28 Sep. 1999 |
| **Nell Davis** Daughter | **BIRTH:** 22 Jan. 1917 **DEATH:** Nov. 2008 |
| **Rachel Frances Davis** Daughter | **BIRTH:** 16 Aug. 1919 **DEATH:** 4 Feb. 2018 |
| **Willie "Billie Thomas Davis-Daughter** | **BIRTH:** 8 Feb. 1923 **DEATH:** 12 Aug. 2006 |
| **Ada Nancy Davis** Daughter | **BIRTH:** 6 Dec. 1924 **DEATH:** 22 Dec. 2015 |

### HIS LIFE

When William Early Davis was born on November 20, 1870, in Tallapoosa, Alabama, his father, Thomas was 30 and his mother, Nancy was 28. He married, Lillie Mills on January 17, 1911, in Williamson County, Tennessee. They had seven children in 13-years. He died on August 27, 1945, in Peytonsville, Tennessee when he was 74-years old. He was buried in the Cool Springs Cemetery in Peytonsville.

# FIELDON A. GLENN
# 1870-1940

## GLENN FAMILY

### HUSBAND'S PARENTS
**John R. Glenn**     **Louisa Virginia Warren**
1836 - 1891                 1838 - 1903

### WIFE'S PARENTS
**George Washington King  Nancy L. Roberts**
1828 - 1914                 1837 - 1911

### HUSBAND
**Fieldon A. Glenn**
**BIRTH:** 27 Dec. 1870, Peytonsville, TN
**DEATH:** 10 Sep. 1940, Peytonsville, TN

### WIFE
**Mary Ada King**
**BIRTH:** 4 July 1868, Peytonsville, TN
**DEATH:** Feb. 1966, Peytonsville, TN

## CHILDREN

**Ila Bell Glenn**
**Daughter**
**BIRTH:** 16 Jan. 1894
**DEATH:** 26 Feb. 1994

**Beatrice Glenn**
**Daughter**
**BIRTH:** 19 Apr. 1896
**DEATH:** May 1985

**Roger Henesker Glenn-Daughter**
**BIRTH:** 6 June 1901
**DEATH:** 27 Nov. 1934

**Richard Wade Glenn**
**Son**
**BIRTH:** 11 Nov. 1904
**DEATH:** 23 Nov. 1960

**Ella Mae Glenn**
**Daughter**
**BIRTH:** 11 Aug. 1908
**DEATH:** 31 Mar. 1995

**John Edward Glenn**
**Son**
**BIRTH:** 9 June 1912
**DEATH:** 4 Nov. 1988

## HIS LIFE

When Fieldon A. Glenn was born on December 27, 1870, in Peytonsville, Tennessee, his father, John was 34 and his mother, Louisa was 32. He married Mary Ada King on July 13, 1892, in Peytonsville. They had six children in 18-years. He died on September 10, 1940, in Peytonsville at the age of 69. He was buried in the King Cemetery in Peytonsville.

# WALTER LEE JOHNSON
# 1871-1944

## JOHNSON FAMILY

### HUSBAND'S PARENTS
**William Lewis Johnson     Elizabeth Allen**
1840 - 1908                 1843 - 1922

### WIFE'S PARENTS
**E. "Standing Bear" Gosey     A.V. Johnson**
1820 - 1887                 1839 - 1900

**Walter Lee Johnson**
**BIRTH:** 20 Mar. 1871, Williamson Co. TN
**DEATH:** 21 Nov. 1944, Peytonsville, TN

WIFE
**Minnie Virginia Gosey**
**BIRTH:** 14 Aug. 1875, Peytonsville, TN
**DEATH:** 17 Dec. 1928, Peytonsville, TN

CHILDREN

| | |
|---|---|
| **Samuel Earl Johnson** Son | **BIRTH:** 20 May 1894 **DEATH:** 24 July 1960 |
| **Sadie A. Johnson** Daughter | **BIRTH:** 6 May 1896 **DEATH:** 27 Jan. 1974 |
| **Blythe Edward Johnson-Son** | **BIRTH:** 8 May 1899 **DEATH:** Unknown |
| **Cora Elizabeth Johnson-Daughter** | **BIRTH:** 21 Feb. 1910 **DEATH:** 29 Jan. 1998 |
| **William Louis Johnson-Son** | **BIRTH:** 4 Dec. 1913 **DEATH:** 8 Aug. 2007 |
| **Murray Lee Johnson** Son | **BIRTH:** 29 May 1918 **DEATH:** 6 Apr. 1971 |

HIS LIFE

When Walter Lee Johnson was born on March 20, 1871, in Williamson County, Tennessee, his father, William was 30 and his mother, Elizabeth was 28. He married Minnie Virginia Gosey on November 10, 1892, in Peytonsville, Tennessee. They had six children in 24-years. He died on November 21, 1944, in Peytonsville at the age of 73. He was buried in the Mount Hope Cemetery in Franklin, Tennessee.

# EWELL CANNON LADD
## 1871-1946

LADD FAMILY

HUSBAND'S PARENTS
**John C. Ladd**   **Mary H. Burge**
1844 - 1924        1845 - ?

WIFE'S PARENTS
**James Lucas Gee**   **Sarah Ann Smithson**
1828 - 1896           1843 - 1915

HUSBAND
**Ewell Cannon Ladd**
**BIRTH:** 28 Mar. 1871, Williamson Co. TN
**DEATH:** 24 May 1946, Franklin, TN

WIFE
**Ola Mai Gee**
**BIRTH:** 17 Dec. 1877, Williamson Co. TN
**DEATH:** 14 Sep. 1943, Franklin, TN

CHILDREN

| | |
|---|---|
| **James Archie Ladd** Son | **BIRTH:** 18 Dec. 1895 **DEATH:** 2 Jan. 1968 |

When Ewell Cannon Ladd was born on March 28, 1871, in Williamson County, Tennessee, his father, John was 27 and his mother, Mary was 26. He married Ola Mai Gee on March 28, 1895, in Peytonsville, Tennessee. They had one child during their marriage. He died on May 24, 1946, in Franklin, Tennessee at the age of 75. He was buried in the Ladd Cemetery.

# THOMAS PRESTON CRAFTON
# 1871-1952

## CRAFTON FAMILY

### HUSBAND'S PARENTS

**John Thomas Crafton**  **Martha J. Johnson**
1835 - 1927  1852 - 1922

### 1ST WIFE'S PARENTS

**David Monroe Tomlin**  **Martha Emma Ford**
1848 - 1933  1855 - 1907

### 2ND WIFE'S PARENTS

**John Abner Tomlin**  **Sarah Elizabeth Tucker**
1855 - 1944  1853 - 1912

### HUSBAND
**Thomas Preston Crafton**
BIRTH: 9 May 1871, Williamson Co. TN
DEATH: 24 June 1952, Franklin, TN

### 1ST WIFE
**Sallie B. Tomlin**
BIRTH: 21 Feb. 1878, Williamson Co. TN
DEATH: Williamson Co. TN

### 2ND WIFE
**Rosie "Tennie" Tomlin**
BIRTH: 15 Oct. 1888, Williamson Co. TN
DEATH: 2 Jan. 1941, Williamson Co. TN

## CHILDREN OF THOMAS AND SALLIE

**Leslie Preston Crafton-Son**
BIRTH: 31 July 1894
DEATH: 22 Dec. 1937

**John David Crafton Son**
BIRTH: 31 Mar. 1897
DEATH: Aug. 1968

**Robert Edward Crafton-Son**
BIRTH: 10 Aug. 1899
DEATH: 3 Jan. 1965

## CHILDREN OF THOMAS AND TENNIE

**Fannie Bell Crafton Daughter**
BIRTH: 17 Aug. 1908
DEATH: 27 June 1959

**Martha Elizabeth Crafton-Daughter**
BIRTH: 23 July 1910
DEATH: 9 May 2007

**Jo Howard Crafton Daughter**
BIRTH: 12 Mar. 1912
DEATH: 30 Oct. 1987

**Rosie Adeline Crafton Daughter**
BIRTH: 1 Sep. 1913
DEATH: 21 Sep. 1933

**Charles Buford Crafton-Son**
BIRTH: 6 Dec. 1914
DEATH: 12 June 1973

**Edward Lee Crafton Son**
BIRTH: 1 Aug. 1916
DEATH: 1978

**Andrew Blythe Crafton-Son**
BIRTH: 15 Sep. 1918
DEATH: 26 June 1981

**Lucy Inez Crafton Daughter**
BIRTH: 30 July 1920
DEATH: 10 May 2008

**Mary Alice Crafton Daughter**
BIRTH: 24 May 1922
DEATH: 20 June 2001

**Cora Louise Crafton Daughter**
BIRTH: 30 June 1924
DEATH: Mar. 1995

**Annie Frances Crafton-Daughter**
BIRTH: 24 Feb. 1926
DEATH: 25 Aug. 2008

**Alpha Pearl Crafton Daughter**
BIRTH: 26 Dec. 1929
DEATH: 8 Oct. 2011

When Thomas Preston Crafton was born on May 9, 1871, in Williamson County, Tennessee, his father, John was 36 and his mother, Martha was 19. He married, Sallie B. Tomlin on October 12, 1893 and they had three children together. Sallie died sometime between 1899 and 1906. Thomas married, Rosie "Tennie" Tomlin on September 9, 1906 in Williamson County. They had 12 children together. He died on June 24, 1952, in Franklin, Tennessee at the age of 81. He was buried in the Cool Springs Cemetery in Peytonsville, Tennessee.

# WILLIAM ALLEN BENNETT
## 1871-?

### BENNETT FAMILY

### HUSBAND'S PARENTS
**Alexander B. Bennett    Minerva Jane Tucker**
1843 - 1908                1844 - 1890

### WIFE'S PARENTS
**Joseph Cook    Anna Osborne**
1865 - ?          1867 - ?

### HUSBAND
**William Allen Bennett**
**BIRTH:** 28 Mar. 1871, Williamson Co. TN
**DEATH:** Peytonsville, TN

### WIFE
**Lilla Cook**
**BIRTH:** 2 Aug. 1885, Williamson Co, TN
**DEATH:** 31 Jan. 1920, Peytonsville, TN

### CHILDREN

**Joe Harrison Bennett    BIRTH:** 11 June 1907
**Son                          DEATH:** 22 Apr. 1990

**Mamie Lou Bennett    BIRTH:** 8 July 1910
**Daughter                 DEATH:** 23 Mar. 1974



When William Allen Bennett was born in 1871 in Williamson County, Tennessee, his father Alexander was 28 and his mother Minerva was 27. He married Lilla Cook on June 25, 1906 in Williamson County. They had two children during their marriage.

# OLIVER CLAIBORNE LILLARD
## 1873-1953

### LILLARD FAMILY

### HUSBAND'S PARENTS
**Monroe Claiborne Lillard    Mary Penny Hay**
1844 - 1891                        1847 - 1917

### 1ST WIFE'S PARENTS
**Thomas Alexander Davis    Nancy E. Ray**
1840 - 1919                       1841 - 1925

### 2ND WIFE'S PARENTS
**James W. Robinson    Malissa A.M. White**
1816 - 1879                  1835 - 1905

### HUSBAND
**Oliver Claiborne Lillard**
**BIRTH:** 15 Sep. 1873, Peytonsville, TN
**DEATH:** 7 Mar. 1953, Peytonsville, TN

### 1ST WIFE
**Greer Jordan Davis**
**BIRTH:** 19 Jan. 1879, TN
**DEATH:** 13 Jun. 1926, Williamson Co. TN

### 2ND WIFE
**Lena Robinson**
**BIRTH:** 1876, TN
**DEATH:** 1961, Davidson Co. TN

## CHILDREN OF OLIVER AND GREER

| | |
|---|---|
| **James Abner Lillard**<br>**Son** | **BIRTH:** 2 Jan. 1897<br>**DEATH:** 15 Feb. 1967 |
| **Mary Rachel Lillard**<br>**Daughter** | **BIRTH:** May 1900<br>**DEATH:** 23 Feb. 1981 |
| **Davis Marion Lillard**<br>**Son** | **BIRTH:** 22 Dec. 1903<br>**DEATH:** 10 Feb. 1938 |
| **Johnnie Oliver Lillard**<br>**Son** | **BIRTH:** 27 Oct. 1906<br>**DEATH:** 25 Dec. 1980 |
| **Rena Lou Lillard**<br>**Daughter** | **BIRTH:** 30 Jan. 1911<br>**DEATH:** 8 Jan. 1981 |

### HIS LIFE

**Ollie Claiborne Lillard story January 13, 1949**

Out in the thirteenth district near Peytonsville, on September 15, 1873, a son was born to Clayborne and Penny Hay LIllard whom they named Ollie Claiborne, but as time went on and three other children were added to the family he became known as O.C and by this has answered for 75 years. He and his siblings gathered around the table three times a day to enjoy the wholesome meals prepared by his mother who knew nothing about vitamins ranging from A to Z, but fed them food which developed sound bones, teeth, brawn and alert minds.

The family lived on a sixty-acre farm which the boys helped to cultivate and attended school at Cool Springs with Joe Stephens, Pat Smithson and Mrs. Mary Moore as teachers. He said he did not remember very much about what knowledge the men teachers imparted but does know they were long on the whipping, one of the greatest offenses being for chewing gum during "books' and he was one of the chief offenders. One of the worst administered was on a day when the teacher was called from the room and a wild scramble ensued to gain possession of the teacher's chair when he unexpectedly returned and every pupil out of his or her seat was soon feeling the sting of a long keen switch,

he of course, in the number, for he never passed up a chance to get into mischief.

In those days, there were no free hot lunches but he was all in favor of them for the present generation and every other improvement for the good of the youth of today. He is not the kind of person who believes "What was good enough for me is good enough for my grandchildren," for if this were true why not revert to the inconveniences of home living and farming facilities? His lunch was carried in a tin bucket and his history, speller, arithmetic and reading books in a satchel made of bed-ticking by his mother who always had their clothes neat and mended when they left home in the morning, but it was a different story when they returned in the afternoon, as they were forever wrestling, fighting, climbing trees or otherwise engaging in strenuous activities.

At the age of 22, Mr. Lillard married a neighborhood girl, Greer Davis, 18-year old daughter of Eck and Nancy Ray Davis, the ceremony taking place in the Davis home. They went immediately to housekeeping in a very meager way in a log house for the groom's wealth consisted of $25 in cash and a plug horse. The money was spent very judiciously for furniture and groceries. He is frank to admit money went much farther in those days than now, and they suffered no special privations for their wants were few. Of their five children four are living. Mrs. Mary Hay and Mrs. Rena Gillespie of Bethesda, J.O. Lillard of Thompsons Station and James who lives with his father.

After the death of his wife Mr. Lillard married Mrs. Lena Robinson, daughter of James and Malissa White Robinson who lived on the road leading from Bethesda to Duplex, and she attended school under about the same conditions as did Mr. Lillard. She is the mother of four children, Jim, Charlie and W.A. Byrd and Mrs. Luverna Tidwell, all of whom live in Nashville. So close are the two sets of children there is little if any difference in the love they have for each other and all appreciate the kindness and consideration Mrs. Lillard bestows upon the brother, James, who lives at home. The same feeling exists between Mr. Lillard's eleven grandchildren and Mrs. Lillard's two, also with her several great-grandchildren. Their plans now are to get the entire family together next summer for a picnic. Mr. Lillard says it is easier to keep the group cool in summer than to keep them warm in winter.

When Mr. and Mrs. Lillard were young they attended school together and were sweethearts, but as they grew older they drifted apart and each married. After their mates were claimed by death their paths again crossed resulting in marriage. As their children were not strangers to each other may partly account for the mutual love and understanding they have always had.

In 1906 Mr. Lillard was elected to the Williamson County Court to represent the thirteenth district, a position held until just before the last election when he resigned and was succeeded by Sam McGee. He and Esquire J.F. Cook went in at the same time, served the same number of terms going out together and were the oldest members of the court. They served under Judges F.C. Russell, H.D. Henderson, J.F. Mays, J.M. Burke, D.B. Graham and Jerre M. Fly and were on several important committees. They saw much improvements in roads and bridges over the county, many schools built and terms extended from three to nine months with teachers' salaries increased from $25 per month to the present standard.

After retiring Mr. Lillard has devoted his time to his farm of 176 acres which he paid for with hard work and penny pinching for he learned, as a boy if he looked after the pennies the dollars would take care of themselves. The two-story brick house is equipped with electricity, which runs the refrigerator, washing machine, stove, other smaller appliances and the radio. They also have electricity in the modern dairy barn where 19 cows are milked and cared for by two

of his grandson's, Walter and Marvin Lillard, sons of Davis, who died several years ago. They and their mother live in a house on the place, both are graduates of Bethesda High School and, as the grandfather expressed it, "are mighty fine industrious boys with no bad habits."

Walter and Marvin cultivate the farm, using mules rather than tractors. They raise hogs for home use and to sell, also raise tobacco, corn and hay.

Mrs. Lillard says she raises Leghorn chickens, and the foxes help the family eat them. They have the children visit them often and never like to run short of food when they come and for that reason try to keep the poultry yard well supplied.

Mr. Lillard seems to think he has been well blessed physically from boyhood on for the only times he was ever sick was when he had typhoid fever as a boy and later a spell of malaria, but was never hospitalized. Financially he has gone from a log cabin heated by a wood fire to the 100-year old two-story, six-room brick kept warm with oil heaters. His swayback horse of his young days long ago gave way to a buggy and that to an automobile, and is now riding in his third one. He is of a quiet, retired disposition, likes to stay at home and listen to the radio. His wife is the only talking member of the family so it falls to him to listen, but, unlike the radio, he can not shut her off.

Both Mr. and Mrs. Lillard are members of Cool Spring Primitive Baptist Church where his grandson, Milton Lillard, is pastor, and Mr. Lillard remarked, "He is a good preacher even if he does have me for a granddad, and I like to hear him."

Neighbors know where to go for help when in need of anything and it isn't convenient to go to town or the neighborhood store. They are neighborly neighbors, like to lend a helping hand and never turn from their door unaided those who need assistance, obeying the admonition, of the greatest of all Teachers, "Freely ye have received, freely give."

Oliver Claiborne Lillard died on March 7, 1953, in Peytonsville, Tennessee at the age of 79. He was buried in the Cool Springs Cemetery in Peytonsville.

FRONT: OLIVER AND JIM, BACK: RENA (LILLARD GILLESPIE, JOHNNY AND MARY (LILLARD) HAY

# WILLIAM "LEE" GARNER
## 1873-1959

### GARNER FAMILY

#### HUSBAND'S PARENTS
**Paul David Garner**  **Mary "Molly" C. Pinkston**
1850 - 1926          1856 - 1920

#### WIFE'S PARENTS
**Alexander B. Bennett**  **Minerva J. Tucker**
1843 - 1908          1844 - 1890

### HUSBAND
**William "Lee" Garner**
BIRTH: 22 Nov. 1873, Williamson Co. TN
DEATH: 9 Mar. 1959, Peytonsville, TN

### WIFE
**Martha Susan Bennett**
BIRTH: 10 Jan. 1879, Peytonsville, TN
DEATH: 10 Apr. 1968, Peytonsville, TN

### CHILDREN

| | |
|---|---|
| **Ermie Irene Garner** Daughter | BIRTH: Sep. 1898 DEATH: 24 May 1918 |
| **Mary Elizabeth Garner**-Daughter | BIRTH: 27 July 1899 DEATH: 17 June 1979 |
| **Maggie Virginia Garner**-Daughter | BIRTH: 2 July 1901 DEATH: 14 Aug. 1969 |
| **Wavie Garner** Daughter | BIRTH: 19 May 1903 DEATH: 28 Nov. 1906 |
| **Bertie May Garner** Daughter | BIRTH: 28 Dec. 1904 DEATH: 3 Mar. 1998 |
| **Elijah Alexander Garner**-Son | BIRTH: 14 Mar. 1907 DEATH: 4 Feb. 1979 |
| **Malcolm Patterson Garner**-Son | BIRTH: 24 Mar. 1910 DEATH: 1 May 1983 |
| **Lenora Garner** Daughter | BIRTH: 25 May 1912 DEATH: 9 Jan. 1913 |
| **Andrew Thomas Garner**-Son | BIRTH: 11 Nov. 1914 DEATH: 24 June 1998 |
| **Susie Lee Garner** Daughter | BIRTH: 1918 DEATH: 19 Dec. 1965 |
| **Lee Garner Jr.** Son | BIRTH: 1919 DEATH: 1919 |
| **Lona Garner** Daughter | BIRTH: 14 Sep. 1920 DEATH: 8 Mar. 1997 |

## HIS LIFE

When William "Lee" Garner was born on November 22, 1873, in Peytonsville, Tennessee, his father, Paul was 23 and his mother, Mary was 17. He married Martha Susan Bennett on October 25, 1896, in Peytonsville, Tennessee. They had 12 children in 22-years. He died on March 9, 1959, in Peytonsville at the age of 85. He was buried in the Bennett Cemetery in Peytonsville.

LEE AND SUSIE (BENNETT) GARNER

# DEE STARNES
# 1873-1959

## STARNES FAMILY

### HUSBAND'S PARENTS

**William Starnes**  **Jane Redmond**
1834 - 1920  1844 - ?

### WIFE'S PARENTS

**Henry Beal**  **Cornelia Parrish**
1850 - 1911  1852 - 1928

### HUSBAND
**Dee Starnes**
BIRTH: 4 Jan. 1873, Williamson Co, TN
DEATH: 2 Jan. 1959, Franklin, TN

### WIFE
**Minnie Beal**
BIRTH: Oct. 1883, TN
DEATH: 13 June 1953, Williamson Co, TN

### CHILDREN

**Hattie Pearl Starnes**  BIRTH: 1903
**Daughter**  DEATH: Mar. 1960

## HIS LIFE

When Dee Starnes was born on January 4, 1873, in Williamson County, Tennessee, his father, William was 38 and his mother, Jane was 29. He married Minnie Beal on January 11, 1902, in Peytonsville, Tennessee. They had one child during their marriage. He died on January 2, 1959, in Williamson County at the age of 85. He was buried in the Beal Cemetery in Williamson County.

# JAMES WATSON KING
# 1874-1940

## KING FAMILY

### HUSBAND'S PARENTS
**George Washington King  Nancy L. Roberts**
1828 - 1914  1837 - 1911

### WIFE'S PARENTS
**William Obidiah Simmons  Margaret A. Spann**
1852 - 1939  1857 - 1933

### HUSBAND
**James Watson King**
BIRTH: 21 Oct. 1874, Peytonsville, TN
DEATH: 12 Oct. 1940, Peytonsville, TN

### WIFE
**Lillie Simmons**
BIRTH: 5 Oct. 1890, Rutherford Co. TN
DEATH: 22 Dec. 1946, Peytonsville, TN

| | |
|---|---|
| **Nancy Ann Elizabeth King-Daughter** | **BIRTH:** 17 Apr. 1913<br>**DEATH:** Aug. 1968 |
| **Ruby Inez King Daughter** | **BIRTH:** 1 Aug. 1914<br>**DEATH:** 2000 |
| **George Washington King-Son** | **BIRTH:** 23 Dec. 1915<br>**DEATH:** 21 May 2009 |
| **James Wade "Dock" King-Son** | **BIRTH:** 9 Feb. 1918<br>**DEATH:** 30 Oct. 1964 |
| **Jesse Milton King Son** | **BIRTH:** 25 May 1919<br>**DEATH:** 4 Oct. 1975 |
| **Francis Wray "Buck" King-Son** | **BIRTH:** 27 Aug. 1921<br>**DEATH:** 31 Aug. 1988 |
| **Jannie C. King Daughter** | **BIRTH:** 1924<br>**DEATH:** Unknown |

## HIS LIFE

When James Watson King was born on October 21, 1874, in Peytonsville, Tennessee, his father, George was 44 and his mother, Nancy was 36. He married Lillie Simmons on May 23, 1912 in Peytonsville. They had seven children in 11-years. He died on October 12, 1940, at the age of 66. He was buried in the King Cemetery in Peytonsville.

# ALVA LEE VADEN
## 1874-1954

### VADEN FAMILY

**HUSBAND'S PARENTS**

**Mark Wilson Vaden**     **Martha J. Johnson**
1840 - 1919                     1845 - 1919

**WIFE'S PARENTS**

**Abram W. Hatcher**   **Martha E. Chriesman**
1835 - 1902                     1844 - 1912

---

## HUSBAND
**Alva Lee Vaden**
**BIRTH:** 24 May 1874, Peytonsville, TN
**DEATH:** 31 Jan. 1954, Peytonsville, TN

## WIFE
**Sarah Alice Hatcher**
**BIRTH:** 14 Aug. 1877, Williamson Co. TN
**DEATH:** 15 Sep. 1940, Peytonsville, TN

## CHILDREN

| | |
|---|---|
| **Martha Elise Vaden Daughter** | **BIRTH:** 22 Sep. 1900<br>**DEATH:** 17 Dec. 1995 |
| **Jennie Vaden Daughter** | **BIRTH:** 19 Nov. 1902<br>**DEATH:** Unknown |
| **Leonard Wilson Vaden-Son** | **BIRTH:** 24 Feb. 1907<br>**DEATH:** 26 Apr. 1986 |

## HIS LIFE

When Alva Lee Vaden was born on May 24, 1874, in Peytonsville, Tennessee, his father, Mark was 34 and his mother, Martha was 29. He married Sarah Alice Hatcher on December 22, 1898, in Peytonsville. They had three children during their marriage. He died on January 31, 1954 in Peytonsville at the age of 79. He was buried in the Mount Hope Cemetery in Franklin, Tennessee.

ALVA AND SARAH (HATCHER)
VADEN

# JAMES HIRAM MATHIS
# 1874-1955

## MATHIS FAMILY

### HUSBAND'S PARENTS
**Jerry Mathis**   **Frances Elizabeth Adair**
1847 - 1927         1849 - 1909

### WIFE'S PARENTS
**Green Burgess**   **Rachel Elizabeth Burgess**
1832 - 1900         1838 - 1883

### HUSBAND
**James Hiram Mathis**
BIRTH: 27 Jun. 1874, Williamson Co. TN
DEATH: 18 July 1955, Franklin, TN

### WIFE
**Eunice Mariah E. Burgess**
BIRTH: Williamson Co. TN
DEATH: 14 Sep. 1957, Franklin, TN

## CHILDREN

**James Walter Mathis**   BIRTH: 25 Feb. 1901
Son                       DEATH: 27 Jan. 1973

**Bertie Mae Mathis**     BIRTH: Feb. 1906
Daughter                  DEATH: 13 Mar. 1948

**Rachel F. Mathis**      BIRTH: Aug. 1907
Daughter                  DEATH: 8 Jan. 1976

**Jerry Braden Mathis**   BIRTH: 21 May 1909
Son                       DEATH: 17 Mar. 1953

## HIS LIFE

When James Hiram Mathis was born on June 27, 1874, in Williamson County, Tennessee, his father, Jerry was 27 and his mother, Frances was 24. He married Eunice Mariah E. Burgess in 1899. They had four children during their marriage. He died on July 18, 1955, in Franklin, Tennessee. He was buried in the Mount Hope Cemetery in Franklin.

JAMES W., RACHEL, JAMES HIRAM,
BERTIE MAE, JERRY BRADEN AND
EUNICE (BURGESS) MATHIS

# RICHARD PALESTINE
# "DICK" WADDEY
# 1874-1962

## WADDEY FAMILY

**John Thomas Waddey**     **Sophronia Low**
1846 - 1911                1850 - 1875


### WIFE'S PARENTS

**John Hal Stephens**     **Emma Jane Giles**
1851 - 1929               1853 - 1883


### HUSBAND
**Richard Palestine "Dick" Waddey**
**BIRTH:** 29 Nov. 1874, Williamson Co. TN
**DEATH:** 14 Oct. 1962, Peytonsville, TN


### WIFE
**Maggie Virginia Stephens**
**BIRTH:** 11 Apr. 1874, TN
**DEATH:** 6 Feb. 1950, Williamson Co. TN


### CHILDREN

**Lee Stanford Waddey**     **BIRTH:** 9 Feb. 1898
**Son**                     **DEATH:** 2 Dec. 1975

**Ira C. Waddey**           **BIRTH:** 31 July 1900
**Son**                     **DEATH:** 27 Mar. 1994

**Margaret Emma**           **BIRTH:** 8 Feb. 1903
**Waddey-Daughter**         **DEATH:** July 1903


### HIS LIFE

When Richard Palestine Waddey was born on November 29, 1874, in Williamson County, Tennessee, his father, John was 27 and his mother, Sophronia was 24.

**From *The Review-Appeal*, February 6, 1941**
**By: Jane Owen**

Tillers of the soil probably get nearer to Mother Nature than those of any other calling. They watch closer her manifold wonders, how a small seed must be nurtured, tended carefully, studied diligently and given every advantage in order that it may develop into the study plant nature intended it to be. The same care is given fowls and animals under their supervision and for this reason boys reared on the farm, who are carefully trained to look for defects, try to correct them and thereby raise better products, oftentimes grow up to make better fathers. This certainly has held true in the case of Richard P. Waddey, better known as plain Dick Waddey, a true dirt farmer in the 13th district.

He is a son of the late Tom and Dolly Low Waddey, of Peytonsville, where he and his brother, John, a bachelor, lived on adjoining farms. Their mother died when the baby, Dick was two months old. The older brother was taken into the home of his grandparents, Gabriel and Viney Low, and reared with the two sons and seven daughters of that family, while the helpless little baby found a safe haven of rest in the arms of his aunt, Virginia Waddey Stanford and her good spouse Cicero Stanford, who were childless and welcomed the small bundle of humanity as a  gift to them from heaven.

The father remarried and by the second union two girls were born and both are dead. At the death of his second wife, he again married and reared a family of six children, four of whom are still living, though badly scattered and rarely heard from. Mr. Waddey was born November 29, 1874, and when he reached school age, he was reluctantly sent by his foster parents to the home of his father to enroll at Ash Hill School as there was no school within walking distance of their home. He stayed seven weeks and each day the separation from his adored aunt and her husband became harder to bear like unto a millstone about his neck, and being a frail child from birth, he began to pine away and refused to be comforted.

In the school and another member of the primer class was an attractive little girl, Maggie Stephens, who noticed his dejected air and tried to cheer him up, even to offering him choice tidbits from her lunch. Though he appreciated her kindness, yet it failed to compensate, one weekend he went home and refused to leave. Though his father and stepmother had been kindness itself, yet he could not endure the separation from his childhood haunts. The aunt and uncle were just as miserable over the situation and were only too happy to have him back. They entered him in Cool Springs School and took turns taking him back and forth, making the trip on horseback with the little fellow riding behind. On these trips he learned more about life and its problems than he did from his books, for they were both true philosophers and never tired of explaining anything concerning life that puzzled the little fellow.

Later he went to Bethesda to such men as Enoch Chest, Joe Stephens and other teachers of that day, famous both as instructors and disciplinarians. Mr. Stephens ancestor was a great hunter and trapper and must have been a successful one for he made enough to pay for his farm of large acreage. His Grandfather (Gabriel) Low, was a ginwright and Grandfather (Ben) Waddey a chair and spinning wheel maker. In Mr. Waddey's home are four chairs made by his grandfather in 1866. His father was a member for three years of Starnes's Regiment during the Civil War, enlisting at the age of 16, and escaped with a wound.

A good definition of Mr. Waddey is well summed up in the word of William Ellery Channing, "A friend is he who sets his heart upon us, is happy in us, and delights in us, —does for what we want, is willing and fully engaged to do all he can for us, on whom we can rely in all cases."

July 30, 1896, Dick Waddey married Maggie Stephens, the same little girl who tried to comfort him in grade school. Together they had three children. He died on October 14, 1962, in Peytonsville, Tennessee at the age of 87. He was buried in the Mount Hope Cemetery in Franklin, Tennessee.

RICHARD PALESTINE "DICK" WADDEY

# SAMUEL MOSES KING
# 1875-1949

### KING FAMILY

### HUSBAND'S PARENTS
**George Washington King**   **Nancy L. Roberts**
1828 - 1914                            1837 - 1911

### WIFE'S PARENTS
**David Monroe Tomlin**   **Martha Emma Ford**
1848 - 1933                          1855 - 1907

### HUSBAND
**Samuel Moses King**
**BIRTH:** 15 Dec. 1875, Peytonsville, TN
**DEATH:** 1 Nov. 1949, Marshall Co. TN

**Ophelia Elizabeth Tomlin**
**BIRTH:** 20 Aug. 1886, Williamson Co. TN
**DEATH:** 20 Apr. 1939, Nashville, TN

## CHILDREN

| | |
|---|---|
| **George Monroe King** Son | **BIRTH:** 18 Feb. 1904 **DEATH:** 13 Apr. 1904 |
| **Ellis Elizabeth King** Daughter | **BIRTH:** 31 July 1905 **DEATH:** 7 Apr. 1999 |
| **Willie Bob King** Son | **BIRTH:** 14 Feb. 1908 **DEATH:** 30 Jan. 1971 |
| **Annie Sue King** Daughter | **BIRTH:** 19 Sep. 1910 **DEATH:** 6 Mar. 1987 |
| **Katy M. King** Daughter | **BIRTH:** 1914 **DEATH:** Unknown |
| **Moses King** Son | **BIRTH:** 21 Feb. 1916 **DEATH:** 1 Oct. 2007 |
| **Joseph King** Son | **BIRTH:** 21 Feb. 1916 **DEATH:** 18 May 1998 |
| **Fealon Claude King** Son | **BIRTH:** 15 Nov. 1918 **DEATH:** 7 July 1949 |
| **Walter Thomas "Bull" King**-Son | **BIRTH:** 2 May 1922 **DEATH:** 7 Aug. 2010 |
| **Kovie Lorene King** Daughter | **BIRTH:** 6 Aug. 1924 **DEATH:** 1 Oct. 1997 |

## HIS LIFE

When Samuel Moses King was born on December 15, 1875, in Williamson County, Tennessee, his father, George was 47 and his mother, Nancy was 38. He married Ophelia Elizabeth Tomlin on August 22, 1902, in Peytonsville, Tennessee. They had 10 children in 20-years. He died on November 1, 1949, in Marshall County, Tennessee at the age of 73. He was buried in the Cool Springs Cemetery in Peytonsville.

# SAMUEL TOLIVER MATHIS
# 1875-1939

MATHIS FAMILY

### HUSBAND'S PARENTS

| **Jerry Mathis** | **Frances Elizabeth Adair** |
|---|---|
| 1847 - 1927 | 1849 - 1909 |

### WIFE'S PARENTS

| **William Henry Crunk** | **Mary Elizabeth Tanner** |
|---|---|
| 1852 - 1918 | 1851 - 1926 |

### HUSBAND

**Samuel Toliver Mathis**
**BIRTH:** 2 Nov. 1875, Marshall Co. TN
**DEATH:** 6 Dec. 1939, Peytonsville, TN

### WIFE

**Martha Louise Crunk**
**BIRTH:** 10 Jan. 1879, Williamson Co. TN
**DEATH:** 20 July 1958, Peytonsville, TN

## CHILDREN

| | |
|---|---|
| **Sammie Lou Mathis** Daughter | **BIRTH:** 19 Dec. 1903 **DEATH:** 13 July 1983 |
| **Johnnie Mae Mathis** Daughter | **BIRTH:** 10 Aug. 1906 **DEATH:** 6 Jan. 1969 |
| **Susie Lee Mathis** Daughter | **BIRTH:** 1912 **DEATH:** 1975 |
| **Charles A. Mathis** Son | **BIRTH:** 1915 **DEATH:** 6 Nov. 1982 |
| **John Mathis** Son | **BIRTH:** 1917 **DEATH:** Unknown |
| **James William Mathis** Son | **BIRTH:** 1918 **DEATH:** 26 May 1981 |
| **Haley Crunk Mathis** Daughter | **BIRTH:** 10 Feb. 1921 **DEATH:** 21 Nov. 1997 |

Samuel Toliver Mathis was born on November 2, 1875, in Marshall County, Tennessee. He married Martha Louise Crunk in 1905. They had seven children in 17-years. He died on December 6, 1939 in Peytonsville, Tennessee at the age of 64. He was buried in the Cool Springs Cemetery in Peytonsville.

# JOHN HENRY CRUNK
# 1876-1956

## CRUNK FAMILY

### HUSBAND'S PARENTS
**John E. Crunk**     **Mary E. Harvey**
1844 - 1904          1847 - 1910

### 1ST WIFE'S PARENTS
**Unknown Father     Unknown Mother**

### 2ND WIFE'S PARENTS
**James Henry Graves     Laura Gertrude Ladd**
1860 - 1928              1860 - 1932

### HUSBAND
**John Henry Crunk**
BIRTH: 6 June 1876, Williamson Co. TN
DEATH: 13 June 1956, Franklin, TN

### 1ST WIFE
**Sallie May Nevils**
BIRTH: 28 July 1880, TN
DEATH: 29 Nov. 1903, Rudderville, TN

### 2ND WIFE
**Annie Belle Graves**
BIRTH: 19 Nov. 1887, Williamson Co. TN
DEATH: 7 Nov. 1945, Thompsons Station, TN

## CHILDREN OF JOHN AND SALLIE

**Fairest Nevils Crunk**     BIRTH: 11 Nov. 1900
**Daughter**                 DEATH: 30 Nov. 1900

**James William Crunk**      BIRTH: 14 Nov. 1903
**Son**                      DEATH: 17 Nov. 1974

## CHILDREN OF JOHN AND ANNIE BELLE

**Mary G. Crunk**       BIRTH: 23 Sep. 1906
**Daughter**            DEATH: July 1985

**Howard P. Crunk**     BIRTH: 25 Dec. 1908
**Son**                 DEATH: 12 June 1994

**Ruby Estelle Crunk**  BIRTH: 20 Sep. 1912
**Daughter**            DEATH: 23 Jan. 1991

**Annie Belle Crunk**   BIRTH: 12 June 1914
**Daughter**            DEATH: 20 May 2001

**John Henry Crunk Jr.**  BIRTH: 29 Mar. 1916
**Son**                   DEATH: 11 Feb. 1975

**Walter E. Crunk**     BIRTH: 2 July 1918
**Son**                 DEATH: 11 Feb. 1978

**Robert H. Crunk**     BIRTH: 29 Feb. 1920
**Son**                 DEATH: 27 Sep. 1965

**Elsie Katherine Crunk**  BIRTH: 17 Mar. 1923
**Daughter**               DEATH: 7 Dec. 2006

## HIS LIFE

When John Henry Crunk was born on June 6, 1876, in Williamson County, Tennessee, his father John was 31 and his mother Mary was 29. He married Sallie May Nevils and they had two children. He then married Annie Belle Graves and they had eight children. He died on June 13, 1956, in Franklin, Tennessee at the age of 80.

JOHN HENRY AND ANNIE BELLE
(GRAVES) CRUNK

# RICHARD M. LILLARD
# 1878-1940

## LILLARD FAMILY

### HUSBAND'S PARENTS
**Monroe Claiborne Lillard**   **Mary Penny Hay**
1844 - 1891        1847 - 1917

### WIFE'S PARENTS
**Thomas A. "Eck" Davis**   **Nancy E. Ray**
1840 - 1919       1841 - 1925

### HUSBAND
**Richard M. Lillard**
**BIRTH:** 29 May 1878, Peytonsville, TN
**DEATH:** 26 Oct. 1940, Franklin, TN

### WIFE
**Lucy Thomas Davis**
**BIRTH:** 8 July 1882, Williamson Co. TN
**DEATH:** 25 Sep. 1969, Franklin, TN

## CHILDREN

**Thomas Clarence Lillard-Son**
**BIRTH:** 26 June 1905
**DEATH:** 5 Dec. 1975

**Woodard M. "Buddy" Lillard-Son**
**BIRTH:** 29 May 1907
**DEATH:** 25 July 1937

**Graham Lillard Son**
**BIRTH:** 1913
**DEATH:** 14 June 1921

**John D. Lillard Son**
**BIRTH:** 28 Apr. 1918
**DEATH:** 11 Feb. 1992

## HIS LIFE

Richard M. Lillard was born on May 29, 1878, in Williamson County, Tennessee. He married Lucy Thomas Davis on December 15, 1904 in Peytonsville, Tennessee. They had four children in 12-years. He died on October 26, 1940, in Franklin, Tennessee at the age of 62. He was buried in the Cool Springs Cemetery in Peytonsville.

# PHILLIP RICHARD "PHIL" BENNETT
# 1878-1982

## BENNETT FAMILY

### HUSBAND'S PARENTS
**Alexander B. Bennett**   **Minerva Jane Tucker**
1843 - 1908       1844 - 1890

### WIFE'S PARENTS
**Sterling Price Harper**   **Martha E. Garner**
1862 - 1930       1868 - 1939

### HUSBAND
**Phillip Richard "Phil" Bennett**
**BIRTH:** 10 Jan. 1878, Peytonsville, TN
**DEATH:** 19 June 1982, Peytonsville, TN

## WIFE
**Maude Frances Harper**
BIRTH: 8 Mar. 1886, Williamson Co, TN
DEATH: 7 Jan. 1947, Peytonsville, TN

### CHILDREN

| | |
|---|---|
| **Ila Mai Bennett** Daughter | BIRTH: 14 Aug. 1905 — DEATH: 15 Feb. 1973 |
| **Floray Bennett** Daughter | BIRTH: 1906 — DEATH: Unknown |
| **Bertha Eunice Bennett-Daughter** | BIRTH: 19 Mar. 1908 — DEATH: 8 Jan. 1975 |
| **Robert Howard Bennett-Son** | BIRTH: 23 May 1910 — DEATH: May 1990 |
| **Fannie Mai Bennett** Daughter | BIRTH: 26 Sep. 1912 — DEATH: 3 Dec. 2002 |
| **Milton H. Bennett** Son | BIRTH: 4 Jan. 1915 — DEATH: 16 Jan. 1957 |
| **Robbie Ela Bennett** Daughter | BIRTH: 5 May 1919 — DEATH: 12 Jan. 2007 |
| **Walter Wade Bennett** Son | BIRTH: 21 Apr. 1921 — DEATH: 9 July 2005 |
| **Ruth Elizabeth Dinah Bennett-Daughter** | BIRTH: 1923 — DEATH: 15 Jan. 2019 |
| **Willie Mae Bennett** Daughter | BIRTH: 19 Jan. 1928 — DEATH: 12 Sep. 1988 |

### HIS LIFE

When Phillip Richard "Phil" Bennett was born on January 10, 1878, in Peytonsville, Tennessee, his father, Alexander was 34 and his mother, Minerva was 33. He married Maude Frances Harper on September 21, 1904, in Peytonsville. They had 10 children in 22-years.

Phil once had a band and played his fiddle at the Grand Old Opry and on the Porter Waggoner Show. He also played frequently with Grand Ole Opry stars, Sam and Kirk McGee. Phil was a resident of Bennett Hollow all his life and was known as the "Mayor of Little Texas".

Phillip Richard "Phil" Bennett died on June 19, 1982, in Peytonsville at the age of 104. He was buried in the Bennett Cemetery in Peytonsville.

# HENRY NATHANIEL HARRISON
# 1878-1948

## HARRISON FAMILY

### HUSBAND'S PARENTS
**Joseph Jones Harrison**     **Mary C. Stegall**
1847 - 1919                   1860 - 1934

### WIFE'S PARENTS
**Samuel Henderson**     **Nettie Harrison**
1855 - ?                 1862 - ?

### HUSBAND
**Henry Nathaniel Harrison**
BIRTH: 15 Mar. 1878, Peytonsville, TN
DEATH: 1948, Franklin, TN

**Mable Catherine Henderson**
**BIRTH:** 21 Apr, 1887, TN
**DEATH:** 13 Mar, 1959, Franklin, TN

## HIS LIFE

When Nathaniel Henry Harrison was born on March 15, 1878, in Williamson County, Tennessee, his father, Joseph was 30 and his mother, Mary was 18. He married Mable Catherine Henderson on May 16, 1912, in Peytonsville, Tennessee. He died in 1948, in Franklin, Tennessee when he was 70-years old.

# WALTER JOSEPHUS PARKS
# 1878-1955

## PARKS FAMILY

### HUSBAND'S PARENTS
**Joe Bennett Parks  Addie Ophelia F. Sweeney**
1850 - 1906        1858 - 1887

### WIFE'S PARENTS
**Mark Wilson Vaden    Martha J. Johnson**
1840 - 1919          1845 - 1919

### HUSBAND
**Walter Josephus Parks**
**BIRTH:** 8 Oct. 1878, Peytonsville, TN
**DEATH:** 13 July 1955, Peytonsville, TN

### WIFE
**Blanche M. Vaden**
**BIRTH:** 21 Apr. 1882, Peytonsville, TN
**DEATH:** 10 Sep. 1943, Williamson Co. TN

### CHILDREN

**Fred Vaden Parks**    **BIRTH:** 21 Aug. 1905
**Son**                **DEATH:** 3 June 1955

**Elizabeth B. Parks**   **BIRTH:** 1908
**Daughter**             **DEATH:** Unknown

**Joe B. Parks**         **BIRTH:** 31 Dec. 1910
**Son**                  **DEATH:** 19 Sep. 1988

## HIS LIFE

When Walter Josephus Parks was born on October 8, 1878, in Peytonsville, Tennessee, his father, Joe was 28 and his mother, Addie was 20.

Walter married Blanche Vaden, a neighborhood girl. They had three children together. He was a teacher and received his elementary work under his father's instruction. He taught at many schools, but spent 16-years teaching at Lankford School.

Walter lived on a part of an original tract of 320-acres granted to his great-grandfather, John Parks, one of the first settlers in the area who came here from North Carolina and built a log house on it. It was in this house his grandfather and father were born, lived and died. He was reared there as well.

Walter Josephus Parks died on July 13, 1955, in Peytonsville, Tennessee at the age of 76. He was buried in the Mount Hope Cemetery in Franklin, Tennessee.

# CHARLES WILLIAM TOMLIN
## 1878-1930

### TOMLIN FAMILY

**HUSBAND'S PARENTS**
**John Abner Tomlin**     **Sarah Elizabeth Tucker**
1855 - 1944                        1853 - 1912

**WIFE'S PARENTS**
**Unknown Father**   **Elizabeth Ann Heathcock**
? - ?                            1835 - 1900

**HUSBAND**
**Charles William Tomlin**
**BIRTH:** 5 Dec. 1878, Peytonsville, TN
**DEATH:** 1930, Peytonsville, TN

**WIFE**
**Agnes Allie Beard**
**BIRTH:** 14 Apr. 1880, Peytonsville, TN

**DEATH:** 8 May 1931, College Grove, TN

### CHILDREN

**Nolie E. Tomlin**
**Daughter**
**BIRTH:** 12 June 1901
**DEATH:** 15 July 1972

**John Lee Lewis**
**Tomlin-Son**
**BIRTH:** 23 Sep. 1903
**DEATH:** 24 June 1931

**Willie Wade Tomlin**
**Daughter**
**BIRTH:** 7 Mar. 1904
**DEATH:** 13 Jan. 1987

**Andrew Thomas**
**Tomlin-Son**
**BIRTH:** 1907
**DEATH:** 1949

**Charles Robert**
**Tomlin-Son**
**BIRTH:** 12 May 1908
**DEATH:** 19 Sep. 1928

**Birdie Mai Tomlin**
**Daughter**
**BIRTH:** 1915
**DEATH:** Unknown

### HIS LIFE

When Charles William Tomlin was born on December 5, 1878, in Williamson County, Tennessee, his father, John was 23 and his mother, Sarah was 25. He married Agnes Allie Beard on April 11, 1898, in Williamson County. They had six children in 14-years. He died in 1930, in Peytonsville, Tennessee at the age of 52. He was buried in the Tomlin Cemetery in Peytonsville.

# CHARLES DAVID TOMLIN
## 1879-1954

### TOMLIN FAMILY

**HUSBAND'S PARENTS**
**David Monroe Tomlin**   **Martha Emma Ford**
1848 - 1933                        1855 - 1907

**WIFE'S PARENTS**
**Frances M. Tomlin**   **Priscilla Golden**
1859 - 1919                    1868 - 1915

## HUSBAND
**Charles David Tomlin**
**BIRTH:** 1 June 1879, Williamson Co. TN
**DEATH:** 1 July 1954, Peytonsville, TN

## WIFE
**Lena Mae Tomlin**
**BIRTH:** 8 Oct. 1886, College Grove, TN
**DEATH:** 25 Oct. 1962, Peytonsville, TN

## CHILDREN

| | |
|---|---|
| **Della Tomlin** Daughter | **BIRTH:** 3 Jan. 1904 **DEATH:** 16 May 1992 |
| **Mildred Virginia Tomlin-Daughter** | **BIRTH:** 18 July 1908 **DEATH:** 10 Aug. 1986 |
| **Emma Frances Tomlin** Daughter | **BIRTH:** 27 Feb. 1910 **DEATH:** 5 Aug. 2002 |
| **James Davis Tomlin** Son | **BIRTH:** 11 Aug. 1913 **DEATH:** 18 Jan. 1998 |
| **Alva Lee Tomlin** Son | **BIRTH:** 21 Sep. 1916 **DEATH:** 4 Mar. 1967 |
| **Jim Franklin Tomlin** Son | **BIRTH:** 25 Mar. 1919 **DEATH:** 2 Feb. 1968 |
| **Lou Ellen Tomlin** Daughter | **BIRTH:** 30 Aug. 1921 **DEATH:** 15 July 1988 |
| **Francis Minerva Tomlin-Daughter** | **BIRTH:** 2 Nov. 1923 **DEATH:** 24 Jan. 1953 |

## HIS LIFE

When Charles David Tomlin was born on June 1, 1879, in Williamson County, Tennessee, his father, David was 30 and his mother, Martha was 23. He married Lena Mae Tomlin on March 28, 1903, in Peytonsville, Tennessee. They had eight children in 19-years. He died on July 1, 1954, in Williamson County at the age of 75. He was buried in the Mount Hope Cemetery in Franklin, Tennessee.

# JOHN L. MCGEE
# 1880-1946

### MCGEE FAMILY

### HUSBAND'S PARENTS
**John Franklin McGee**    **Mary Elizabeth Truett**
1857 - 1944                1859 - 1941

### 1ST WIFE'S PARENTS
**John W. Anderson**    **Tennessee S. Graham**
1853 - ?                1854 - 1933

### 2ND WIFE'S PARENTS
**Thomas Roberson**    **Minnie Maddox**
? - ?                  ? - ?

### HUSBAND
**John L. McGee**
**BIRTH:** 21 Nov. 1880, Peytonsville, TN
**DEATH:** 27 May 1946, Peytonsville, TN

**1ST WIFE**
**Willie Eunice Anderson**
BIRTH: 8 Dec. 1885, TN
DEATH: 27 May 1936, Peytonsville, TN

**2ND WIFE**
**Pauline R. Roberson**
BIRTH: 31 Mar. 1911, Franklin, TN
DEATH: 16 May 1999, Franklin, TN

**CHILDREN OF JOHN AND WILLIE EUNICE**

| | |
|---|---|
| **Henry Wade McGee** Son | **BIRTH:** 15 Jan. 1906 **DEATH:** 19 Mar. 1993 |
| **Clyde L. McGee** Son | **BIRTH:** 14 July 1909 **DEATH:** 25 July 2003 |
| **Flossie Ella McGee** Daughter | **BIRTH:** 2 Oct. 1913 **DEATH:** 20 Mar. 1999 |
| **William Herbert McGee-Son** | **BIRTH:** 1916 **DEATH:** Unknown |
| **John Herman McGee** Son | **BIRTH:** 1917 **DEATH:** 26 May 2001 |

**HIS LIFE**

When John L. McGee was born on November 21, 1880, in Williamson County, Tennessee, his father, John was 23 and his mother, Mary was 21. He married Willie Eunice Anderson and they had five children together. Willie died on May 27, 1936. John married Pauline R. Roberson on April 4, 1937, in Williamson County. He died on May 27, 1946, in Peytonsville, Tennessee at the age of 65. He was buried in the Cool Springs Cemetery in Peytonsville.

# ESCAR KNOTT SMITHSON
## 1881-1951

**SMITHSON FAMILY**

**HUSBAND'S PARENTS**

| Charles C. Smithson | Sarah C. Smithson |
|---|---|
| 1837 - 1890 | 1845 - 1896 |

**WIFE'S PARENTS**

| Charles Meek | Mary Ann Gillispie |
|---|---|
| 1857 - 1917 | 1859 - 1891 |

**HUSBAND**
**Escar Knott Smithson**
BIRTH: 26 Aug. 1881, Marshall Co. TN
DEATH: 29 Sep. 1951, Peytonsville, TN

**WIFE**
**Josephine V. Meek**
BIRTH: 21 May 1886, Williamson Co. TN
DEATH: 3 Aug. 1957, College Grove, TN

**CHILDREN**

| | |
|---|---|
| **Charles Herbert Smithson-Son** | **BIRTH:** 14 June 1910 **DEATH:** 23 June 1994 |
| **Agnes Smithson** Daughter | **BIRTH:** 1911 **DEATH:** Unknown |
| **Mary Kathryn Smithson-Daughter** | **BIRTH:** 28 Apr. 1912 **DEATH:** 16 June 1978 |
| **Leland Knott Smithson-Son** | **BIRTH:** 28 Mar. 1914 **DEATH:** 30 May 1953 |
| **Robert Frank Smithson-Son** | **BIRTH:** 24 Mar. 1916 **DEATH:** 11 Sep. 1988 |
| **Bennie Thelma "Doll" Smithson-Daughter** | **BIRTH:** 10 May 1918 **DEATH:** 19 Sep. 1996 |
| **Nora Agnes Smithson** Daughter | **BIRTH:** 1921 **DEATH:** 19 July 2006 |
| **Ralph Meek Smithson** Son | **BIRTH:** 9 May 1923 **DEATH:** 12 May 1991 |
| **Grace Christene Smithson-Daughter** | **BIRTH:** 17 Aug. 1926 **DEATH:** 4 Aug. 2016 |
| **Marjorie Carolyn Smithson-Daughter** | **BIRTH:** 7 June 1930 **DEATH:** 30 Sep. 1997 |

| Joe Ennis Smithson | BIRTH: 12 Nov. 1932 |
| Son | DEATH: 20 July 2002 |

## HIS LIFE

When Escar Knott Smithson was born on August 26, 1881, in Marshall County, Tennessee, his father, Charles was 43 and his mother, Sarah was 35. He married Josephine V. Meek on August 29, 1909. They had 11 children in 22-years. He died on September 29, 1951, in Williamson County, Tennessee at the age of 70. He was buried in the Mount Hope Cemetery in Franklin, Tennessee.

# WALTER B. BEARD
# 1882-1961

## BEARD FAMILY

### HUSBAND'S PARENTS

| Lewis Jackson Beard Jr. | Amanda E. Young |
| 1859 - 1943 | 1861 - 1893 |

### WIFE'S PARENTS

| William O. Simmons | Margaret A. Spann |
| 1852 - 1939 | 1857 - 1933 |

## HUSBAND
### Walter B. Beard
BIRTH: 8 Mar. 1882, Williamson Co. TN
DEATH: 22 Oct. 1961, Williamson Co. TN

## WIFE
### Sarah Rebecca Simmons
BIRTH: 3 Feb. 1882, Rutherford Co. TN
DEATH: 7 July 1951, Franklin, TN

## CHILDREN

| Mary Sue Beard | BIRTH: 24 Sep. 1904 |
| Daughter | DEATH: 24 May 1971 |

| William Jackson "Willie" Beard-Son | BIRTH: 13 May 1906 |
| | DEATH: 14 Nov. 1965 |

| Amanda "Myrtle" Beard-Daughter | BIRTH: 14 Aug. 1907 |
| | DEATH: 14 Aug. 1934 |

| Lillie Florence Beard | BIRTH: 27 Mar. 1909 |
| Daughter | DEATH: 1 Aug. 1910 |

| Addie Lee Beard | BIRTH: 16 Apr. 1912 |
| Daughter | DEATH: 3 Sep. 1982 |

| Henry Claud Beard | BIRTH: 23 June 1913 |
| Son | DEATH: 20 Apr. 2007 |

| Era Mai Beard | BIRTH: 4 Jan. 1916 |
| Daughter | DEATH: 9 Oct. 2003 |

| Allie Elizabeth Beard | BIRTH: 16 Sep. 1917 |
| Daughter | DEATH: 6 Aug. 1995 |

| Gladys Beard | BIRTH: 23 Nov. 1918 |
| Daughter | DEATH: 28 Oct. 2007 |

| James Walter Beard | BIRTH: 12 Nov. 1920 |
| Son | DEATH: 29 Feb. 1988 |

## HIS LIFE

When Walter B. Beard was born on March 8, 1882, in Williamson County, Tennessee, his father, Lewis was 22 and his mother, Amanda was 21. He married Sarah Rebecca Simmons on December 20, 1903, in Peytonsville, Tennessee. They had 10 children in 16-years. He died on

October 22, 1961, in Williamson County at the age of 79. He was buried in the Cool Springs Cemetery in Peytonsville.

---

# JOHN ANDREW WARREN
# 1883-1936

### WARREN FAMILY

### HUSBAND'S PARENTS
**Drewey Hamilton Warren**      **Judie E. Vaugh**
1852 - 1902                     1866 - 1949

### WIFE'S PARENTS
**Thomas S. Williams**      **Susanna A. Graham**
1868 - 1918                 1873 - 1904

### HUSBAND
**John Andrew Warren**
**BIRTH:** 1 May 1883, Williamson Co. TN
**DEATH:** 25 Feb. 1936, Williamson Co. TN

### WIFE
**Lela Maud Williams**
**BIRTH:** 2 Mar. 1896, Williamson Co. TN
**DEATH:** 27 Nov. 1975, Peytonsville, TN

### CHILDREN

**Virginia Warren**
**Daughter**
**BIRTH:** 11 Dec. 1918
**DEATH:** 12 Dec. 1918

**Gerald Warren**
**Son**
**BIRTH:** 27 June 1921
**DEATH:** 28 June 1921

**Jewell Warren**
**Daughter**
**BIRTH:** 19 June 1924
**DEATH:** 24 June 1924

**Herschel Clifton Warren-Son**
**BIRTH:** 3 Mar. 1926
**DEATH:** 14 July 1926

### HIS LIFE

When John Andrew Warren was born on May 1, 1883, in Williamson County, Tennessee, his father, Drewey was 30 and his mother, Judie was

16. He married, Lela Maud Williams on December 31, 1913, in Williamson County. They had four children. He died on February 25, 1936, in Williamson, County at the age of 52. He was buried in the Mount Hope Cemetery in Franklin, Tennessee.

---

# LEONARD LEE LADD
# 1883-1949

### LADD FAMILY

### HUSBAND'S PARENTS
**William Price Ladd Sr.**      **Martha F. Burnett**
1847 - 1915                     1847 - 1930

### WIFE'S PARENTS
**Thomas S. Williams**      **Susanna A. Graham**
1868 - 1918                 1873 - 1904

### HUSBAND
**Leonard Lee Ladd**
**BIRTH:** 4 Sep. 1883, Williamson Co. TN
**DEATH:** 8 July 1949, Peytonsville, TN

### WIFE
**Bessie Alta Williams**
**BIRTH:** 15 Sep. 1892, Williamson Co. TN
**DEATH:** 3 Dec. 1918, Peytonsville, TN

### CHILDREN

**Alma Estella Ladd**
**Daughter**
**BIRTH:** 8 Apr. 1912
**DEATH:** 1992

### HIS LIFE

When Leonard Lee Ladd was born on September 4, 1883, in Williamson County, Tennessee, his father, William was 36 and his mother, Martha was 36. He married Bessie Alta Williams on November 14, 1910, in Williamson County. They had one child during their marriage. He died on July 8, 1949, in

Peytonsville, Tennessee at the age of 65. He was buried in the Ladd Cemetery in Peytonsville.

# JOHN BEAL
# 1883-1958

### BEAL FAMILY

#### HUSBAND'S PARENTS
**Henry Beal**    **Cornelia Parrish**
1850 - 1911      1852 - 1928

#### WIFE'S PARENTS
**Walter T. Ewing**    **Clora Perkins**
1862 - 1928           1862 - 1936

#### HUSBAND
**John Beal**
**BIRTH:** 17 May 1883, Williamson Co. TN
**DEATH:** 29 Sep. 1958, Peytonsville, TN

#### WIFE
**Lena Sadie Ewing**
**BIRTH:** 1892, Williamson Co. TN
**DEATH:** 27 Feb. 1953, Nashville, TN

#### CHILDREN

**Louise Beal**
Daughter
**BIRTH:** 21 Aug. 1915
**DEATH:** 23 June 2016

**Carey Beal**
Daughter
**BIRTH:** 24 Feb. 1926
**DEATH:** 22 May 2009

### HIS LIFE

When John Beal was born on May 17, 1883, in Williamson County, Tennessee, his father, Henry was 32 and his mother, Cornelia was 30. He married Lena Sadie Ewing on December 28, 1907, in Peytonsville, Tennessee. They had two daughters during their marriage. He died on September 29, 1958, in Williamson County at the age of 75. He was buried in the Beal Cemetery in Peytonsville.

JOHN BEAL

# GEORGE WASHINGTON
# BRUCE
# 1884-1969

### BRUCE FAMILY

#### HUSBAND'S PARENTS
**George W. Bruce**    **Mary E. Bruce**
1847 - ?               1844 - ?

#### 1ST WIFE'S PARENTS
**George B. Young**    **Sarah Ann Nichols**
1854 - 1933           1856 - 1935

#### 2ND WIFE'S PARENTS
**Charlie D. Tomlin**    **Dessie May Reynolds**
1880 - 1964             1882 - 1961

#### 3RD WIFE'S PARENTS
**Walter B. Beard**    **Sarah Rebecca Simmons**
1882 - 1961           1882 - 1951

264

**George Washington Bruce**
**BIRTH:** 29 Oct. 1884, Williamson Co. TN
**DEATH:** 15 Sep. 1969, Peytonsville, TN

**1ST WIFE**
**Bessie Maude Young**
**BIRTH:** 19 Jan. 1892, TN
**DEATH:** 4 Jan. 1916, TN

**2ND WIFE**
**Myrtle Tomlin**
**BIRTH:** 12 Mar. 1901, TN
**DEATH:** 15 Nov. 1979, Williamson Co. TN

**3RD WIFE**
**Gladys Beard**
**BIRTH:** 23 Nov. 1918, Williamson Co. TN
**DEATH:** 28 Oct. 2007

**CHILDREN OF GEORGE AND BESSIE**

| | |
|---|---|
| **Clifton H. Bruce**<br>Son | **BIRTH:** 1914<br>**DEATH:** 1999 |
| **George Milton Bruce**<br>Son | **BIRTH:** 4 Jan. 1916<br>**DEATH:** Oct. 1981 |

**CHILDREN OF GEORGE AND GLADYS**

| | |
|---|---|
| **Jewell Elizabeth Bruce**-Daughter | **BIRTH:** 22 Jan. 1936<br>**DEATH:** 27 June 2011 |
| **Private Bruce** | **BIRTH:**<br>**DEATH:** |
| **John Wade Bruce**<br>Son | **BIRTH:** 2 Aug. 1944<br>**DEATH:** 5 Aug. 1944 |

## HIS LIFE

When George Washington Bruce was born on October 29, 1884, in Williamson County, Tennessee, his father, George was 37 and his mother, Mary was 40. He was married three times and had four sons and one daughter. He died on September 15, 1969, in Peytonsville, Tennessee at the age of 84. He was buried in the Williamson Memorial Gardens Cemetery in Franklin, Tennessee.

# HENRY DAVE TOMLIN
# 1884-1969

**TOMLIN FAMILY**

**HUSBAND'S PARENTS**
| Robert Tomlin | Mary Elizabeth McGee |
|---|---|
| 1851 - ? | 1856 - 1910 |

**WIFE'S PARENTS**
| William B. Skinner | Narcissa "Sissy" White |
|---|---|
| 1859 - ? | 1869 - 1904 |

**HUSBAND**
**Henry Dave Tomlin**
**BIRTH:** 10 Aug. 1884, Williamson Co. TN
**DEATH:** 6 Dec. 1969, Peytonsville, TN

**WIFE**
**Bessie Skinner**
**BIRTH:** 10 May 1890, Williamson Co. TN
**DEATH:** 21 Aug. 1947, Franklin, TN

**CHILDREN**

| | |
|---|---|
| **Albert Lee Tomlin**<br>Son | **BIRTH:** 26 Nov. 1904<br>**DEATH:** 8 Oct. 1983 |
| **Hattie Louise Tomlin**<br>Daughter | **BIRTH:** 19 Dec. 1911<br>**DEATH:** 30 June 1987 |
| **William Marvin Tomlin**<br>Son | **BIRTH:** 12 Dec. 1913<br>**DEATH:** 27 Feb. 1980 |
| **Mildred Tomlin**<br>Daughter | **BIRTH:** 10 May 1916<br>**DEATH:** 29 Apr. 1990 |
| **Virginia Tomlin**<br>Daughter | **BIRTH:** 17 June 1920<br>**DEATH:** Apr. 2018 |

| **Howard Leonard Tomlin-Son** | **BIRTH:** 4 Mar. 1922 <br> **DEATH:** 7 Apr. 2018 |
| --- | --- |
| **Dorothy Lorraine Tomlin-Daughter** | **BIRTH:** 20 Dec. 1925 <br> **DEATH:** 13 June 2006 |
| **Bettie Kathleen Tomlin-Daughter** | **BIRTH:** 11 Mar. 1930 <br> **DEATH:** 14 July 1926 |
| **Marion Dan Tomlin Son** | **BIRTH:** 14 Nov. 1934 <br> **DEATH:** Apr. 1995 |
| **Mary Ann Tomlin Daughter** | **BIRTH:** 14 Nov. 1934 <br> **DEATH:** 12 Oct. 1995 |

## HIS LIFE

When Henry Dave Tomlin was born on August 10, 1884, in Williamson County, Tennessee, his father, Robert was 33 and his mother, Mary was 28. He married Bessie Skinner on October 25, 1903, in Williamson County. They had ten children in 29-years. He died on December 6, 1969, in Peytonsville, Tennessee. He was buried in the Mount Hope Cemetery in Franklin, Tennessee.

DAVE TOMLIN AND DAUGHTERS, BETTY, ANN, MILDRED, LOUISE, DOROTHY AND VIRGINIA

DAVE TOMLIN AND SONS, DAN, HOWARD, ALBERT AND MARVIN

# JOHN SMITHSON
# 1885-1964

### SMITHSON FAMILY

**HUSBAND'S PARENTS**

| Wash Smithson | Susan Beal |
| --- | --- |
| 1848 - ? | 1848 - ? |

**1ST WIFE'S PARENTS**

| Unknown Father | Unknown Mother |
| --- | --- |

**2ND WIFE'S PARENTS**

| Joseph Mayberry | Cherry Russell |
| --- | --- |
| 1865 - 1956 | 1890 - 1952 |

### HUSBAND
**John Smithson**
**BIRTH:** 24 May 1885, Peytonsville, TN
**DEATH:** 30 Nov. 1964, Peytonsville, TN

### 1ST WIFE
**Elnora Starnes**
**BIRTH:** 1887, Peytonsville, TN
**DEATH:** 17 Nov. 1915, Peytonsville, TN

### 2ND WIFE
**Nannie B. Mayberry**
**BIRTH:** 21 Nov. 1906, Williamson Co. TN
**DEATH:** Mar. 1984, Nashville, TN

### CHILDREN OF JOHN AND ELNORA

| | |
|---|---|
| **John Robert Smithson-Son** | **BIRTH:** 19 May 1914<br>**DEATH:** 8 Sep. 1930 |

### CHILDREN OF JOHN AND NANNIE

| | |
|---|---|
| **Private Smithson** | **BIRTH:**<br>**DEATH:** |
| **Private Smithson** | **BIRTH:**<br>**DEATH:** |

### HIS LIFE

When John Smithson was born on May 24, 1885, in Williamson County, Tennessee, his father, Wash was 37 and his mother, Susan was 37. He married Elnora Starnes on January 5, 1908, and they had one son together. Elnora passed away on November 17, 1915, in Williamson County at the age of 28. They had been married seven-years. On April 5, 1931, John married Nannie B. Mayberry. They had two children together. John Smithson died on November 30, 1964, in Peytonsville, Tennessee at the age of 79.

### WIFE'S PARENTS

| | |
|---|---|
| **William C. Beech** | **Michael D. Young** |
| 1869 - 1929 | 1869 - ? |

### HUSBAND
**Henry W. Simmons**
**BIRTH:** 5 Feb. 1885, Peytonsville, TN
**DEATH:** Mar. 1971, Peytonsville, TN

### WIFE
**Lena Elizabeth Beech**
**BIRTH:** 2 Oct. 1895, TN
**DEATH:** 11 Sep. 1958, Peytonsville, TN

### CHILDREN

| | |
|---|---|
| **Frances Simmons Daughter** | **BIRTH:** 28 Oct. 1916<br>**DEATH:** 6 June 1970 |
| **Hattie Elizabeth Simmons-Daughter** | **BIRTH:** 1 May 1923<br>**DEATH:** 9 Jan. 2014 |

### HIS LIFE

When Henry W. Simmons was born on February 5, 1885, in Peytonsville, Tennessee, his father, William was 32 and his mother, Margaret was 27. He married Lena Elizabeth Beech on December 24, 1915, in Peytonsville. They had two children during their marriage. He died in March, 1971, in Peytonsville at the age of 86. He was buried in the Simmons Cemetery in Peytonsville.

# HENRY W. SIMMONS
# 1885-1971

## SIMMONS FAMILY

### HUSBAND'S PARENTS

| | |
|---|---|
| **William O. Simmons** | **Margaret A. Spann** |
| 1852 - 1939 | 1857 - 1933 |

# HENRY THOMAS WARREN
## 1885-1967

### WARREN FAMILY

### HUSBAND'S PARENTS
**Drewey H. Warren**  **Judie Ellen Vaughn**
1852 - 1902        1866 - 1949

### WIFE'S PARENTS
**Newman S. Bennett**  **Elizabeth Tomlin**
1860 - 1944          1865 - ?

### HUSBAND
**Henry Thomas Warren**
BIRTH: 28 Aug. 1885, Peytonsville, TN
DEATH: 15 Apr. 1967, Franklin, TN

### WIFE
**Mary Ellen Bennett**
BIRTH: 4 Aug. 1887, Williamson Co. TN
DEATH: 8 May 1944, Nashville, TN

### CHILDREN

| | | |
|---|---|---|
| **Claud C. Warren** Son | BIRTH: 1901 | DEATH: Unknown |
| **Louise Warren** Daughter | BIRTH: 1904 | DEATH: 27 Nov. 1925 |
| **Lucille Thomas Warren-Daughter** | BIRTH: 23 Aug. 1906 | DEATH: Unknown |
| **Raymond Edgar Warren-Son** | BIRTH: 1909 | DEATH: Nov. 1966 |
| **Henry Ralph Warren** Son | BIRTH: 23 Sep. 1911 | DEATH: 29 Dec. 1983 |
| **Thelma Lorene Warren-Daughter** | BIRTH: 1915 | DEATH: 1 Aug. 1985 |
| **Claude Roland Warren-Son** | BIRTH: 7 Aug. 1922 | DEATH: 11 Apr. 1994 |

### HIS LIFE

When Henry Thomas Warren was born on August 28, 1885, in Williamson County, Tennessee, his father, Drewey was 32 and his mother, Judie was 19. He married Mary Ellen Bennett on July 12, 1903, in Peytonsville, Tennessee. They had seven children in 21-years. He died on April 15, 1967, in Franklin, Tennessee at the age of 81. He was buried in the Mount Hope Cemetery in Franklin.

# ALLEN L. BRUCE
## 1885-1957

### BRUCE FAMILY

### HUSBAND'S PARENTS
**James W. Bruce**  **Belle V. Garner**
1857 - 1932        1861 - 1944

## WIFE'S PARENTS
**John Frizzell**    **Rosa Goins**
1870 - ?        1875 - 1897

## HUSBAND
**Allen L. Bruce**
**BIRTH:** 27 Aug. 1885, Bon Aqua, TN
**DEATH:** 19 Sep. 1957, Peytonsville, TN

## WIFE
**Pearl E. Frizzell**
**BIRTH:** 17 Apr. 1896, Bon Aqua, TN
**DEATH:** 1 Dec. 1946, Peytonsville, TN

## CHILDREN

**Rosie Bruce**
Daughter
**BIRTH:** 1915
**DEATH:** 21 Nov. 1962

**Bertha Bruce**
Daughter
**BIRTH:** 14 Apr. 1917
**DEATH:** 23 Oct. 2005

**Percy Bud Bruce**
Son
**BIRTH:** 29 July 1919
**DEATH:** 15 July 1981

**Ruby Hazel Bruce**
Daughter
**BIRTH:** 26 June 1921
**DEATH:** Apr. 1998

**John Allen Bruce**
Son
**BIRTH:** 16 Oct. 1924
**DEATH:** Jan. 1979

**Alton Bruce**
Son
**BIRTH:** 23 Jan. 1927
**DEATH:** 11 Jan.1928

## HIS LIFE

When Allen L. Bruce was born on August 27, 1885, in Bon Aqua, Tennessee, his father, James was 28 and his mother, Belle was 24. He married Pearl E. Frizzell on March 1, 1913, in Hickman County, Tennessee. They had six children in 12-years. He died on September 19, 1957, in Peytonsville, Tennessee at the age of 72. He was buried in the Bon Aqua Cemetery in Hickman County.

# DICUS "DYKE" DAVID BENNETT
# 1886-1976

## BENNETT FAMILY

## HUSBAND'S PARENTS
**John Reece Bennett**    **Martha Ann Garner**
1851 - 1941        1854 - 1929

## 1ST WIFE'S PARENTS
**Patrick Henry Smithson**    **Susan Gillespie**
1870 - 1944        1872 - 1907

## 2ND WIFE'S PARENTS
**T.R. Ingram**    **Capitola Smithson**
? - ?        1871 - 1918

**Jim Frank Garner**    **Jessie Carroll Hargrove**
1876 - 1942                1873 - 1944

## HUSBAND
**Dicus "Dyke" David Bennett**
**BIRTH:** 28 Jan. 1886, Peytonsville, TN
**DEATH:** June 1976, Peytonsville, TN

## 1ST WIFE
**Eunice Ethel Smithson**
**BIRTH:** May 1892, Williamson Co. TN
**DEATH:** 21 Aug. 1916, Williamson Co. TN

## 2ND WIFE
**Gertrude Ingram**
**BIRTH:** 1903, TN
**DEATH:** 10 Feb. 1937, Williamson Co. TN

## 3RD WIFE
**Grace Garner**
**BIRTH:** 1912, TN
**DEATH:** 16 Jun. 1989

## CHILDREN OF DYKE AND EUNICE

| | |
|---|---|
| **Mattie Lee "Bunt" Bennett-Daughter** | **BIRTH:** 13 Nov. 1907  **DEATH:** 4 Jan. 1999 |
| **Henry C. Bennett Son** | **BIRTH:** 1909  **DEATH:** Unknown |
| **Annie Ethel Bennett Daughter** | **BIRTH:** 16 Mar. 1912  **DEATH:** 15 Jan. 2006 |

## CHILDREN OF DYKE AND GERTRUDE

| | |
|---|---|
| **Charles "Buck" H. Bennett-Son** | **BIRTH:** 17 Aug. 1910  **DEATH:** June 1986 |
| **James Oscar Bennett-Son** | **BIRTH:** 28 Apr. 1913  **DEATH:** 17 July 1943 |
| **James David Bennett Son** | **BIRTH:** 24 May 1923  **DEATH:** 25 Dec. 1948 |
| **Josie Elise Bennett Daughter** | **BIRTH:** 22 Sep. 1925  **DEATH:** 2 Mar. 2008 |

## CHILDREN OF DYKE AND GRACE

| | |
|---|---|
| **Lewis Alvin Bennett Son** | **BIRTH:** 28 Feb. 1933  **DEATH:** 2 Feb. 1991 |

## HIS LIFE

When Dicus "Dyke" David Bennett was born on January 28, 1886, in Peytonsville, Tennessee, his father, John was 36 and his mother, Martha was 31. He was married three times and had five sons and three daughters. He died in June 1976, in Peytonsville at the age of 90.

DICUS "DYKE", HENRY "BUCK",
MARTHA LEE, EUNICE (SMITHSON)
HOLDING ANNIE BENNETT

# JOHN THOMAS HUGHES
# 1887-1954

## HUGHES FAMILY

### HUSBAND'S PARENTS
**William Hughes**    **Charlotte Adair**
1846 - 1905            1861 - ?

### WIFE'S PARENTS
**George Marion King**    **Tennessee Skinner**
1857 - 1945                1858 - 1942

## HUSBAND
**John Thomas Hughes**
**BIRTH:** 6 Jan. 1887, Williamson Co. TN

**DEATH:** 13 Feb. 1954, Peytonsville, TN

### WIFE
**Ercelle King**
**BIRTH:** 1891, Peytonsville, TN
**DEATH:** 17 Oct. 1979, Peytonsville, TN

### CHILDREN

| | |
|---|---|
| **Marion Thomas Hughes-Son** | **BIRTH:** 10 Jan. 1918<br>**DEATH:** 30 Oct. 1931 |
| **Gladys Rebecca Hughes-Daughter** | **BIRTH:** 1920<br>**DEATH:** 29 Jan. 2013 |
| **James Malcolm Hughes-Son** | **BIRTH:** 10 Dec. 1922<br>**DEATH:** 22 Apr. 1983 |
| **Mary Hughes Daughter** | **BIRTH:** 25 Apr. 1926<br>**DEATH:** 31 Jan. 2016 |
| **Melvin Hughes Son** | **BIRTH:** 4 Oct. 1928<br>**DEATH:** 31 Jan. 1992 |

### HIS LIFE

John Thomas Hughes was born on January 6, 1887, in Williamson County, Tennessee. He married Ercelle King on December 24, 1916, in Peytonsville, Tennessee. They had five children in 10-years. He died on February 13, 1954, in Peytonsville at the age of 67. He was buried in the Cool Springs Cemetery in Peytonsville.

# OZIE LEE SMITHSON
# 1888-1930

## SMITHSON FAMILY

### HUSBAND'S PARENTS
**Wash Smithson**      **Susan Beal**
1848 - ?                    1848 - ?

### WIFE'S PARENTS
**John Henry Hayes**      **Laura Janie Morrow**
1860 - ?                        1867 - ?

### HUSBAND
**Ozie Lee Smithson**
**BIRTH:** 1 June 1888, Williamson Co. TN
**DEATH:** 27 Apr. 1930, Peytonsville, TN

### WIFE
**Daisy Lee Hayes**
**BIRTH:** 14 Dec. 1891, TN
**DEATH:** 2 Nov. 1975, Franklin, TN

### CHILDREN

| | |
|---|---|
| **Mattie Jane Smithson Daughter** | **BIRTH:** 30 Mar. 1912<br>**DEATH:** 22 Dec. 1991 |
| **Osie Lee Smithson Daughter** | **BIRTH:** 4 July 1915<br>**DEATH:** 8 July 1948 |
| **Gussie Smithson Daughter** | **BIRTH:** 1917<br>**DEATH:** Unknown |
| **Pearl Smithson Daughter** | **BIRTH:** 29 Dec. 1918<br>**DEATH:** 29 Nov. 1948 |
| **Lizzie Smithson Daughter** | **BIRTH:** 1919<br>**DEATH:** Unknown |
| **George W. Smithson Son** | **BIRTH:** 8 Aug. 1921<br>**DEATH:** 3 Apr. 1976 |
| **Thomas Richard Smithson-Son** | **BIRTH:** 25 Nov. 1928<br>**DEATH:** 12 Apr. 1985 |

### HIS LIFE

When Ozie Lee Smithson was born on June 1, 1888, in Williamson County, Tennessee, his father, Wash was 40 and his mother, Susan was 40. He married Daisy Lee Hayes on December 31, 1910, in Williamson County, Tennessee. They had seven children in 16-years. He died on April 27, 1930, in Williamson County at the age of 41. He was buried in the Westwood Cemetery in Peytonsville, Tennessee.

# PERRY EVANS JOHNSON
## 1888-1939

### JOHNSON FAMILY

#### HUSBAND'S PARENTS
**Jesse H. Johnson**    **Ophelia Zorilda Sprott**
1842 - 1914                1851 - 1917

#### WIFE'S PARENTS
**James W. Thompson**    **Mary E. Camus**
1844 - 1929                1851 - 1907

#### HUSBAND
**Perry Evans Johnson**
**BIRTH:** 21 Sep. 1888, Peytonsville, TN
**DEATH:** 14 June 1939, Peytonsville, TN

#### WIFE
**Ozzie Thompson**
**BIRTH:** 26 Feb. 1895, Davidson Co. TN
**DEATH:** 6 Nov. 1972, Franklin, TN

### CHILDREN

| Perry G. Johnson | **BIRTH:** 26 Jan. 1918 |
| Son | **DEATH:** 16 Mar. 1969 |

| Jesse W. Johnson | **BIRTH:** 16 Dec. 1925 |
| Son | **DEATH:** 7 Jan. 1985 |

### HIS LIFE

When Perry Evans Johnson was born on September 21, 1888, in Williamson County, Tennessee, his father Jesse was 45 and his mother Ophelia was 37. He married Ozzie Thompson on March 17, 1917, in Williamson County. They had two children during their marriage. He died on June 14, 1939 in Peytonsville, Tennessee at the age of 50 and was buried in Mount Hope Cemetery in Franklin, Tennessee.

# JOHN WESLEY TOMLIN
## 1889-1951

### TOMLIN FAMILY

#### HUSBAND'S PARENTS
**Elijah Tomlin**    **Nancy Elizabeth Hay**
1853 - 1934           1863 - 1947

#### WIFE'S PARENTS
**Robert Lindsey Stevens**    **Sarah A. Ladd**
1851 - 1943                     1850 - 1935

#### HUSBAND
**John Wesley Tomlin**
**BIRTH:** 14 Mar. 1889, Peytonsville, TN
**DEATH:** 22 May 1951, Peytonsville, TN

#### WIFE
**Cleo Stephens**
**BIRTH:** 26 Nov. 1891, Williamson Co. TN
**DEATH:** 17 June 1976, College Grove, TN

| | |
|---|---|
| **Mildred Tomlin** Daughter | **BIRTH:** 9 Aug. 1911 **DEATH:** 29 Aug. 1994 |
| **Paul Otto Tomlin** Son | **BIRTH:** 4 Jan. 1913 **DEATH:** 14 Aug. 1961 |
| **William Price Tomlin** Son | **BIRTH:** 25 Aug. 1915 **DEATH:** 9 Aug. 1993 |
| **Sarah E. Tomlin** Daughter | **BIRTH:** 13 Feb. 1921 **DEATH:** 17 Apr. 2016 |
| **Mary Norine Tomlin** Daughter | **BIRTH:** 1 Sep. 1924 **DEATH:** 26 June 2007 |
| **Velma Louise Tomlin** Daughter | **BIRTH:** 21 Aug. 1925 **DEATH:** 19 Sep. 2008 |

## HIS LIFE

When John Wesley Tomlin was born on March 14, 1889, in Williamson County, Tennessee, his father Elijah was 35 and his mother Nancy was 25. He married Cleo Stephens on October 5, 1910, in Peytonsville, Tennessee. They had six children in 14-years. He died on May 22, 1951 in Franklin, Tennessee at the age of 62.

# BEN GIPSON SMITHSON
# 1889-1972

## SMITHSON FAMILY

### HUSBAND'S PARENTS
**Charles C. Smithson    Sarah C. Smithson**
1837 - 1896                1845 - 1896

### WIFE'S PARENTS
**Fountain E. McMahon    Nellie McMahon**
1868 - ?                      1875 - ?

### HUSBAND
**Ben Gipson Smithson**
BIRTH: 11 Jan. 1889, Marshall Co. TN

DEATH: 22 Nov. 1972, Franklin, TN

### WIFE
**Maggie Lee McMahon**
BIRTH: 13 Nov. 1898, TN
DEATH: 10 Dec. 1995

## HIS LIFE

When Ben Gipson Smithson was born on January 11, 1889, in Marshall County, Tennessee, his father, Charles was 51 and his mother, Sarah was 43.

From *Who's Who in Williamson County*
By Jane Owen, *The Review-Appeal*
October 11, 1951

To see Ben G. Smithson as he goes about his self-imposed duties at Quality Market where his cousins, Martha Kinnard and Nelle Mosley, sisters, are proprietors, you'd never suppose he is a happy-go-lucky, carefree kind of person. He likes to dance, swim, play bridge and engage in other pastimes.

Visited one evening recently at his home on Jennings Street he and his wife were most hospitable and greeted their guests quite cordially.

Mr. Smithson said, "I was born in Marshall County near Lunn's Store, about ten miles from Chapel Hill. My parents were Charles and Sallie Kate Smithson. They were both Smithsons as were my grandparents on both sides. As far back as I can trace them no surname enters in except Smithson. I can't say it goes back that way to any of the Ark for the Bible does not give that name to any of Noah's sons, so I do not know when it originated."

"I was one of nine children, two girls and four boys, all are dead except a younger sister and me. She, Addie Smithson, lives in Janesville, Ark., And I have not seen her for the past 35 years. We do not correspond regularly either. But we have never known each other very well. My parents died less than a week apart when I was seven years of age. The older children were grown or about able to fend for themselves. My sister was taken into the family of one uncle and I found a home with Uncle Benjamin Smithson, for whom I was named, and here I grew up out at Peytonsville."

"There were four children in the family and when I went there to live I was accepted as one of them. We attended school at Peytonsville and when we came home in the afternoon W.H. (father of Nelle and Martha), Van, Syl and I shared the chores. I have a picture of my uncle and aunt taken together hanging over my bed and every day I look at them, remembering their kindness and how much pains they took to teach me how to live right and instilled good principles into all of us. They never allowed us to use bad language or use strong drink."

"When I reached the age of 19 my benefactors died and I went to live with W.H. or Billy, as we called him. I was living there when Martha was born, and I suppose that is why I love her so. All the children call me "Uncle Ben" for they were taught that from infancy. I lived for a while with my brother, Escar, who died recently, and Like Smithson, grandfather of Frank Woodward Smithson. It was with him I was making my home when World War One caught up with me."

"It was on May 11, 1918, I left for Fort Oglethorpe, Ga., for training. I left there for Long Island, New York, where I spent two weeks before leaving for overseas on July 6, of that same year. You see they did not give the raw recruits any more training than they do now. We were eleven days going over, dodging submarines all the way. I was certainly glad when we arrived at Liverpool, England, all in one piece. I saw service in England, France and Germany for a year, and that was two years too long for me. There were only two Franklin boys, Sidney L. Pratt and Gilbert Walton, along with me and we stuck together all the way."

"After Armistice Day we were sent to Germany on guard duty on the Rhine. Our coming home was much more pleasant mentally and physically. We were on the Leviathan; you see it framed there on the wall. It was the largest and fastest ship then afloat and we made it back in six days. We were given only two meals a day, breakfast at 8 o'clock and dinner at 4 in the afternoon. But that was enough as we had nothing to do but loll around and talk."

"My health was greatly impaired while overseas and when I came home, I was sent to the government hospital in Augusta, Georgia, where I spent the next 20 years. I made many friends there and have often returned to visit them. I was transferred to Murfreesboro where I was discharged three months later."

"When I was a small boy going to school at Peytonsville there was a little girl, Maggie Lee McMahon, and a boy Pink Johnson, who were my classmates. Both Pink and I gave all our red apples to Maggie Lee, but somehow, he always had the inside edge on me, won out, and in 1915 they were married. I did not blame Maggie Lee for her choice for he was a fine fellow."

"Pink died in 1936 and ten years later Maggie Lee and I were married. We lived in Peytonsville, where I farmed and ran a dairy until 1949 when we bought this house of six rooms and moved in. We rented our farm to James Goodman, a mighty good man and a splendid farmer. We get fresh vegetables from the farm all during the growing season and fresh eggs the year round."

"After we got settled with everything in place and I'd helped my wife with a good size flower garden I kinder tired of sitting around all day, so I began going down to Quality Market. I just couldn't stand seeing Martha going around with her tongue hanging out and I sitting idly by watching her, so I said, 'Honey, give me an apron and let me help you.' Little by little I began taking more and more off the shoulders of the little girl I rocked to sleep as a baby and now I go to work each morning as regularly as the others. It does my heart good to hear Martha ask, 'Uncle Ben, will you do this, that or the other for me?' And I'm always only too happy to do it. I know it would please her father, Billy, if he could know it. I owe a lot to her grandparents and this is one way I can show my appreciation."

Mr. Smithson, though 62 years of age, is still full of life. Every time there is a square dance in town, even if it on the Square, he is right in the thick of it. He also is found swimming. Last summer he and his wife went to Florida taking in both coasts, going as far south as Key West. He spent much time in the ocean but could not persuade his wife to follow him. Returning they took in the mountains of North Georgia and East Tennessee and visited his friends in Augusta. They are looking forward to returning this winter. Next summer, if all goes well, they are planning to load up their car and head for California, visiting all the interesting places in between and relatives in Texas.

They both like young people and have many in their home for visits or drop in for meals, as cooking is one of Mrs. Smithson's many hobbies. They are both members of Epworth Methodist Church and go back every Sunday for both Sunday school and Church services. Mr. Smithson serves as a steward and is a member of S.I. Vaden's class while his wife is in Mrs. J.N. Boxley's and is past vice-president of the Women's Society of Christian Service. She is also a charter member of Peytonsville Home Demonstration Club and has enjoyed the work from Miss Carson on down to Miss Crowley. Every demonstration given, in which she is interested she tries out when she gets home. She has an electric machine and enjoys sewing. On the floor in her bedroom is a beautiful oval crocheted rug in floral designs. The kitchen linoleum was showing wear, so she painted it solid green and then worked out a floral design for it also, making a most restful pattern. A beautiful Afghan, embroidered pieces over the house and other handiwork shows she is never idle. She is a good hand at playing croquet and holds all her young neighbors in awe of her skill when they have games together.

In speaking of his early life Mr. Smithson said, "I was an old bachelor when I married. This was partly due the fact that when I started going with a girl it was not long before she was married to another fellow. When I was in France, I studied French for a while, and it was not long before I thought I knew enough to speak like a native. I saw a pretty girl on the street and addressed her in her native tongue. She becomes convulsed with laughter. When I found an interpreter and told him what I had said he also began to laugh and told me I had only said "Good morning, good night, Mademoiselle," After that I stuck to my good old American English, good or bad."

While living in Augusta Mr. Smithson was a member of the American Legion but he did not keep it up when he came back to Franklin. He does not dwell on those war days back of him but thinks of the future. He and Mrs. Smithson like to go to their farm on Sundays to see how things are progressing. They have a nice house with her father, F.E. McMahon, a rock mason and carpenter, designed and built. They were sorry to leave it but found work on the farm much easier for both of them in their new home.

Mr. Smithson said, "I waited a long time to marry but I certainly made no mistake when I did. I didn't carry all those red apples to school for nothing as a boy. Nobody can cook a better pie, cake, steak, biscuit or anything else than Maggie Lee. If you don't believe it just come and eat with us some day." And he meant it.

### The following is his obituary:
Franklin, Tenn.
SMITHSON, Ben G. - Age 83, Nov. 22, 1972. Survived by wife, Mrs. Maggie Lee Smithson; 7 nieces; 6 nephews. Remains are at Franklin Memorial Chapel, where services will be conducted at 2:30 o'clock p.m., Fri., Nov. 24, by Rev. Michael D. O'Bannon. Burial in Mt. Hope

Cemetery. Honorary pallbearers: Alva Vaden Sunday school Class, James & Frank Boyd, Reedy Edgmon, J.W. Garrett, Bob Sewell, Eddie House, Lawrence Hussey, Bob Waller, Leon Smith, Douglas York, William Miller, John Reynolds, Charles Clemmons, Jim Robert McMahon, Herman & Howard Smithson, George Boyd, Ernest Epperson & Joe Smithson. Active pallbearers: Herbert, Frank, Ralph, Joe, Charles & Ben T. Smithson, Roy King, John Horner, Jim Nycewonder, Lewis Stanfield & J.R. King. FRANKLIN MEMORIAL CHAPEL.

# CHARLES MARTIN MATHIS
## 1890-1943

### MATHIS FAMILY

## HUSBAND'S PARENTS
**Jerry Mathis**     **Frances Elizabeth Adair**
1847 - 1927              1849 - 1909

## WIFE'S PARENTS
**Thomas Henry Pate**     **Mary Ellen Tomlin**
1867 - 1941                      1877 - 1914

## HUSBAND
**Charles Martin Mathis**
**BIRTH:** 3 Nov. 1890, Williamson Co. TN
**DEATH:** 17 Feb. 1943, Davidson Co. TN

## WIFE
**Mary Clifton Pate**
**BIRTH:** 17 Sep. 1900, Franklin, TN
**DEATH:** 4 Feb. 1971, Williamson Co. TN

### HIS LIFE

When Charles Martin Mathis was born on November 3, 1890, in Williamson County, Tennessee, his father, Jerry was 43 and his mother, Frances was 41. He married Mary Clifton Pate on January 12, 1919, in Williamson County. He died on February 17, 1943, in Davidson County, Tennessee at the age of 52. He was buried in the Cool Springs Cemetery in Peytonsville, Tennessee.

# JESSE MARSHALL WARREN
## 1891-1979

### WARREN FAMILY

## HUSBAND'S PARENTS
**James Lee Warren**     **Sarah Ann Jamison**
1868 - 1947                      1871 - 1947

## 1ST WIFE'S PARENTS
**John Hugh Duff**     **Mary Elizabeth Vaughan**
1859 - 1931                  1862 - 1929

## 2ND WIFE'S PARENTS
**Elijah Thompson Hassell**   **Mary Jane Ragan**
1840 - 1930          1858 - 1949

## HUSBAND
**Jesse Marshall Warren**
**BIRTH:** 17 Dec. 1891, Nashville, TN
**DEATH:** 23 Oct. 1979, Peytonsville, TN

## 1ST WIFE
**Amelia Mell Duff**
**BIRTH:** Nov. 1895, Williamson Co. TN
**DEATH:** 27 Aug. 1943, Williamson Co. TN

## 2ND WIFE
**Elizabeth M. Hassell**
**BIRTH:** 6 Nov. 1897, Houston Co. TN
**DEATH:** Mar. 1986, Nashville, TN

## CHILDREN OF JESSE AND AMELIA

**Alta Mercille Warren**   **BIRTH:** 1920
**Daughter**                      **DEATH:** 7 Jan. 1991

**Private Warren**   **BIRTH:**
**Daughter**              **DEATH:**

**Lloyd Duff Warren**   **BIRTH:** 19 Jun. 1922
**Son**                         **DEATH:** 23 Jan. 2003

## HIS LIFE

When Jesse Marshall Warren was born on December 17, 1891, in Nashville, Tennessee, his father, James was 23 and his mother, Sarah was 20. He married Amelia Mell Duff on January 21, 1919, and they had three children together. Amelia died on August 27, 1943. He died on October 23, 1979, at the age of 87. He was buried in the Mount Hope Cemetery in Franklin, Tennessee.

# JAMES DEE BENNETT
# 1892-1982

## BENNETT FAMILY

## HUSBAND'S PARENTS
**John A. Bennett**   **Sarah Elizabeth McGee**
1865 - 1900          1877 - 1970

## WIFE'S PARENTS
**Wade Hampton Jay**   **May Jane Jay**
1859 - 1939          1860 - 1920

## HUSBAND
**James Dee Bennett**
**BIRTH:** 12 Nov. 1892, TN
**DEATH:** 12 Nov. 1982, Peytonsville, TN

## WIFE
**Beatrice Lucille Jay**
**BIRTH:** 3 July 1895, Howe, TX
**DEATH:** 25 Jan. 1974, Franklin, TN

## CHILDREN

**Margaret Alline**   **BIRTH:** 30 Apr. 1918
**Bennett-Daughter**   **DEATH:** 24 Apr. 1928

**Jewel Bennett**   **BIRTH:** 18 July 1920
**Daughter**          **DEATH:** 4 Mar. 2016

**James "Jimmie" Dee**   **BIRTH:** 1922
**Bennett-Son**             **DEATH:** 8 Nov 2020

**Paris Bennett**   **BIRTH:** 1924
**Son**                 **DEATH:** 25 July 2019

**Private Bennett**   **BIRTH:**
                            **DEATH:**

**Johnnie Richard**   **BIRTH:** 2 July 1929
**Bennett-Son**          **DEATH:** 20 July 2016

**Janie Rachel Bennett**   **BIRTH:** 3 July 1929
**Daughter**                    **DEATH:** 29 Aug. 2015

## HIS LIFE

When James Dee Bennett was born on November 12, 1892, in Tennessee, his father, John was 27 and his mother, Sarah was 15. He married Beatrice Lucille Jay on February 6,

1916, in Pontotoc, Oklahoma. They had seven children in 11-years. He died on November 12, 1982, in Williamson County, Tennessee at the age of 90. He was buried in the Williamson Memorial Gardens Cemetery in Franklin, Tennessee.

JIMMIE DEE AND BEATRICE (JAY) BENNETT

# JAMES MOSES BRUCE
## 1892-1963

### BRUCE FAMILY

**HUSBAND'S PARENTS**
**James W. Bruce**    **Belle V. Garner**
1857 - 1932          1861 - 1944

**WIFE'S PARENTS**
**William "Lee" Garner**   **Martha Susan Bennett**
1873 - 1959               1879 - 1968

### HUSBAND
**James Moses Bruce**
BIRTH: 29 Jan. 1892, Hickman Co. TN
DEATH: 10 May 1963, Peytonsville, TN

### WIFE
**Mary Elizabeth Garner**
BIRTH: 27 July 1899, Peytonsville, TN
DEATH: 17 June 1979, Peytonsville, TN

### CHILDREN

| | |
|---|---|
| **James Helton Bruce** Son | BIRTH: 3 Sep. 1923<br>DEATH: 6 Dec. 1994 |
| **Garrett Walls Bruce** Son | BIRTH: 1 Nov. 1925<br>DEATH: 15 Jan. 1963 |
| **George Washington Bruce-Son** | BIRTH: 22 Feb. 1928<br>DEATH: 7 Jan. 1975 |
| **Sue Willie Bruce** Daughter | BIRTH: 9 Apr. 1930<br>DEATH: 7 Sep. 1993 |
| **Filmore Mutt Bruce** Son | BIRTH: 24 May 1932<br>DEATH: 27 Feb. 2000 |
| **Betty Catherine Bruce** Daughter | BIRTH: 27 Sep. 1935<br>DEATH: 11 June 2016 |
| **Mary Yvonne Bruce** Daughter | BIRTH: 1938<br>DEATH: 2020 |
| **James Moses Bruce** Son | BIRTH: 19 Jun, 1939<br>DEATH: 4 Jun, 1995 |
| **Private Bruce** Daughter | BIRTH:<br>DEATH: |

### HIS LIFE

When James Moses Bruce was born on January 29, 1892, in Hickman County, Tennessee, his father, James was 43 and his mother, Belle was 30. He married Mary Elizabeth Garner on September 24, 1922, in Williamson County, Tennessee. They had eight children in 15-years. He died on May 10, 1963, in Peytonsville, Tennessee at the ager of 71. He was buried in the Simmons Cemetery in Peytonsville.

# SAM FLEMING MCGEE
# 1894-1975

## MCGEE FAMILY

### HUSBAND'S PARENTS
**John Franklin McGee**      **Mary Elizabeth Truett**
1857 - 1944                              1859 - 1941

### WIFE'S PARENTS
**William Lundy Pate**    **Sophia Alice J. Farrow**
1858 - 1935                          1863 - 1950

### HUSBAND
**Sam Fleming McGee**
**BIRTH:** 1 May 1894, Peytonsville, TN
**DEATH:** 21 Aug. 1975, Peytonsville, TN

### WIFE
**Mary Elizabeth Pate**
**BIRTH:** 7 Mar. 1897, Franklin, TN
**DEATH:** 27 Mar. 1976, Franklin, TN

## CHILDREN

**Mildred A. McGee Daughter** — **BIRTH:** Mar. 1915 **DEATH:** 3 Nov. 1920

**Sam Fleming McGee Jr.-Son** — **BIRTH:** 1917 **DEATH:** 15 May 1959

**James Mabron "Macky" McGee-Son** — **BIRTH:** 4 Aug. 1922 **DEATH:** 9 Oct. 1988

**William Sebastian "Bass"McGee-Son** — **BIRTH:** 1 Dec. 1925 **DEATH:** 4 Feb. 2009

**Clifton Reese McGee Son** — **BIRTH:** 3 Nov. 1934 **DEATH:** 12 Dec. 2006

## HIS LIFE

When Sam Fleming McGee was born on May 1, 1894, in Peytonsville, Tennessee, his father, John was 36 and his mother, Mary was 34.

Sam inherited the love of music and the talent to compose from his father, John R. McGee. At a very young age Sam played the banjo with his father and it was not long until he was able to compose.

Sam and his brother, Kirk were famous comedians, appearing on Nashville radio. As small boys an uncle made them a fiddle from cigar boxes and the music coming from the crude instruments was close to marvelous. They played at dances and with the money they earned, purchased better musical instruments. In later days they traveled to many locations, doing concerts and bringing cheer to thousands. They eventually became members of the Grand Ole Opry and were on the radio on Saturday nights over WSM at the Ryman Auditorium where large crowds were present to hear them perform in person.

Sam and Kirk toured the United States and visited nearly every state. They made appearances in theaters, town halls and auditoriums. They were also among the oldest recording artists, their first being made in 1925 with Uncle Dave Macon. When they first began to perform, their services were free, but when they found they could make money from their singing and playing, they went on the road. They played every coal mining camp in Virginia, West Virginia and East Kentucky. Later they appeared at Carnegie Hall, the Newport Jazz Festival and the Festival of American Folklife.

The McGee brothers and sisters attended Harpeth School where most of them began their education under Miss Susie (Baugh) Scales. Kirk said "The influence Miss Susie had on our lives cannot be estimated."

Sam had two farms at Peytonsville totaling 600-acres. He kept busy there when he wasn't in the studio or touring. On July 19, 1914, he married, Mary Elizabeth Pate in Peytonsville. They had five children in 19-years.

Sam has been called by music historians, "the most influential guitar player in the early history of country music." He played a big part in the international development of this music which was a significant chapter in Williamson County history.

On August 21, 1975, Sam McGee died as the result of an accident on his farm. He was 81-years old. He just lacked one month from being on the Opry for 50-years. He was buried in Williamson Memorial Gardens Cemetery in Franklin, Tennessee.

ELIZABETH (PATE) AND SAM MCGEE

# SAMUEL EARL JOHNSON
## 1894-1960

### JOHNSON FAMILY

**HUSBAND'S PARENTS**
**Walter Lee Johnson   Minnie Virginia Gosey**
1871 - 1944                1875 - 1928

**WIFE'S PARENTS**
**Samuel Toliver Mathis   Martha Louise Crunk**
1875 - 1939                1879 - 1958

**HUSBAND**
**Samuel Earl Johnson**
**BIRTH:** 20 May 1894, Peytonsville, TN
**DEATH:** 24 July 1960, Clearwater, FL

**WIFE**
**Sammie Lou Mathis**
**BIRTH:** 19 Dec. 1903, Peytonsville, TN
**DEATH:** 13 July 1983, Williamson Co. TN


**CHILDREN**

| | |
|---|---|
| Earl Mathis Johnson Son | **BIRTH:** 1924 <br> **DEATH:** 21 July 1977 |
| Frances Louise Johnson-Daughter | **BIRTH:** 18 Jan. 1925 <br> **DEATH:** 31 Jan. 2009 |
| Richard Eugene Johnson-Son | **BIRTH:** 19 Oct. 1926 <br> **DEATH:** 14 May 1998 |
| Martha Virginia Johnson-Daughter | **BIRTH:** 8 Dec. 1927 <br> **DEATH:** 26 Feb. 2007 |
| Gerald Lewis Johnson-Son | **BIRTH:** 8 Dec. 1930 <br> **DEATH:** 14 Nov. 2010 |

**HIS LIFE**

When Samuel Johnson was born on May 20, 1894, in Peytonsville, Tennessee, his father, Walter was 23 and his mother, Minnie was 18. He married Sammie Lou Mathis on November 19, 1922, in Peytonsville. They had five children during their marriage. He died on July 24, 1960, at the age of 66. He was buried in Woodlawn Memorial Cemetery in Nashville, Tennessee.

# JAMES ELMER GRAVES
# 1894-1958

**GRAVES FAMILY**

**HUSBAND'S PARENTS**
James Henry Graves    Laura Gertrude Ladd
1860 - 1928          1860 - 1932

**WIFE'S PARENTS**
John Wesley Boyd    Francis Henrietta Dodson
1864 - 1923        1864 - 1912

---


**HUSBAND**
**James Elmer Graves**
**BIRTH:** 11 June 1894, Peytonsville, TN
**DEATH:** 11 Dec. 1958, Franklin, TN

**WIFE**
**Johnnie D. Boyd**
**BIRTH:** 24 Aug. 1903, Peytonsville, TN
**DEATH:** 2 Oct. 1970


**CHILDREN**

| | |
|---|---|
| James Elmer Graves Jr.-Son | **BIRTH:** 19 Dec. 1925 <br> **DEATH:** 29 Nov. 1991 |
| Harold Boyd Graves Son | **BIRTH:** 1928 <br> **DEATH:** 9 Sep. 2020 |
| Margaret Ann Graves Daughter | **BIRTH:** 21 Feb. 1930 <br> **DEATH:** 16 Feb. 1999 |
| Private Graves | **BIRTH:** <br> **DEATH:** |
| Private Graves | **BIRTH:** <br> **DEATH:** |

**HIS LIFE**

When James Elmer Graves was born on June 11, 1894, in Peytonsville, Tennessee, his father, James was 34 and his mother, Laura was 34. He married Johnnie D. Boyd on March 24, 1925, when he was 30-years old. They had five children together. James died on December 11, 1958, in Franklin, Tennessee at the age of 64. He was buried in the Mount Hope Cemetery in Franklin.

# ROY GILLIAM MEEK
# 1895-1967

### MEEK FAMILY

### HUSBAND'S PARENTS
**Thomas Richard Meek**  **Lena Allen Smithson**
1870 - 1957          1872 - 1913

### WIFE'S PARENTS
**Charles Wilson Vaden**  **Nora E. Pennington**
1896 - 1935          1874 - 1942

### HUSBAND
**Roy Gilliam Meek**
**BIRTH:** 10 Mar. 1895, Williamson Co. TN
**DEATH:** 13 Nov. 1967, Franklin, TN

### WIFE
**Lera Mae Vaden**
**BIRTH:** 30 July 1903, Peytonsville, TN
**DEATH:** 11 July 1985, Lawrence Co. TN

### CHILDREN

| | |
|---|---|
| **Lena Alice Meek** Daughter | **BIRTH:** 20 May 1927 **DEATH:** 28 Mar. 2016 |
| **Charles Richard Meek** Son | **BIRTH:** 14 May 1929 **DEATH:** 29 June 2008 |

### HIS LIFE

When Roy Gilliam Meek was born on March 10, 1895, in Williamson County, Tennessee, his father, Thomas was 25 and his mother, Lena was 22. He married Lera Mae Vaden and they had one son and one daughter together. He died on November 13, 1967, in Franklin, Tennessee at the age of 72. He was buried in the Williamson Memorial Gardens Cemetery in Franklin.

# JAMES ARCHIE LADD
# 1895-1968

### LADD FAMILY

### HUSBAND'S PARENTS
**Ewell Cannon Ladd**  **Ola Mai Gee**
1871 - 1946          1877 - 1943

## HUSBAND
**James Archie Ladd**
BIRTH: 18 Dec. 1895, Peytonsville, TN
DEATH: 2 Jan. 1968, Peytonsville, TN

## WIFE
**Pamelia Stanfield**
BIRTH: 12 Mar. 1902, TN
DEATH: 27 Dec. 1984, Franklin, TN

## CHILDREN

| | |
|---|---|
| **Gordon Brown Ladd** Son | BIRTH: 21 June 1934 DEATH: 28 June 2013 |

## HIS LIFE

When James Archie Ladd was born on December 18, 1895, in Williamson County, Tennessee, his father, Ewell was 24 and his mother, Ola was 18. He married Pamelia Stanfield on November 30, 1933, in Peytonsville, Tennessee. They had one child during their marriage. He died on January 2, 1968, in Williamson County at the age of 72. He was buried in the Williamson Memorial Gardens Cemetery in Franklin, Tennessee.

# WILLIAM BRYAN DODD
# 1896-1978

## DODD FAMILY

### HUSBAND'S PARENTS
**William Albert Dodd**   **Anna Elizabeth Owen**
1868 - 1943              1867 - 1953

### WIFE'S PARENTS
**John Wesley Boyd**   **Francis Henrietta Dodson**
1864 - 1923            1864 - 1912

## HUSBAND
**William Bryan Dodd**
BIRTH: 5 Nov. 1896, Rockvale, TN
DEATH: 28 June 1978, Peytonsville, TN

## WIFE
**Myrtle Alene Fagan**
BIRTH: 5 Jan. 1905, Chapel Hill, TN
DEATH: 31 Mar. 1957, Peytonsville, TN

## CHILDREN

| | |
|---|---|
| **William Harold Dodd** Son | BIRTH: 20 Jan. 1925 DEATH: 30 Jan. 1990 |
| **Henry Elbert Dodd** Son | BIRTH: 18 May 1927 DEATH: 4 Oct. 1933 |
| **John Albert Dodd** Son | BIRTH: 22 Sep. 1929 DEATH: 13 Aug. 1993 |
| **Eleanor Ruth Dodd** Daughter | BIRTH: 6 July 1931 DEATH: 7 Feb. 2018 |
| **Mary Elizabeth Dodd** Daughter | BIRTH: 9 Oct. 1932 DEATH: 14 Dec. 2018 |
| **James Roy Dodd** Son | BIRTH: 12 Nov. 1936 DEATH: 31 Aug. 2018 |
| **Gerald Smith Dodd** Son | BIRTH: 16 July 1939 DEATH: 21 Jan. 2020 |
| **Private Dodd** Son | BIRTH: DEATH: |
| **Private Dodd** Daughter | BIRTH: DEATH: |
| **Private Dodd** Daughter | BIRTH: DEATH: |
| **Private Dodd** Son | BIRTH: DEATH: |

## HIS LIFE

When William Bryan Dodd was born on November 5, 1896, in Rockvale, Tennessee, his father, William was 28 and his mother, Lizzie was

29. He married Myrtle Alene Fagan on November 27, 1928, in Williamson County, Tennessee. They had eleven children in 14-years. He died on June 28, 1978, at the age of 81. He was buried in the Mount Hope Cemetery in Franklin, Tennessee.

MYRTLE (FAGAN) AND WILLIAM BRYAN DODD

# ODELIA CROWDER
## 1896-1972

### CROWDER FAMILY

**HUSBAND'S PARENTS**

| Martin Crowder | Anna Gibson |
|---|---|
| 1853 - 1915 | 1851 - 1926 |

**WIFE'S PARENTS**

| Reuben B. Reynolds | Mary Jane Hughes |
|---|---|
| 1850 - ? | 1873 - 1925 |

**HUSBAND**
**Odelia Crowder**
**BIRTH:** 2 May 1896, Peytonsville, TN
**DEATH:** Nov. 1972, Franklin, TN

**WIFE**
**Amelia Reynolds**
**BIRTH:** 1895, TN
**DEATH:** Apr. 1973, Franklin, TN

### CHILDREN

| | |
|---|---|
| **Louise Crowder** Daughter | **BIRTH:** 1919 **DEATH:** 20 Aug. 1997 |
| **James Ewing Crowder-Son** | **BIRTH:** 13 Dec. 1919 **DEATH:** 1995 |
| **Mamie Crowder** Daughter | **BIRTH:** 1920 **DEATH:** |
| **Josephine Crowder** Daughter | **BIRTH:** 1923 **DEATH:** 8 Feb. 2018 |
| **John H. Crowder** Son | **BIRTH:** 1925 **DEATH:** 17 Jan. 1987 |
| **Minnie Marie L. Crowder-Daughter** | **BIRTH:** 12 Nov. 1926 **DEATH:** 30 Aug. 2012 |
| **Marion Wesley Crowder-Son** | **BIRTH:** 31 Aug. 1931 **DEATH:** 19 Feb. 1972 |
| **Mary Ann Crowder** Daughter | **BIRTH:** 1936 **DEATH:** |

### HIS LIFE

When Odelia Crowder was born on May 2, 1896, in Williamson County, Tennessee, his father, Martin was 42 and his mother, Anna was 44. He married Amelia Reynolds on February 2, 1918, in Peytonsville, Tennessee. They had eight children in 17-years. He died in November, 1972, in Franklin at the age of 76.

AMELIA (REYNOLDS) AND ODELIA CROWDER

# GRANT LUSTER JR.
## 1896-1981

### LUSTER FAMILY

**HUSBAND'S PARENTS**
**Grant Luster Sr.**    **Anna Patton**
1864 - 1931          1865 - 1915

**1ST WIFE'S PARENTS**
**Noble Curtis Carothers**    **Hattie M. Jordan**
1865 - ?                    1875 - ?

**2ND WIFE'S PARENTS**
**Ozie Lee Smithson**    **Daisy Lee Hayes**
1888 - 1930           1891 - 1975

**HUSBAND**
**Grant Luster Jr.**
BIRTH: 27 Nov. 1896, Williamson Co. TN
DEATH: 27 Apr. 1981, Williamson Co. TN

**1ST WIFE**
**Nellie Lea Carothers**
BIRTH: 1903, Williamson Co. TN
DEATH: 11 Apr. 1933, Williamson Co. TN

**2ND WIFE**
**Mattie Jane Smithson**

BIRTH: 30 Mar. 1912, TN
DEATH: 22 Dec. 1991

### CHILDREN OF GRANT AND NELLIE

**James Lee Luster**    BIRTH: 10 May 1922
Son                  DEATH: Aug. 1985

**Nelson Noble Luster**    BIRTH: 27 Sep. 1924
Son                     DEATH: 25 Sep. 2014

**William T. Luster**    BIRTH: 2 Dec. 1929
Son                   DEATH: Feb. 1969

### HIS LIFE

When Grant Luster was born on November 27, 1896, in Williamson County, Tennessee, his father, Grant was 32 and his mother, Anna was 31. He married Nellie Lea Carothers and they had three children together. Nellie died on April 11, 1933. Grant married Mattie Jane Smithson on September 20, 1933, in Williamson County. He died on April 27, 1981, in Peytonsville, Tennessee at the age of 84. He was buried in the Luster Cemetery in College Grove, Tennessee.

MATTIE (SMITHSON) AND GRANT LUSTER JR.

285

⌣

# JOHN EDWARD PRATT
## 1897-1977

### PRATT FAMILY

**HUSBAND'S PARENTS**
**Samuel Houston Pratt**      **Mary Frances Wood**
1868 - 1904                              1876 - 1942

**WIFE'S PARENTS**
**Thomas Richard Meek**   **Lena Allen Smithson**
1870 - 1957                              1872 - 1913

**HUSBAND**
**John Edward Pratt**
**BIRTH:** 7 Dec. 1897, Peytonsville, TN
**DEATH:** 9 Feb. 1977, Franklin, TN

**WIFE**
**Addie Louise Meek**
**BIRTH:** 6 June 1902, TX
**DEATH:** 9 Jan. 1968, Williamson Co. TN

### CHILDREN

| | |
|---|---|
| **Thomas Houston Pratt-Son** | **BIRTH:** 18 Nov. 1922 <br> **DEATH:** 16 May 2003 |
| **Lena Frances Pratt Daughter** | **BIRTH:** 15 Feb. 1924 <br> **DEATH:** 22 Oct. 2007 |
| **Catherine Louise Pratt-Daughter** | **BIRTH:** 1925 <br> **DEATH:** 18 Dec. 2020 |
| **Samuel Leon Pratt Son** | **BIRTH:** 29 June 1928 <br> **DEATH:** 18 Dec. 2016 |
| **John Edward Pratt Jr. Son** | **BIRTH:** 26 Aug. 1932 <br> **DEATH:** 28 Feb. 1964 |
| **Private Pratt Daughter** | **BIRTH:** <br> **DEATH:** |
| **Private Pratt Son** | **BIRTH:** <br> **DEATH:** |
| **Private Pratt Son** | **BIRTH:** <br> **DEATH:** |

### HIS LIFE

When John Edward Pratt was born on December 7, 1897, in Williamson County, Tennessee, his father, Samuel was 29 and his mother, Mary was 21. He married Addie Louise Meek on December 24, 1921, in Peytonsville, Tennessee. They had eight children in 21-years. He died on February 9, 1977, in Franklin, Tennessee at the age of 79. He was buried in Williamson Memorial Gardens Cemetery in Franklin.

JOHN EDWARD, ADDIE LOUISE (MEEK) AND PAUL M. PRATT

⌣

# WILLIE JO BUFORD
## 1897-1966

### BUFORD FAMILY

**Calvin Tate Buford    Ida Turner**
1875 - 1957       1879 - 1930

WIFE'S PARENTS
**James R. Crafton    Leade "Lee" White**
1878 - 1949       1878 - 1958

HUSBAND
**Willie Jo Buford**
**BIRTH:** 24 Aug. 1897, Maury Co. TN
**DEATH:** 1 Dec. 1966, Peytonsville, TN

WIFE
**Vera Elizabeth Crafton**
**BIRTH:** 20 May 1905, TN
**DEATH:** 4 Dec. 1983, Franklin, TN

CHILDREN

| | | |
|---|---|---|
| **Willie Joe Buford Jr.** Son | **BIRTH:** 19 Aug. 1921 | **DEATH:** 16 Feb. 1992 |
| **Alvin Lee Buford** Son | **BIRTH:** 23 Apr. 1923 | **DEATH:** 28 Aug. 1998 |
| **Leslie Davis Buford** Son | **BIRTH:** 14 Apr. 1925 | **DEATH:** 25 Sep. 2012 |
| **Esther Elizabeth Buford-Daughter** | **BIRTH:** 19 Mar. 1927 | **DEATH:** 5 Oct. 2001 |
| **Lucy Pearl Buford** Daughter | **BIRTH:** 3 Aug. 1929 | **DEATH:** 14 Dec. 2014 |
| **Gladys Rebecca Buford-Daughter** | **BIRTH:** 30 Nov. 1930 | **DEATH:** 10 May 2015 |
| **Geneva Louise Buford-Daughter** | **BIRTH:** 26 Jan. 1934 | **DEATH:** 26 Feb. 1935 |
| **James Calvin Buford** Son | **BIRTH:** 1939 | **DEATH:** 26 Dec. 2020 |

HIS LIFE

When Willie Jo Buford was born on August 24, 1897, in Maury County, Tennessee, his father, Calvin was 22 and his mother, Ida was 17. He married Vera Elizabeth Crafton on December 25, 1919, in Williamson County, Tennessee. They had eight children in 18-years. He died on December 1, 1966, in Williamson County at the age of 69.

# CLAUDE DOUGLAS YORK
## 1898-1980

YORK FAMILY

HUSBAND'S PARENTS
**Claude York    Josephine Stevens**
1869 - 1947       1872 - 1956

WIFE'S PARENTS
**Samuel Houston Pratt   Mary Frances Wood**
1868 - 1904          1876 - 1942

HUSBAND
**Claude Douglas York**
**BIRTH:** 2 Mar. 1898, Nolensville, TN
**DEATH:** Oct. 1980, Williamson Co. TN

WIFE
**Sadie Florence Pratt**
**BIRTH:** 21 July 1902, Peytonsville, TN
**DEATH:** 26 Aug. 1980, Williamson Co. TN

HIS LIFE

When Claude Douglas York was born on March 2, 1898, in Nolensville, Tennessee, his father, Claude was 28 and his mother, Josephine was 25. He married Sadie Florence Pratt on December 21, 1922, in Williamson County, Tennessee. He died in October, 1980, in Williamson County at the age of 82. He was buried in the Williamson Memorial Gardens Cemetery in Franklin, Tennessee.

# THOMAS LITTLE
# 1898-1972

### LITTLE FAMILY

#### HUSBAND'S PARENTS
**John Wallace Little**    **Florence Johnson**
1869 - 1901                1874 - 1946

#### 1ST WIFE'S PARENTS
**George Dahnke**    **Elanor Maria Noffman**
1866 - 1921          1870 - 1953

#### 2ND WIFE'S PARENTS
**William M. Hannah**    **Margaret S. Claiborne**
1878 - 1964              1881 - 1972

#### HUSBAND
**Thomas Little**
**BIRTH:** 27 Sep. 1898, Peytonsville, TN
**DEATH:** 20 June 1972, Nashville, TN

#### 1ST WIFE
**Helen Dahnke**
**BIRTH:** 1901, Nashville, TN
**DEATH:** 24 Dec. 1938, Nashville, TN

#### 2ND WIFE
**Lillian Mae Hannah**
**BIRTH:** 29 Mar. 1906, Harriman, TN
**DEATH:** 10 Apr. 2000, Nashville, TN

### HIS LIFE

When Thomas Little was born on September 27, 1898, in Peytonsville, Tennessee, his father, John was 29 and his mother, Florence was 24.

***Biographies of the 13th District***
**Tom Little, Pulitzer Prize Winner**
**By Ann Beasley Johnson**
***The Review-Appeal,*** **June 28, 1998**

Tom Little, the "Southpaw from Snatch," is one of Williamson County's most illustrious sons. Recognized nationally and abroad from his newspaper work, it seems logical that he be recognized in his native county along with others who are included in the Bicentennial Honor Roll.

Born in the tiny village of Peytonsville, Tenn., on Sept. 27, 1898, to John Wallace and Florence Johnson Little, Tom, after the death of his father, lived with his grandmother and grandfather Johnson in this rural community and attended school there for a short time.

In Goodspeed's "*History of Tennessee*" is recorded this interesting fact; "it is a matter of record that in 1936 Peytonsville was called Snatchett, or as the public now (1886) have it— Snatch. Its name originated in the fact, it is said that one individual owed another $10, and the creditor being unable to collect the debt seized the opportune moment and snatched the money from the unsuspecting debtor."

(Local color of other areas of the county is magnified by the place names by which they have been known for years. Included in such a list are: Possom Trot, Lousy Level, Mudsink, Henpeck Lane, Pumpkin Center and Little Texas.)

Tom, and his mother, "Miss Florence," lived in Franklin for a few years on Third Avenue. During these years Miss Florence worked at Roberts Store (later known as Draper and Darwin). Tom Little's aunt, his mother's sister, Mrs. T.O. Murrey, was the former Miss Myrtle Johnson.

Later, Mrs. Little and her son moved to Nashville. Miss Florence worked in the ladies' ready-to-wear department of Lebeck's (later known as Harvey's), and Tom attended Montgomery Bell Academy. While still in high school, Little and a buddy went to see the city editor of *The Tennessean* about a job. There was one job available, so they took it and divided the $15 weekly salary. From this 'sobering salary, Tom began his life-long love affair with newspapers."

In 1957 Tommy Little was awarded the coveted Pulitzer Prize for his cartoons which appeared for 33 years in the *Nashville Tennessean*. It was in 1956 that Tom sent out his message through his now famous cartoon of a crippled boy on crutches watching his buddies play football.

The caption was: "Wonder why my parents didn't give me the Sabin Shots?" It was this cartoon which helped him win the Pulitzer award.

On Feb. 17, 1958, at the Richland Country Club in Nashville, a rousing tribute was paid Mr. Little by more than 400 friends in recognition of his 46 years with *The Tennessean* as a reporter, editor and cartoonist. Many of these cartoons "drew a sharp image of issues that bothered city, state and nation."

Guests on this occasion included scores of Tom's Nashville friends, newspaper men representing many of this nation's dailies, and a group of past and present political figures. Those coming from a distance had doggedly stuck by the airlines struggling with snow and zero temperature to get them to Nashville.

Decorations for the dinner included tablecloths on which Little's more famous cartoons had been printed, the entire wall behind the speakers' table was covered with a giant cartoon strip in color, and on the speakers' table were figurines of characters from Little's "*Sunflower Street.*"

Louise Davis, *The Tennessean's* special news writer, in 1973 reported the acquisition of 4.000 to 5,000 original Tom Little cartoons by the Joint University Library. Mrs. Lillian Hannah Little, wife of Tom, made this magnanimous gift to Vanderbilt University.

"This collection was much sought after by several universities that were interested in them as an art form and as a valuable source for historians interpreting the era." It will be housed in the same special collections room where original manuscripts of the Fugitives and the Grantland Rice manuscripts are preserved.

"I'm glad it's here," said Mrs. Little. "It had to be in Tennessee. It wouldn't seem right any other way for Tom."

Quoting from the "*Vanderbilt Alumnus*" Autumn 1973: "That Tom's drawings would end up in the archives of a university was probably the last thing in the minds of relatives when he was growing up in Williamson County. He started drawing when he was still a toddler, lying on his stomach in front of the fire, and doing his pictures with his left hand."

"Little Tommy Little" was truly a tall man. He was praised by Coleman A. Harwell with these words: 'His life and works are a source of pride and inspiration to every newspaperman. He has the bigness of modesty, the charm of sincerity, and the impact of courage..."

Included in "*Who's Who in the South and Southeast*" and in "*Who's Who in America*" are awards to Little for various achievements such as: Editorial award 1947; Christopher Award 1953, Foundation metal 1955 and 1956, Pulitzer Prize for Cartoons 1957. Also included in the above named: "*Who's Who*" were the memberships held by Mr. Little in many professional civic and social clubs.

The "Southpaw from Snatch" was a tall man who cast a long shadow.
(Information from Mrs. Tom Little and Miss Katie Lou Gatlin.)

Thomas Little died on June 20, 1972, in Nashville, Tennessee when he was 73-years old.

THOMAS LITTLE



# MIKE GARNER SIMMONS
## 1899-1968

### SIMMONS FAMILY

#### HUSBAND'S PARENTS
**William O. Simmons**   **Margaret A. Spann**
1852 - 1939              1857 - 1933

#### WIFE'S PARENTS
**Thomas J. Wray**   **Sallie Wray**
1852 - ?             1873 - ?

#### HUSBAND
**Mike Garner Simmons**
**BIRTH:** 21 Dec. 1899, Peytonsville, TN
**DEATH:** 22 Mar. 1968, Peytonsville, TN

#### WIFE
**Alice Wray**
**BIRTH:** 15 Dec. 1900, TN
**DEATH:** 2 Jun. 1981, Peytonsville, TN

### CHILDREN

| | |
|---|---|
| **Mary Alice Simmons** Daughter | **BIRTH:** 10 Jan. 1922 **DEATH:** 14 Sep. 1940 |
| **Sarah Ann Simmons** Daughter | **BIRTH:** 1 Feb. 1924 **DEATH:** 20 June 1938 |
| **Hazel Virginia Simmons-Daughter** | **BIRTH:** 17 Mar. 1926 **DEATH:** 3 Mar. 1999 |
| **Gerald Mike Simmons-Son** | **BIRTH:** 1928 **DEATH:** 22 Mar. 1958 |

### HIS LIFE

When Mike Garner Simmons was born on December 21, 1899, in Peytonsville, Tennessee, his father, William was 47 and his mother, Margaret was 42. He married Alice Wray on February 27, 1921, in Peytonsville. They had four children together. He died on March 22,

1968, in Peytonsville at the age of 68. He was buried in the Simmons Cemetery in Peytonsville.

# BLYTHE EDWARD JOHNSON SR.
# 1899-?

## JOHNSON FAMILY

### HUSBAND'S PARENTS
**Walter Lee Johnson**  **Minnie Virginia Gosey**
1871 - 1944          1875 - 1928

### WIFE'S PARENTS
**Samuel Oliver Mathis**  **Martha Louise Crunk**
1875 - 1939          1879 - 1958

### HUSBAND
**Blythe Edward Johnson Sr.**
BIRTH: 8 May 1899, Peytonsville, TN
DEATH: Williamson Co. TN

### WIFE
**Johnnie Mai Mathis**
BIRTH: 10 Aug. 1906, Williamson Co. TN
DEATH: 6 Jan. 1969

### CHILDREN

**Blythe Edward Johnson Jr.-Son**
BIRTH: 2 June 1923
DEATH: 12 July 1974

**Infant Johnson Daughter**
BIRTH: 22 Dec. 1924
DEATH: 23 Dec. 1924

**Mary Elizabeth Johnson-Daughter**
BIRTH: 1927
DEATH: 2 Mar. 1929

**Samuel Richard Johnson-Son**
BIRTH: 1929
DEATH: 1987

### HIS LIFE

When Blythe Edward Johnson was born on May 8, 1899, in Peytonsville, Tennessee, his father, Walter was 28 and his mother, Minnie was 23.

He married Johnnie Mai Mathis on September 21, 1921. They had four children together. He died in Williamson County, Tennessee.

# WAVERLY "DOC" LABAN WILLIAMS
# 1901-1975

## WILLIAMS FAMILY

### HUSBAND'S PARENTS
**Thomas S. Williams**  **Susanna A. Graham**
1868 - 1918          1873 - 1904

### WIFE'S PARENTS
**Ed Lee Skinner**  **Bettie Mangrum**
1884 - 1967        1888 - 1961

### HUSBAND
**Waverly "Doc" Laban Williams**
BIRTH: 19 Oct. 1901, Williamson Co. TN
DEATH: May 1975, Peytonsville, TN

### WIFE
**Birdie Mai Skinner**
BIRTH: 1910, Williamson Co. TN
DEATH: 10 July 1993

### CHILDREN

**Private Williams**
BIRTH:
DEATH:

### HIS LIFE

When Waverly "Wave" "Doc" Labon Williams was born on October 19, 1901, in Williamson County, Tennessee, his father, Thomas was 32 and his mother, Susanna was 27. He married Birdie Mai Skinner on April 15, 1931, in Williamson County. They had one daughter together. He died in May, 1975, in Peytonsville, Tennessee at the age of 73. He was buried in the

Williamson Memorial Gardens Cemetery in Franklin, Tennessee.

# RICHARD WADE GLENN
## 1904-1960

### GLENN FAMILY

#### HUSBAND'S PARENTS
**Fieldon A. Glenn**    **Mary Ada King**
1870 - 1940              1868 - 1966

#### WIFE'S PARENTS
**Thomas Henry Pate**    **Mary Ellen Tomlin**
1867 - 1941              1877 - 1914

#### HUSBAND
**Richard Wade Glenn**
**BIRTH:** 11 Nov. 1904, Williamson Co. TN
**DEATH:** 23 Nov. 1960, Williamson Co. TN

#### WIFE
**Ercelle Odell Pate**
**BIRTH:** 28 July 1908, Williamson Co. TN
**DEATH:** 28 July 1957, Peytonsville, TN

### CHILDREN

**Thomas Feldon Glenn** **BIRTH:** 9 Oct. 1927
Son                       **DEATH:** 4 Oct. 2002

**Mary Joyce Glenn**     **BIRTH:** 3 Feb. 1930
Daughter                  **DEATH:** 15 Aug. 1988

**Jerald Richard Glenn** **BIRTH:** 4 May 1932
Son                       **DEATH:** 3 May 2001

**Private Glenn**        **BIRTH:** 1944
Son                       **DEATH:**

### HIS LIFE

When Richard Wade Glenn was born on November 11, 1904, in Peytonsville, Tennessee, his father, Fieldon was 33 and his mother, Mary was 36. He married Ercelle Odell Pate on November 28, 1926, in Peytonsville. They had four children in 17-years. He died on November 23, 1960 in Peytonsville when he was 56-years old. He was buried in the Mount Hope Cemetery in Franklin, Tennessee.

ERCELLE ODELL (PATE) AND
RICHARD WADE GLENN

# JAMES OSCAR BOYD
## 1905-1989

### BOYD FAMILY

### HUSBAND'S PARENTS
**John Wesley Boyd**  **Francis Henrietta Dodson**
1864 - 1923          1864 - 1912

### WIFE'S PARENTS
**Walter Lee Johnson**   **Minnie Virginia Gosey**
1871 - 1944              1875 - 1928

### HUSBAND
**James Oscar Boyd**
**BIRTH:** 20 Sep. 1905, Peytonsville, TN
**DEATH:** 6 Feb. 1989, Franklin, TN

### WIFE
**Cora Elizabeth Johnson**
**BIRTH:** 21 Feb. 1910, Peytonsville, TN
**DEATH:** 29 Jan. 1998, Franklin, TN

### CHILDREN

| | |
|---|---|
| **James William Boyd**<br>Son | **BIRTH:** 1928<br>**DEATH:** 2004 |
| **Robert Johnson Boyd**-Son | **BIRTH:** 3 June 1930<br>**DEATH:** 28 Apr. 2020 |
| **Private Boyd** | **BIRTH:**<br>**DEATH:** |
| **Private Boyd** | **BIRTH:**<br>**DEATH:** |
| **Private Boyd** | **BIRTH:**<br>**DEATH:** |
| **Sarah Janis Boyd**<br>Daughter | **BIRTH:** 29 Nov. 1945<br>**DEATH:** 23 Sep. 1949 |

### HIS LIFE

James Oscar Boyd was born on September 20, 1905, in Peytonsville, Tennessee; the son of Francis and John. He married Cora Elizabeth Johnson on May 8, 1927, in Nashville, Tennessee when he was 21-years old. They had six children together. He died on February 6, 1989, in Franklin, Tennessee when he was 83-years old. He was buried in Mount Hope Cemetery in Franklin.

# JOHNNIE OLIVER
# LILLARD
## 1906-1980

### LILLARD FAMILY

### HUSBAND'S PARENTS
**Oliver Claiborne Lillard**   **Greer Jordan Davis**
1873 - 1953                    1879 - 1926

### WIFE'S PARENTS
**John Henry Crunk**    **Annie Belle Graves**
1876 - 1956             1887 - 1945

**Johnnie Oliver Lillard**
**BIRTH:** 27 Oct. 1906, Peytonsville, TN
**DEATH:** 25 Dec. 1980, Williamson Co. TN

WIFE
**Annie Belle Crunk**
**BIRTH:** 12 June 1914, TN
**DEATH:** 20 May 2001, College Grove, TN

CHILDREN

| | |
|---|---|
| **Harry Albert Lillard**<br>Son | **BIRTH:** 19 Mar. 1936<br>**DEATH:** 8 Apr. 2002 |
| **James Oliver Lillard**<br>Son | **BIRTH:** 9 Oct. 1937<br>**DEATH:** 6 June 2012 |
| **Private Lillard** | **BIRTH:**<br>**DEATH:** |
| **Linda Marie Lillard**<br>Daughter | **BIRTH:** 13 Feb. 1945<br>**DEATH:** 5 Sep. 2019 |

## HIS LIFE

When Johnnie Oliver Lillard was born on October 27, 1906, in Peytonsville, Tennessee, his father, Ollie was 32 and his mother, Greer was 27. He married Annie Belle Crunk on February 27, 1935. They had four children during their marriage. He died on December 25, 1980, in Williamson County, Tennessee at the age of 74. He was buried in the Mount Hope Cemetery in Franklin, Tennessee.

BROTHERS, DAVIS MARION AND JOHNNIE OLIVER LILLARD

# HOLLIS VIRGIL WARF
# 1906-1998

## WARF FAMILY

### HUSBAND'S PARENTS
**Samuel Gentry Warf**     **Sidney D. McCord**
1868 - 1954                1878 - 1966

### 1ST WIFE'S PARENTS
**William Reed Richards**  **Etta P. Pendergrass**
1879 - 1956                1887 - 1964

### 2ND WIFE'S PARENTS
**James W. Luckett**       **Rosa M. Sullivan**
1898 - ?                   1900 - ?

**Hollis Virgil Warf**
BIRTH: 21 Jan, 1906, Hickman Co. TN
DEATH: 21 Nov, 1998, Franklin, TN

1ST WIFE
**Annie Lee Richards**
BIRTH: 9 Mar. 1906, TN
DEATH: 22 Jan. 1951, Franklin, TN

2ND WIFE
**Lettie Mai Luckett**
BIRTH: 19 Oct. 1922, Williamson Co. TN
DEATH: 6 Aug. 1999, Franklin, TN

## CHILDREN OF HOLLIS AND ANNIE LEE

**Alma Jean Warf**
**Daughter**
BIRTH: 5 May 1929
DEATH: Unknown

**Private Warf**
BIRTH:
DEATH:

**Mary Ruth Warf**
**Daughter**
BIRTH: 29 Nov. 1931
DEATH: 26 Feb. 2005

**Ola Christine Warf**
**Daughter**
BIRTH: 4 Dec. 1933
DEATH: 1 Feb. 2016

**Private Warf**
BIRTH:
DEATH:

**Private Warf**
**Son**
BIRTH:
DEATH:

**Private Warf**
BIRTH:
DEATH:

**Private Warf**
BIRTH:
DEATH:

## CHILDREN OF HOLLIS AND LETTIE

**Private Warf**
BIRTH:
DEATH:

**Private Warf**
BIRTH:
DEATH:

## HIS LIFE

When Hollis Virgil Warf was born on January 21, 1906, in Hickman County, Tennessee, his father, Samuel was 37 and his mother, Sidney was 28. He married Annie Lee Richards on January 1, 1926, when he was 19-years old. They had eight children together. His wife, Annie Lee passed away on January 22, 1951, in Franklin, Tennessee when she was 44. They had been married 25-years. Hollis married Lettie Mai Luckett in Williamson County, Tennessee on January 29, 1957, when he was 51-years old. They had two children together. Hollis Virgil Warf died on November 21, 1998, in Franklin at the age of 92. He was buried in the Mount Hope Cemetery in Franklin.

HOLLIS VIRGIL AND ANNIE LEE
(RICHARDS) WARF

# LEONARD WILSON VADEN
## 1907-1986

### VADEN FAMILY

**HUSBAND'S PARENTS**
**Alva Lee Vaden**     **Sarah Alice Hatcher**
1874 - 1954                 1877 - 1940

**WIFE'S PARENTS**
**Ralph Gilman Cutler**     **Lena M. Sievert**
1891 - ?                             1896 - ?

**HUSBAND**
**Leonard Wilson Vaden**
**BIRTH:** 24 Feb. 1907, Peytonsville, TN
**DEATH:** 26 Apr. 1986, Peytonsville, TN

**WIFE**
**Evelyn Cutler**
**BIRTH:** 14 Oct. 1920, IL
**DEATH:** 9 Dec. 2010, Peytonsville, TN

### CHILDREN

| | |
|---|---|
| **Private Vaden** Daughter | BIRTH: DEATH: |
| **Private Vaden** Son | BIRTH: DEATH: |
| **Private Vaden** Son | BIRTH: DEATH: |
| **Private Vaden** Son | BIRTH: DEATH: |

### HIS LIFE

When Leonard Wilson Vaden was born on February 24, 1907, in Peytonsville, Tennessee, his father, Alva was 32 and his mother, Sarah was 29. He married Evelyn Cutler and they had four children together. He died on April 26, 1986, in Peytonsville when he was 79-years old. He

was buried in the Mount Hope Cemetery in Franklin, Tennessee.

LEONARD, EVELYN (CUTLER), SARA, MIKE, PAUL AND JIM VADEN

# ELIJAH ALEXANDER "BUSTER" GARNER
## 1907-1979

### GARNER FAMILY

**HUSBAND'S PARENTS**
**William "Lee" Garner**     **Martha S. Bennett**
1873 - 1959                         1879 - 1968

**WIFE'S PARENTS**
**William Allen Bennett**     **Lillian Cook**
1867 - ?                                 1885 - 1920

**HUSBAND**
**Elijah Alexander "Buster" Garner**
**BIRTH:** 14 Mar. 1907, Peytonsville, TN
**DEATH:** 4 Feb. 1979, Peytonsville, TN

## WIFE
**Mamie Lou Bennett**
**BIRTH:** 8 July 1910, Williamson Co. TN
**DEATH:** 23 Mar. 1974, Williamson Co. TN

### CHILDREN

| | |
|---|---|
| **Susie Florence Garner-Daughter** | **BIRTH:** 1929 <br> **DEATH:** |
| **Mary Ethel Garner Daughter** | **BIRTH:** 31 Dec. 1930 <br> **DEATH:** 25 Nov. 2011 |
| **Willie Dean Garner Daughter** | **BIRTH:** 9 Nov. 1934 <br> **DEATH:** 9 Jan. 2006 |
| **William Alton Garner Son** | **BIRTH:** 7 Jan. 1937 <br> **DEATH:** 5 Mar. 1980 |
| **Robert Raybon Garner-Son** | **BIRTH:** 27 May 1938 <br> **DEATH:** 23 May 2020 |
| **James Franklin Garner-Son** | **BIRTH:** 3 Dec. 1939 <br> **DEATH:** 28 May 1995 |
| **Arthur Allen "Tater" Garner-Son** | **BIRTH:** 12 Jan. 1943 <br> **DEATH:** 7 Mar. 2011 |
| **Linda Darnell Garner Daughter** | **BIRTH:** 26 May 1945 <br> **DEATH:** 19 Dec. 2003 |
| **Della Lourine Garner Daughter** | **BIRTH:** 5 Nov. 1947 <br> **DEATH:** 27 Mar. 2011 |

### HIS LIFE

When Elijah Alexander "Buster" Garner was born on March 14, 1907, in Peytonsville, Tennessee, his father William was 33 and his mother, Martha was 28. He married Mamie Lou Bennett on September 5, 1926, in Peytonsville. They had nine children in 18-years. He died on February 4, 1979, in Peytonsville at the age of 71. He was buried in the Bennett Cemetery in Peytonsville.

# JOE HARRISON BENNETT
## 1907-1990

### BENNETT FAMILY

### HUSBAND'S PARENTS
**William Allen Bennett**   **Lilla Cook**
1871 - ?                     1885 - 1920

### WIFE'S PARENTS
**Columbus L.G. Hartley**   **Adelia Ann Veach**
1888 - 1963                  1892 - 1971

### HUSBAND
**Joe Harrison Bennett**
**BIRTH:** 11 June 1907, TN
**DEATH:** 22 Apr. 1990, Bethesda, TN

### WIFE
**Catherine Hartley**
**BIRTH:** 26 Sep. 1911, TN
**DEATH:** 7 Mar. 2003, Franklin, TN

### CHILDREN

| | |
|---|---|
| **Estelle R. Bennett Daughter** | **BIRTH:** 25 Mar. 1929 <br> **DEATH:** 20 May 1987 |
| **Delia "Dellie" Bennett Daughter** | **BIRTH:** 22 June 1932 <br> **DEATH:** 6 Mar. 2021 |
| **Joe Allen Bennett Son** | **BIRTH:** 31 May 1934 <br> **DEATH:** 22 June 1984 |
| **Lilla Mai Bennett Daughter** | **BIRTH:** 10 Nov. 1935 <br> **DEATH:** 12 Jan. 1987 |
| **Betty Mai C. Bennett Daughter** | **BIRTH:** 26 Jan. 1938 <br> **DEATH:** 5 Jan. 2014 |
| **Robert W. Bennett Son** | **BIRTH:** 13 Feb. 1942 <br> **DEATH:** 6 Jan. 2010 |

When Joe Harrison Bennett was born on June 11, 1907, in Tennessee, his father William was 36 and his mother Lilla was 21. He married Catherine Hartley on October 13, 1928, in Williamson County, Tennessee. They had six children in 12-years. He died on April 22, 1990 in Bethesda, Tennessee at the age of 82. He was buried in the Williamson Memorial Gardens Cemetery in Franklin, Tennessee.

JOE HARRISON, LILLA (COOK) AND MAMIE BENNETT

# JAMES MONROE GENTRY
## 1908-1981

### GENTRY FAMILY

**HUSBAND'S PARENTS**
**John Tyler Gentry**    **Josephine Thompson**
1868 - 1958                1877 - 1928

**WIFE'S PARENTS**
**Solomon Woods**    **Martha Swancy**
1882 - 1964              1882 - 1958

### HUSBAND
**James Monroe Gentry**
**BIRTH:** 24 July 1908, Williamson Co. TN
**DEATH:** 15 Jan. 1981, Peytonsville, TN

### WIFE
**Jessie Bee Woods**
**BIRTH:** 14 Mar. 1909, Williamson Co. TN
**DEATH:** 27 July 2007, Peytonsville, TN

### CHILDREN

**Private Gentry**          **BIRTH:**
                            **DEATH:**

**Jessie James Gentry**   **BIRTH:** 31 Mar, 1935
**Son**                    **DEATH:** 3 Mar, 1993

**Private Gentry**          **BIRTH:**
                            **DEATH:**

### HIS LIFE

When James Monroe Gentry was born on July 24, 1908, in Williamson County, Tennessee, his father, John was 39 and his mother, Josephine was 30. He married Jessie Bee Woods on January 22, 1933, in Peytonsville, Tennessee. They had three children together. He died on January 15, 1981, in Williamson County at the age of 72. He was buried in the Gentry Cemetery in Peytonsville.

# ARTHUR HENRY STEELE KINNARD
## 1908-1982

### KINNARD FAMILY

#### HUSBAND'S PARENTS
**Enoch Kinnard Sr.**  **Mollie Ella Southall**
1881 - 1952  1886 - 1970

#### WIFE'S PARENTS
**Richmond Smith Jr.**  **Catherine Belle**
1865 - 1940  1876 - 1935

#### HUSBAND
**Arthur Henry Steele Kinnard**
**BIRTH:** 20 May 1908, Franklin, TN
**DEATH:** 15 June 1982, Franklin, TN

#### WIFE
**Era Mae Elizabeth Smith**
**BIRTH:** 11 Jan. 1911, Franklin, TN
**DEATH:** 21 Jan. 1988, Franklin, TN

### CHILDREN

| | |
|---|---|
| **Rosa Mae Kinnard** Daughter | **BIRTH:** 23 Sep. 1930 **DEATH:** 7 Apr. 2001 |
| **Arthur Henry Kinnard Jr.-Son** | **BIRTH:** 15 Apr. 1933 **DEATH:** 16 Feb. 2011 |
| **Richmond E. Kinnard** Son | **BIRTH:** 15 Jan. 1935 **DEATH:** 7 Aug. 2020 |
| **Private Kinnard** | **BIRTH:** **DEATH:** |
| **Private Kinnard** | **BIRTH:** **DEATH:** |
| **Private Kinnard** | **BIRTH:** **DEATH:** |
| **Private Kinnard** | **BIRTH:** **DEATH:** |
| **Private Kinnard** | **BIRTH:** **DEATH:** |
| **Private Kinnard** | **BIRTH:** **DEATH:** |

### HIS LIFE

**From: *Biographies of the 13th District***
**Arthur H. Sr., & Era Smith Kinnard**
***Williamson County in Black & White***
**Rick Warwick, Editor**
**Williamson County Historical Society**
**Journal No. 31, 2000**

The Kinnards can claim Tennessee State University as "my school" in the true sense of an earned possession.

Nine children of the Williamson County farm family of Mr. and Mrs. Arthur H. Kinnard have persevered through economic and physical obstacles to become TSU graduates spanning a period of 21 years.

"Mr. and Mrs. Arthur H. Kinnard celebrated their 50th wedding anniversary this year. But the

Kinnards have a lot more than that milestone to celebrate," said a report in the current *Cupolian*, TSU's official magazine.

"From 1948 to 1969, 21 years,' it says, "there was at least one of their nine children attending classes at Tennessee State University."

The story of the family's quest for education is told by one of the first, Katie Kinnard White, to receive an under-graduate degree in 1952. She now is a member of the TSU biology faculty.

In addition to relating the support and encouragement the elder Kinnards gave their children, the story tells how the father and mother received eighth-grade certificates in 1966 after attending classes at Franklin High School adult education program.

Mrs. Kinnard put her newly gained training to use by teaching her children their ABC's, numbers and reading to prepare them for elementary school. "We lived on a farm in the country so far away from a school that there was no way we could walk and get back each day, so my sister and I lived with my grandmother (in Franklin), because we were very close to the age of her youngest daughter," Mrs. White said.
She said their father would take them to Franklin on Sunday night and return them to the farm on Friday. "We would do the washing and ironing during that time so that we would be ready to go back and forth each week. Sometimes we would even carry food from the garden to help supplement my grandmother's food bill. This is how we managed."

Mrs. White, who holds a doctorate degree, recalls events as the Kinnard children went through grade school and college each level of attainment made through hard work, help from their parents and from the older children as they finished college and obtained jobs.

Mrs. White said when she and her sister-Rosa M. Kinnard Cason, also a 1952 graduate-entered

TSU as freshmen, she was able to get campus work and an off-campus job.

"My sister and I graduated together." Mrs. White noted, "I never did go to summer school because I didn't have the money, I had to work. We had to get out (of college) in four years. There was just no such thing as an extra year. And my brothers did the same thing."

Arthur H. Kinnard, Jr. '55, coordinator of the international curriculum program and professor of history at Mississippi Valley State University, Itta Bena, Mississippi; the Rev. Richmond E. Kinnard, '57, professor of agronomy at Langston University, Okla., and pastor of research for the Veterans Administration in the United States and Puerto Rico.

Martha K. Kinnard Forston, '61, teacher in the Washington D.C. school system; Sophia Beamon, '63, guidance counselor at East Nashville High School; Anna Kinnard Broome, '66, '69, licensed psychological examiner for the adult day hospital program at Meharry medical College.

Mrs. Cason, formerly an elementary school teacher in Williamson County, is a Murfreesboro housewife.

***Editor's note:*** Arthur Kinnard, Sr. (1908-1982) was the son of Enoch and Mollie Southall Kinnard. After many years as farm manager of the Matt Dobson farm on Hillsboro Road at Berry's Chapel, Arthur Kinnard was able to buy a 29-acre farm on Arno Road in the 13th District in the 1950s. Mr. Kinnard practiced good farming techniques and made the most of his small farm. The Kinnards were a welcomed addition to the Millview community.

Arthur Henry Steele Kinnard died on June 15, 1982, in Franklin, Tennessee when he was 74-years old. He was buried in the Toussaint L'Ouverture Cemetery.

ERA (SMITH) AND ARTHUR KINNARD

# JOSEPH WESLEY YORK
## 1909-1997

### YORK FAMILY

#### HUSBAND'S PARENTS
**Claude York**   **Josephine Stevens**
1869 - 1947        1872 - 1956

#### WIFE'S PARENTS
**Joseph Thomas Finchum  Carrie L. Anderson**
1879 - 1952                    1886 - 1968

#### HUSBAND
**Joseph Wesley York**
**BIRTH:** 2 June 1909, TN
**DEATH:** 28 Dec. 1997, Peytonsville, TN

#### WIFE
**Nellie G. Finchum**
**BIRTH:** 22 Oct. 1916, Williamson Co. TN
**DEATH:** 20 Dec. 1975, Franklin, TN

#### CHILDREN

| | |
|---|---|
| **Gary Wesley York**<br>**Son** | **BIRTH:** 11 Nov. 1942<br>**DEATH:** 21 June 2018 |
| **Private York** | **BIRTH:**<br>**DEATH:** |
| **Private York** | **BIRTH:**<br>**DEATH:** |
| **Private York** | **BIRTH:**<br>**DEATH:** |
| **Private York** | **BIRTH:**<br>**DEATH:** |

### HIS LIFE

When Joseph Wesley York was born on June 2, 1909, in Williamson County, Tennessee, his father, Claude was 39 and his mother, Josephine was 36. He married Nellie G. Finchum on February 14, 1941, in Peytonsville, Tennessee. They had five children during their marriage. He died on December 28, 1997, in Peytonsville at the age of 88. He was buried in the Williamson Memorial Gardens Cemetery in Franklin, Tennessee.

NELLIE (FINCHUM) AND JOSEPH WESLEY YORK

## CHARLES H. "BUCK" BENNETT
### 1910-1986

### BENNETT FAMILY

**HUSBAND'S PARENTS**
**Dicus David Bennett**   **Eunice E. Smithson**
1886 - 1976                1892 - 1916

**WIFE'S PARENTS**
**Phillip Richard Bennett**   **Maude F. Harper**
1878 - 1982                   1886 - 1947

**HUSBAND**
**Charles H. "Buck" Bennett**
**BIRTH:** 17 Aug. 1910, Peytonsville, TN
**DEATH:** June 1986, Peytonsville, TN

**WIFE**
**Fannie Mai Bennett**
**BIRTH:** 26 Sep. 1912, Peytonsville, TN
**DEATH:** 3 Dec. 2002, Peytonsville, TN

### CHILDREN

| | |
|---|---|
| **Private Bennett** | **BIRTH:**<br>**DEATH:** |
| **Private Bennett** | **BIRTH:**<br>**DEATH:** |
| **Private Bennett** | **BIRTH:**<br>**DEATH:** |

### HIS LIFE

Charles H. "Buck" Bennett was born on August 17, 1910, in Peytonsville, Tennessee. He married Fannie Mai Bennett on December 23, 1928, in Peytonsville. They had three children during their marriage. He died in June, 1986, in Peytonsville at the age of 75. He was buried in the Williamson Memorial Gardens Cemetery in Franklin, Tennessee.

## THOMAS WADE SMITHSON
### 1910-1960

### SMITHSON FAMILY

**HUSBAND'S PARENTS**
**Thomas Walter Smithson**   **Ella Vaden**
1864 - 1926                  1879 - 1952

**WIFE'S PARENTS**
**Barney Wade Stanfield**   **Ava Virginia Stanfield**
1865 - 1943                 1872 - 1943

**HUSBAND**
**Thomas Wade Smithson**
**BIRTH:** 16 Mar. 1910, Peytonsville, TN
**DEATH:** 30 Jan. 1960, Peytonsville, TN

**WIFE**
**Martha Permelia Stanfield**
**BIRTH:** 26 Aug. 1910, Nashville, TN
**DEATH:** 24 Apr. 1992, Rutherford Co. TN

### CHILDREN

| | |
|---|---|
| **Martha Virginia Smithson-Daughter** | **BIRTH:** 6 Aug. 1930<br>**DEATH:** 28 July 2001 |
| **Gene Thomas Smithson-Son** | **BIRTH:** 3 Dec. 1933<br>**DEATH:** 24 Jan. 2007 |

### HIS LIFE

When Thomas Wade Smithson was born on March 16, 1910, his father, Thomas was 45 and his mother, Ella was 30. He married Martha Permelia Stanfield on May 11, 1929, when he was 19-years old. They had two children together. He died on January 30, 1960, in Peytonsville, Tennessee when he was 49-years old. He was buried in the Mount Hope Cemetery in Franklin, Tennessee

THOMAS WADE SMITHSON

# CHARLES HERBERT SMITHSON
## 1910-1994

### SMITHSON FAMILY

#### HUSBAND'S PARENTS
**Escar Knott Smithson**    **Josephine V. Meek**
1881 - 1951                         1886 - 1957

#### WIFE'S PARENTS
**Allen Reece McGee**    **Nancy Jane Ingram**
1879 - 1952                      1887 - 1959

#### HUSBAND
**Charles Herbert Smithson**
**BIRTH:** 14 June 1910, Williamson Co. TN
**DEATH:** 23 June 1994, Peytonsville, TN

#### WIFE
**Maggie Virginia McGee**

**BIRTH:** 24 Mar. 1910, Williamson Co. TN
**DEATH:** 24 Dec. 1997, Peytonsville, TN

### CHILDREN

**Charles Reece Smithson-Son**
**BIRTH:** 29 Jan. 1934
**DEATH:** 7 May 2014

**Harriet Jane Smithson-Daughter**
**BIRTH:** 15 Dec. 1940
**DEATH:** 2 June 2017

**Private Smithson**
**BIRTH:**
**DEATH:**

### HIS LIFE

When Charles Herbert Smithson was born on June 14, 1910, in Williamson County, Tennessee, his father, Escar was 28 and his mother, Josephine was 24. He married Maggie Virginia McGee on September 10, 1932, in Williamson County. They had three children together. He died on June 23, 1994, in Williamson County at the age of 84. He was buried in the Poteete Cemetery.

# PAUL JACKSON
## 1910-1972

### JACKSON FAMILY

#### HUSBAND'S PARENTS
**Robert Walter Jackson**    **Janie E. Jackson**
1869 - 1948                         1876 - 1941

#### WIFE'S PARENTS
**Charles T. Jackson**    **Josephine E. Poteete**
1870 - 1946                      1885 - 1926

#### HUSBAND
**Paul Jackson**
**BIRTH:** 12 Oct. 1910, Williamson Co. TN
**DEATH:** 23 June 1972, Peytonsville, TN

#### WIFE
**Mary Lorene Jackson**

**BIRTH:** 8 May 1913, Williamson Co. TN
**DEATH:** 12 July 2004, Peytonsville, TN

### CHILDREN

| | |
|---|---|
| Henry Allen Jackson<br>Son | **BIRTH:** 15 Nov. 1932<br>**DEATH:** 15 Dec. 2011 |
| Private Jackson<br>Daughter | **BIRTH:**<br>**DEATH:** |
| Private Jackson<br>Son | **BIRTH:**<br>**DEATH:** |
| Private Jackson<br>Son | **BIRTH:**<br>**DEATH:** |

### HIS LIFE

When Paul Jackson was born on October 12, 1910, in Williamson County, Tennessee, his father, Robert was 41 and his mother, Janie was 33. He married Mary Lorene Jackson on January 24, 1931, in Peytonsville, Tennessee. They had four children together. He died on June 23, 1972, in Peytonsville at the age of 61. He was buried in the Williamson Memorial Gardens Cemetery in Franklin, Tennessee.

# HOWARD PARKS SMITHSON
# 1911-1994

## SMITHSON FAMILY

### HUSBAND'S PARENTS
**Sylvanus Andrew Smithson**   **Beulah Beasley**
1879 - 1947                    1887 - 1969

### WIFE'S PARENTS
**Green Gallio Cook**   **Minnie Myrtle Sullivan**
1875 - 1969             1875 - 1956

### HUSBAND
**Howard Parks Smithson**

**BIRTH:** 9 Feb. 1911, Peytonsville, TN
**DEATH:** 28 May 1994, Williamson Co. TN

### WIFE
**Lenora Doris Cook**
**BIRTH:** 24 May 1911, Williamson Co. TN
**DEATH:** 16 Oct. 1993, Williamson Co. TN

### CHILDREN

| | |
|---|---|
| Jimmy A. Smithson<br>Son | **BIRTH:** 22 Apr. 1933<br>**DEATH:** 8 Nov. 2013 |
| Private Smithson | **BIRTH:**<br>**DEATH:** |
| William Andrew<br>Smithson-Son | **BIRTH:** 21 Dec. 1942<br>**DEATH:** 11 Aug. 1987 |
| Private Smithson | **BIRTH:**<br>**DEATH:** |

### HIS LIFE

When Howard Parks Smithson was born on February 9, 1911, in Williamson County, Tennessee, his father, Sylvanus was 31 and his mother, Beulah was 23. He married Lenora Doris Cook on December 23, 1930, in Williamson County. They had four children together. He died on May 28, 1994, in Peytonsville, Tennessee at the age of 83. He was buried in the Mount Hope Cemetery in Franklin, Tennessee.

HOWARD PARKS SMITHSON

## JOHN EDWARD GLENN
## 1912-1988

### GLEN FAMILY

#### HUSBAND'S PARENTS
**Fieldon A. Glenn**     **Mary Ada King**
1870 - 1940              1868 - 1966

#### WIFE'S PARENTS
**John Henry Poteete**     **Effie Pearl Reynolds**
1880 - 1921                1883 - 1933

#### HUSBAND
**John Edward Glenn**
**BIRTH:** 9 June 1912, Peytonsville, TN
**DEATH:** 4 Nov. 1988, Peytonsville, TN

#### WIFE
**Odell Poteete**
**BIRTH:** 1916, Williamson Co. TN
**DEATH:** 20 Sep. 1999, Peytonsville, TN

#### CHILDREN
**Private Glenn**     BIRTH:
                      DEATH:

**Private Glenn**     BIRTH:
                      DEATH:

### HIS LIFE

When John Edward Glenn was born on June 9, 1912, in Peytonsville, Tennessee, his father, Fieldon was 41 and his mother, Mary was 43. He married Odell Poteete on October 7, 1933, in Peytonsville. They had two children together. He died on November 4, 1988, in Peytonsville at the age of 76. He was buried in the Williamson Memorial Gardens Cemetery in Franklin, Tennessee.

## DENNIS GRADY SKINNER
## 1913-1977

### SKINNER FAMILY

#### HUSBAND'S PARENTS
**Ed Lee Skinner**     **Bettie Mangrum**
1884 - 1967            1888 - 1961

#### WIFE'S PARENTS
**Unknown Father**     **Unknown Mother**

#### HUSBAND
**Dennis Grady Skinner**
**BIRTH:** 23 Aug. 1913, TN
**DEATH:** 9 Sep. 1977, Peytonsville, TN

#### WIFE
**Stella Mae Skinner**
**BIRTH:** 13 Apr. 1927, Williamson Co. TN
**DEATH:** 14 July 2016, Peytonsville, TN

#### CHILDREN
**Private Skinner**     BIRTH:
                        DEATH:

**Private Skinner**     BIRTH:
                        DEATH:

**Private Skinner**     BIRTH:
                        DEATH:

### HIS LIFE

When Dennis Grady Skinner was born on August 23, 1913, in Tennessee, his father, Ed was 28 and his mother, Bettie was 25. He married Stella Mae Skinner and they had three children together. He died on September 9, 1977, in Williamson County, Tennessee at the age of 64. He was buried in the Williamson Memorial Gardens Cemetery in Franklin, Tennessee.

# WALTER WILSON VADEN SR.
## 1913-1980

### VADEN FAMILY

#### HUSBAND'S PARENTS
**Charles Wilson Vaden**　**Nora E. Pennington**
1869 - 1935　　　　　　　1874 - 1942

#### WIFE'S PARENTS
**John William Golden**　**Sallie Elizabeth McGee**
1878 - 1958　　　　　　　1877 - 1970

ROBERTA (GOLDEN) AND WALTER WILSON VADEN

#### HUSBAND
**Walter Wilson Vaden**
**BIRTH:** 7 Mar. 1913, Peytonsville, TN
**DEATH:** 30 Apr. 1980, Peytonsville, TN

#### WIFE
**Roberta Bess Golden**
**BIRTH:** 1 Oct. 1914, Williamson Co. TN
**DEATH:** 31 July 1995, Peytonsville, TN

#### CHILDREN

| | |
|---|---|
| Private Vaden | BIRTH:<br>DEATH: |
| Private Vaden | BIRTH:<br>DEATH: |

### HIS LIFE

When Walter Wilson Vaden was born on March 7, 1913, in Peytonsville, Tennessee, his father, Charles was 43 and his mother, Nora was 38. He married Roberta Bess Golden in 1930, in Elizabethtown, Kentucky when he was 17-years old. They had two children together. He died on April 30, 1980, in Peytonsville at the age of 67. He was buried in the Williamson Memorial Gardens Cemetery in Franklin, Tennessee.

# WILLIAM MARVIN TOMLIN
## 1913-1980

### TOMLIN FAMILY

#### HUSBAND'S PARENTS
**Henry Dave Tomlin**　**Bessie Skinner**
1884 - 1969　　　　　　1890 - 1947

#### WIFE'S PARENTS
**William E. Walton**　**Mollie Gee**
1870 - 1925　　　　　　1866 - 1961

#### HUSBAND
**William Marvin Tomlin**
**BIRTH:** 12 Dec. 1913, Peytonsville, TN
**DEATH:** 27 Feb. 1980, Peytonsville, TN

#### WIFE
**Nell Gee Walton**
**BIRTH:** 9 July 1917, Peytonsville, TN
**DEATH:** 9 Apr. 2014, Peytonsville, TN

#### CHILDREN

| | |
|---|---|
| **Barbara Ann Tomlin**<br>**Daughter** | BIRTH: 23 Oct. 1934<br>DEATH: 2 Dec. 2020 |

Private Tomlin            BIRTH:
                          DEATH:

Private Tomlin            BIRTH:
                          DEATH:

Private Tomlin            BIRTH:
                          DEATH:

## HIS LIFE

When William Marvin Tomlin was born on December 12, 1913, in Williamson County, Tennessee, his father, Henry was 29 and his mother, Bessie was 23. He married Nell Gee Walton on February 14, 1934, in Williamson County. They had four children together. He died on February 27, 1980, in Peytonsville at the age of 66. He was buried in the Williamson Memorial Gardens Cemetery in Franklin, Tennessee.

# DR. HARRY JASPER GUFFEE
# 1913-1996

## GUFFEE FAMILY

### HUSBAND'S PARENTS
**Albert Pierce Guffee**     **Martha Jane McGee**
1867 - 1957                  1885 - 1982

### WIFE'S PARENTS
**John Edward Brady**     **Elizabeth W. Dowlen**
1884 - 1934               1887 - 1973

### HUSBAND
**Harry Jasper Guffee**
**BIRTH:** 19 Feb. 1913, Williamson Co. TN
**DEATH:** 16 Mar. 1996, Franklin, TN

### WIFE
**Dorothy Brady**
**BIRTH:** 24 Aug. 1914, Springfield, TN
**DEATH:** 27 Apr. 1993, Franklin, TN

## CHILDREN

**Paul Owen Guffee**     **BIRTH:** 27 Oct. 1943
Son                      **DEATH:** 15 Mar. 1968

**John Brady Guffee**     **BIRTH:** 1945
Son                       **DEATH:** 4 Apr. 2018

**Infant Guffee**     **BIRTH:** 1 Nov. 1946
Son                   **DEATH:** 1 Nov. 1946

**Private Guffee**     **BIRTH:**
                       **DEATH:**

**Private Guffee**     **BIRTH:**
                       **DEATH:**

## HIS LIFE

### Rodeo brings back memories of Dr. Guffee
### By: Hudson Alexander

If you go back to the earliest days of frontier medicine, even back to a time when Dr. John Sappington set up the first medical practice here, around 1802, you'd discover hundreds of physicians who dedicated their professional lives to helping the people of Williamson County.

And one of the most popular of all time, among that group, would be Dr. Harry Guffee.

According to family legend, it was only by a stroke of fate that the Guffee family ever settled in Williamson County. Dr. Guffee's grandfather was moving his family from East Tennessee to Texas, so the story goes, when his wife suddenly went into labor while passing through Franklin.

They stopped, intending to stay only long enough for the baby to be born but they never left.

Harry Jasper Guffee was born in 1913. He attended the Franklin schools and later graduated from Battle Ground Academy. He had always planned to study architectural engineering at Georgia Tech. But, once again, a stroke of fate intervened: those plans were drastically altered when his brother, Paul, was killed in a tragic motorcycle accident. Guffee vowed that he would dedicate all his energies toward helping those in need of medical care.

Guffee began his college studies at Vanderbilt University in 1930. During his undergraduate years, he was noted as an outstanding student-athlete. He played both offense and defense on some of the best Commodore football teams ever coached by legendary field generals Ray Morrison and Dan McGugin. He was captain of the 1934 Vandy football team.

Determined to make good on his pledge to pursue the field of medicine, Guffee then entered the Vanderbilt Medical School. After his second year of study, he was married to the former Miss Dorothy Brady of Springfield. In 1939, he received his medical degree. And the following year, 1940, he returned to Franklin, where he entered into a medical practice with Dr. Dan German and Dr. Tandy Rice at the Dan German Hospital on Fourth Avenue South.

World War II interrupted Guffee's early medical career. He hadn't much more than gotten started, when he suddenly found himself in the 84 U.S. Infantry Division, assigned to a specialty medical unit called the Blackout Express Convoy. This unit made regular trips to assist soldiers wounded at the front line. At Normandy, where thousands of American soldiers were killed storming the beaches, Guffee was with a group of about 1000 soldiers who were taken prisoner.

The weeks that followed really took their toll on Guffee. He lost down from 180 pounds to only about 118 pounds. But he was lucky to have survived at all. The 84th Division started the war with 3,500 men; when it ended, Guffee was one of only 32 survivors.

After the war, Dr. Guffee once again returned to Franklin, where he resumed his medical practice with Dr. Tandy Rice at the Dan German Hospital.

And for the next 30 years, he maintained one of the most successful family medical practices in Williamson County.

In 1962, Dr. Guffee began sharing a medical office, on Carter's Creek Pike, with Dr. A. Joel Lee. They were assisted for many years by Lottie Haffner, whose nursing career dated back to the days of the Dan German Hospital. They made a great medical team back in those days.

Many old-timers still hold fond memories of Dr. Guffee. He was a unique man: he was a very skilled surgeon, but he also possessed an uncanny ability to ease the fears and apprehensions for his patients. He is also remembered for the house calls he made to the rural parts of the county, where patients could not be reached by automobile. On these occasions, he would hook his horse trailer to his Jeep. He'd drive as far as he could, and then continue on horseback, with his medical bag slung across the saddle. There were times when he would even deliver babies in backwoods cabins, some with dirt floors.

Every year when the Franklin Rotary Club holds their annual rodeo, I can't help but think of Dr. Guffee. The rodeo was always one of his favorite projects. For many years, he especially enjoyed the calf-roping competition. And, as long as he was able, Dr. Guffee enjoyed leading the rodeo parade on horseback through the streets of downtown Franklin.

By the time Dr. Guffee retired from his active medical practice in 1975, it was estimated that he had delivered 4,342 babies in Williamson County. I was one of them, along with my brother and two sisters.

Dr. Harry Guffee died, following a lengthy battle with Alzheimers Disease, on March 16, 1996. He was buried in the Mount Hope Cemetery.

DR. HARRY GUFFEE VISITING JERRY CARROLL IN WADDELL HOLLOW ABOUT 1956

# JAMES MADISON MAXWELL 1916-1972

## MAXWELL FAMILY

### HUSBAND'S PARENTS
**Felix M. Maxwell**   **Ethel Cothran**
1877 - 1957          1885 - ?

### WIFE'S PARENTS
**John L. McGee**   **Willie Eunice Anderson**
1880 - 1946        1885 - 1936

### HUSBAND
**James Madison Maxwell**
**BIRTH:** 9 Jan. 1916, Maury Co. TN
**DEATH:** 1 Dec. 1972, Peytonsville, TN

### WIFE
**Flossie Ella McGee**
**BIRTH:** 2 Oct. 1913, Peytonsville, TN
**DEATH:** 20 Mar. 1999, Peytonsville, TN

## CHILDREN

**James Madison Maxwell Jr.-Son**   **BIRTH:** 16 Mar. 1938
**DEATH:** 27 Mar. 2018

**Private Maxwell**   **BIRTH:**
**DEATH:**

## HIS LIFE

When James Madison Maxwell and his twin brother, John Edward "Ed" were born on January 9, 1916, in Maury County, Tennessee, their father, Felix was 38 and their mother, Ethel was 31. He married Flossie Ella McGee on September 7, 1935, in Williamson County, Tennessee. They had two children together. He died on December 1, 1972, in Peytonsville, Tennessee at the age of 56. He was buried in the Williamson Memorial Gardens Cemetery in Franklin, Tennessee.

FLOSSIE (MCGEE) AND JAMES MADISON MAXWELL

309

## PERRY G. JOHNSON
## 1918-1969

### JOHNSON FAMILY

#### HUSBAND'S PARENTS
**Perry Evans Johnson**     **Ozzie Thompson**
1888 - 1939                 1895 - 1972

#### WIFE'S PARENTS
**Edward O. Dodson**     **Rosa Lee Hughes**
1878 - 1954              1884 - 1960

#### HUSBAND
**Perry G. Johnson**
**BIRTH:** 26 Jan. 1918, Peytonsville, TN
**DEATH:** 16 Mar. 1969, Peytonsville, TN

#### WIFE
**Nora Lee Dodson**
**BIRTH:** 8 Sep. 1915, TN
**DEATH:** 4 Aug. 1979

#### CHILDREN

**Private Johnson**     **BIRTH:**
                        **DEATH:**

### HIS LIFE

When Perry G. Johnson was born on January 26, 1918, in Williamson County, Tennessee, his father Perry was 29 and his mother Ozzie was 22. He married Nora Lee Dodson on September 21, 1938, in Williamson County. They had one child during their marriage. He died on March 16, 1969 in Peytonsville, Tennessee at the age of 51. He was buried in the Williamson Memorial Gardens Cemetery in Franklin, Tennessee.

## RICHARD POTEETE
## 1918-1998

### POTEETE FAMILY

#### HUSBAND'S PARENTS
**John Henry Poteete**     **Effie Pearl Reynolds**
1880 - 1921               1883 - 1933

#### WIFE'S PARENTS
**Sam Preston Crawford**     **Alta Garrett Lovins**
1895 - 1964                 1892 - 1967

#### HUSBAND
**Richard Poteete**
**BIRTH:** 8 Aug. 1918, Peytonsville, TN
**DEATH:** 20 Apr. 1998, Peytonsville, TN

#### WIFE
**Virginia Gertrude Crawford**
**BIRTH:** 31 Jan. 1930
**DEATH:** 16 Dec. 2018, Williamson Co. TN

#### CHILDREN

**Charles Richard**     **BIRTH:** 9 Sep. 1950
**Poteete-Son**         **DEATH:** 20 June 2007

**Private Poteete**     **BIRTH:**
                        **DEATH:**

**Private Poteete**     **BIRTH:**
                        **DEATH:**

**Private Poteete**     **BIRTH:**
                        **DEATH:**

### HIS LIFE

When Richard Poteete was born on August 8, 1918, in Williamson County, Tennessee, his father, John was 38 and his mother, Effie was 35. He married Virginia Gertrude Crawford and they had four children together. He died on April 20, 1998, in Peytonsville, Tennessee at the age of 79. He was buried in the Poteete Cemetery in Peytonsville.

# PERCY BUD BRUCE
## 1919-1981

### BRUCE FAMILY

#### HUSBAND'S PARENTS
**Allen L. Bruce**   **Pearl E. Frizzell**
1885 - 1957       1896 - 1946

#### WIFE'S PARENTS
**Mike Garner Simmons**   **Alice Wray**
1899 - 1986             1900 - 1981

#### HUSBAND
**Percy Bud Bruce**
BIRTH: 29 July 1919, Hickman Co. TN
DEATH: 15 July 1981, Peytonsville, TN

#### WIFE
**Hazel Virginia Simmons**
BIRTH: 17 Mar. 1926, Peytonsville, TN
DEATH: 3 Mar. 1999, Nashville, TN

#### CHILDREN

| | |
|---|---|
| **Michael Allen Bruce** Son | **BIRTH:** 1949 **DEATH:** 25 Apr. 2018 |
| **Richard Earl Bruce** Son | **BIRTH:** 27 Mar. 1952 **DEATH:** July 1987 |
| **Jackie Jerald Bruce** Son | **BIRTH:** 28 Sep. 1957 **DEATH:** 5 July 2014 |
| **Private Bruce** | **BIRTH:** **DEATH:** |
| **Private Bruce** | **BIRTH:** **DEATH:** |
| **Private Bruce** | **BIRTH:** **DEATH:** |

### HIS LIFE

When Percy Bud Bruce was born on July 29, 1919, in Hickman County, Tennessee, his father, Allen was 33 and his mother, Pearl was 23. He married Hazel Virginia Simmons on January 10, 1948, in Peytonsville, Tennessee. They had six children together. He died on July 15, 1981, in Peytonsville at the age of 61.

# JAMES EWING CROWDER
## 1919-1995

### CROWDER FAMILY

#### HUSBAND'S PARENTS
**Odelia Crowder**   **Amelia Reynolds**
1896 - 1972        1895 - 1973

#### WIFE'S PARENTS
**John Ham Roberts**   **Mattie Lizzie McEwen**
1885 - ?             1875 - 1968

#### HUSBAND
**James Ewing Crowder**
**BIRTH:** 13 Dec. 1919, Peytonsville, TN
**DEATH:** 1995, TN

#### WIFE
**Julia Ethel Roberts**
**BIRTH:** 27 May 1921, Williamson Co. TN
**DEATH:** 4 Mar. 1998, Franklin, TN

### CHILDREN

**Private Crowder**      BIRTH:
                        DEATH:

**Private Crowder**      BIRTH:
                        DEATH:

**Private Crowder**      BIRTH:
                        DEATH:

### HIS LIFE

When James Ewing Crowder was born on December 13, 1919, in Williamson County, Tennessee, his father, Odelia was 23 and his mother, Amelia was 24. He married Julia Ethel Roberts on September 29, 1956, in Peytonsville, Tennessee. They had three children together. He died in 1995, at the age of 76. He was buried in the Reynolds Cemetery in Williamson County.

JULIA (ROBERTS) AND JAMES EWING CROWDER

# L. T. MAUPIN
## 1919-2004

### MAUPIN FAMILY

#### HUSBAND'S PARENTS
**Unknown Father    Unknown Mother**

#### WIFE'S PARENTS
**Walter B. Beard**   **Sarah Rebecca Simmons**
1882 - 1961         1882 - 1951

#### HUSBAND
**L. T. Maupin**
**BIRTH:** 4 July 1919, Williamson Co, TN
**DEATH:** 7 Dec. 2004, Peytonsville, TN

#### WIFE
**Era Mai Beard**
**BIRTH:** 4 Jan. 1916, TN
**DEATH:** 9 Oct. 2003, Peytonsville, TN

## CHILDREN

**Private Maupin**     BIRTH:<br>
                                  DEATH:

**Private Maupin**     BIRTH:<br>
                                  DEATH:

## HIS LIFE

L. T. Maupin was born on July 4, 1919, in Williamson County, Tennessee. He married Era Mai Beard on February 4, 1939, in Williamson County. They had two children together. He died on December 7, 2004, in Peytonsville at the age of 85. He was buried in the Williamson Memorial Gardens Cemetery in Franklin, Tennessee.

IN FRONT: GERALD SIMMONS, L.T. MAUPIN, JOHNNY BRUCE, BACK: MIKE SIMMONS, BERRY HARGROVE, PERCY BRUCE, HENRY SIMMONS AND TOM DAVIS

# THOMAS HOUSTON PRATT
## 1922-2003

PRATT FAMILY

## HUSBAND'S PARENTS
**John Edward Pratt**    **Addie Louise Meek**<br>
1897 - 1977            1902 - 1968

## WIFE'S PARENTS
**Garner M. Maxwell**    **Katie M. Patterson**<br>
1885 - 1941            1891 - 1963

## HUSBAND
**Thomas Houston Pratt**<br>
**BIRTH:** 18 Nov. 1922, Peytonsville, TN<br>
**DEATH:** 16 May 2003, Peytonsville, TN

## WIFE
**Catherine Maxwell**<br>
**BIRTH:** 15 Dec. 1927<br>
**DEATH:** 27 Sep. 2011, Williamson Co. TN

## CHILDREN

**Anthony Wayne Pratt**   **BIRTH: 25 Jan, 1948**<br>
**Son**                      **DEATH: 8 Oct, 2010**

**Private Pratt**        BIRTH:<br>
                                  DEATH:

**Private Pratt**        BIRTH:<br>
                                  DEATH:

## HIS LIFE

When Thomas Houston Pratt was born on November 18, 1922, in Williamson County, Tennessee, his father, John was 24 and his mother, Addie was 20. He married Catherine Maxwell on November 30, 1943, in Georgia. They had three children together. He died on May 16, 2003, in Peytonsville, Tennessee at the age of 80. He was buried in the Williamson Memorial Gardens Cemetery in Franklin, Tennessee.

THOMAS HOUSTON PRATT

# BLYTHE EDWARD JOHNSON JR.
## 1923-1974

### JOHNSON FAMILY

#### HUSBAND'S PARENTS
**Blythe E. Johnson Sr.**  **Johnnie Mai Mathis**
1899 - ?  1906 - 1969

#### WIFE'S PARENTS
**Unknown Father**  **Unknown Mother**

#### HUSBAND
**Blythe Edward Johnson**
**BIRTH:** 2 June 1923, Peytonsville, TN
**DEATH:** 12 July 1974, Franklin, TN

#### WIFE
**Sue Eloise Duggins**
**BIRTH:** 24 Jan. 1922, Franklin, TN

**DEATH:** 7 Feb. 1996, Franklin, TN

### CHILDREN

**Blythe Edward**  **BIRTH:** 8 July 1945
**"Butch" Johnson-Son DEATH:** 2007

**Private Johnson**  **BIRTH:**
**DEATH:**

### HIS LIFE

When Blythe Edward Johnson was born on June 2, 1923, in Peytonsville, Tennessee, his father, Blythe was 24 and his mother, Johnnie was 16. He married Sue Eloise Duggins and they had two children together.

Blythe served as Sheriff in 1960-1962 for Williamson County. He was also a State Trooper with the Tennessee Highway Patrol for 11-years.

Blythe Edward Johnson died on July 12, 1974, in Franklin, Tennessee when he was 51-years old. He was buried in the Williamson Memorial Gardens Cemetery in Franklin.

BLYTHE EDWARD JOHNSON, II

314

# JESSIE EDWARD "JESS" CRAWFORD
## 1923-2020

### CRAWFORD FAMILY

#### HUSBAND'S PARENTS
**Sam Preston Crawford**    **Alta Garrett Lovins**
1895 - 1964                  1892 - 1967

#### WIFE'S PARENTS
**Leonard Lee Ladd**    **Bessie Alta Williams**
1883 - 1949              1892 - 1918

#### HUSBAND
**Jessie Edward "Jess" Crawford**
**BIRTH:** 16 Apr. 1923, Marshall Co. TN
**DEATH:** 25 Mar. 2020, Franklin, TN

#### WIFE
**Alma Estella Ladd**
**BIRTH:** 8 Apr. 1912, Williamson Co. TN
**DEATH:** 1992, Franklin, TN

### CHILDREN

| Private Crawford | BIRTH: |
| | DEATH: |
| Private Crawford | BIRTH: |
| | DEATH: |
| Private Crawford | BIRTH: |
| | DEATH: |
| Private Crawford | BIRTH: |
| | DEATH: |
| Private Crawford | BIRTH: |
| | DEATH: |
| Private Crawford Son | BIRTH: |
| | DEATH: |

### HIS LIFE

When Jessie Edward Crawford was born on April 16, 1923, in Marshall County, Tennessee, his father, Sam was 28 and his mother, Alta was 31. He married Alma Estella Ladd on May 29, 1943, in Williamson County, Tennessee. They had six children together. He died on March 25, 2020, in Williamson County at the age of 96. He was buried in the Williamson Memorial Gardens Cemetery in Franklin, Tennessee.

CLIFTON AND DONALD VEACH, JESSIE CRAWFORD, FRANK VEACH AND DEWARD FORRESTER

# THOMAS FELDON GLENN
## 1927-2002

### GLENN FAMILY

#### HUSBAND'S PARENTS
**Richard Wade Glenn**    **Odell Pate**
1904 - 1960              1908 - 1957

**Paul Everett Clark**   **Fannie Mai Mangrum**
1883 - 1949          1916 - 1999

## HUSBAND
**Thomas Feldon Glenn**
**BIRTH:** 9 Oct. 1927, Peytonsville, TN
**DEATH:** 4 Oct. 2002, Peytonsville, TN

## WIFE
**May Ellen Clark**
**BIRTH:** 14 Dec. 1937, Franklin, TN
**DEATH:** 11 Sep. 2005, Peytonsville, TN

## HIS LIFE

When Thomas Feldon Glenn was born on October 9, 1927, in Peytonsville, Tennessee, his father Richard was 22 and his mother Odell 19. He married May Ellen Clark. Thomas Feldon Glenn died on October 4, 2002, in Peytonsville at the age of 74. He was buried in the Mount Hope Cemetery in Franklin, Tennessee.

MAY ELLEN (CLARK) AND THOMAS FELDON GLENN

---

## CHARLES RICHARD MEEK
## 1929-2008

### MEEK FAMILY

### HUSBAND'S PARENTS
**Roy Gilliam Meek**   **Lera Mae Vaden**
1895 - 1967          1903 - 1985

### WIFE'S PARENTS
**Robert T. Sanders**   **Beulah Galdys Null**
1903 - 1980          1911 - 1984

### HUSBAND
**Charles Richard Meek**
**BIRTH:** 14 May 1929, Peytonsville, TN
**DEATH:** 29 June 2008, Peytonsville, TN

### WIFE
**Roberta Ruth Sanders**
**BIRTH:** 15 May 1929, Putnam Co. WV
**DEATH:** 21 Apr. 2016, Peytonsville, TN

### CHILDREN

| | |
|---|---|
| **Private Meek** | BIRTH:<br>DEATH: |
| **Private Meek** | BIRTH:<br>DEATH: |
| **Private Meek** | BIRTH:<br>DEATH: |

### HIS LIFE

When Charles Richard Meek was born on May 14, 1929, in Peytonsville, Tennessee, his father, Roy was 34 and his mother, Lera was 25. He married Roberta Ruth Sanders in 1956, in Putnam County, West Virginia. They had three children together.

Charles was born in the Peytonsville Community and was a successful dairy farmer. He served faithfully for 20-years as Williamson County Commissioner and another 20-years as Williamson County Highway Superintendent. He was a life-long member of the Peytonsville Church of Christ, and served as an elder there.

He died on June 29, 2008, in Peytonsville at the age of 79. He was buried in the Williamson Memorial Gardens Cemetery in Franklin, Tennessee

# ELLIS WILMONT "BILLY" MANGRUM
# 1930-2006

## MANGRUM FAMILY

### HUSBAND'S PARENTS

**Cammie Reed Mangrum**    **Susie Z. Martin**
1904 - 1992                       1911 - 1991

### 1ST WIFE'S PARENTS

**Joe Harrison Bennett    Catherine Hartley**
1907 - 1990                       1911 - 2003

### 2ND WIFE'S PARENTS

**Mike Stampfli    Mary B. Barnes**

### HUSBAND

**Ellis Wilmont "Billy" Mangrum**
**BIRTH:** 9 Feb. 1930, Williamson Co. TN
**DEATH:** 21 May 2006, Williamson Co. TN

### 1ST WIFE

**Delia "Dellie" Bennett**
**BIRTH:** 22 June 1932, Peytonsville, TN
**DEATH:** 6 Mar. 2021, Peytonsville, TN

### 2ND WIFE

**Marian Pauline Stampfi**
**BIRTH:** 11 Mar. 1938, Williamson Co. TN
**DEATH:** 24 Apr. 2020, Murfreesboro, TN

### CHILDREN OF BILLY AND DELLIE

**Timothy H. "Timbo"** **BIRTH:** 16 Apr. 1959
**Mangrum-Son** **DEATH:** 1 Aug. 1979

**Private Mangrum** **BIRTH:**
**DEATH:**

### HIS LIFE

When Ellis Wilmont "Billy" Mangrum was born on February 9, 1930, in Williamson County, Tennessee, his father Cammie was 26 and his mother Susie was 19. He married Delia "Dellie" Bennett and they had two children together. He then married Marian Pauline Stampfi on July 3, 1997, in Williamson County. He died on May 21, 2006, in Williamson County at the age of 76. He was buried in the Williamson Memorial Gardens Cemetery in Franklin, Tennessee.

DELIA "DELLIE" (BENNETT) AND ELLIS WILMONT "BILLY" MANGRUM

GOLDIE HARRISON

## MUSICIANS OF THE 13TH DISTRICT

Music seems to be in the water in the 13th District. Musical families flourished as talent for playing the guitar, banjo, fiddle and singing pure country passed through bloodlines of many families in the district.

The state of Tennessee once had a strong old-time music tradition. The early days of the Grand Ole Opry featured banjo players, fiddle players and string bands from middle Tennessee and some of them came right out of the 13th District. There was scarcely a family gathering that didn't include some type of music.

CHASE WEBSTER ON THE RYMAN STAGE IN 1961

JOHN FRANKLIN MCGEE AND SAM

BLYTHE POTEETE

DOC BENNETT, SIS BENNETT AND
CALVIN VEACH

JOHN HARVEY HASSELL

DIXIELINERS: SAM MCGEE, ARTHUR SMITH AND KIRK MCGEE

RACHEL VEACH OF PEYTONSVILLE PLAYED BANJO WITH ROY ACUFF AND THE SMOKY MOUNTAIN BOYS ON THE GRAND OLE OPRY FROM 1939 UNTIL 1950

T.K. BENNETT OF THE LITTLE TEXAS COMMUNITY

WILLIAM LOGAN AND LACY (JOHNSON) WILLIAMS

FIDDLING AT 104 - PHIL BENNETT, DR. HARRY GUFFEE, KIRK MCGEE AND FULLER ARNOLD

# ALEXANDER B. BENNETT
## 1843-1908

### BENNETT FAMILY

#### HUSBAND'S PARENTS
**Newman L. Bennett**     **Seinee O.F. McGee**
1810 - ?                  1821 - ?

#### WIFE'S PARENTS
**John A.W. Tucker**     **Rachel Ann Graves**
1820 - 1893             1820 - 1908

#### HUSBAND
**Alexander B. Bennett**
BIRTH: 25 Dec. 1843, Williamson Co. TN
DEATH: 30 Nov. 1908, Peytonsville, TN

#### WIFE
**Minerva Jane Tucker**
BIRTH: 8 Mar. 1844, Williamson Co. TN
DEATH: 14 Oct. 1890, Peytonsville, TN

### CHILDREN

**John A. Bennett**
Son
BIRTH: 1865, TN
DEATH: 6 Nov. 1900

**Mollie Bennett**
Daughter
BIRTH: 20 Oct. 1866
DEATH: 24 Sep. 1897

**Marry E. Bennett**
Daughter
BIRTH: 1867
DEATH: Unknown

**James T. Bennett**
Son
BIRTH: 1868
DEATH: 1914

**Williams Bennett**
Son
BIRTH: 1869
DEATH: Unknown

**William Allen Bennett**
Son
BIRTH: 1871
DEATH: Unknown

**Cenia Jane Bennett**
Daughter
BIRTH: 6 Sep. 1871
DEATH: 27 Apr. 1946

**Allie Bennett**
Son
BIRTH: 7 Aug. 1872
DEATH: Unknown

**Laura C. Bennett**
Daughter
BIRTH: 7 Aug. 1872
DEATH: 2 Sep. 1926

**Luanda Jane Bennett**
Daughter
BIRTH: 1873
DEATH: Unknown

**Matilda C. Bennett**
Daughter
BIRTH: 1876
DEATH: Unknown

**Phillip Richard "Phil" Bennett-Son**
BIRTH: 10 Jan. 1878
DEATH: 19 Jun. 1982

**Martha Susan Bennett**
Daughter
BIRTH: 10 Jan. 1879
DEATH: 10 Apr. 1968

**Felix Moore Bennett**
Son
BIRTH: 30 Aug. 1887
DEATH: 14 May 1971

### HIS LIFE

When Alexander B. Bennett was born on December 25, 1843, in Williamson County, Tennessee, his father Newman was 33 and his mother Seinee was 22. He married Minerva Jane Tucker on November 22, 1864 in Williamson County. They had 14 children in 21-years. He died on November 30, 1908, in Peytonsville, Tennessee at the age of 64. He was buried in the Bennett Cemetery in Peytonsville.

# SNAPSHOTS OF OUR PEYTONSVILLE FAMILY

CHASE WEBSTER - AKA, GARY BRUCE

RICHARD P. "DICK" WADDEY

RACHEL STARNES

SUSIE (BEAL) STARNES

THOMAS WADE SMITHSON

DR. HARRY GUFFEE WITH MARY DORTON
AND CHILD

JIMMY DEE BENNETT

RACHEL VEACH FAMILY

WESLEY CROWDER

ALLEN, RICHARD AND TOM
BENNETT, BABY UNKNOWN

MARTHA (BURNETT), ROBERT N. AND
WILLIAM PRICE LADD, SR.

DEE AND DOLLY STANFIELD

WILLIAM AND RACHEL (VEACH)
WATSON

CROWDER PICNIC

GEORGE BRUCE, FATHER OF GARY BRUCE

WILL AND MATILDA (JOHNSON) MARLIN, BESSIE (SKINNER) AND DAVID TOMLIN

WILL AND ALICE (VADEN) JONES

STANDING IN BACK: PAUL, PAT, TOMMY, IN FRONT: JIM ED, JIM FRANK AND JEFF GARNER

JANE MCGEE, ANN VEACH, MARGARET
ANN WILLIAMS, RIGHT END BARBARA
ROBINSON, BACK RIGHT, CAROL
MAXWELL

HERMAN GENTRY WWII, SON OF J.T.
GENTRY

OBEDIAH S. AND SALLY SIMMONS
FAMILY - STANDING: HENRY, MIKE,
OPHELIA, OSCAR, ROBERTS, LILLIE
(SIMMONS) KING

HENRY SIMMONS, OPHELIA (SIMMONS)
YOUNG, ALICE (RAY) SIMMONS, MIKE
SIMMONS

MALACHI STARNES

SAMUEL CHEATHAM SMITHSON, JR.

HENRY AND ALICE SIMMONS WITH
CAROLYN, HAZEL AND GERALD
SIMMONS

MUSSIE (ANDERSON) POTEETE

WILLIAM EARLY AND LILLIE (MILLS) DAVIS
AND KIDS, RACHEL IN FRONT, ADA,
BILLIE, JONAH, FLORENCE, NELL AND
MARY

BUCK AND FANNIE MAY BENNETT
WITH GRANDDAUGHTER, BRENDA

JOHN
HATCHER

CORNELIUS GENTRY

TWINS, JAMES MADISON
AND JOHN EDWARD
MAXWELL

THOMAS WADE, MAMIE AND THOMAS WALTER
SMITHSON

RACHEL GERTRUDE ANDERSON

ALLEN MCGEE AND ROBERT BRUCE

JOHN LORENZO MCGEE AND HIS GRANDSON, JIM MAXWELL

ALMA BENNETT, FRANCES SIMMONS, BILL AND ROBERT TOMLIN

LEFT: WILLIAM DODSON HATCHER, SON OF A.W. HATCHER

DR. J.C. HATCHER, SON OF A.W. HATCHER

CLYDE, HERMAN, WADE, HERBERT AND FATHER, JOHN LORENZO MCGEE

ABRAM WOOLRIDGE HATCHER FAMILY HOME ON ARNO ROAD

GEORGE ABRAM HATCHER

THELMA (PATTON) SCRUGGS, DAUGHTER OF FELIX AND SOPHRONIA PATTON

FELIX PATTON

WALTER J. PARKS (TEACHER) AT PEYTONSVILLE SCHOOL

JIMMIE (VADEN) WYATT

THE PEYTONSVILLE CARDINALS WERE WILLIAMSON COUNTY LITTLE LEAGUE CHAMPS IN 1957. BACK ROW: MILTON HINSON, BOBBY HOLT, GARY YORK, MANAGER JOHNNY PRATT, 2ND ROW: DONALD GLENN, ARTHUR GARNER, HENRY ROBINSON, JESSIE CRAWFORD, PAUL PRATT, 1ST ROW: TOMMY KING, BILLY MCGEE, TONY PRATT AND JACK HOLT

ELIJAH AND NANCY (HAY) TOMLIN AND GRANDCHILDREN

THOMAS A. "ECK", NANCY E. (RAY), SON WILLIAM EARLY DAVIS HOME
WAS ON ARNO ROAD.

CLAUDE DOUGLAS YORK AND JOHN E. PRATT WERE TO LEAVE FRANKLIN LATER IN THE DAY. AFTER BEING SWORN IN, THEY RECEIVED NOTICE THAT WORLD WAR I WAS OVER AND THEY WERE GIVEN A DISCHARGE THAT SAME DAY.

WILLIE D. STARNES AND MALACHI STARNES JR.

DORIS (COOK) SMITHSON

SOPHIA (FARROW) PATE, WILLIAM EARLY DAVIS AND LUCY (DAVIS) LILLARD

OZIE LEE (SMITHSON) STARNES WITH
WILLIE AND MALACHI STARNES, JR.

OLLIE JOHNSON

JESSE MATHIS

MATTIE JANE (SMITHSON) LUSTER
AND DAISY LEE SMITHSON

JANE (ALSTON) MARTIN

STELLA (SMITHSON) LADD AND GEORGE WEST

OUDORA (HARRISON) CLAYTON

MARY E. MCGEE AND ROBERT TOMLIN

ELIJAH "BUSTER", MARTHA SUSAN (BENNETT) AND PAT GARNER ON HORSE

JOHN EDWARD, ADDIE LOUISE (MEEK)
AND PAUL M. PRATT

JAMES F. MARTIN

W.P. AND STELLA (SMITHSON) LADD FAMILY: ALFRED, MARY
KATE ZIMMERMAN, W.P., GOLDIE, STELLA, BILL, ED,
MARTHA ALEXANDER, BOBBY T. LADD

337

OSCEANA FEATHERSTONE (BENNETT)
MCGEE

WRITE BENNETT, BROTHER OF DYKE

DAISY LEE SMITHSON AND
CHILD

MINNIE VIRGINIA GOSEY

DAVID AND MARY (POLK) PINKSTON

SAMUEL HENDERSON, LAWTON, LUVENIA (ADAIR), LLOYD HENDERSON, MANON CLAUD AND BEULAH SMITHSON

SON AND HATTIE BRUCE

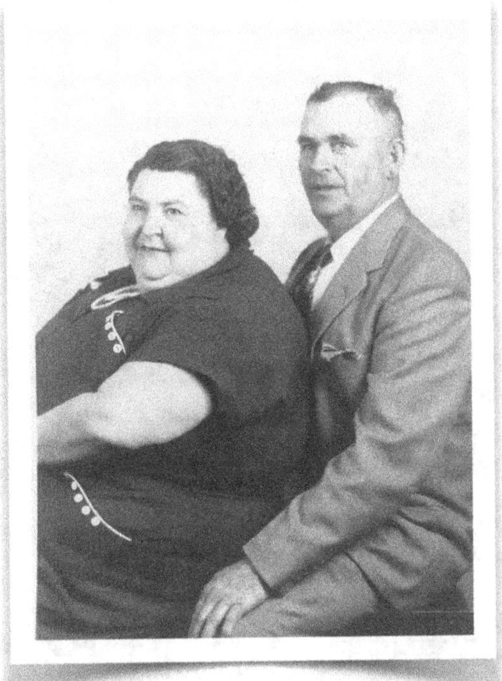

BERTHA AND SAM BENNETT

LEFT: RICHARD PALESTINE "DICK" WADDEY, CICERO STANFORD AND VIRGINIA (WADDEY) STANFORD

RIGHT: SAM AND ELIZABETH (PATE) MCGEE

LEFT: REESE AND DESSIE TOMLIN

JAMES TURNER PINKSTON

JAMES N. AKIN AND MAMIE SMITHSON

DAN VEACH, ANN VEACH, JANE MCGEE AND BELOVED COOK, NANNIE B. SMITHSON
AT PEYTONSVILLE SCHOOL

PATRICK HENRY SMITHSON FAMILY

LEFT: LOGAN, CALVIN, WILLIAM AND
IRENE "SIS" VEACH

KATIE LOU GATLIN

LEONARD, EVELYN, SARA, MIKE, PAUL AND JIM VADEN

CHARLES JOHNSON

DR. BRICE MARTIN

CHARLES WOODARD

LEFT: HENRY AND MIKE SIMMONS, STANDING: JIM YOUNG AND ROBERT SIMMONS